Tokugawa Village Practice

A

Philip E. Lilienthal (signature)

∎   ∎   ∎

BOOK

The Philip E. Lilienthal imprint
honors special books
in commemoration of a man whose work
at the University of California Press from 1954 to 1979
was marked by dedication to young authors
and to high standards in the field of Asian Studies.
Friends, family, authors, and foundations have together
endowed the Lilienthal Fund, which enables the Press
to publish under this imprint selected books
in a way that reflects the taste and judgment
of a great and beloved editor.

Tokugawa Village Practice

Class, Status, Power, Law

HERMAN OOMS

University of California Press

BERKELEY   LOS ANGELES   LONDON

University of California Press
Berkeley and Los Angeles, California

University of California Press, Ltd.
London, England

© 1996 by
The Regents of the University of California

Library of Congress Cataloging-in-Publication Data

Ooms, Herman
    Tokugawa village practice : class, status, power, law / Herman
Ooms.
        p.   cm.
    "A Philip E. Lilienthal book."
    Includes bibliographical references and index.
    ISBN 0-520-20209-0 (acid-free paper)
        1. Japan—Social conditions—1600–1868.   2. Japan—Politics and
    government—1600–1868.   3. Social classes—Japan—History.
    4. Villages—Japan—History.   5. Villages—Law and legislation—
    Japan—History.   I. Title.
    HN723.067   1996
    306'.0952—dc20   95-41444
                                                          CIP

Printed in the United States of America
9 8 7 6 5 4 3 2

In memoriam Maria De Buyser, boerendochter

Contents

Illustrations

Plates

Figures

Maps

Tables

Acknowledgments

A number of people have assisted me in giving shape to this book, personally through comments, unknowingly through publications, or anonymously through institutions. I wish here to gratefully acknowledge their contributions.

My greatest intellectual debt is to Pierre Bourdieu for helping me to think my way through a number of important subjects taken up here. His writings, of great help in orienting my interpretations in *Tokugawa Ideology,* provided me with fresh angles of analytical vision in the present work as well. A second scholar to whom I owe my thanks, first for his writings and then for his personal assistance, is the local historian Ozaki Yukiya from the city of Ueda in Nagano prefecture. The heavy concentration in this book of material from Kita-Saku district in Nagano is due in part to his publications. I am grateful for his generous assistance in gathering data in Mochizuki during a brief visit in the summer of 1991 and his readiness to reduce my ignorance by answering numerous queries.

Once the manuscript had taken form, Tom Keirstead and Anne Walthall generously offered their comments at a critical moment when, simply happy that it was all on paper, I had lost all perspective on the project. Also of great help were those who read and commented on particular chapters: my wife Emily Groszos Ooms, Mark Ramseyer, and graduate students at UCLA. I would like to mention especially Christine Schoppe, who was always putting things together in unexpected ways, and Jason Creigh, a close reader of texts. Others I have to thank collectively for engaging with my ideas when I presented some of the chapters as papers: at Harvard University; at a mini-conference called "Learning the Rules: Schooling, Law, and the Reproduction of Social Order in Early Modern Eurasia" at the University of Minnesota; at two international workshops on the topic "Social Embeddedness of Japanese Law" at the University of California, Los Angeles; at a seminar at Otani University in Kyoto organized by Professor Ōkuwa Hitoshi, where Maeda Ichirō's critique changed my thinking on some important points. I also owe my thanks to Yoshiko Kainuma, Eiko Ikegami, and Kurozumi Makoto for assistance in deciphering and translating some recalcitrant material, to Frank Upham for some helpful suggestions, and to Chase Langford for producing the map of the Kita-Saku area.

Finally, this study was made possible by financial support from a number of institutions over almost a decade: a fellowship from the Japan Foundation, a research fellowship from the National Endowment for the Humanities, a research grant from the Social Science Research Council, a research travel grant from the U.S.-Japan Friendship Commission, travel and research funds from the UCLA Center for Japanese Studies, and UCLA Academic Senate research funds.

Abbreviations

KDJ   *Kokushi daijiten* 国史大辞典. Edited by Kokushi daijiten henshū iinkai 国史大辞典編集委員会. 15 vols. Yoshikawa kōbunkan, 1979–94.

MK   *Mibun to kakushiki* 身分と格式. Nihon no kinsei 日本の近世, 7. Edited by Asao Naohiro 朝尾直弘. Chūōkōronsha, 1992.

NAK-KS2 (1)   *Nagano-kenshi: Kinsei shiryō-hen, Vol. 2, Tōshin chihō* 長野県史：近世史料偏，2：東信地方. Edited by Nagano-ken 長野県. Pt. 1. Nagano-shi: Nagano-kenshi kankōkai, 1978.

NAK-KS2 (2)   *Nagano-kenshi: Kinsei shiryō-hen, Vol. 2, Tōshin chihō* 長野県史：近世史料偏，2：東信地方. Edited by Nagano-ken 長野県. Pt. 2. Nagano-shi: Nagano-kenshi kankōkai, 1979.

NAK-T 4   *Nagano-kenshi: Tsūshi 4 (Kinsei 1)* 長野県史：通史4（近世1). Edited by Nagano-ken 長野県. Nagano-shi: Nagano-kenshi kankōkai, 1987.

NAK-T 5   *Nagano-kenshi: Tsūshi 5 (Kinsei 2)* 長野県史：通史5（近世2). Edited by Nagano-ken 長野県. Nagano-shi: Nagano-kenshi kankōkai, 1988.

NAK-T 6   *Nagano-kenshi: Tsūshi 6 (Kinsei 3)* 長野県史：通史6（近世3). Edited by Nagano-ken 長野県. Nagano-shi: Nagano-kenshi kankōkai, 1989.

NKR 12   *Kinsei no jikata-machikata monjo* 近世の地方・町方文書. Nihon komonjogaku ronshū 日本古文書学論集, 12 (Kinsei 近世 2). Edited by Nihon komonjo gakkai 日本古文書学会. Yoshikawa kōbunkan, 1987.

NNS 3   *Ken'i to shihai* 権威と支配. Nihon no shakaishi 日本の社会史, 3. Iwanami shoten, 1987.

NNS 4 *Futan to zōyo* 負担と贈与. Nihon no shakaishi 日本の社会史, 4. Iwanami shoten, 1986.

NNS 5 *Saiban to kihan* 裁判と規範. Nihon no shakaishi 日本の社会史, 5. Iwanami shoten, 1987.

NRT 3 *Kinsei* 近世. Nihon rekishi taikei 日本歴史大系, 3. Edited by Kodama Kōta 児玉幸多, Nagahara Keiji 長原慶二, et al. Yamakawa shuppan, 1988.

NSSS 14 *Buraku* 部落. Nihon shomin seikatsu shiryō shūsei 日本庶民生活史料集成, 14. Edited by Harada Tomohiko 原田伴彦 et al. San'ichi shobō, 1971.

NST 27 *Kinsei buke shisō* 近世武家思想. Nihon shisō taikei 日本思想大系, 27. Iwanami shoten, 1974.

NST 36 *Ogyū Sorai* 荻生徂徠. Nihon shisō taikei 日本思想大系, 36. Iwanami shoten, 1973.

TKKk *Tokugawa kinreikō kōshū* 徳川禁令考後集. Edited by Ishii Ryōsuke 石井良助. 4 vols. Sōbunsha, 1959–61.

TKKz *Tokugawa kinreikō zenshū* 徳川禁令考前集. Edited by Ishii Ryōsuke 石井良助. 6 vols. Sōbunsha, 1959–61.

Aki 48
Awa 42
Awa (Bōshu) 13
Awaji 41
Bingo 50
Bitchū 49
Bizen 51
Bungo 63
Buzen 62
Chikugo 64
Chikuzen 61
Echigo 16
Echizen 20
Etchū 18
Harima 52
Hida 24
Higo 66
Hitachi 8
Hizen 65
Hōki 58
Hyūga 67
Iga 32
Inaba 56
Ise 33
Iwaki 6
Iwami 60
Iwashiro 7
Iyo 44
Izu 28
Izumi 37
Izumo 59
Kaga 19
Kai 26
Kawachi 38
Kazusa 12
Kii (Kishū) 35
Kōzuke 10

Mikawa 30
Mimasaka 57
Mino 23
Musashi 15
Mutsu 1
Nagato 47
Noto 17
Ōmi 22
Ōsumi 69
Owari 31
Rikuchū 2
Rikuzen 4
Sagami 14
Sanuki 45
Satsuma 68
Settsu (Sesshū) 40
Shima 34
Shimōsa 11
Shimotsuke 9
Shinano (Shinshū) 25
Suruga 27
Suō 46
Tajima 55
Tamba 53
Tango 54
Tosa 43
Tōtōmi 29
Ugo 3
Uzen 5
Wakasa 21
Yamashiro 39
Yamato 36

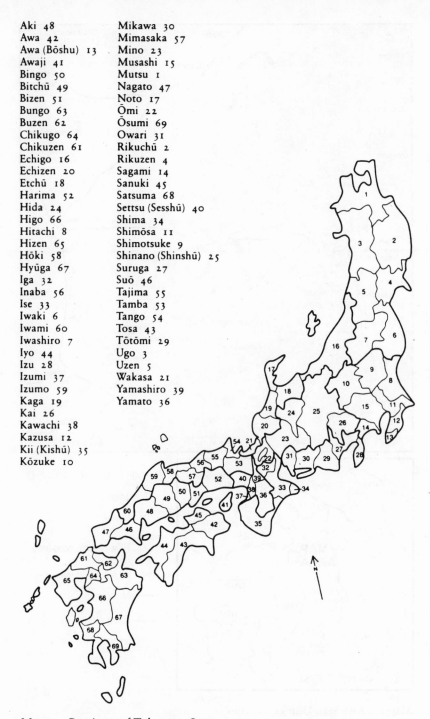

Map 1.   Provinces of Tokugawa Japan

SOURCE: Conrad Totman, *Green Archipelago: Forestry in Pre-Industrial Japan* (Berkeley: University of California Press, 1989).

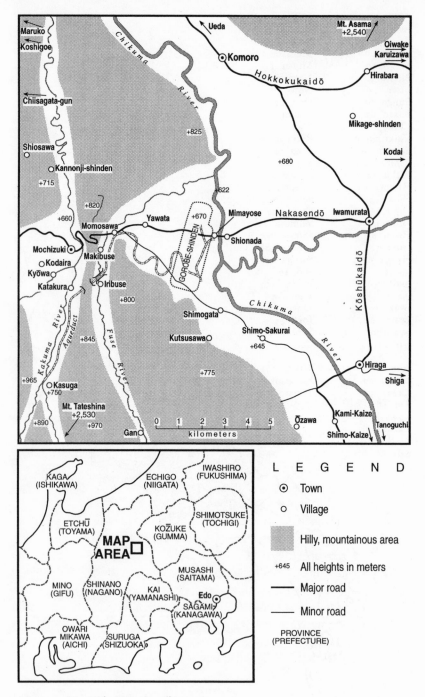

Map 2. Kita-Saku District, Shinano

Introduction

Class, status, power, and law are not new topics to non-Japanese macrostructural treatments of Tokugawa society (1600–1868). Scholars have described well their historical specificity, though often without discussing their interrelationship. Together, as a cluster of general questions, they constitute a Marxian-Weberian problematic perhaps so familiar that it seems disingenuous to persist in treating them still as questions. Indeed, one might ask what the point is of returning to them if they are in reality answers given long ago posturing posthumously as questions—an "answeramatic" disguised as a problematic. How is this book situated within the fields of Tokugawa history and general sociological theory? A second question a reader acquainted with my previous interest in Tokugawa ideology might raise concerns my new orientation.[1] Why this shift from intellectual history and representations of reality to social history and institutional practice?

Post factum justifications for what one has gotten into in the first place without clearly knowing why, except that it looked interesting, partake of retrospective fiction. This is especially true for questions regarding one's intellectual trajectory. With the proviso that reflections of this genre never get at real reasons, I can offer some rationale that one may expect from an introduction.

Previous scholarship, including my own analysis of ideological constructs, approached the issues of class, status, domination, and so on, from a position that was located in the political center. The scholar's

---

1. My book *Tokugawa Ideology: Early Constructs, 1570–1680* was published by Princeton University Press in 1985.

totalizing perspective—"modernist" some would call it now—from such a vantage point is the cognitive equivalent of the rulers' reach of dominion. Past works described how the system of governance was set up, how it functioned, reproduced itself, collapsed—and begat modernity. Even when I argued that the ideology of the times was not produced or even commissioned by the rulers, my emphasis was clearly that it served their interests. Perhaps less explicitly, I also implied that ideas or social representations mattered as much as they did because of their direct link to practice.

I formulated some of those structuralist and functionalist interpretations on the basis of insights gained from Pierre Bourdieu's writings. His writings have further led me to turn my attention to ways in which institutions, like laws, not only constitute sites of ideological embodiment but also define fields of practice and power contests. To a considerable extent, institutions circumscribe, directly, with less mediation by ideology than one might think perhaps, what people are, do, can be, can do, or feel instinctively to be unthinkable or impracticable. This simple truth calls for a kind of history that focuses on what people do within and with institutions. In regard to Tokugawa Japan, this insight translated for me into a desire to examine what peasants did and could do in their villages. How did the institutional setting of a military regime influence intravillage power distributions? Conversely, did village politics affect institutions?

Questions of this genre have received hardly any attention in Western scholarship, and although Japanese historians have produced a staggering amount of work about local rural history, very little of it has crossed the language barrier. Thomas C. Smith's admirable classic *The Agrarian Origins of Modern Japan* touches only briefly on intravillage politics. Scholars writing about peasant resistance (Bix, Kelley, Vlastos, and Walthall) deal mainly with what peasants did when they left their villages to protest extravillage authority and only occasionally with the allocation, use, and contestation of power within villages. These studies are also limited to the mid and late Tokugawa period, when the most dramatic collective protests took place.

Class has been discussed far more than status by these scholars, who either emphasize its growing importance or argue its irrelevance. Either way, the assumption has been that status may explain collective action in the first Tokugawa century but not later, when class interests prevailed (or, according to an anticlass argument, when less stable group alliances cut across various social strata). Schematically, class either replaced status as the motor of social stratification or failed to do so contrary to expectations. In either case the issue was class, not status.

My critique of this kind of diachronic dichotomizing is inspired by Bourdieu's reworking of the Weberian categories of class, status, and power through his flexible model of convertible capital (economic, social, and symbolic). Within this perspective, class and status, far from being mutually exclusive, constitute forms of power that are complementary and occasionally substitutable for each other. Chapters 2 and 3 of this book address this class-status question and, like the two concepts, are hard to separate. In chapter 2 I concentrate on the role of class-based rural power even in the early period, following in this principally the lead taken by the Japanese historian Mizumoto Kunihiko. In chapter 3 I examine the manipulation of power through status positions in village political struggles throughout the period.

Some time ago class ceased to be an almost obligatory subject for social historians, many of whom were attracted to insights promised by discourse analysis or the new cultural history. Bourdieu's work, however, has opened up possibilities to engage the topic anew by "bringing in" status. In an interesting turnabout, in 1992 the well-known British historian David Cannadine also called for a reengagement with class analysis, via the study of status.[2] I share this point of view.

When discussing class, it is important to maintain the distinction, however elementary, between objective socioeconomic conditions shared by a number of people or groups and subjective awareness or practice (not to be taken for granted) based upon a recognition of those conditions. Too often, either a subjective class is postulated automatically on the basis of the existence of objective conditions (in doctrinaire Marxism) or the significance of an objective class is belittled because of the absence of class agents (in anti-Marxist arguments). An objective class is an analytical construct that is simultaneously the initial impetus for a query and its final result. Although classes in seventeenth-century Japan (or France) obviously do not look the same as modern classes—a

2. See David Cannadine, "Cutting Classes," *New York Review of Books,* Dec. 17, 1992, 52–57, esp. 57.

fact that is often forgotten in class analyses of Tokugawa Japan—their absence clearly is hard to argue.[3] An example of an objective class in this study is the *dogō*, or rural magnates, which Japanese historians, long interested in class, have identified as existing as an identifiable socioeconomic stratum from the sixteenth through the eighteenth century. Yet even the term that names and thus constitutes this group as a group is a modern scholarly creation. When, however, dogō organized armed resistance against land surveys in certain regions toward the end of the sixteenth century they acted subjectively as a class.

In the seventeenth century there are numerous instances of peasants agitating around issues of village governance. Analysis identifies these peasants as belonging successively to different socioeconomic strata and acting to further shared interests by submitting group petitions. In this instance also, it is justified to speak both of an objective property class and a subjective social class, although their membership is not identical. The objective class may be identifiable across whole provinces, while peasant demands were always limited to the immediate environment; thus theirs was a social class consciousness expressed in practice but embedded in and circumscribed by the village.

Often these village disputes concerned issues of status. At a macro and official level, Tokugawa Japan was, of course, a society of "orders" (*Stände*), legally defined status groups. Thus, all villagers were commoners, and most of them belonged to the status order of peasants. Yet this commonality, sanctioned legally by the state (from a distant center), should not be reconfigured into an equally distant image of village solidarity. On closer examination, it is clear that villagers always differentiated among themselves within a clearly marked hierarchy comprising multiple status gradations. This status was in part indirectly sanctioned legally by overlords (and thus an "order"), in part locally generated (and thus closer to the modern meaning of social standing).

This intravillage status hierarchy, expressed in prescribed forms of social interaction and normative gradations of material consumption, was closely related to economic power as either an addition to or a

---

3. For a cogent defense of the need for a class analysis of seventeenth-century France, a "society of orders" like Tokugawa Japan, see William Beik, *Absolutism and Society in Seventeenth-Century France: State Power and Provincial Aristocracy in Languedoc* (Cambridge: Cambridge University Press, 1985), chap. 1, esp. 7–9.

substitute for it. That economic power translates into political control, which it supplements with privileges (often based on tales of ancestry), thus creating and securing rare status positions, is not difficult to understand. Once the dog grew a tail, however, the tale could whip the dog. Status could be made to function as a first line of defense of political privilege, even when economic underpinnings had given way, by holding off new claimants who, pointing to their new wealth, insisted on a share in the control of village affairs. This tug of war for political power between peasants differentiated by economic and social status can be documented throughout the Tokugawa period.

The discussion of status and power in villages is limited in this book to those aspects of this dyad that were the subject of explicit written regulations and contestations. This means that the players discussed here are households, not individuals. It goes without saying that within households too power was distributed and exercised according to status, in this case along gender and age differentials. This is the area of (mostly un- or undercodified) dispositional habits, which does not belong to a study of explicit social and economic stratification that, moreover, extends beyond intrafamilial roles.

This limitation does not mean that I hold a monolithic view of human agency. Individual identities are plural, not singular, because they are constituted by multiple differences in kin, gender, age, lineage, neighborhood, and regional systems. In the public political realm, however, such multiple identities are simplified and channeled to create single group agents in accordance with the needs of policymakers—or their challengers. In Tokugawa Japan this was especially true of households, neighborhoods, and lineages. They were politically overdetermined by extravillage lordly authority. Many a village dispute centered around the way power was distributed through these institutions.

Status is a system of stratification through socially recognized honor, esteem, and privilege. The positive connotation of these terms, however, is misleading since such a description of a status system is the work of an outside observer who perceives grades of more or less honor, esteem, and privilege and relates to the whole hierarchy at once. This structuralist gaze is of a different quality than the experience of those who occupy a position within the status system. Status holders always relate to the system differentially, from a specific position that determines the scope and intensity of their interest in other positions, especially neighboring ones. One can at least say that, while they enjoyed public social honor and esteem from those below them (and private envy and resentment as well), status holders must look down upon occupants of lower positions (with fear perhaps) as undeserving of such recognition, as embodiments of dishonor. Things are obviously more complicated than this dichotomy indicates. Even in a rigidly stratified society like Tokugawa Japan not all of the aspects of social interaction were patterned on status prescriptions. For instance, the "outcastes," too often still referred to by the pejorative term *eta,* were not treated as polluted in every social encounter. The point is that a status system is always also a system of socially sanctioned dishonor.

This is particularly true in the case of the outcastes, victims not only of social disrespect but also of stigmatizing ostracism and outright discrimination. For the last two decades, Japanese historians have produced a monumental body of research about the Tokugawa history of today's *burakumin* (in part descendants of the outcastes), a subject virtually untouched by non-Japanese scholars. This record, however, is not only a collection of particular histories of individuals, families, or communities. It also reveals changes and developments in the status of outcastes as such over the whole Tokugawa period and suggests that other factors besides cultural prejudice were at work.

Obviously, a study of status cannot neglect the subject of outcastes, although I almost did. Only after the other chapters were written did I become aware of the need to address this difficult issue. This near oversight is not without its own significance. The outcastes lived with their own headmen in hamlets near but apart from peasant villages and, in eastern Japan since the 1720s, under the direct jurisdiction of their seminational leader, or Danzaemon (an office name), in Edo. Since they formed a "society outside society," as Japanese historians often put it, they have usually been treated separately in modern historiography as well. Their serious study has been a ghettoized subdiscipline until very recently. Thus, it is possible to read endlessly about status, class, and power within Tokugawa villages without encountering them. And yet, as I argue in chapter 5, the treatment of these outcastes in Tokugawa and modern times constitutes perhaps the clearest and ugliest example of the operation of status.

The topography of power within villages was not shaped solely by intravillage factors. Extravillage lordly authority helped draw some of the lines over which confrontations took place. This authority interfered as a source of prestige and power, directly by creating "titled peasants" and the village offices of headman and neighborhood heads and by issuing village laws, indirectly by allowing the officialization of village-generated statuses as they appeared on documents drawn up locally and by sanctioning through noninterference separate, "autonomous" village codes.

Nevertheless, it has often been said that villages were self-governing to a very high degree. A headman and the neighborhood heads who assisted him constituted the core of the village council (where only titled peasants had a seat), which took care of all public affairs, foremost the delivery of tribute and corvée to the overlord's district intendant but also many judicial and penal matters. In domains of the daimyo and shogun a district intendant (a bannerman in the shogunal houseland, a special portion of the shogunal domain) was in charge of from a dozen to over a hundred villages. Often there were also village group headmen, who channeled communication between the headmen of a number of villages and the intendant. Tribute and population registers were kept at both the village and the district level. Matters that could not be settled by the neighborhood heads or by the village council or headman could be taken to the district intendant (via the village group headman) in the form of petitions or suits or, ultimately, to shogunal or domainal higher-ups, usually in Edo. Defendants were routinely invited to respond to the accusations in writing, thus completing the record of the plaintiff's lawsuit. The written testimonies of witnesses or interested parties would be taken into consideration by the authorities as they tried to reach a solution—a verdict or an ordered settlement. It should be understood that at all these levels administrative and judicial functions overlapped; Tokugawa Japan did not have an independent judiciary and was a society without lawyers.

Although the sketch above may blur distinctions between locality and center, the degree to which Tokugawa villages enjoyed autonomy has long been debated among Japanese historians. This debate has centered mainly on the structural position of village regulations within the overall power distribution of society. Did these codes constitute limits to, or were they vehicles for, the penetration of supravillage authority within the village? I engage this question in chapter 4, where I supplement the traditional approach, which is based almost exclusively on the study of legal texts, with an analysis of actual practice. This perspective emphasizes the articulation within a single juridical domain of two specific legal authorities, a supra- and an intravillage authority, which created a distinct space that allowed each one to choose whether to use the other explicitly or implicitly.

This strategic area, where village headmen or district intendants exercise some discretion in deciding which laws to apply, overlook, or subvert (and to what extent) is, of course, hard to explore. We usually know only the outcomes of such deliberations, not the processes by which they were reached. Local historians, however, have discovered diaries, notes, and queries by village headmen that reveal strategies they weighed or used in applying, interpreting, or circumventing existing regulations. All too often one feels obliged to choose between a "naive" view that equates written law with actual practice and a skepticism that questions the effectiveness of laws. Headmen's private papers provide an escape from this simplistic dilemma. They reveal judicious appraisals by historical actors of the relative power of law and other circumstantial constellations of forces.

The approach to the study of Tokugawa law followed here is twofold and aims at the interplay between the normative power of laws and actual social practice. On the one hand, in the final chapter I attempt to sketch a general macro picture, not of Tokugawa laws, but of the juridical field and the specific power generated by laws. On the other hand, most of the other chapters are constructed to a large extent around lawsuits and law cases, where one can witness how laws figured in various local power struggles and contestations. To change unwanted situations, the peasants relied far more frequently on suits and petitions than on mass protests or uprisings. One cannot avoid the impression that lawyerless Tokugawa Japan was far more litigious than the Japan of today.

Even though contention often took the form of litigation, one should keep in mind that the distinction between petitions or requests and what we would call suits or legal action is not at all clear. There are several reasons for this. Suits were always drawn up according to an official format in a formal language of entreaty ("with fear and trembling") as supplications professing in advance willing subjection to the good will of the authorities.[4] Furthermore, there were no attorneys

---

4. The phrases "formal language of entreaty" and "willing subjection" are taken from Geoffrey Koziol, *Begging Pardon and Favor: Ritual and Political Order in Early Medieval France* (Ithaca: Cornell University Press, 1992), 8, 45. His description of tenth- and eleventh-century France applies well to Tokugawa

available, and the governing authorities (village councils or overlords) were the "judges." The outcomes of suits/petitions, rather than being "verdicts," were often conciliations or compromises without clearcut winners or losers, reached with the help of appointed ad hoc mediators. Because restoring social order was more important than conforming to an abstract rule of law or justice, apologies were often the decisive moment in legal closure.

Since petitioning or litigating is only one way for individuals or groups to exercise power, a regional study of such action viewed against a detailed background of other forms of social and economic power would be ideal. I was led to explore that possibility after coming across a particularly well documented case of a poor peasant woman engaged in a protracted confrontation against all levels of village and even supravillage authority. The woman was from a village in Kita-Saku district in eastern Shinano (Nagano prefecture). I begin the book with her story.

Ultimately, however, my goal was a more comprehensive statement than an area study would allow. Although much is to be gained from regionally controlled research, I abandoned this way of organizing my project. Nevertheless, I was able to use much of the material thus gathered, often in the form of other cases presented throughout this book, giving it a strong regional emphasis. Thus, in good part, this is a study *in* rather than *of* a region.

A legal case usually yields a narrative, a fragment revealing what people cared about and why. Knowledge of circumstantial detail is often essential for an adequate understanding of the issue. An analysis of practice through a number of case studies with ever-changing actors and settings, however, can be taxing to the reader. The detail can at times be bewildering and overwhelming. Yet, the alternative of a quick summary of the issues to please the hurried reader sacrifices too much of what makes history—an old-fashioned idea—interesting and what reminds us that cases are about people.

It is just as appropriate to remind oneself that we get to know those

---

Japan, perhaps not surprisingly given the "feudal" character of these two societies: "Petition and concession, humility and grace, dependence and domination; these were the categories that expressed the fundamental political relations of the tenth and eleventh centuries" (81).

people because others, namely, local historians, have retrieved their stories. Without their assiduous efforts, a study like this, which touches upon the history of many locales, would be impossible. With this in mind, I have chosen not to relegate their names to footnotes in order to protect a seamless narrative and uninterrupted analysis. The reader will have to bear with this reminder in the text that it is the work of these historians that carries the study forward.

To a considerable extent, this book is a collection of essays that can be read independently and in almost any sequence. Linking the different topics and chapters, however, is the fact (and I use the term without hesitation) of inequality and often the reality (again, no apologies) of social suffering as they were institutionalized in the communities of Tokugawa villages. The frequent description of villages as harmonious and consensual is a misrecognition if not an outright denial of these realities.

I

"Mountains of Resentment"

One Woman's Struggle against
Tokugawa Authority

Follow your judgment.
                    Ken, 1757

In this study I often rely on data from Nagano prefecture, formerly Shinano province, especially from the Saku district in the east (since 1624 split into a northern, Kita-, and a southern, Minami-, half). This is in part accidental and in part by design and deserves an explanation. (For provinces, see map 1; for Kita-Saku, see map 2.)

Learning of my interest in Tokugawa village law, my colleague Anne Walthall recommended an article about a peasant woman who sued officials in Makibuse, a village in Kita-Saku. As it turned out, this case provided an unusually well documented entry into village politics. Additional reading drew me further into a study of the region, which, I soon found, had been explored by many prominent historians of the early Tokugawa period, including Kodama Kōta, Miyagawa Mitsuru, Ōishi Shinzaburō, and the pathbreaking local historian Ichikawa Yū-ichirō. Independent scholars continue this tradition of local history today. Ozaki Yukiya is one of them.

Like Ichikawa before him, Ozaki until recently supported his passion for local history by his work as a high school teacher. He wanted to become a professional historian, but in the immediate postwar period his father, convinced that science was the wave of the future, steered his son in the direction of physics and chemistry. Fortunately, Ozaki was able to squeeze some courses on Tokugawa documents into his schedule at the university. When I established contact with him in 1991, he was teaching high school science by day and researching and writing local history by night and on weekends.

Initially interested in questions of discrimination against *burakumin,* Japan's indigenous minority, Ozaki organized a club in the mid seventies to explore the history of Mochizuki, the town into which Makibuse has been incorporated. He taught this small group of retired history buffs how to read the difficult Tokugawa texts, and together they began collecting, cataloging, and reading tens of thousands of documents from the storehouses of descendants of Tokugawa village headmen in the area.[1]

In the storehouse of the descendant of Makibuse's headman, Ozaki came across dozens of documents referring to a woman named Ken. Intrigued, he devoted a great deal of time to piecing together the fragments of her story. I retell it here, following the trail of documents, supplemented with relevant historical data from other sources.[2]

THE REGISTRATION INCIDENT: 1761–1763

Our point of entry into Ken's story is an incident involving the population register of Makibuse that is neither the beginning nor the end of Ken's story (see table 6 for a chronology of Ken's life). I chose this incident because often long-simmering questions regarding status surface in the historical record as disputes around the proper entry in village population registers, which were updated every year. These registers recorded not only a person's name but also his or her social and

1. Currently the group is writing a multivolume history of the town and its surrounding villages. In the fall of 1992 Ozaki resigned from his high school teaching position to accept an appointment with Nagano's new prefectural museum, scheduled to open near Nagano city at the time of the 1998 Winter Olympics. As director of historical acquisitions for the Tokugawa period, he is at last pursuing his passion for local history on a full-time basis.

2. Today Makibuse is part of Mochizuki, a township with some 3,100 households and a population of 11,300 that since 1959 has included a number of surrounding villages, each of which in turn comprises what were once several Tokugawa villages. For the materials on Mochizuki, see Mochizuki-machi kyōiku iinkai, *Mochizuki no burakushi*, nos. 1–5 (1976–79), and *Mochizuki no chōmin no rekishi*, nos. 6–15 (1980–91). The documents related to Ken are still in the possession of the descendant of the Tokugawa headman of Makibuse village, who was reluctant to allow me access to them on my visit there in the summer of 1991. Fortunately, Ozaki had made copies, which he graciously put at my disposal. Ozaki published his findings on Ken in two partly overlapping but mostly complementary articles: "Kenjo oboegaki: Kinsei nōson joseishi e no kokoromi," *Mochizuki no chōmin no rekishi* 8 (1983): 61–100; and "Shinshū Saku-gun Makibuse-mura Kenjo ikken—Kinsei nōson joseishi shikiron to shite," *Rekishi Hyōron* 419 (1985): 45–66. References to sources other than those directly pertaining to Ken's story are my own. The story has become famous locally through a play based on it.

legal status. Individuals contesting their status might cause delays in the village headman's submission of the registers to the higher authorities, or they might escalate the confrontation into a lawsuit, in either case leaving evidence for historians to examine. In Ken's case, we are well informed about the immediate issue she was raising and the pressures applied to her to conform. Behind this incident, however, lies the story of a peasant family, which adds a number of other dimensions to this incident.

Population registers, along with village laws and land cadasters (chronologically the earliest of the three), were the most important documents the supravillage authorities ordered the village headmen to keep up-to-date. Titled peasants had to signal agreement with the registers and laws for themselves and their dependents by affixing their seals.[3] In principle, the laws were read at least once a year to all the villagers, sometimes, as in Makibuse, at every formal meeting of the village council.[4] The list of signatures attached to these laws eventually evolved into separate, complete population registers (*jinbetsu aratamechō*). The earliest such register in Kita-Saku dates from 1642. A record of Buddhist affiliation, required nationwide since 1665, was first added to these population registers but came to be drawn up separately and known as *shūmon aratamechō*.[5] These lists often functioned as population registers with increasingly detailed information on the age, provenance, and whereabouts of each co-resident of each household and his or her relationship to the household head. By the 1720s a full-fledged, nationwide population census was being conducted every six years. The headman, assisted by the *kumi* heads (the heads of the official neigh-

3. On the process of diffusion of these laws from the lord to the peasants and their ratification by the village, see Yokota Fuyuhiko, "Kinsei sonraku ni okeru hō to okite," (*Kōbe Daigaku daigakuin bunkagaku kenkyūka*) *Bunkagaku nenpō* 5 (1986): 150–55.

4. Ichikawa Yūichirō, *Saku chihō Edo jidai no nōmin seikatsu* (Nagano-ken Minami Saku-gun Nozawa-machi: Saku Insatsujo, 1955), 24. As is so often the case with Tokugawa institutions, however, some of these laws antedated the *bakufu* order: the oldest one in Shinano is from Kyōwa, a village five kilometers west of Makibuse, and dates from 1628 (ibid., 15).

5. For an introduction to the *shūmon aratamechō*, see L. L. Cornell and Akira Hayami, "The *shūmon aratame chō*: Japan's Population Registers," *Journal of Family History* 11, no. 4 (1986): 311–28. For a recent discussion of the development of population registers, see Yokota Fuyuhiko, "Kinseiteki mibun seido no seiritsu," in *Mibun to kakushiki*, ed. Asao Naohiro, Nihon no kinsei, 7 (Chūōkōronsha, 1992), 41–78, esp. 55–78 (hereafter MK).

borhood groups, the *goningumi*), was responsible for drawing up a new register every year and having each entry properly verified and certified with each household head's seal. (For special terms, please consult the Glossary.)

In Kita-Saku district, as elsewhere in *bakufu*, or shogunal, territories, the yearly population check took place in the third month.[6] A copy of the register remained with the headman, the original being forwarded to the lord's chargé d'affaires, who for Makibuse in 1763 was quartered at an office in Shimogata village, the administrative center for a shogunal bannerman's (*hatamoto*) small fief by the same name.[7]

Thus, on 1763/2/8,[8] a woman named Ken refused to certify her household's entry with her seal. A yearly routine had taken on the dimensions of an event. No doubt greatly annoyed by this flagrant case of insubordination by a mere woman, which would reflect badly on his own governance and certainly trigger an investigation from above, the headman, one Chūemon, had no way of concealing the matter, so he reported it to the Shimogata office.

Why was a woman's seal required? Usually the male head of the household held legal authority for all its members, whether affines, cognates, or other co-residents. And Ken was neither single nor a widow. In 1756, then thirty-seven, Ken had married a man a few years her elder. He was from Mochizuki, a way station on the Nakasendō inland highway between Edo and Kyoto, located across a low range of hills

6. Ichikawa Yūichirō, *Saku chihō*, 70.
7. Between 1702 and 1765, Makibuse was one of thirteen villages in the area that together constituted the five-thousand-*koku* fief of Shimogata (see Nagano-ken, ed., *Nagano-kenshi: Kinsei shiryō-hen*, Vol. 2, *Tōshin chihō*, pt. 1 [Nagano-shi: Nagano-kenshi kankōkai, 1978], 724 [hereafter NAK-KS2 (1)]). Its overlord history, like that of most villages in the fertile Kita-Saku plain, is a complex one. Villages were shifted numerous times, sometimes even divided, among various lords. Makibuse started as a village of the *fudai* domain of Komoro (first under the Sengoku house, 1590–1622; then under the shogun's brother Tadanaga, 1622–24; then under a Matsudaira, 1624–47). Between 1648 and 1661 it was entrusted as a shogunal possession (*azukaridokoro*) to the Aoyama. Subsequently it was part of the Kōfu Tokugawa domain until 1700. After two years of incorporation in the shogunal domain proper (*tenryō*) under an intendant (*daikan*), it was transferred to the jurisdiction of the Shimogata bannerman's fief until 1765. From that year until the end of the Tokugawa period it was again part of the tenryō.
8. Dates are referred to by year first, followed by the lunar month and the day according to the traditional Japanese calendar.

some two and a half kilometers due west of Makibuse. His name was Rokuemon, formerly Yohachi. Two years before the incident, however, in the winter of 1761, he had left Ken, and his whereabouts were unknown.

At the time of the first registration after her husband's disappearance, in the spring of 1762, Ken requested to keep him on the rosters as the *in absentia* household head. The following year, however, she officially petitioned the headman, in a document legalized with the seals of her relatives and kumi members (the same persons, since in Makibuse lineages overlapped with neighborhood kumi),[9] to take him off the rosters, leaving her the head of a single-member household, for her parents were no longer alive and she had no heir.

This Ken did on 2/6, that is, only two days before she surprised the headman by refusing to affix her seal to the population register. Had her relatives suspected the trouble she was to cause, they certainly would never have signed the petition. Instead, they would have placed her under the fiduciary authority of one of them, as she had been before her marriage. Did they not know Ken well enough to foresee this? Was this why she had sought legal authority? What lay behind this surprise move?

In his report to the Shimogata magistrate, the headman carefully explained the futile efforts by the village authorities (himself and the four kumi heads) to make this recalcitrant woman comply with shogunal law and also recorded Ken's reason for her behavior:

> Ken did not affix her seal to this year's population register. What was the reason for this delinquency? We asked her to please affix her seal, there being regulations concerning the population register. Even if I did it, [she said,] come fall I intend to leave the village, so there is no need for my seal. In any case, [we said,] it is an offense not to affix your seal this year. All the village officials urged her strongly to quickly affix her seal, but no matter what, she did not listen and [just] went home.[10]

The headman also mobilized the members of the next authority level down, namely, Ken's kumi members / relatives, asking them to persuade

---

9. *Kumi* is short for *goningumi*, the term for a five-household neighborhood association, an official administrative subdivision of a village. Their membership was supposed to cut across, rather than overlap with, lineage membership. Makibuse had four kumi.

10. Ozaki, "Kenjo ikken," 47–48.

her, but they were equally powerless. He finally ordered her to appear in person in Shimogata, about seven kilometers to the east of Makibuse, across the hills, in the open plateau of Kita-Saku, on the other side of Gorobe-shinden, near the Chikuma River.

But Ken did not budge. "If this is an offense, then it is one I have been looking for that suits me well (*ochido ni ainarisōrō mo, saiwai nozomu tokoro ni gozarō*)," she replied, according to the headman's report, "and even if I receive the death penalty or banishment, no matter what punishment [might await me], I have thought this over very well [and taken all such possibilities into consideration]." Thus Ken not only categorically refused to appear before the Shimogata magistrate—she interpreted the order to do so as a threat—but used the occasion to impress upon the headman again the depth of her determination, countering his order/threat by warning him that threats would be of no use. At least this is the headman's view of the confrontation, aimed at impressing his superior with the particular difficulties he was having with this woman.

Ken's leaving the village would result in the disappearance of a household, which was always an extremely grave matter, for it affected the distribution of tribute that the village as a whole owed the lord. The lord, who "owned" the land, which "owned" the people on it, did not let them go easily. Yet the land under Ken's name was minuscule, a mere 0.19 *koku*, three-quarters of it a dry plot attached to the homestead.[11] The reassignment of her land to another peasant in order to produce the apportioned part of the village tribute quota could not have been the only thing at stake. As we shall see, there were in the village poverty-stricken peasants in need of land who presumably would have gladly taken over the holding. It seems particularly nasty of the headman to deny this woman her request to leave the village. Was he getting back at her for some unspecified reason?

When moving to a domicile out of one's locale of registration (village or township), one had first to secure a certificate of leave (*okurijō*, or "sending document") in order to properly register in one's new resi-

11. The term *koku*, a measure of volume equivalent to 180 liters or 44.8 gallons, refers to the putative rice yield of fields, the basis for the computation of tribute. All property, including dry fields and homesteads, was converted into koku equivalents for tribute purposes. Ken's property was thus registered as equivalent to a mere 34 liters of rice.

dence. Ken knew the procedure; she had followed it a year earlier, without, however, being granted her wish. This time she seemed to have changed strategy, hoping, perhaps, to force the hand of the village authorities or at least to cause trouble by exploiting the jurisdictional division between village and district.[12]

In 1762/3, only a year earlier and thus around the registration time when she had kept her absent husband recorded as household head, Ken had petitioned to leave the village but the petition had not been granted, possibly because her husband still held legal authority for the household. In 1763, however, she held the title and seal of household head. The petition of 1762 read as follows:

> In the winter I was asked [by her lineage and kumi members and possibly also by the village officials] to establish a successor for the household [through adoption of an heir or remarriage], but I do not want to do that. I want to work the fields but cannot even become a tenant. So I have no alternative because I have trouble paying the tribute and performing cor-vée. Thus I request to donate the residence land, paddies, dry fields and woodland, all of it, to my family temple, the Baikei-in [in the adjoining village of Iribuse]. If this request is honored, then I and Rokuemon [my husband] will have to be taken from the population register. I want to leave Makibuse. By making this request, [I hope] I am putting an end to your order [to establish a successor]. There is no need to call me and talk to me about this again and again. Would you please examine my pro-posal.[13]

This petition throws some light on the headman's ill will. He refused to grant Ken's request to leave after commending her property to a temple because she had balked at his order to establish an heir. There is evidence here of the same uncompromising, blunt determination that comes through in her refusal to sign the register a year later, when she defiantly told the headman that "I do not care for my life, no matter

12. Peasants crossing domain boundaries en masse resorted to a similar strategy on a larger scale. Perhaps the most famous such mass exodus was an 1853 crossing from Nanbu to Sendai domain led by Miura Meisuke (see Herbert Bix, "Miura Meisuke, or Peasant Rebellion under the Banner of 'Distress,'" *Bulletin of Concerned Asian Scholars* 10, no. 2 [1978]: 18–28).

13. Ozaki, "Kenjo ikken," 48. Makibuse did not have a temple. The village may have split off at some time from Iribuse, where, according to the 1671 population register, 74 of the 133 inhabitants of Makibuse were registered with the Baikei-in; 49 were registered with a temple in Mochizuki (doc. 351 in NAK-KS2 [1]: 779–80).

what happens to me; I am not in the least afraid; there is no need for me to go to the [Shimogata] office."[14]

This was an angry woman who, all by herself, challenged every level of authority: the shogunal magistrate, the village headman, the kumi heads, her kumi members, and her relatives. She stood up against them by refusing to straighten out the succession of the house, sign the register, and appear before the Shimogata magistrate. The headman reports that when her lineage members put pressure on her in the registration incident, "it was useless, she would not consent and started even saying slanderous and irresponsible things." Taking another tack, they pleaded understanding for their own plight: as the group responsible and liable for its members' behavior they would face difficulties because of this incident. But she responded to this plea as she had to the headman's threat, retorting that this was precisely the point: "I have been waiting for this opportunity with the population register in order to cause trouble for the goningumi (*goningumi nangi itashisōrō tame ni gochōmen inkei no setsu to aimachi makari arisōrō*)." Ken had planned this. What in Ken's past had brought her to this bold confrontation?

Goningumi, or official neighborhood groups, were not supposed to overlap with family networks: the first article of laws of some villages in the area, like Makibuse also under bakufu jurisdiction, specified that these kumi ought not to include only kinsmen or close friends, kith and kin (*shinrui naka yoki mono*).[15] This rule obviously was aimed at preventing collusion of interests and increasing local control. In the neigh-

14. Ozaki, "Kenjo ikken," 49.
15. Ichikawa Yūichirō (*Saku chihō*, 13–63) studied forty-one *goningumichō zensho*, or village laws, of Saku district covering the whole Tokugawa period. Included in these are four versions of the Makibuse village laws, from 1687, 1784, 1801, and 1857. He discovered great similarities, if not complete identity, among many of them across jurisdictions (domains and bakufu territories of various kinds) in three chronologically distinct periods separated by the 1660s and the second decade of the eighteenth century. He appended to his study the full text of the standard version of each period: the laws of the bakufu village of Shimo-Sakurai, nine kilometers east of Makibuse, of 1640 (21 articles), 1662 (56 articles), and 1766 (also 56 articles). (The first two of these laws are translated in appendixes 2 and 3.) Among the Makibuse laws, the one of interest to us is the first one, dated 1687, which according to Ichikawa is identical, down to the number of articles, to the 1662 version from Shimo-Sakurai. When citing articles of the village law of Makibuse, it is to this text (appendix 3) that I refer. The article about the proper composition of goningumi is the first one in the 1640 version of Shimo-Sakurai village law (appendix 2).

boring village of Kodaira, kin-exclusive kumi had led to trouble;[16] in Makibuse also family networks and kumi overlapped: the six households of Ken's lineage all belonged to the same kumi. In this region, shogunal law clearly had failed to break the power of the local self-governing bodies of the lineages.

ONE OF MAKIBUSE'S POOR PEASANTS: 1719–1744

Ken was a native of Makibuse, the daughter of a peasant named Rihei, whom we shall refer to as Rihei II since her grandfather bore the same name (hence we will call the grandfather Rihei I). Born in 1719, she was forty-four at the time of the registration incident. Her mother was from Yawata village, a station on the Nakasendō two and a half kilometers east of Makibuse (the last station in the Kita-Saku plateau before the highway winds its way westward into the mountains to the next station, Mochizuki, where Ken's husband had come from); Makibuse's northern border also touched the Nakasendō. In 1694, at the age of sixteen, slightly earlier, perhaps, than was usual for girls, Ken's mother had married Rihei II.[17] She bore him a son, Shinzō, in 1700; a daughter, Ine, twelve years later; and finally Ken, her last child, seven years after that, in 1719.

Ken's father died the year she was born. By then Shinzō was nineteen, old enough to work the fields, and Ine, seven, could help care for her baby sister. At age fifteen, rather young, Ine married out to Yawata, where her mother (and paternal grandmother)[18] were from, perhaps to reduce the number of mouths to be fed in the family.[19] Ken's first

16. See the discussion of this issue in chapter 3.

17. Ichikawa Yūichirō (*Saku chihō*, 113) found that the average marriage age in the area was twenty-three to twenty-four for men and sixteen to seventeen for women. These are a couple of years lower than Hayami's findings for another district in Nagano or Smith's findings in his study of Nakahara (Hayami Akira and Nobuko Uchida, "Size of Household in a Japanese County throughout the Tokugawa Era," in *Household and Family in Past Time*, ed. Peter Laslett [Cambridge: Cambridge University Press, 1972], 502; Thomas C. Smith, *Nakahara: Family Farming and Population in a Japanese Village, 1717–1830* [Stanford: Stanford University Press, 1977], 94–96).

18. See the sixth entry in the 1671 population register of Makibuse, in NAK-KS2 (1): 771.

19. Smith (*Nakahara*, 93–95) found that daughters of wealthier families married considerably younger than those of poor families. He suggests that this may have to do with the fact that the poor spent time as servants to supplement

Plate 1. Makibuse Village. Facing west toward Mochizuki, some three hundred meters south of the Nakasendō. Photograph by author.

marriage, in 1737 at age eighteen, brought her to Mimayose, two kilometers beyond Yawata on the Nakasendō, leaving her mother and unmarried brother in Makibuse.

Shinzō's bachelor status at age thirty-seven needs some comment, although a specific psychological or other personal explanation is not available. Perhaps he had been married and was divorced; we do not know. The thought that he might have been an unattractive prospect seems culturally incongruent. Males must have had the strategic advantage in a society like that of Tokugawa Japan. It is possible that Shinzō could not afford a wife, that the reason of his bachelorhood was sociostructural rather than personal. In 1671, at least, the only bachelors of marriageable age in the village were indentured ser-

family income. In other circumstances, however, early marriage of daughters may have been a solution to the problem of too many mouths to feed.

vants.[20] A socioeconomic explanation would thus point to the near-poverty situation of the family, although even "landless," that is, tenant, peasants did marry, as did Ken.[21]

Outmarriage was quite common in Kita-Saku district from fairly early in the Tokugawa period, contrary to Smith's assumption of a "village rule of endogamy except for high-placed families who had to go outside the village to find marriage partners of comparable family rank."[22] The 1671 population register of Makibuse recorded thirty-two peasant households (including fourteen titled peasants), all but two headed by couples (see table 1). In addition, there were seven married sons, brothers, and nephews of titled peasants co-residing with their main families in an extended-family pattern, which makes a total of thirty-seven couples. Only seven of the thirty-seven wives were from Makibuse; all the others had inmarried from villages in the same district or, in one case, from another district. Yawata tops the list of villages as sources for wives, with five. As for outmarriage, fourteen daughters or sisters of current household heads married out. Only two Makibuse women married out to the Kita-Saku plain; the rest settled in the mountain area. On the other hand, ten wives came from the plain. All twenty-three bond servants (*genin* and *fudai*) came from the mountain area, from within a radius of eight kilometers.

Thus, the number of women marrying within the village (seven) was

20. According to the population register of 1671, none of the bond servants (genin and fudai) were married. There were nineteen indentured servants (genin) in Makibuse—twelve males ranging in age from thirteen to thirty-four and seven females between fourteen and twenty-three—and four lifetime servants (fudai) between the ages of nine and twenty-two (see NAK-KS2 [1]: 771–80).

21. Smith (*Nakahara*, 92) found that the probability of male celibacy in lower-class peasant families (those with holdings of less than four koku) was from two to ten times as high as that among wealthier peasants (67 percent for the cohort aged thirty to thirty-four and 41 percent for those aged thirty-five to forty-nine). Pierre Bourdieu discusses the structural necessity of bachelorhood of nonsuccessor males for reproducing the social system in the late nineteenth century in the Béarn in southern France in "Célibat et condition paysanne," *Études rurales*, nos. 5–6 (1962): 32–135.

22. Thomas C. Smith, *The Agrarian Origins of Modern Japan* (Stanford: Stanford University Press, 1959), 61, 62–63 n. 1. My occasional critique of this excellent study should be understood in light of the vast amount of Japanese scholarship produced in the last thirty years. In *Nakahara* (133–34, 143) Smith reports only that "nearly all daughters were married out of the family" but gives no figures for out-village marriage. See also the following note.

Table 1. Population of Makibuse, 1671–1764

	Population				Households				[Kokudaka]
	Male (genin)	Female (genin)	Total	Horses	Honbyakushō	Kakae	Mizunomi	Total	
1671	73 (13)	60 (10)	133	—	14	18	0	32	[175]
1700	93 (18)	80 (10)	173	—	16	24	0	40	
1717	121 (12)	104 (10)	225	18	13	30	4	47	[205]
1725	129 (14)	99 (11)	228	16	12	33	3	48	
1737	136 (15)	112 (9)	248	16	12	38	2	52	
1750	130 (11)	112 (9)	242	12	11	35	2	48	[205]
1764	129 (11)	115 (9)	244	10	11	43	3	57	

SOURCES: Adapted from Ozaki, "Kenjo oboegaki," table 9 (p. 97); the population for 1671 is from NAK-KS2 (1): 771–80, and the kokudaka is from NAK-KS2 (2), appendix p. 53.

NOTE: Land development seems to have reached its capacity in the late seventeenth century. The kokudaka of 205 was first recorded in 1704 (NAK-KS2 [1]: 613); between 1704 and 1834 another 16 koku were added.

only half of that marrying out, and this in a community where thirty-seven wives were needed for households to reproduce. If one adds all marital liaisons in and out of the village, the total is fifty-one, out of which only seven, or 14 percent, were endogamous to the village.[23] This contrasts sharply with 50 percent and 75 percent for other villages in the area (Komiyayama in 1669 and Wada in 1713, respectively), as Ichikawa Yūichirō relates.[24] He also concludes that the average marriage age in the district was twenty-three to twenty-four for men and sixteen to seventeen for women, and he notes that almost all of the indentured servants (genin) and lifetime servants (fudai) were unmarried.[25] In 1671 none of Makibuse's nineteen genin or four fudai were married.[26]

Let us return to the narrative. In 1742, five years after her first marriage, Ken's name reappears on Makibuse's family register, which means that she had left Mimayose and her husband, although it is unknown whether this was a divorce. The household she returned to, however,

---

23. Finding a wife appropriate to one's economic status, which might necessitate liaisons outside the village, does not seem to have been a motive either. After the 1670s the overwhelming majority of the peasants in Makibuse were very small landholders. The seven marriages within Makibuse that were recorded on the 1671 population register were as follows (*honbyakushō* means "titled peasant"; *kakae* refers to a branch house in a lineage):

1. Headman (29 koku) and daughter of honbyakushō (5 koku; 21 koku before partition)
2. Honbyakushō's son (6) and kakae (4) daughter
3. Kakae (2) and kakae (5) daughter
4. Kakae (2) and kakae (5) daughter
5. Honbyakushō (5; 23 before partition) and kakae (5) daughter
6. Kakae (5) and honbyakushō (7) daughter
7. Honbyakushō (7) and kakae (10) daughter

24. Ichikawa Yūichirō, *Saku chihō*, 83. On the other hand, Makibuse's geographic distribution of spousal provenance is very similar to that of Kodaira (a village studied in more detail in chapter 3), some four kilometers to the east. The latter's population register of 1694 lists fifty-four couples, in only six of which both partners had been born in Kodaira; in the other forty-eight, one spouse, usually the wife, came from within a radius of twelve kilometers, thirty-six from within a radius of four kilometers (see Komonjo kenkyūkai dai ni han, "Genroku-ki no shūmon aratamechō o miru," *Mochizuki no chōmin no rekishi* 12 [1988]: 64–65).

25. Ichikawa Yūichirō, *Saku chihō*, 110, 113.

26. See n. 20. For comparative data on lifetime servants and indentured servants in the area, see ibid., 108, 120 ff.

consisted now only of herself and her mother. Shinzō's name had disappeared from the register. The possible reasons for such disappearance are limited to a few: death, outmarriage to another locale (temporary employment elsewhere would be duly recorded and not cause removal of the name), petition by relatives and kumi members for reasons of disinheritance (kandō or kyūri), or abscondence to an unknown destination. The authorities kept a close tab on the whereabouts of all subjects.

The previous year's register offers no clue about Shinzō's fate. Ken's return, however, may have been prompted by the need to take care of her mother, then sixty-four years old (or seventy, according to the entry of that year), and the minuscule plot of land (0.19 koku, the equivalent of 2 ares or 0.04 acres, of medium-quality dry fields) for which her mother was responsible in the village. Or was this a pretext to get out of a marriage that was not working? Ken was left completely alone when her mother died in 1744, two years after her brother's disappearance. She was then twenty-five.

The death of her mother brought a change in Ken's "civic" status, as we know from the next year's entry. Until then the household had been registered as a kakae, or branch family, of her uncle Gendayū, her deceased father's younger brother. Kakae literally means "embrace" or "hold in one's arms" and refers to the client-patron relationship of dependency between branch and main houses; the term will be rendered hereafter as "branch house," "fully established branch house," or simply "client." Now she was legally incorporated into her uncle's household and entered under his name (she was thus chōnai, or "on [his] register," that is, co-resident), although it is unclear whether she actually moved into his house, since she had one of her own.

In order to grasp the significance of this change, one needs to understand the highly structured village social and political hierarchy. First, there was the great divide between peasants and nonpeasants, perhaps as great as the divide between rulers and ruled in the society at large. The nonpeasant population increased throughout the Tokugawa period as craftsmen, doctors, and others took up residence in the countryside in increasing numbers.[27] But these nonpeasants were marked in the registers as belonging to an inferior class: all of them were registered as clients or bond servants (genin).[28]

27. For Saku district, see ibid., 144–46.
28. Ibid., 128.

The first article in the village laws, including Makibuse's, reveals this hierarchy in the context of certifying that no Christians were present in the village: "Art. 1. Re: Christians. Following the investigations of the past, each and every one, down to the last person, has been thoroughly examined: not only (*mōshioyobazu*) house owners [but also] men, women, children, servants and semi-independent branch houses (*kadoya*), renters, fully established branch houses (kakae), down to (*sono ta ... itaru made*) Buddhist monks, Shinto priests, mountain priests (*yamabushi*), ascetics, mendicant monks with flutes or bells, outcastes, common beggars and registered beggars (*hinin*, "nonhumans"), etc...." (see appendix 3). This comprehensive list is clearly hierarchized; none of these undesirables seem to have resided in Makibuse.

Nonpeasants were second-class citizens within the village, yet some peasants also fell into this category. At the bottom were *mizunomi-byakushō*, literally, "water-drinking peasants," without land of their own, pure tenants whose number increased over time. Next were nontitled landholders, who, although they were autonomous proprietors, were incorporated into a political dependency relationship as real or fictitious fully established branch houses (kakae) to main families, lineage heads, or patrons (*kakaeoya*). Thus were constituted lineages and sublineages, crisscrossing or overlapping the kumi (as in Makibuse). All landowning peasants, even immigrants, belonged to a "lineage." Prior to Ken's mother's death, her household was a kakae under her uncle Gendayū.

The titled peasants (*honbyakushō*) constituted the village council, and all lineage heads were titled peasants. In the eyes of overlords, they were the official tribute deliverers. The two categories of landowning peasants—fully established branch houses and lineage heads—often had a number of dependents: lifetime (fudai) and indentured (genin) servants, semi-established branch families living in a separate dwelling on the premises (kadoya), renters, and dependent co-resident members, like Ken after her mother's death.

This multilayered class, status, and social hierarchy, which allowed for some controlled mobility (specified later for Makibuse), was thus from the bottom up: nonpeasants, lifetime servants, indentured servants, co-residents, pure tenants, semi-established branch houses, fully established branch houses, titled peasants (who allowed for further power combinations with the suprahousehold authority positions of lineage head, kumi head, and headman).

In 1721 Makibuse counted thirteen titled peasants (the same number as in 1647 but three fewer than in 1700 [see table 4]) and thirty-six others, among whom were four landless peasants who first appear on the rosters around 1710 (see table 1). In 1721, moreover, of the forty-five landholding peasants sixteen had holdings of less than 1 koku, eighteen had between 1 and 4 koku, and eleven had 5 or more koku. Ken's household was among the poorest in Makibuse. With its 0.19 koku, it was dangerously close to landless status. Ken was not a titled peasant, and her shift in status from fully established branch house (kakae) to co-resident (chōnai) meant the loss of an already very circumscribed control over her own life.

FAILED MARRIAGES, MISFIRED FORGERIES: 1745–1756

A year after her mother's death, in the winter of 1745, Ken married someone from Kannonji-shinden, six kilometers northwest of Makibuse, into the mountains. This second marriage, however, was not one that would provide her house with a male head or successor because she had married *out*. Apparently, in this case, unlike in 1762–63, the village authorities put no obstacles in the way of Ken's leaving. Could the only difference have been that this time she seems to have had no plans to transfer her land to a temple? Ken was supposed to take up residence with her husband in Kannonji-shinden. Yet, oddly enough, she did not seize this opportunity to leave the village, because she either returned very soon to Makibuse or remained there all along.

The reason for this short-lived union was recorded as having to do with Ken's husband's postponing the building of their new house because of some problems with its proper geomantic orientation. One is led to believe that there was procrastination and deliberate reluctance on Ken's part because her patron uncle and relatives showed impatience, making her sign a promise in 1746/3 "to move without fail (sōmaku) to Kannonji-shinden by next spring." This time her lineage wanted her out badly, but she did not want to go—the opposite of the situation in 1762–63. The population register of two years later (1748), however, indicates no change: Ken had not moved to Kannonji-shinden, and she remained listed as co-resident under her uncle Gendayū. Ken's return did not signal a firm determination to remain in Makibuse, though, because she went on a three-year stint as a servant in two places quite different from Kannonji-shinden: Hirabara and Komoro. This absence, however, did not sever her ties with Makibuse, where she remained registered.

Kannonji-shinden was a very small village of Komoro domain, that never amounted to much as it expanded quickly to its full capacity of a meager sixty-four koku.[29] Ken's places of employment were not in the mountains but in the wealthier Kita-Saku plain. She worked first for one year in Hirabara, some fifteen kilometers northeast of Makibuse, then for two years in the castle town of Komoro, the center of the small fudai domain some thirteen kilometers almost due north (gradually reduced by 1700 to 15,000 koku from an original 50,000), of which Makibuse was a part for some time (1590–1647). Both Hirabara (a sizable village of 1,474 koku in 1647, 2,018 in 1834, with a population of 602 in 1760) and the town of Komoro (with 357 households and a population of 3,620 in 1746) were situated on the Hokkokukaidō, the highway that splits off to the north from the Nakasendō in Oiwake at the foot of Mount Asama (see map 2).

It seems that, after her misfortunes, Ken sought to escape from her kin and had no intention of continuing the household by adopting an heir or remarrying.[30] Nor did she want to leave the village for good by marrying out to a rather remote place in the mountains like Kannonji-shinden. After her service, she reappears on the village register in 1752 as a resident, and then we lose track of her until her third marriage, in 1756.

There is a short document dated 1755/12 that was signed by the priest of a temple from Koshigoe, some sixteen kilometers northeast of Makibuse, beyond the mountains in the neighboring district of Chiisa-

29. Originally, Kannonji-shinden was part of Innai village, which in 1624 had a *kokudaka* of 526 koku, to which 88 koku of new fields (*shinden*) had been added by 1703. It remained unchanged until the end of the Tokugawa period (at least until 1834). By 1703 Kannonji-shinden had split off as a separate village with 64 koku, which also remained unchanged. Its population was registered as seventy-nine in 1760. For these figures, see NAK-KS2 (1): 7, 27, 120; and Nagano-ken, ed., *Nagano-kenshi: Kinsei shiryō-hen*, Vol. 2, *Tōshin chihō*, pt. 2 (Nagano-shi: Nagano-kenshi kankōkai, 1979), app. 53 (hereafter NAK-KS2 [2]).

30. There may have been some affinal connection explaining Ken's choice of Hirabara, although this is sheer speculation. According to the 1671 population register, Heijirō's wife came from there and Heijirō (C[4] of fig. 1) was a brother of Rihei I (C[1]), Ken's grandfather.

gata, south of Ueda city. It is a certificate of leave addressed to Maki-buse village officials, and it mentions Shinzō's name. Ozaki Yukiya discovered several irregularities in the composition of this certificate, especially when compared with a similar one dated a mere eight months later (1756/8):

Paper (*issatsu no koto*)

Re: this Shinzō. He is a person who was born in the village of Naka-Maruko. There is no question that [his family] has been registered with this temple for generations. Now he is moving to your village as a suc-cessor [to a house there]. Therefore, as the original guarantor of his reli-gious affiliation, [I submit] the above document.

Hōreki 5/12 [1755/12], Koshigoe village
Zenbō-in temple (seal)
[*To:*] Makibuse village officials.

Certificate of Leave for Rokuemon

Certificate of leave Re: Yohachi, 39 years old
The above mentioned person was born in this village and is certified as such. He is moving to your honorable village as successor to Rihei. Please add him to your population register and put him under your jurisdiction. For future reference, this sending document is as stated above.

Hōreki 6/8 [1756/8],
The [Nakasendō] Station of Mochizuki,
Ōmori Hisazaemon, headman (seal)
[*To:*] Makibuse headman, Tsuchiya Chūemon[31]

The second document is addressed to Makibuse's headman (not to the village officials, as the first document is) by the headman of origin, Mochizuki (and not by the person's family temple, as in the first docu-ment), where the person in question, Yohachi (or Rokuemon), was reg-istered. It records Rokuemon's age and the house (Rihei's) to which he will succeed in Makibuse, both of which are missing in the former docu-ment, and requests that his name be added to the population register in that capacity (also missing in the former document). The second docu-ment is more formal and complete.

Next to be noted is the name of Shinzō, the same name as Ken's brother, who had disappeared thirteen years earlier, leaving the house

31. Both documents are cited only in Ozaki, "Kenjo oboegaki," 67, 68. The title of the second document was added on a separate sheet by the headman for filing purposes.

without a male head. Ken's two divorces and her seeming reluctance to adopt another husband had put the continuity of that house in jeopardy. If someone by that name were now to be recorded in Ken's household, it would appear that the original Shinzō had returned. Everything points to a forgery in the making. Ultimately the attempt must have been abandoned, because no Shinzō appears on subsequent population registers in Makibuse, and the forged document might inadvertently have been filed among the headman's papers. As noted, only one year later, in 1756/8, Ken married Yohachi/Rokuemon from Mochizuki (her third husband).[32] The second document is the one Rokuemon brought with him when he moved to Makibuse (the Rihei mentioned is none other than Ken's father).

It should be pointed out that this kind of document, a notification of a marriage union, does not mention the wife. Is it too much to interpret this as indicating the absence of a legal status for women as contributing to a man's identity as his wife? The two legal entities that are united here are a male and a house. Presumably, if the person being sent were a woman, she would be spoken of as joining a male, as acquiring a new identity as someone's wife. Is the phrase "successor to a house," as Bourdieu suggests, writing of Berber heirs in a similar situation, "an official euphemism allowing people to name the unnameable, that is a man who could only be defined, in the house that receives him, as the husband of his wife"?[33]

Rokuemon's arrival brought another change in Ken's "civic" status: she was promoted from co-resident to head of a fully established branch house (kakae). Moreover, her patron/lineage head was now Jūzaemon (E^4 of fig. 1), not her uncle Gendayū, her legal guardian for twelve years, since her mother's death.

SHIFTING POWER WITHIN A LINEAGE: 1670–1756

At the time, Ken's lineage was subdivided into two sublineages, headed by two patrons: Gendayū and Jūzaemon. It had not always been that

32. Anne Walthall, upon reading this, made the interesting remark that while Shinzō was presumably too destitute (0.19 koku) to take a wife, Ken succeeded in adopting a husband, which was supposed to be more difficult than marrying a woman. Ken's obviously strong personality may perhaps partly explain this.

33. Pierre Bourdieu, *The Logic of Practice* (Stanford: Stanford University Press, 1991), 179.

Fig. 1. Genzaemon's Lineage, 1629–1756

$\vert$	lineal succession
$\Vert$	same person

Year							
1629			A(20)^a				
1650			B(20)^a				
1671	C^{5,c}	C^{4,c}					C^{1,b}
1677		(4.8)^c	(10)^c				(8)^{b,c}
1684		(4.8)^c	C^3(5)^c	C^2(5)^c			(8)^{b,c}
1690		(4.3)^c	(4.3)^c	(1.2)^c			(8)^{a,b,c}
1700		D^5(6.3)^{b,d,e}	D^4(5)^{d,e}	D^3(1.2)^c	D^2(6.3)^{c,e}		D^1(2.9)^{b,c}
1721		D^6(6.3)^{b,d,e}	E^2(3.4)^d	E^1(2.8)^d	(7.3)^{b,c}		SHINZŌ(1.9)^c
1741		E^3(7.1)^{b,d,e}	(8.9)^{d,e}	(5.7)^{d,e}	(7.3)^{b,c}		(0.19)^c
1756	E^5(3.7)^d	(3.8)^d E^4(3.9)^{b,d,e}	F(4.5)^{d,e}	(4.5)^{d,e}	(2.07)^{b,c}		KEN (0.18)^d

Age	23	47	29	29	59	76	37

^{a} village headman (plus lineage head and titled peasant)
^{b} lineage or sublineage head
^{c} household in dependent relationship with C line lineage
^{d} household in dependent relationship with D line sublineage
^{e} possession of one horse

SOURCE: Adapted from Ozaki, "Kenjo ikken," table 4 (p. 57).

NOTES: The total yield of the lineage property held by Genzaemon (A) in 1629 is 20 koku; that held by 7 households in 1756 is 22 koku. Note that Ken switched sublineages: she is not dependent on D^2 but on E^4.

way. Originally Ken's paternal ancestors had headed the lineage. Since around 1670 there had been four households, headed then by Rihei I, Ken's grandfather (C^1 of fig. 1). Around 1700 there were five households (D^1—D^5) headed by two patrons, Ken's father, Rihei II (D^1), being patron to two units, and Rihei's cousin (D^5), to one. By the 1750s, however, power within the lineage had shifted further away from Rihei's line, for now Rihei II's cousin's son Jūzaemon (E^4) was patron to four households (E^1, F, E^3, E^5), while the other "patron," Gendayū (D^2), had Ken "registered under him," but not as a fully established branch house, so that he was, properly speaking, no longer patron of a segment of the lineage.

As mentioned above, the patron-client (or main house–branch house) lineage structure was a strictly internal village affair, not regulated by shogunal law (although disputes concerning it, unresolvable in the village, could come before intendants). That it was private or informal from the lord's point of view does not mean that lineage practice was not formalized and regulated locally. The distinction between private and public does not pertain to the presence or absence of political regulation as such; rather, it defines the modality of jurisdictional recognition between two social units one of which encompasses the other. Thus the famous revenge of the forty-seven *rōnin* of Akō, masterless samurai who avenged their lord, was for the bakufu not a private but a public act and therefore under its jurisdiction. The bakufu left lineages alone, recognizing as legal entities only neighborhood kumi as public institutions at the subvillage level. Nevertheless, as we shall see repeatedly, lineages were crucial for the communal organization of villages.

Every peasant household in the Kita-Saku area had to be accounted for intramurally in a patron-client relationship; none could function otherwise. Even new settlers from outside had first to secure a sponsoring patron in addition to the village council's approval. Since political power was limited to titled peasants, who held access shares to irrigation, common grass or mountain land, and so on, and lineage heads were always titled peasants, a client's access to power and its benefits was totally dependent on his or her relationship to a patron and the latter's position and standing among the titled peasants. A client who had serious complaints about his or her patron or lineage head could ask the village council to switch the household to a different patron.[34] Such change, together with the reasons for it, was duly recorded in the village.

Ken was able to elevate her status from co-resident back to branch house, as it had been when her brother and mother were still alive, by securing a male head and eventual successor to the house through marriage. This increased her autonomy vis-à-vis her lineage patron. Ken's switch to Jūzaemon as her new patron was a double blow for

34. For examples of newcomers seeking a patron, clients wanting to switch lineages (in the neighboring villages of Gorobe-shinden and Yawata), and other cases illustrating the position of clients, see Ōishi Shinzaburō, *Kinsei sonraku no kōzō to ie seido* (Ochanomizu shobō, 1968), 125–37.

Gendayū, for now he lost control over Ken's household and his status as patron, for he had no other clients. The whole lineage, except for himself, because he was a titled peasant, was now controlled by Jūzaemon, who had five branch houses as his clients.

The reason for this change was recorded as "disharmony (*fuwa*)" between Ken and her uncle: "Hōreki 6 [1756]. Ken is taken out as coresident from under Gendayū. There being disharmony with her uncle [Gendayū], Ken is also removed as client and will be client of her cousin [in reality her linealogical third cousin] Jūzaemon." Ken's failed marriages and her three-year absence from the village must have been related as cause or effect to this "disharmony," but relations must have been very strained for her to want and to be granted severance from her uncle. We know the real reason from a petition she submitted to the headman in the summer of 1757, a year after her marriage to Rokuemon.

AN OPEN SECRET PUBLICIZED AFTER SEVENTEEN YEARS: 1757

On 1757/7/22 Ken made the rounds of all her kumi/lineage members, the three kumi heads and the headman, in other words, all the authority figures in Makibuse. She told them that she had a request to make. This was obviously a serious matter, because that day the headman started keeping notes of meetings, recording also the absence of any officials and the reason for it, as well as occasional quotations of who said what.[35] He obviously was creating a paper trail to cover himself, for Ken's request concerned the violent death of her brother, Shinzō. The headman recorded that he consulted with two villagers that same evening. Two days later he got in touch with the Shimogata magistrate.

Thus prepared, before Ken had even made her request officially known, and most likely having agreed among themselves on a strategy, the village officials took the first steps four days later, on 7/28. On that

35. Ozaki shared with me a copy of this diary, which he used for his narrative. I have supplemented some details after reading the diary (with the help of Kainuma Yoshiko, whose assistance I gratefully acknowledge). The document is called "Oken mōshidashisōrō ichigi nikki" and runs from 1757/7/22 to 11/18. The original is with the house of Tsuchiya Shingorō, descendant of the Tokugawa headman, in Makibuse.

day the gathered officials (the headman and the four kumi heads) called all Ken's relatives for a hearing. When Rokuemon, Ken's husband, was asked whether he agreed with Ken, he replied that "she had not involved him at all (*watakushi e wa issai kamawase mōsazu sōrō*)." While his answer may sound implausible, it is not impossible that he knew nothing about this matter. He had moved to Makibuse to marry Ken only eleven months earlier. His answer was important, however, because it was certainly irregular for a wife to engage in public action that took on the appearance of a lawsuit without her husband's consent, since he held legal authority over the household.

The interrogators must have known that this was a wedge they could possibly drive into Ken's intentions. In Rokuemon's written affidavit taken three weeks later, it is indeed clearly stated that "I did not know anything about it" and that "I am not of the same mind [as Ken] on this (*ichien dōshin tsukamatsurazu*)."

His wife's pursuit of a lawsuit, with or without his knowledge or assent, must have humiliated Rokuemon, for it showed his inability to keep order in his own household as was his duty. Moreover, lawsuits were to be avoided at all cost. Those who resorted to them were written about in the village law as being on a par with other troublemakers and thus as people who should be reported: "Art. 16. People who are not engaged in cultivation, trade, or any other occupation, or withdraw from consultation with the village, or like quarrels and lawsuits, or do all kinds of bad things should not be hidden [but reported]" (see appendix 3).

Rokuemon left Ken in 1759/2, a year and a half after Ken's lawsuit. He may have returned to his native Mochizuki, which was very close. There is also a written pledge from around this time to stay away from sake; his problems must have led him to drink. All his in-laws and the household heads of the Jūzaemon group tried in vain to bring him back. Shortly thereafter, Ken added her voice and persuaded him to return.[36]

Obviously, life in Makibuse had become unbearable for Rokuemon, yet Ken prevailed for a while in keeping him home. Finally, he could not take it any longer, and two years later, in 1761, he disappeared for good. Ken, however, must have had problems too, for around the same time she started petitioning to leave the village. Indeed, as we shall see,

36. The history of Rokuemon's earlier disappearances is discussed only in Ozaki, "Kenjo oboegaki," 72.

her first request coincides with the moment she understood that her suit had failed.

As mentioned above, Ken directed her accusations against her relatives, among others, especially against her uncle and former guardian, Gendayū. This suit, which had been on her mind for some time, sheds light on Ken's second and third marriages. Her second one came to a quick end because her move to another village under a different jurisdiction (Komoro domain) would have made a suit nearly impossible. This marriage would have removed the only voice critical of what had happened to Shinzō.

Perhaps Ken sensed that this arranged marriage was an exile in disguise, which may explain her resistance under the flimsy pretext of inauspicious geomantic matters. Yet her reinstatement as Gendayū's co-resident robbed her of the voice she needed if she intended to file a suit, especially a suit against him. Once registered under him, Ken was legally as incompetent as a child, and "hierarchy suits," in which children might sue fathers or retainers might sue their superiors, were outlawed.[37]

Ken's third marriage, to Rokuemon, however, solved the problem of legal voice, because it gave her back her status as a member of an autonomous household. It is quite possible that through this marriage she intended not so much to put the minds of her relatives to rest by securing the succession to her house (especially since later she would categorically refuse to take the necessary steps for establishing an heir) as to dissolve her total dependency on Gendayū, block any interference by him, and gain the necessary authority to act publicly.[38] Rokuemon, perceived by others and perhaps himself as having been used by a scheming woman, lost his bearings, fell apart, ran away, and finally fled for good.

Ken was present at the hearing of 2/28, but she was not asked about

37. Dan Fenno Henderson, *Conciliation and Japanese Law, Tokugawa and Modern*, 2 vols. (Seattle: University of Washington Press, 1965), 1:118: "Whether they were family or feudal, the rule was that suits brought by inferiors were not accepted."

38. I would like to record Professor Yokota Fuyuhiko's cautious reservation as he communicated it to me in Kyoto in the summer of 1994 regarding my interpretation of the legal dimension of Ken's third marriage. In his opinion, universal registration in Tokugawa Japan created, *in principle,* the notion that everybody had the right to petition or sue, a "right" that was, however, thwarted in many practical ways. In this view, strictly speaking, Ken would not have needed that marriage to give her legal voice.

her "request." Instead, she was told that an oral request would not do: if she had a petition to make, she should put it in writing. The next day, a report of the investigation was sent to Shimogata, probably under the assumption that things had been taken care of. By insisting on a written petition, the officials must have aimed at more than a postponement of the case, calculating that without her husband's consent and assistance, and with the whole village against her, Ken would be unable to draft a formal document.

Ken, however, was a resourceful woman. A week later, on 8/5, in the evening, she delivered a written petition to the village authorities via the proper channel, that is, via Jūzaemon, her patron and kumi head. Early the next morning, Jūzaemon rushed the document to the headman, who convened the village officials that same evening. Ten days later the document was forwarded to Shimogata.

The first half reads as follows:

> This is a request to hold the seventeenth memorial service for my elder brother Shinzō. I have mountains and mountains of grudges against Mr. Chūemon [the headman]. He called my relatives and he called the whole village together, deliberated with them, gave detailed instructions, and [thus] the innocent peasant of my house [my brother] was killed. If he had been guilty [of some crime], my mother or myself would have been told the details by my relatives. [But] because he was blameless they kept silent to us. He was killed [because the headman] had wondered what [other misbehavior Shinzō] might engage in next, given the things he had been doing. Spite and vexation about this murder have piled up mountain high, which I kept in my heart until this year. I want to pray for the repose of his soul with a memorial offering so that your descendants may not suffer divine retribution. Anyhow, following my judgment (*nanibun ni mo kono kata no zonji yori ni*), I request that a memorial service be held.
>
> On 1741/11/6 [a week after the murder], my relative Shinzaemon [E[1] of fig. 1] called people together and I went [Ken must have returned to Makibuse from Mimayose] and heard details about this. Shinzaemon said that an order had come from the headman to have a memorial service held, since Shinzō had been killed. I returned home and told my mother the details [of what I had heard]. My sister also came from Yawata station [where she had married]. Anyhow, we thought of filing a suit for punishment with the shogunal authorities (*gokōgisama*). But I was young [twenty-three] and mother lost her mind because this had been too much for her, so that I abandoned the plan until this year.
>
> I have mountains of resentment against Mr Gendayū [my uncle; D[2]] in this matter. [At one point, Shinzō] lost the horse of my sister's husband Jingoemon from Yawata and came to borrow money [to pay back his

brother-in-law], but my mother refused because they both [her son and son-in-law] were her children [she said], so he went to Gendayū, who lent him the money [on the condition] that [Shinzō] henceforward stop dealing with horse people. All the relatives signed a note to that effect.

In addition, on 1741/16 his uncle had entrusted his own horse [to Shinzō], who had [mishandled] it, so that it could not be sold. For this reason [he] did not [dare to] come home. If he were to come home, my uncle, Mr. Gendayū, threatened to kill him. This being the case, Shinzō pondered setting out for another province, but the thought of leaving his old mother behind alone held him back. So he hung around in the area and stayed at a dry field [owned by the family] at the foot of Ichiyama. There, everybody [got together] and a big crowd drove him out, and so on 1741/10/31, in the evening, it was inevitable that he was killed (*uchikorosaresōrō wa hitchō gozarō*) beyond the great bridge of Momozawa.

Shinzaemon [E^1] delivered the first blow with a club, for which I heaped mountains of hatred on him. But now, after seventeen years, I shall forgive him. [They] were told [to kill] this innocent man by the headman, but they should [simply] have banished him. Dan'emon, who delivered blows, after seventeen years I can forgive. Uheiji [F] is without blame, but Bunkyūrō [his brother], who died, he also delivered blows and is guilty. I do not know about Chōkyūrō [E^3], Naoemon [peasant representative; 1.b of table 5], Iheie [kumi head; 5.F of table 5], Kichizaemon [kumi head; 13.v of table 5] and the people of the village. But those who participated in this murder must know about them.[39]

Thus, the reason for the disappearance of Shinzō's name from the village population register in the spring of 1742 was that he had been clubbed to death by his relatives and fellow villagers a few months earlier. Ken heard about it, although perhaps not in great detail, at the time of the memorial service ordered by the headman, very likely to protect himself and all accomplices against Shinzō's avenging spirit. Together with her sister and mother, Ken had pondered the possibility of pressing charges with the shogunal authorities, a plan she abandoned, but only for seventeen years, as it turned out. Over time, Ken probably picked up bits and pieces of the story, which was a public secret. Realizing Gendayū's role in her brother's murder must have made life under him unbearable, a situation so perfectly euphemized by calling it *fuwa*, disharmony.

Ken's most serious accusations, however, were directed at the head-

39. Ozaki, "Kenjo ikken," 50–51. The second half of this document is discussed below.

man for allegedly ordering the murder of a man who, although admittedly a troublemaker, certainly did not deserve the fate that befell him. Ken deduced Shinzō's "innocence" from the silence of those who should have informed her and her mother of the reason for his death. Shinzō's troubles had centered around horse trading and gambling, both activities that were disapproved. Article 51 of the village law specifically warns against horse thieves and go-betweens in horse trading (see appendix 3). This angered most of all his uncle Gendayū, who seems to have used Shinzō as a middleman to sell his own horse, which Shinzō somehow must have spoiled.[40] Understandably angry, Gendayū threatened to kill Shinzō, which implicates him heavily in this "death almost foretold," as Gabriel Garcia Márquez might put it. According to Ken, there had been malign intention to kill her brother: an order by the headman and a threat by Gendayū. She blames her relatives for having followed a death order rather than simply expelling Shinzō, and she names people who might know more about other participants in the murder. Although Ken stated her accusation within the context of a professed desire to hold a memorial service and a willingness to pardon some of those involved in the crime (about which more will be said later), she was seeking at least some justice—from the accused—for a crime committed seventeen years earlier.

If the village officials had ordered the murder as a punishment, they were in double or even triple jeopardy: for contracting a murder, for committing it, and for going beyond the bounds of their penal jurisdiction by issuing a death verdict, if, in fact, that is what they did. This last point is important, for as we know, in principle, "private justice" was forbidden by shogunal law.

The historian Mizumoto Kunihiko lists seventeenth-century laws (which did not change during the next century) at various jurisdictional

---

40. In 1737 there were 16 horses in Makibuse, which then counted 12 titled peasants out of a total of 52 households, with a total population of 248. In 1750 the figures were slightly different: 12 horses, 11 titled peasants out of a total of 48 households, and a population of 242 (see table 1); thus there was almost one horse per titled peasant. The price of a horse is discussed as follows by Tanaka Kyūgū (1662–1729) in his *Minkan seiyō* of 1721: "Peasants need horses, but their price has gone up in recent years. In the past, one could get a horse for one or two *ryō*. Now, however, there are no horses for that price ... now one cannot even get them for ten ryō" (*Nihon keizai sōsho*, ed. Takimoto Sei'ichi, vol. 1 [Nihon keizai sōsho kankōkai, 1914], 261). In article 13 of appendix 4, a price of "from 3 *bu* to one ryō" is referred to in 1665.

levels prohibiting punishments such as wounding or killing by villagers: shogunal laws issued for intendants to be applied in their districts, bannerman laws for their fiefs, and bakufu-ordered village laws.[41] The heaviest penalty allowed at the village level was banishment, although, as we shall see in chapter 4, scholars have recently discovered a small number of exceptions. In addition, Mizumoto cites instances of enforcement of such laws: in Okayama domain a headman was beheaded for having "secretly" (i.e., "privately" on his own initiative, without reporting it to the higher authorities), and with the help of others, killed a thief (1676); village officials in a shogunal fief were fined in 1778 for having "secretly" banished a thief to another province. Makibuse's village law explicitly prohibited the killing of evildoers (article 4) or the plotting by peasants of evil things (article 17; see appendix 3).

The officials in Makibuse saw their options for getting rid of this case disappearing fast once an official accusation of murder had been made. If behind the attempt to have Ken married out to Kannonji-shinden lay the intention to get rid of the one dissident voice against them, they had failed. Doing away with the evidence by eliminating the litigant was obviously much too extreme and risky. Besides, the recommended punishment for such a crime in shogunal courts was the death penalty, followed by gibbetting of the severed head.[42] Persuading Ken to withdraw her suit did not work either. Hence, they had to transmit the suit to the Shimogata office because murder was a matter beyond village jurisdiction and the investigation and punishment had to be left to the higher authorities.

What the village officials resorted to, as already mentioned, was seeking secret advice from the Shimogata magistrate on how to handle this

41. Mizumoto Kunihiko, "Kōgi no saiban to shūdan no okite," *Saiban to kihan*, Nihon no shakaishi, 5 (Iwanami shoten, 1987), 285–86 (hereafter NNS 5); the information on village punishment in the following paragraphs comes from p. 286.

42. *Kujikata osadamegaki* (1742), art. 71, par. *shi, tsuika* of 1744 (*Tokugawa kinreikō kōshū*, ed. Ishii Ryōsuke, 4 vols. [Sōbunsha, 1959–61], 3:419 [hereafter TKKk]). For an English translation of book 2 of the *Kujikata osadamegaki*, see John C. Hall, "Japanese Feudal Laws III: Tokugawa Legislation, Part IV, The Edict in 100 Sections," *Transactions of the Asiatic Society of Japan* 41, pt. 5 (1913): 683–804. For a German translation of the whole work, see Otto Rudorff, "Tokugawa-Gesetz-Sammlung," *Mittheilungen der Deutschen Gesellschaft für Natur- und Völkerkunde Ostasiens in Tokio*, supplement to vol. 5 (April 1889).

case before officially transmitting the suit to him. That much we know from Makibuse's headman's diary, but he did not record the nature of this advice. We can only follow the developments surmising what it might have been.

The shogunal legislation that would be applied in an eventual trial was as follows. The law provided for severe punishments, graded according to the nature of the murder, the perpetrators, their motives, their degree of participation, and the status of the victim. For example, accidentally killing a nephew was punished by banishment; but if the murder had been premeditated for gain, it was punished by death (*shizai*). Contracting a murder was punished by death (*geshunin*); executing a contract murder, by banishment. Among accomplices, the one who struck the first blow received the death penalty (geshunin), those who assisted were banished, and those who did not physically participate in the crime were punished by medium deportation (10 miles).[43]

There existed some half-dozen different death penalties, of which shizai and geshunin were the lowest two. Death penalties were always beheadings, to which various additional degrees of nastiness could be added, such as exposure of the criminal, gibbetting, and so on. Shizai always entailed the availability of the corpse for sword practice (*tameshimono*) by samurai and confiscation of the criminal's property (*kessho*). Geshunin, as a rule reserved only for commoners, was based on the retribution principle calling for the taking of a life if a murder has been committed; the corpse and property were left intact.[44]

INVESTIGATING AN ALLEGATION

On 8/16, a week after Ken's document was forwarded to Shimogata, Ken's relatives were called together by the village officials to ascertain their intentions. As was to be expected, they disagreed with Ken's statement, which again left her alone to face the whole village and its authorities. She had no allies.

The next day Ken was summoned by the headman and informed of her relatives' intention not to back her up, to which Ken apparently retorted, "If my request is not settled after submitting it to the [Shi-

43. Ibid.
44. Hiramatsu Yoshirō, *Edo no tsumi to batsu* (Heibonsha, 1988), 94.

mogata] public office (*Goyakushosama negai age*), I shall go all the way to the Edo office (*Edohyō*)."[45] The headman's ploy to keep the lid on this case foundered on Ken's forceful counterthreat to bring the case to court in Edo. Always upping the ante in her confrontations with authority, Ken invariably found ways to respond to official threats with threats of her own. Thus, the Shimogata office was officially informed of Ken's suit.

On 8/21 life came to a halt in Makibuse. Early that morning all those involved in Ken's suit, practically the whole village (the headman, the kumi leaders, and all the members of the kumi), were summoned to Shimogata for interrogation. Yet the question addressed to Ken was not about her allegations. It concerned Shinzō's relationship to his household and Ken's knowledge thereof: did Ken know that her brother had been disinherited? She testified that she had never been informed about it but added that if Shinzō had indeed been disinherited, "what I have said will have difficulty standing up (*watakushi mōsu bun aitachinikui tatematsuri zonji sōrō*)." In other words, her indictment might be null and void.

Ken had married and left home four years before her brother's disappearance. Therefore, it is possible that she did not know that Shinzō had indeed been disinherited only a few months before he was killed. Shinzaemon, however, produced then and there the disinheritance deed. Seeing that the killers would escape prosecution, Ken spat out, "Now I hate you even more." We shall return later to this question of disinheritance (kyūri). Let us first follow the investigation to its conclusion.

A second question pressed upon Ken was how she had drawn up the lawsuit. Her ability to do this, after all, had thwarted the village officials' plan to ever let it come this far. Ken admitted that she had paid someone to draft the document, but she was fierce in her refusal to reveal the name of the person who had assisted her. "I won't tell you," she fired back, "even if I lose my head for it."

A war was being waged here over knowledge of documents. The disinheritance deed nullified Ken's suit, and she was ultimately accused of lying when she maintained her ignorance of its existence. The officials, on the other hand, tried to prevent her from producing a docu-

45. Ozaki, "Kenjo oboegaki," 76.

ment, the suit, in order to avoid an investigation, and they insisted (in vain) on knowing who had composed it. Ken's ignorance was the weapon used by the officials against Ken (she should have known about the disinheritance), that she was quick to use against them when she refused to reveal the name of the scribe.

Of course, we do not know who helped Ken. It is unlikely that it was someone from the village. If she had to find help elsewhere, however, she would not have had to search far. Her family temple in Iribuse, to which she intended to commend her property, was only one kilometer away. She could have gone to Yawata, where her sister was living and where her mother and grandmother had come from. By this time in the Tokugawa period there were literate people in most villages, some even with scholarly pretensions. For example, in Katakura village, two and a half kilometers beyond the hills west of Makibuse, one of the village officials had a collection of books and manuscripts, even a copy of a work by Yamagata Shūnan, one of Ogyū Sorai's disciples.[46]

There were thus ways to circumvent the village elite's monopoly on writing and on writing in proper form (which meant power in a regime that governed through documents). Ken's "petition," nevertheless, was not in proper form, for it gave too much vent to her resentment and hatred and was devoid of the obligatory deferential formulae, besides being extremely difficult to understand. It looks like a draft for a suit and allows a rare glimpse at a commoner's feelings, and rarer still, at a woman's confrontation with authority.

At this juncture, a senior retainer (*karō*) from Shimogata joined the case and examined the evidence. Ken gave up her lawsuit, owing to the legal point made of Shinzō's disinheritance, and then requested to leave the village. She must have realized that life there would be hell, and those with the power to decide whether to release her or to consign her to the village for life must have realized it as well. She was given no final answer; instead, she was "entrusted" to her husband Rokuemon, a euphemism for house confinement. This closed the first round of the investigation. Now that Ken's allegations had been thoroughly discredited, the matter of Shinzō's violent death could be taken up—rather safely, one should add.

46. Nagano-ken, ed., *Nagano-kenshi: Tsūshi 5 (Kinsei 2)* (Nagano-shi: Nagano-kenshi kankōkai, 1988), 251 (hereafter NAK-T 5).

A whole month went by before, on 9/21, Gendayū testified and admitted to the murder as follows:

> Shinzō was doing evil things [gambling] roaming about the mountain where he lived. Therefore, the lineage and the whole village banished him. They drove him out beyond the bridge at Momozawa, at which point Shinzō turned around, and because he raised his hand against me, I had to hit him with the club I held in my hand. In the commotion that followed, it was hard to tell who was doing what (*dare to mōsu koto mo naku bō nite uchimōshisōrō*). Blows fell, resulting in his death.[47]

Gendayū's legal ground for defense was built into his testimony, perhaps on the Shimogata officials' private advice. Shinzō had started the fight, and his death was therefore not premeditated; it was a rebuttal of Ken's attempt to impute intention to the accused. Moreover, he had been thrown out of the village for good reason (gambling), and it was his resistance to this punishment that had led to the tragedy. On Ken's own admission, the headman had wondered "what would be next, given that he does all these things."

That Shinzō "raised his hand first" was most likely crucial to Gendayū's defense—insofar as a defense was still needed. This had two legal consequences. First, it turned Shinzō's violent death into something other than murder: an unfortunate accident for which the victim was to blame (he had resisted expulsion from the village). And second, the alibi introduced an element that today would be labeled "justified and legal self-defense."

One article of the shogunal penal code read: "When, due to the unreasonable behavior of one party, one has no choice but to cut him or her down, if it is certain that the relatives and village headman of the victim acknowledge that he or she was ordinarily unlawful in behavior, offer no excuses for the person in question, and beg that the killer be pardoned, the punishment is to be medium deportation [i.e., a lessening of the sentence]."[48] Moreover, although in principle arrests of criminals by official or private parties had to take place without the infliction of harm, if it happened that the criminals got killed under certain circumstances, the killers would not be held responsible.[49]

---

47. Ozaki, "Kenjo ikken," 52.
48. *Kujikata osadamegaki*, art. 72 (TKKk 4:1).
49. Hiramatsu Yoshirō, *Kinsei keiji soshōhō no kenkyū* (Sōbunsha, 1960), 683.

Gendayū could not have known of this particular article of the penal code, because the code had been written that same year and was secret, meant only as a set of guidelines for judicial officers of the shogunate.[50] However, the code was also based on previous practice, and an awareness of mitigating circumstances must have existed, at least among bakufu officials.

Perhaps advised by the officials at Shimogata, Gendayū may have aimed his testimony toward legitimate self-defense against an opponent of dubious reputation for whom nobody would speak up. There certainly was enough time to structure Gendayū's testimony that way, since a month had elapsed between the first and second hearings.

A DUBIOUS CASE OF DISINHERITANCE

At this point the question of disinheritance comes in. Kyūri was a distinctive Tokugawa form of disinheritance, different from an older type (kandō) although often confused with it even in Tokugawa times.[51] It drastically changed one's "civic" status and is best understood in conjunction with other laws.

Japanese disinheritance practice has changed over time. Its main forms were *gizetsu,* kandō, and kyūri. In antiquity, gizetsu ("cutting the obligation") meant expulsion from home and loss of all inheritance rights. During the Kamakura period (1185–1333) it was gradually replaced by kandō ("right measure after examination"), applied for unfilial behavior to escape vicarious responsibility for crimes one is afraid one's children might commit, especially when their whereabouts are not known, or simply when parents decide to exercise this right. The descendant had to leave the house and was freed from all filial obligations and rights, including protection, but was not barred from official posts; and the decision could be revoked by the parents. In the Tokugawa period, official permission was required for kandō, but now

---

50. Dan Fenno Henderson, "Introduction to the Kujikata Osadamegaki (1742)," in *Hō to keibatsu no rekishiteki kōsatsu,* ed. Hiramatsu Yoshiro hakushi tsuito ronbunshū henshū iinkai (Nagoya: Nagoya Daigaku shuppankai, 1987), 504–8.

51. For the information that follows, see *Kokushi daijiten,* ed. Kokushi daijiten henshū iinkai, 15 vols. (Yoshikawa kōbunkan, 1979–94), 4:253 ("kyūri") and 3:884 ("kandō") (hereafter KDJ). See also F. Joüon des Longrais, *L'Est et l'Ouest: Institutions du Japon et de l'Occident comparées (six études de sociologie juridique)* (Tokyo: Maison Franco-japonaise, 1958), 387–90.

there was also kyūri ("separation for a long duration" or "old separation"). Kyūri had the same prophylactic function against the consequences of possible crimes by absconded offspring. Official ratification
was by the parents, kumi, village officials, and the intendant who ultimately permitted the fugitive to be taken from the population rosters,
which automatically dissolved marriage and blocked any possibility of
holding office.

Laws and institutions often have ambiguous functions. They steer
practice along norms and paths to produce good and just behavior,
which, however, may only be good and just in some respects but not in
others. Hence, they also produce a need for additional laws and institutions to correct these "dysfunctions." Kyūri can be understood in
such a way, as a response to the undesirable effects of two other laws.
One was the stipulation, inherent in the Tokugawa feudal configuration
of power, that crimes be judged in the jurisdiction of the criminal's registration. The simplest of these were domains or fiefs for peasants and
samurai. Matters were more complicated for uncommon commoners
like priests, registered beggars, outcastes, and the registered blind or
for uncommon cases that involved two jurisdictions.[52] The other legal
practice with a direct bearing on kyūri was the custom of vicarious
guilt or communal responsibility for misbehavior (enza): the relatives,
the kumi, or sometimes the village could be punished for a crime committed by any of its members. Hence they could suffer for a crime
committed by someone who had absconded and over whom they had
thus lost control.

Legally separating an absconder from the group responsible for him
or her through official disinheritance prevented such injustice. Kyūri
was thus both a punishment in absentia for someone who had illegally
left the village and a protection against possible prosecution of his or
her relatives and kumi members for crimes he or she might commit.[53] It
should be noted that in the second half of the Tokugawa period com-

52. See Henderson, Conciliation, vol. 1, chap. 4, esp. pp. 86–92.
53. Ōishi Hisakata (1725–94) discusses kyūri and kandō in these terms. A
former village group headman from Kyūshū who traveled widely in Ōmi, Shinano, and the Kantō, he was hired in 1783 as coordinator of rural administration in the Takasaki domain (Gunma prefecture, east of Kita-Saku), where
he composed for his lord a very detailed vade mecum for rural administrators,
the Jikata hanreiroku (see Ōishi Hisakata, Jikata hanreiroku, ed. Ōishi Shinzaburō, 2 vols. [Kondō shuppansha, 1969], 2:123–54).

munal responsibility was activated only for the most extreme crimes: killing one's lord or one's parent. Hence, "disinheritance" was rather dormant as protection for the legally accountable group.[54] It served mostly as a means for the person legally responsible for an absconder to evade social criticism within the village. Also, kyūri could not be enacted against a status superior: one could not "disinherit" one's absconding parent. Such disinheritance was a publicly certified act. It had to be approved by the local headman, and valid reasons had to be stated. Since someone thus "disinherited" was erased from the village registers, this measure needed to be sanctioned by the higher authorities. It changed the official status of the person in question. A disinherited person was thus legally a nonperson and, because he or she was not attached to a legal group, perhaps the village equivalent of a rōnin, or masterless samurai. Such a person was thus cut off from the village in all possible ways, having neither obligations to the village nor privileges, including the privilege of protection. He was an outlaw.

A remedy to the possible ill effects of another law, kyūri itself was insufficiently corrected by further laws against its own possible negative effects—except for the important general provision, central but implicit to Ken's argument, that life could not be taken. Article 4 of the Makibuse village law made this clear: "People who have killed someone, or strange people who hang out in shrines, forests, and mountains: the villagers, together with people from neighboring villages, should set out, arrest them, tie them up, and hand them over. If it is difficult to catch them there on the spot, then you have to pursue them however far and catch them where they settle. But no matter what kind of person they are, you cannot kill them" (see appendix 3). Kyūri's only other softening aspect was that it was revokable if the person affected by it mended his or her ways.[55] In Shinzō's case we see how kyūri could be manipulated to prevent a violent death from being categorized as murder.

The next questions to be addressed are the reasons for Shinzō's punishment of disinheritance and banishment. Why the disinheritance, which was an action that ultimately only Shinzō's mother could have sanctioned? And why did the villagers and lineage members mete out

---

54. KDJ 4:253.

55. For an example of documents reversing prior verdicts of disinheritance and banishment, see Dan Fenno Henderson, *Village "Contracts" in Tokugawa Japan* (Seattle: University of Washington Press, 1975), 190–91, 194.

what turned out to be, in Ken's eyes, deadly punishment for Shinzō—without trial, verdict, or, as reported by Ken, stated reasons? Ultimately, Ken was arguing degrees of appropriate punishment and maintained that they had no right to kill Shinzō.

Two documents exist requesting the disinheritance of Shinzō: one, signed by his mother and relatives, is addressed to the village officials and dated 1741/7; the other, bearing the seals of the village officials, is the one the village officials forwarded to the Shimogata office and is dated 1741/7/21, or barely three months before the murder. Since these documents were so crucial in the murder case, it is of course not unthinkable that they were fabricated post factum for that purpose—after the murder and even after Ken presented her suit.

If the disinheritance deed was a forgery, one might wonder how Shinzō's mother's seal was secured. The modern presumption that seals were always kept at home, however, does not apply universally to Tokugawa Japan. Ishii Ryōsuke writes that it was not uncommon for a village headman to keep all the seals of all the households; some village laws even warned against the possible abuses of entrusting one's seal to others, even relatives.[56]

Shinzō's mother's request reads as follows:

Written Petition Submitted in Fearful Deference

My son Shinzō, who made a living as a horse trader, was fond of heavy drinking and misbehaved in various places. Moreover, he did not engage in agriculture. In particular, last fall he left fallow the small dry field we have, leaving me almost starving [the following spring]. Again and again the lineage, united in its views, requested him [to change his ways], but it was of no use whatsoever and the problems remained.

This year on 4/13, he disappeared with Gendayū's horse without leaving a trace. I asked the lineage to look for him everywhere, but he has not been found to this day, and this matter has [still] not been settled. It is hard to gauge what other evil things he might be up to next. I therefore request the shogunal authorities to take him, starting this year, from the population register and disinherit him.

1741/7 The village of Makibuse
Shinzō's mother (seal)[57]

This petition served as the basis for the official document forwarded to Shimogata, which is in three parts: Shinzō's mother's (rewritten) peti-

56. Ishii Ryōsuke, *Inban no rekishi* (Akashi shoten, 1991), 182, 184.
57. This document to be found only in Ozaki, "Kenjo oboegaki," 77–78.

tion, an endorsement by her four kumi members/relatives testifying to the truth of her statement, and an addendum by the village officials including further explanations. The first two parts read as follows:

Written Petition

My son Shinzō has not worked in recent years and not supported me, which has made life very hard for me. Moreover, on 4/13 he disappeared, which is why I asked the lineage to look for him everywhere, but to this day he has not been found, and even if we look further, I am alone with nobody to support me. Therefore, I petition to remove [my son] from the population register.

The mother of Makibuse's Shinzō
1741/7/21

The abovementioned Shinzō, as stated in his mother's petition, made an unsubstantial living (*fujittai yue yowatari*), which caused great hardship to his mother. Then, on 4/13, he disappeared with his uncle Gendayū's horse. We immediately started a search everywhere without results. On 5/21 we sought an official warrant [for an official search], and we ordered the neighborhood kumi to look for him. We have searched until today but not found him, and nobody has reported him, so that nobody from either the lineage or the kumi has been able to lay a hand on him.

The above is without fallacy. Without any discrepancy do the relatives and kumi endorse the mother's petition. Deferentially looking upward to the shogun (*gokōgisama*), we humbly request the removal [of Shinzō's name] from the population register.

1741/7/21 The village of Makibuse
petitioner Gendayū (seal)
petitioner Chōkyūrō (seal)
same Shin'emon (seal)
same Masaemon (seal)
[*To:*] The village headman
The elders [i.e., kumi leaders][58]

According to these documents, Shinzō had ceased to work the fields and instead had gotten involved in horse trading, with the result that he was unable to support his mother. He drank too much and caused trouble. Moreover, he disappeared with his uncle's horse. (Ken also refers to this matter in her petition, although rather obliquely). Private searches failed to locate him. After one month a complaint was filed; the kumi ordered an official search, with no results.

58. This document is available only in Ozaki, "Kenjo ikken," 53.

Fleeing became legal absconding only after a certified effort had been made to apprehend the fugitive. A certain amount of time (officially, six periods of thirty days) was fixed during which active searches were repeatedly ordered by the village or supravillage authorities.[59] Hence the mention of the failed search in the disinheritance document (although fewer than six months seem to have elapsed between Shinzō's absconding and the disinheritance): disinheritance, as mentioned earlier, was a legally certified "punishment" for absconding, while absconding was the legally certified status of a fugitive.

The official petition, signed by Shinzō's mother and endorsed by her relatives, was forwarded to the Shimogata office by the village officials, who appended a note with more details to complete the work of character assassination. They mention his asocial conduct with reverberations in the community: drunkenness, general misbehavior, noncompliance with the "will of the lineage," mentioned by Shinzō's mother. Moreover, in the context of an investigation of theft conducted six years earlier (in 1735) by another shogunal office (one in Hiraga, some fifteen kilometers east, in the Kita-Saku plain), Shinzō had been questioned because he was a horse trader (*bakurō*). Although Shinzō seems not to have been involved in the 1735 theft (otherwise it would certainly have been used more fully against him), and although this matter was six years old, one surmises that it was made part of the record to give more weight to the argument for disinheritance by establishing, through innuendo, a long record of misbehavior and bad companions. Following this investigation, the lineage had made him promise to abandon horse trading and return to tilling the fields, a promise he had not kept. This, presumably, was "the will of the lineage."

The previous fall, the officials also related, his absence of over twenty days had made him miss the wheat sowing time, which had endangered his mother's food supply. Moreover, on 4/13 he had led his uncle's horse away to sell it and had disappeared wearing his uncle's clothes. This last detail testifies, perhaps, to Shinzō's poverty: members of branch houses often relied on their patrons for material gifts or loans of daily necessity, so these clothes may or may not have been "given" to him by his uncle. His relatives looked for him quietly for one month, but then the kumi was ordered to undertake a formal search, which it did for an-

59. Mizumoto, "Kōgi no saiban," 307; see also Ōishi Hisakata, *Jikata hanreiroku*, 2:113, 114, 119.

other month, without results. Fearing what Shinzō might be up to next, his mother had requested the removal of his name from the register.

The case against Shinzō is made again and again in these documents, at ever higher levels of authority: by his mother, his lineage, the village officials. This reiteration no doubt had a reinforcing effect, solidifying the case against him. Clearly, things were presented so as to put the blame for the removal of Shinzō's name from the registers and the concomitant disinheritance on Shinzō himself. But one senses also the pressure the lineage put on Shinzō's mother to take this drastic step. At this point, however, she could not have foreseen the tragic outcome only three months away. And perhaps neither did anyone else in the village, although there was the alleged threat by Gendayū. Moreover, since kyūri could be revoked, perhaps Shinzō's mother hoped for such a reversal when she consented to the disinheritance—if the document is genuine.

THE DECLINE OF A PROMINENT PEASANT HOUSEHOLD

In her disinheritance request, Shinzō's mother mentioned that the family's landholdings were minuscule. Indeed, they may have been too small to support her and her son, so that Shinzō had sought additional income in horse trading and perhaps also in gambling. How small was the property?

The family holdings Shinzō inherited at the death of his father in 1719, when he was nineteen, amounted to no more than 1.9 koku, or 1.6 *tan*, the equivalent of less than 0.4 acres. (His father, Rihei II, had not managed the property too well: he had lost one third of it, since he had started out with 2.9 koku.) One koku of rice was the amount needed to feed an adult for one year, and one able-bodied adult could normally cultivate three tan.[60] Shinzō was obviously a very poor peas-

60. Nakane Chie, *Kinship and Economic Organization in Rural Japan*, London School of Economics Monographs on Social Anthropology, 32 (London: Athlone Press, 1967), 59. See also Ōishi Shinzaburō, *Kyōhō kaikaku no keizai seisaku: Dai ichibu, Kyōhō kaikaku no nōson seisaku* (Zōhoban: Ochanomizu shobō, 1978), 20. A similar estimate is given in NAK-T 5:143, where it is stated that a couple could cultivate seven to eight *tan* (the equivalent of about ten koku). Thomas C. Smith quotes a less productive ratio: four or five adults for one *chō* of arable (one chō equals ten tan), eight or nine for two, and twelve for three (*Agrarian Origins*, 6). A holding's kokudaka is only an indirect

Table 2. Disposal of Shinzō's Holdings in Koku, 1727–1740

| Holdings | First-grade | | Homestead | |
	Paddies	Dry Fields	Dry Fields	Total Holdings
At start of 1727	1.03	0.79	0.14	1.97[a]
Disposed in				
1727	0.43	—	—	
1729	—	0.14	—	
1735	—	0.6	—	
1736	0.26	—	—	
1737	0.17	—	—	
1739	0.15	—	—	
1740	0.02	—	—	
At end of 1740	0	0.05	0.14	0.19[b]

[a] 1.97 koku = 0.414 ACRES
[b] 0.19 koku = 0.042 ACRES

SOURCE: Adapted from Ozaki, "Kenjo ikken," table 9 (p. 63).

NOTE: The fields were sold to two distant cousins, E^1 and E^2, belonging to the other sublineage, headed by D^5. The 0.14 koku of dry fields constitutes newly developed fields; the remaining 0.05 koku is also made up of newly developed dry fields. All paddies, plus the 0.60 koku of dry fields, are main fields or honden (fields registered on the original seventeenth-century land surveys).

ant with insufficient land to keep him fully occupied, but in this he was not alone in the village. With 1.9 koku, his was among the twenty-seven households, out of a total of forty-nine, with holdings under two koku.

In 1727, Shinzō started to dispose of the little land he had (see table 2), until by 1740 all the *honden* ("original paddies": first-grade paddies and first-, second-, and third-grade dry fields) and three-fourths of the newly developed dry fields were sold to two distant cousins (E^1 and E^2 of fig. 1, who, it should be noted, in the 1720s and 1730s more than doubled their property, to 8.9 koku and 5.7 koku, respectively). Shinzō

reflection of its size, for it refers to the computed putative yield of all products converted into rice equivalents, on the basis of which the tribute was calculated. This tribute, in turn, was paid neither in rice nor in any other natural products. After 1726, in all bakufu land in Shinano, the tribute amount, calculated as a percentage of the kokudaka, was converted into a cash amount at the going conversion rate (NAK-T 5:86).

kept only a tiny lower-grade dry field in the mountains and the superior-grade dry fields of residence land, a total of 0.19 koku, or 0.04 acres. In other words, he wound up selling 90 percent of the land he had inherited, making him no better off than a landless peasant, as mentioned earlier. In her petition of 1757, Ken stated that her brother Shinzō "went to live in the mountain on his plot of land." This plot of land, at the northern outskirts of the village, beyond the Nakasendō, was the only one he had left besides the residence land. He was killed a year after he sold his last paddy.

In table 2 one can see that in 1727 Shinzō must have suddenly been in great need of cash. This was when he sold almost half of his prime paddy to his cousin. Two years later he disposed of all the newly developed (low-grade) dry fields, except for the tiny plot in the mountains, which he kept until the end. The next spurt of sales occurred between 1735 and 1740: first the main (honden) dry fields all at one time in 1735, then the remaining precious paddy piece by piece.

It is not clear when Shinzō began horse trading, but it is unlikely that he did so before he started to dispose of the land, in 1727. Until then he must have been working the fields he had inherited seven years earlier. In 1727 he fell into a spiraling circle of horse trading, gambling, drunkenness, and land sales. At least this is the picture one gets from the disinheritance document the village officials submitted to the Shimogata office. Yet these hardships seem to have come in spurts: the first one in 1727–29 (loss: 0.57 koku), the second and seemingly the greatest in 1735–37 (loss: 1.03), the last in 1739–40 (loss: 0.17). Ozaki surmises that Shinzō's "reprehensible" behavior was most likely not the cause but the result of hardships that may have had something to do with the marriages of his two sisters. His sister Ine got married in this first period, his sister Ken in the second period.[61]

These data Ozaki culled from records unrelated to the case. However, the 1763 incident (with the population register) triggered an investigation, possibly ordered by the Shimogata office. The report reveals a wider background to Ken's lineage and introduces us to some social and political dimensions of the history of Makibuse.

According to this report, Ken's ancestors had been peasants in Maki-

---

61. Smith (*Nakahara*, 97) writes that for peasants "dowry was not normally a significant form of property." His source is late Tokugawa. Yet, the "chest of personal belongings" the bride usually took may have seriously taxed a poor peasant's resources.

buse for several generations, starting in the early 1600s with Genzae-mon [A of fig. 1], headman at the time of the land survey in 1629. His holdings were listed at 20 koku, among the four largest land holdings, each between 20 and 24 koku. For four generations, down to Ken and Shinzō's father, Rihei II, the family had been very prominent in the vil-lage and no doubt jealous of its prestige, which may help explain the resentment provoked by Shinzō's behavior. What happened to the family between Genzaemon's time and Shinzō's? The story mirrors the fate of many families in the area. One has only to remember that down to 1662 only three out of twelve families had holdings of under ten koku, while after 1721 that number was forty-six out of forty-nine (and thirty-four of the forty-six had three koku or less [see table 4]).

In the second generation, in the late 1640s, the successor (B) lost the village headship because of an unspecified village conflict, but his hold-ings were not affected negatively; in fact, they grew even larger (ac-cording to the resurvey of 1669–70, he had twenty-three koku).[62] The third-generation successor (C^1, or Rihei I) also held the village headship for one year, in 1689. In the transition from the second to the third generation, in 1684, the property was split among four sons. The suc-cessor to the lineage headship (C^1, then the oldest son) received about one-third of the land, and the other three (C^2, C^3, and C^4) each received one-fifth. However, partitioning had already started more than a decade earlier. According to the population register, in 1671 the family had been split into four separate households: Rihei I (C^1, then the sec-ond oldest son), Shinzaemon (B, the father), Heishirō (C^4, the youngest son), and Chōemon (C^5, the oldest son, who disappears from the regis-ters thereafter). The latter three, *including the father,* were all clients of Rihei I, their patron and also the only titled peasant in the lineage.[63]

<hr />

62. Ozaki has discovered no further details concerning the village conflict that caused the headship to be lost to another lineage. The research by Mizu-moto Kunihiko and Saitō Yoshiyuki, introduced in chapter 2, suggests that most of the village disturbances of the 1640s were directed against the arbitrary use the village headman had made of the new power the lords had vested in them (Mizumoto Kunihiko, *Kinsei no mura shakai to kokka* [Tōkyō Daigaku shuppankai, 1987], esp. chaps. 1 and 3 [hereafter *Mura shakai*]; idem, "Mura-kata sōdō," *Chūsei no minshū undō,* Chūseishi kōza, 7 [Gakuseisha, 1985], 289–307; Saitō Yoshiyuki, "Kinsei shoki no nōmin tōsō to muraukesei: nen-gukanjō sōdō o sozai to shite," *Rekishi hyōron,* no. 475 [1989]: 42–60).

63. Ozaki ("Kenjo ikken," 57) charts the 1671 generation as one compris-ing three brothers (Rihei, 37; Shinzaemon, 64; and Heijirō, 34) and a fourth

It should be noted that the father moved out (a pattern of retirement sometimes called *inkyo bunke,* literally, "retirement branch house"), and the headship was passed on to a house that branched off but was legally the head of the lineage and inherited also the status of titled peasant. Primogeniture was by no means the rule in this region or, indeed, in most of rural Japan in the seventeenth century.

MORE AND SMALLER PEASANTS

In 1734 a bakufu official sketched a picture of the optimal ratio of land to people in an ideal village. Such a model community would have 200 koku (half paddies and half dry fields) and a population of 120 divided into 24 households, 60 males and 60 females, as well as 12 craftsmen or merchants and 6 horses.[64] In terms of arable, Makibuse met this standard: in 1750 it had 205 koku (see table 1). Its population, however, was double what it should have been: 48 households with a total of 242 members and 21 horses.

This model was put forward at the time of the first of three large-scale reforms, the Kyōhō Reforms of the 1730s, which attempted to arrest developments that had weakened the bakufu's economic base. The earlier edicts prohibiting the sale of land (1643) and the division of land into holdings of less than 10 koku (in the case of headmen, 20 koku) (1673) had failed to strengthen the rulers' grip on agricultural surplus. A significant increase in the number of large landholdings syphoned off part of that surplus as land rent paid to landlords by tenant farmers without land, or with too little land to support their households. The history of these two prohibitions—"thou shalt not accumulate" and "thou shalt not divide"—and their implementation is a complex one.[65] Put simply, it is clear that the laws were circumvented in various ways.

---

person (Chōemon, 39), whose relationship to the other three is unspecified (respectively, C^1, B, C^4, and C^5 in fig. 1). Three of these four were relatively close in age, but the fourth, Shinzaemon, was twenty-five years older than the oldest of the trio, which makes it possible that he was their father—assuming also that Chōemon is a sibling. According to Ozaki's table, this Shinzaemon was the son of another Shinzaemon. My reasoning is based on the assumption that there is only one Shinzaemon, son of Genzaemon (A) and father of Rihei I and his brother(s).

64. Nakane, *Kinship,* 42.
65. See Ōishi, *Kyōhō kaikaku.*

The limitation on land partitioning was dealt with locally by officially (*tatemae*) limiting the number of titled peasants and recording branch houses as working part of the main family's land (*buntsuke*). This practice can also be found in Makibuse, for instance in Genzaemon's lineage. The 1677 cadaster shows the land registered under Rihei I's name and indicates the amount tilled separately (buntsuke) by each household of the lineage.

Ōishi Hisataka, the eighteenth-century local administrator of Takasaki domain in a neighboring province, explained this "partition" as marking the division of inheritance but not separately established branch houses (*bunke*).[66] If branch houses were established, their heads would be titled peasants and would pay tribute and corvée directly, he wrote. In Makibuse, however, those households marked as buntsuke in the 1677 *land* cadaster had already been registered six years earlier in the 1671 *population* register as branch houses (kakae), that is to say, as separate branch houses under a patron. It is not clear whether these houses paid their tribute directly, as Ōishi Hisataka suggested, or through their patron. What is certain, however, is that they were branch houses *without* being titled peasants. Over time, the number of titled peasants in Makibuse decreased somewhat, while the number of households providing tribute and corvée increased dramatically. Thus the bakufu's definition of a titled peasant (as seen through Ōishi's eyes) was at variance with the village's. In the village of Makibuse, the title became a privilege and a mark of political, not economic, power. Like shares or stock that could be sold, titles were transmissible and negotiable. In order to purchase one, an individual needed "economic capital," but as figure 2 indicates, one could hold on to it as symbolic (and political) capital even if one's holding was less than 2 koku. Note that household L of figure 2 had only 0.4 koku, whereas the village headman had 33 koku, and they were both titled peasants.

As in the case of neighboring Kodaira, which is analyzed in detail in chapter 3, partitioning leveled economic differences between titled peasants or patrons and (nontitled) branch houses. Such partitioning of the lineage's holdings by establishing branch houses was a common practice in Makibuse. Other examples are the Iemon and Kichisaburō lineages (see table 3 and fig. 2).

66. Ōishi Hisakata, *Jikata hanreiroku*, 2:110. On Ōishi, see above, n. 53.

Table 3. Holdings of Iemon's Lineage in Koku, 1719–1736

	Lineage Households						
Lineage Patron and Co-residents	A	B	C	D	E	G	K
1719 A + d/e/f/g/h (5 sons)	13	4	5				
1723 H + d/e/f/g (4 sons) + k/m (2 fudai)	14	4	4				
1729 H + f/g (2 sons) + k (1 fudai)	7	4	4	3	3		
1731 H + f (1 son) + k (1 fudai)	4	4	3	3	3	3	
1736 F	3	4	3	3	3	3	0

SOURCE: Adapted from Ozaki, "Kenjo ikken," table 3 (p. 55).

NOTE: Over a span of thirteen years, between 1723 and 1736, the lineage, headed by A, added four households, D–K; by 1719, B and C already existed as autonomous households. The position of economic prominence of the main house over the branch houses disappeared as its size dropped from 14 koku to 3 and its holdings were equalized with those of all the other units of the lineage. Notice that H, the successor to A, was the youngest of five sons (d–h) and that the holding was divided equally among them.

Of the two fudai of 1723, the female (*m*) had disappeared from the registers by 1729; the remaining male fudai (*k*) was eventually established as branch house K without land (mizunomibyakushō) in 1736. It was quite usual for fudai to marry and have families of their own after being set up as a separate branch. Thus, the practice of branching off of fudai must have led to a population increase.

The same leveling trend was manifested throughout the village (see table 4). Between 1647 and 1662 the distribution of holdings among titled peasants remained stable: four units had holdings of 20–24 koku (one of them being the A and B generations of Genzaemon's lineage), five units had 10–14 koku, two had 5–9 koku, and one had 3 koku. The one household with less than 1 koku in 1647 had disappeared from the registers three years later, leaving a total of twelve titled peasant households by 1662.

By 1677, however, the situation had changed drastically, although official registration maintained a fiction of continuity: four households were shown to have more than 20 koku, four to have 10–14 koku, seven to have between 4 and 9 koku, and one with 1 koku, bringing the total to sixteen, an (official) increase of four. Yet, in reality, seven out of this total of sixteen holdings (each officially registered under one house) were divided among two to five households, usually evenly, resulting in a massive (unofficial) increase in the number of households owning 1–10 koku of land. The distribution was as follows: one house of 29 koku (that of Chūemon, the village headman); one of 11 koku and one

Fig. 2. Kichisaburō's Lineage, 1700–1758

	lineal succession	L	nephew of F
‖	same person	M	younger brother of K
D	younger brother of A	N	nephew of M
G/H	younger brothers of F		

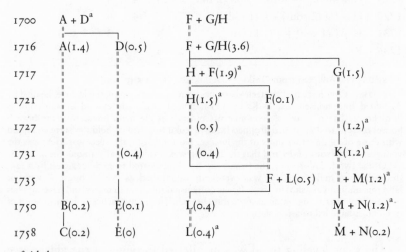

^a titled peasant

SOURCE: Adapted from Ozaki, "Kenjo ikken," table 7 (p. 61).

NOTES: Notice the kokudaka of 0.4 of title peasant L in 1758. It will be remembered that the headman, also a titled peasant, had over 30 koku. Smith (*Agrarian Origins*, 39 n. d) states that to "ignore the minimum [below which partition was not practical] was to invite ruin." Yet this is precisely what seems to have been happening here and elsewhere in the village. Hayami Akira wrote that there were no cases of holdings under 5 koku being divided ("The Myth of Primogeniture and Impartible Inheritance in Tokugawa Japan," *Journal of Family History* 8, no. 1 [1983]: 23).

of 10 koku; thirteen in the 5–9 koku range; and fifteen in the 1–4 range, bringing the actual total to thirty-one households, an increase of nineteen over the 1662 total.

In subsequent decades the partitioning of lineage lands continued. By 1721 the total number of households had risen to forty-nine (thirteen titled peasants, thirty-two branch houses, and four landless peasants), with two holdings above 30 koku; one of 14 and one of 10 koku; seven in the 5–9 koku range; eighteen in the 1–4 koku range; and sixteen with less than 1 koku. Four peasants were registered as without land of their own.

By 1700, when Ken's grandfather Rihei I divided his property (increased by 1 koku to a total of 9), some branches of Genzaemon's lineage were struggling to survive on very diminished holdings. Ken's father, Rihei II (D^1), received only 2.9 koku, and her uncle Gendayū (D^2), 6.3 koku. Her father's cousin (D^3), with only 1.2 koku, soon disappeared from the land register. The other branch of the lineage was doing better: another cousin of her father's (D^5, who held 6.3 koku) formed a sublineage with yet another cousin (D^4, holding 5 koku) and the latter's two successors (E^2 and E^3).

In 1703 Ken's father, Rihei II, transferred half of his already small holdings to his brother Gendayū, retaining only 1.5 koku for himself. He must have been experiencing financial difficulties, an indication that the decline of this line did not start with Ken's brother, Shinzō. Peasants in this situation had few options. Obviously, they lacked the means to develop substantial new fields. Moreover, the terrain may not have allowed further development. Over more than four generations, between 1627 and 1756, the lineage's holdings increased by a mere 2 koku.

One solution was part-tenancy, but it is not clear whether this was an option in Makibuse. There were only a few holdings large enough to use labor beyond the nuclear family (two holders of more than 30 koku, one of 14 koku, and one of 10 koku [see table 4]), labor that may have been provided by hereditary or indentured servants who do not seem to disappear, even though the population grew considerably and at a much faster rate than the village kokudaka (see table 1). On the other hand, branch house or client status no doubt included some duties for the lineage head or patron that may have been remunerated; indeed, some clients may have been quasi-tenants.

Another solution for surplus members of the household was to seek regular employment in towns or cities or short-term employment during the slack winter season.[67] This is what Rihei II did. In 1712 he left his wife and daughter Ine (Ken was not yet born) and took twelve-year-old

67. Seasonal employment in Edo during the winter months was customary in some areas in Nagano, even for villages far north, such as Yomase in Takai district. Documents show Yomase villagers petitioning to go to Edo from the ninth to the third month in 1701–2. In 1757 in Otsukoto (Suwa district), which had 130 households, the number of those who officially petitioned to spend the winter months in Edo was 33 (NAK-T 5:366). In Kodaira (see n. 24), exactly half of the peasants (9 out of 20 titled peasants and 18 out of 36 kakae) were themselves listed as being in service outside the village (all titled peasants but one, and no kakae, went to Edo); this, in addition to 11 of their children (see Komonjo kenkyūkai, "Genroku-ki," 67).

Table 4. Family Holdings in Koku, 1647–1721

Koku	1647	1650	1662	1677 Officially	In reality	1721
33						Z (1)
32						
31						Y (1)
30						
29				Z	Z	
28						
27				X		
26						
25				W		
				[3]	[1]	
24	Z	Z	Z			
23	X	X	X	C[1]		
22						
21	W	W	W			
20	A	B	B			
	[4]	[4]	[4]	[1]		
19						
18						
17						
16						
15						
	[0]	[0]	[0]	[0]		
14	1	1	1	V		1 (1)
13		1	1	T		
12	3	2	1 V	S		
11		S		1	1	
10	S		S		B	1 (1)
	[5]	[5]	[5]	[4]	[2]	[2]
9				1	1 x	2 (1)
8	1	1	1	1 M	1 x C[1]	1 (1)
7				1	1 v v	1 (1)
6	1	1	1	1	1 m	2 (2)
5					x w w	1
	[2]	[2]	[2]	[5]	[13]	[7]

Table 4 (continued)

Koku	1647	1650	1662	1677 Officially	1677 In reality	1721
4				2	2 w w w t t t s s s C⁴	1
3	1	1	1			7 (2)
2					m	3
1				1	1 x	7 (1)
0+	1					16 (1)
	[2]	[1]	[1]	[3]	[15]	[34]
0						4
Total	13	12	12	16	16 + 15 = 31	49 (13)

SOURCE: Adapted from Ozaki, "Kenjo ikken," table 5 (p. 58).

NOTE: Letters A–C refer to households of the Genzaemon lineage (fig. 1), M–Z to households of other lineages; small letters refer to households that are branch houses of capital-letter lineages that were officially listed in 1677 under the patron families. Numbers indicate households whose relationship over time could not be traced between 1647 and 1662. Totals of 1647 through "1677 (Officially)" all refer to titled peasants; those of "1677 (In reality)" comprise the same 16 titled peasants and their 15 branch houses after partition; the totals for 1721 are for the number of households and, in parentheses, the number of titled peasants.

The number of households almost quadrupled between 1647 and 1721 (from 13 to 49), although the aggregate yield remained more or less the same: approximately 166 koku in 1647 and 186 koku in 1721. (Numbers have been rounded to the nearest even number.) Cf. table 1.

The increase in small and minuscule holdings was dramatic. Landless peasants appeared in 1721 (4), when another 23 households with less than 2 koku were very close to becoming landless. In 1647 only 4 out of 13 households held less than 10 koku; in 1721 that number was 45, and only 4 held more than 10 koku.

Shinzō with him to Edo (some 180 km, or twenty-four way stations on the Nakasendō, away), where they worked together for two years. After his father returned home, Shinzō stayed in Edo another three years; then he worked a year in the tiny village of Gan (at the southern end of Makibuse's valley, some 7 km from home).

These efforts proved somewhat successful, for in 1716 Rihei II was able to "buy back" 0.5 koku from his brother, increasing his holdings to 1.9 koku. This is the amount of land Shinzō inherited three years later. However, when Rihei II sold part of his land to his younger brother Gendayū in 1703, he also relinquished, or very likely sold, to him his inherited lineage headship and his status as titled peasant.[68] Also, when Rihei II left for Edo, he had to step down from the village office of kumi leader, an office he would be unable to recuperate upon his return because he lacked the prerequisite status of titled peasant. Rihei II, whose great-grandfather and grandfather had been village headmen and whose father, Rihei I, had held the office for one year in 1689, had become an impoverished, untitled peasant.

A brief excursus is called for here regarding the link between village office and peasant status in Makibuse. As table 5 indicates, in the first half of the eighteenth century the number of titled peasants in the village decreased by one-third, from sixteen to eleven. These five households became clients of other titled peasants (household numbers 2, 4, 10, 14, and 15). On the other hand, some clients became titled peasants, trading status with their patrons. This is what happened between Rihei II (D^1) and his younger brother (D^2), and they obviously were not the only ones: see the three switches in the Kichisaburō lineage recorded in 1717, 1735, and 1764 (line 11 of table 5); see also figure 2. This table and figure also show younger brothers superseding their older brothers (e.g., in lines 7, 8, 11, and 12 of table 5), although one must here distinguish between shifting the status to a different household headed by a younger brother (D^1 and D^2 in line 7) and keeping the status within the same household with the younger brother succeeding his older brother as the head of the household (K and M in line 11). It is also clear that these shifts do not occur in the more well-to-do lineages (lines 1, 3, and 5), which also are able to hold on to village offices more durably. It should be noted that after 1735 the office of elder was combined with that of kumi leader (which meant the lineage head, since kumi here were constituted along lineage lines).

LINEAGE TENSIONS

Let us recapitulate Ken's story in light of this information. Some time between his marriage in 1694 and the birth of Shinzō in 1700, Rihei II set up a separate household, leaving his younger brother Gendayū with

68. In Kasuga, a village southwest of Makibuse, across the hills, the village law stipulated the price a client had to pay to his patron in order to be set free and become a titled peasant as 20 ryō (Nagano-ken, ed., *Nagano-kenshi: Tsūshi* 4 [*Kinsei* 1] [Nagano-shi: Nagano-kenshi kankōkai, 1987], 466 [hereafter NAK-T 4]). For a study of land pawning and redemption, see Shirakawabe Tatsuo, "Kinsei shichichi ukemodoshi kankō to hyakushō takashoji," *Rekishigaku kenkyū*, no. 552 (1986): 17–32.

Table 5. Titled Peasants and Village Offices, 1700–1764

Tables and Figures	1700	1717	1725	1735	1750	1764
1 Table 4.Y	Y	a	Y_{31}	(Y)	(b)	(b)
2 Table 4.s	s_4 ——┘					
3 Table 4.Z	Z_{33}	c	c	d	d	c
4 Table 4.T	T_4 ——┘					
5 Table 4.V	A_{13}	A_{13}	H_{14}	F_3	F	F
6 Table 3	e	f*	f	g	g	h
7 Table 4.A–C⁴ Fig. 1	$D^1{}_{2.9}$	$D^{2*@}{}_{6.3}$	$D^2{}_{7.3}$	$D^2{}_{7.3}$	$D^2{}_2$	$D^2 son_2$
8 Table 4.A–C⁴ Fig. 1	$D^5{}_{6.3}$	$i_{6.3}$	$D^6{}_{6.3}$	$D^6{}_{6.3}$	$E^3{}_{3.8}$	$j^@{}_{3.8}$
9 Table 4.X	X_9	X	X	k	k	l*
10	m	n*	n	n ——┘		
11 Fig. 2	$A_{1.9}$	$H^*{}_{1.9}$	$H_{1.9}$	$K^*{}_{1.2}$	$M^@{}_{1.2}$	$L^*{}_{0.4}$
12	o	p	p	$q^@$	r*	r
13	s	t	t	u	u	v
14	w	w ——┘				
15	x ——┘					
16	y	y	y	y	z	a
Total	16	13	12	12	11	11

SOURCE: Adapted from Ozaki, "Kenjo ikken," table 8 (p. 62).

NOTE: Column one is a guide to lineages diagrammed in other tables (for example, Table 4.Y = table 4, lineage Y). Letters representing household heads that appear in other tables are capitalized. All other peasants are represented by lowercase letters in alphabetical order. === = village headman; ( ) = otonabyakushō, which according to NAK-T 4:57 means *hyakushō sōdai*, or peasant representative, usually a small peasant, but not in Makibuse or in Irebuse before 1760 as discussed in chapter 2; ___ = village elder, after 1735 kumi head; * = earlier client status with preceding titled peasant; @ = younger brother of preceding peasant; ⌐ = becomes client of next titled peasant (note the decreasing number of titled peasants). Subscript figures indicate koku.

their mother. In 1700 Rihei was thirty-seven and Gendayū was eighteen. The division of the property greatly favored Gendayū, perhaps because he took care of the mother: Rihei received 2.9 koku, while Gendayū received 6.3, or more than twice Rihei's portion. As we have seen, the succession rules in the village were not hard and fast, least of all that of primogeniture. Nevertheless, because his brother got the lion's share, Rihei had to find ways to prevent his economic situation from declining further. It was perhaps as a means to reassert symbolically the importance of his line over his brother's that Rihei adopted his father's name, thereby resurrecting his forebear and affirming his claim to the latter's power and position inherited as titled peasant, patron, and kumi head. Yet economic reality prevailed: Rihei wound up selling his titles and office to Gendayū, which further increased the gap between the two families, this time in terms of political power. This was part of the legacy he left Shinzō when he died at age fifty-six.

Shinzō's stay in Edo during his adolescent years must have changed his outlook on the world. He returned to a life as a poor peasant without hope of improving his lot by working the fields. To the great dismay of his lineage members, who counted village headmen among their ancestors, he sought his fortune in horse trading. Worse, he courted the company of gamblers and suspected thieves.

From Shinzō's perspective, however, it must have appeared that part of the reason for his misery lay with his uncle Gendayū, who had wound up with most of the family's property and with the family's titles. It should be noted that none of the land Shinzō sold in his seven separate sales went to Gendayū: it all went to the competing and rising sublineage (see table 2). The constant criticism of his ways by the lineage and their attempts to make him change his style of life must have further alienated Shinzō.

But the advice his relatives gave him carried more import than that of an ordinary uncle or aunt: as members of his kumi, they were responsible for his behavior in the eyes of the community and the authorities. Their opinions, therefore, constituted official admonitions. The head of his kumi was the representative of the village headman, behind whom stood the authority of the bannerman and ultimately the shogun. This being the case, it was difficult for Shinzō's mother to defend her son, and her agreement to request the disinheritance, if it was her doing, undoubtedly signified her public disapproval of Shinzō's course of action. She had to align herself with the village authorities. Yet, even thus isolated, Shinzō could not bring himself to leave the village, for which he paid with his life.

As Ken pointed out in her lawsuit, the legal grounds for killing Shinzō were open to question. The official effect of disinheritance was to relinquish communal responsibility, but it was revocable. Although expulsion from the village could have been a justifiable punishment for habitual gambling, it should not have meant irreversible exile. Yet it was pushed in that direction, ordered by the headman, given full lin-

Table 6. Chronology of Ken's Life

1694		Rihei II [D¹ of fig. 1] (30), lineage head, titled peasant, son of village head, member of village council, marries young woman from Yawata (16)
1700		Rihei (36) and Gendayū [D²] (20) set up separate households; Shinzō born
1712		Ine born; Rihei and Shinzō (12) leave for Edo; Rihei stays two years; Shinzō stays five years and then works in Gan village one year
1719		Rihei dies; Ken born
1727		Ine (15) marries and moves to Yawata
1737		Ken (18) marries and moves to Mimayose
1741		Shinzō (42), Gendayū's client
	4/13	Shinzō disappears with Gendayū's horse
	7/21	Shinzō disinherited by his mother (63)
	10/31	Shinzō dies
1742		Ken returns and becomes Gendayū's client (kakae)
1745		Ken's mother dies; Ken under Gendayū's tutelage (chōnai)
		Winter: Ken (26) marries man from Kannonji-shinden
1746		Ken returns to Makibuse; lives alone
1749		Ken in service at Hirabara
1750–52		Ken in service in Komoro, then returns to Makibuse and lives alone
1756		Ken (37) marries Rokuemon (39), from Mochizuki; leaves Gendayū's tutelage
1757	7/22	Ken's oral petition for a memorial service for her brother; headman starts keeping diary (until 11/18)
	8/5	Ken's written petition
	8/16	Affidavit by Rokuemon
1759	2/24	Rokuemon disappears
	3/25	Written promise by Rokuemon to abstain from sake
	4/15	Rokuemon returns
1761	9/–	Rokuemon (44), disappears for good
1762	3/–	Ken (40), requests to leave Makibuse
	3/6	Succession question for Ken
	3/7	Ken requests to leave Rokuemon on population register
1763	2/6	Ken requests to take Rokuemon off the population register
	2/8	Ken refuses to sign the population register
1795	1/8	Ken dies

NOTE: Ages are given in parentheses.

eage support. That Shinzō resisted expulsion is understandable, but his resistance, if we believe Gendayū's version, resulted in his death.

Ken bitterly resented the outcome. Yet, when she challenged its legality, the disinheritance document saved the accused by giving Shinzō's violent death justification legitimized by authority (the Shimogata magistrate).

PROTECTION AGAINST AN AVENGING SPIRIT

In her efforts to bring this affair into the open and question its legality, Ken obviously could not count on any cooperation from within the village. She said she paid someone to draft the suit, although that may not have been true. Payment, however, made the relationship between herself and the scribe a business one, exculpating the scribe from any charge of sympathy for her case. But bringing it into the open must also have been a catharsis for Ken, as the second half of her petition/suit shows:

> As for his memorial service, following my judgment (*nanibun ni mo kono kata no zonji yori ni*), it should be held so that none of your descendants might suffer retribution. The service itself should consist of daily recitations at Zenkōji in perpetuity (*kono yo aran kagiri*) and, also at Zenkōji, a forty-nine-day ritual; daily recitations in perpetuity at Kōyasan and a lantern; at the family temple of Baikei-in, recitation of one thousand sutras in perpetuity.[69] If things turn out that way, I shall sponsor all this. I shall go to Zenkōji [to arrange] for the service. I shall bring money from you and I shall contribute my own part (*sesshagi mo kono setsu dōdō itasu beku sōrō*). Kōyasan is a place where women are not allowed, hence my husband Rokuemon will represent me. He will also, in a similar fashion, collect money, including travel expenses.
>
> Although I am talking like this, I do not want to request even one sen. It would not be proper to do [as I say] if each and every one is not convinced [that it is the right thing to do]. You should all get together and follow your judgment (*zonji yori ni nasaru beku*). I also am following my own. If you are convinced [of the rightness of this case], then Chūemon [the village headman], Gendayū, Shinzaemon [E^1 of fig. 1], Dan'emon,

69. The forty-nine-day "ritual (*tsukare*)" probably refers to the period after death during which a number of purifying exorcisms are performed. The lantern may refer to a standard stone lantern or to one used in memorial services. Zenkōji was famous as a Pure Land to which all souls were said to go immediately following death. On Zenkōji, see Donald F. McCallum, *Zenkōji and Its Icon: A Study in Medieval Japanese Religious Art* (Princeton: Princeton University Press, 1994).

Uheiji [F] should write a deed [of apology for the murder]. If that is what they think is right, then I shall write a document [to forgive them]. I also want a deed [of apology] from Chōkyūrō [E³] and all the other officials, and then I in turn shall write a document [to forgive them]. I [shall] feel no [further] resentment toward my relatives. I have no resentment toward Jūzaemon [E⁴], Heihachi [E⁵], and, among the officials, toward Tadasuke [kumi head; 9.1 of table 5; the other two kumi heads were mentioned as guilty in the first half of the petition]. As for the people of the village who did not show up here today, I do not need their monetary contribution for the service. I have nothing else to say. As stated above.

1757/8 Ken (seal)
[To:] The village headman
The officials[70]

Thus Ken had devised a number of rather extraordinary memorial events—perhaps commensurate in her eyes to the crime to be expiated—in order that the descendants of her brother's murderers might not suffer divine retribution. She hints at supernatural retribution and vents her resentment but is also determined and resourceful to overcome a difficulty she, as a woman, might encounter in executing her plan. Ken would take charge of it all and collect monetary contributions from everyone, but she wanted these only if people were convinced that the murder had been a mistake and were ready to apologize for it in writing. She appealed to everyone's conscience. She wanted a verdict from a tribunal less than she wanted an apology from everyone. That, however, she would not get.

For all those involved in Shinzō's murder, the deed of disinheritance had wrapped up the case. On 9/21, accused of false testimony concerning her lack of knowledge of the disinheritance, Ken was "entrusted" to her kumi; that is, she was restricted in her comings and goings and put under surveillance. A month later, on 10/26, she was summoned before the Shimogata authorities again and told that her suit was an "unspeakably impudent petition (*iwarezaru daitan naru negai*)" that on principle ought to be investigated. Instead, she was told, in the condescending voice of paternalistic authority, "you are forgiven because you are a woman [but] will be ordered house confinement because of your offense."

When the village officials received this order, they used it to restore

70. This second half of Ken's petition is to be found only in Ozaki, "Kenjo oboegaki," 93–94.

"peace" in the village. Through the priest of her family temple, they promised Ken that they would not enforce the house arrest order if she reconciled herself with her relatives, that is, if she stopped harassing them—a second put-down, turning the victim into the cause of the trouble. This new proposal made Ken furious, and at first she resisted it forcefully. Finally, perhaps recognizing that it would be futile to further resist her relatives and the whole village, backed as they were by bakufu authority, Ken stated her intention to comply with their demands.

The failure to obtain an apology or win her lawsuit had not broken Ken's spirit. The trouble arising from her refusal to affix her seal to the population register in 1763 proves this. That year, it so happened, was the twenty-third anniversary (according to Japanese reckoning) of Shinzō's death, something that must not have escaped Ken. (Individual dead are memorialized with more than the annual rites at special anniversaries—the seventh, eleventh, thirteenth, and twenty-third.) This time Ken did not accuse her relatives or the village of wrongdoing, but pleaded hardship in having to work the fields, pay tribute, and perform corvée. She asked for understanding for her plight and proposed a solution, namely, that the fields she was supposed to work be removed from the tax register and commended to her temple and that she leave the village. In fact, Ken's solution was another expression of her total rejection of her relatives and her village, no doubt prompted by her unwillingness to accept their denial of any wrongdoing in her brother's murder.

In this she resisted, of course, the solution proposed by the village authorities, namely, to provide for an heir. This threw them into confusion once again, but they could not let a woman who had caused them so much trouble have her own way. The two sides were at an impasse again. The village wanted a successor to Ken's house and therefore did not want to let her go, so that the land would remain in the village. She did not want to stay, nor did she want her land to go to anyone in the village. There seems to have been more behind village officials' insistence that she establish an heir (part of a new agreement Ken signed, in which she also promised to continue as a peasant and keep the peace) than, as Ozaki surmises, a desire to comply with overlord law not to let peasant houses die out. Ken was not even a titled peasant; her holding was tiny, and many families could have used more land.

What came of this promise? Twenty years later, according to Makibuse's population register of 1782, Ken was still living alone. She also appears on the tax register of 1792 as a tribute payer. She still had not complied with the wishes of the authorities. Ken's tombstone, next to her mother's and Shinzō's, perhaps erected by her lineage in fear of their avenging spirits, records the date of her death as 1795/1/8. She lived alone in Makibuse until she was seventy-six. One can only imagine what her life must have been like during those last thirty years. The best way to describe it, leaving room for the imagination, is the way her life under Gendayū was described: *fuwa,* without harmony.

CONCLUSION

Through the story of Ken we have made the acquaintance, in unusually vivid detail, of a peasant woman and some salient events in her life. Ken's life and that of her family were tied to a past of increased economic hardship, which many others shared. It also unfolded in a wide geographic setting beyond the village, reaching all the way to Edo. There her father and brother hoped to accumulate savings to alleviate the family's plight, and there Ken thought she might eventually find justice. Ken was a stubborn and strong woman who followed her own conscience (see the several instances of *kono kata no zonji yori ni* in her petition). Her sense of justice was reflected in a trail of documents recording a series of confrontations with authority at various levels: her husband, her relatives as a lineage and as a neighborhood kumi, the village officials, the headman, and shogunal representatives.

Ken's sense of justice clashed with the authorities' concern for order. With a firm grasp of the system of governance, geared toward the maintenance of order, Ken succeeded more than once in strategically subverting it to pursue what she judged to be just. She manipulated two of her marriages this way. Although illiterate, she produced an important document, in format a petition for a memorial service, in reality a demand for justice in the form of an apology from the village authorities, in effect a lawsuit against them for murder. She knew how to gain a public voice to lodge this suit and how to embarrass the headman and her kumi. She threatened to wield the symbolic weapons provided by religion and by the courts to find retribution and justice from two faraway centers that she must have imagined as detached from the nasty world she experienced: Zenkōji, a nonsectarian Buddhist pilgrim center

Plate 2.   Ken's Tomb. *Left to right:* the tombstones of Ken, her mother, and Shinzō. Photograph by author.

and also a transit point for the souls of the recently deceased; and Edo, a political center where powers and authorities converged and to some degree lost their local character.

Ultimately, this match between a woman seeking justice and a system seeking "harmony" was uneven. Authority was not to bend to law, and law was not to bow to reason, according to a Tokugawa saying. In practice, therefore, authorities did not issue public apologies, because only subjects could be in the wrong. Ken, who thought justice might be a concern of the shogunal authorities, found that they functioned with the same logic as her village superiors. Once she publicly forced the issue of an apology, the two levels of authority, intra- and extravillage, formed a common front. Then Ken's resistance turned passive. Within the village that became her prison, she kept control over her property and her life until the end of her days by not adopting an heir or a husband as her superiors would have had her do.

Power in a village, as we see it used by both sides in Ken's story, is social power that is steeped in public, official power. One's relatives and lineage provide an immediate social framework that has at the same time a public character, because it overlaps with the official neighborhood system and its internal hierarchy of main and branch houses, which takes on an official dimension by the distinction between titled and nontitled peasant households. In addition, the manipulation of power at the village level has wider dimensions because of the strategic possibilities offered by the intersection of intra- and extravillage authorities. Here we can mention the attempts by the village authorities to prevent the petition/suit from leaving the village; the threats by Ken either not to appear before the extramural authorities (in the registration incident) or to bring her suit to them (in the murder case); the collusion between the intramural and extramural authorities with regard to the investigation of the murder; and the pressure on the part of the village authorities to extort promises by granting suspension of a punishment (house confinement) decided beyond the village.

Because Ken was a woman, her interactions with village authorities and the expectations she confronted must have been those of patriarchal power. Yet, in apparent control of her three marriages, firm and outspoken in her confrontations with her kumi members and village officials, and countering the headman's threats with some of her own, Ken flaunted those expectations. When the officials finally dug in their heels, denying Ken her request to leave the village and transfer her land to a temple, they put her in her place *as a woman,* which was to secure males (a husband or an heir) on the land to produce tribute. Ken, however, was equally firm in sticking to her earlier warning: "There is no need to come and speak about this to me again."

Ken must have been scolded often by her relatives and superiors. One clear instance was when the Shimogata authorities told Ken that she was not given the full punishment she deserved for her "unspeakably impudent" suit because she was a woman. Here condescendence yields, by way of scolding, the double profit of a feigned compassion and understanding and a real punishment. Scolding is perhaps the first means to activate explicitly when threatened, the (usually unformulated) power of *doxa* or common sense, which as it is used here is that of gender-asymmetrical propriety.

In all moves made by parties in the power field encompassing both village and supravillage authorities, written documentation played a crucial role. Conflicts and disputes revolved around, and were ultimately resolved by, the creation of legally recognized documents; for example, in the case of the headman's diary, the record of steps taken by him could eventually be used in court. The following instances of the crucial role of documentation come to mind: the ability to write petitions in proper form; the manipulation of population records; the importance of *written* and certified disinheritance documents that were forwarded beyond the village; a petition for a memorial service that could not be suppressed because it contained a charge of murder; the many occasions where written promises were exacted (to not drink sake, to establish an heir, to move in with a new husband in another village, to live in harmony, to work the fields, etc.). Documents were indispensable for regulating conduct within the village. Village life was highly legalistic and formalized, a far cry from a Gemeinschaft governed by informal understandings, where the spoken word is binding.

Moreover, intervillage linkages of various kinds played an important role in defining networks that could be exploited for a number of purposes. Not only was Makibuse exogamous to a very high degree but some of its inhabitants spent long periods of time working outside the village. Its position on a major highway made Edo appear available and within reach to the villagers and must have increased the flow of information that could be put to use in various ways. Villages were less isolated than often imagined.

The question of village autonomy has been debated back and forth by Japanese historians, most of whom choose either to defend it or to deny that it had any substance. The Tokugawa political landscape, being neither homogeneous (which would make the village insubstantial) nor divided into two heteronomous spheres (which would disregard the grave imbalance of power between villages and lords), is perhaps best visualized as two fields of power that created at their intersection a space for manipulation from either side.

2
Class Politics

Privileges associated with past status are acknowledged, but times
have changed.

Bannerman to village headman, 1650s

Class and status are introduced in two separate chapters in this book.
The distinction between the two, however, hard to justify even analytically, should certainly not be taken as an objective separation, as the
epitaph on status in this chapter on class suggests. It is merely a question of emphasis, of foregrounding one against the other. The simulta-
neous economic and political decline of Ken's line in Makibuse illustrates how inextricably related the two could be in Tokugawa village
life. Yet status obviously is not a mere reflection of class: some of Ken's
neighbors, although impoverished, were able to hold on to the status of
titled peasant and the political power that came with the title. That
micro narrative was firmly anchored locally, venturing only occasionally beyond the confines of the village. In this chapter the analysis
moves inward toward the village from the wider class and power con-
figurations that were shaping society mainly in the first half of the
Tokugawa period.

A cardinal feature of Tokugawa society was the concentration of
the new warrior rulers in urban centers, separated from the land and
the people they had conquered in the last decades of the sixteenth century. The rulers' self-enforced spatial separation from the fruits of their
conquest, which resulted in domination from a distance, made particularly acute the need for reliable, quantifiable data for the full exploitation of their new sources of revenue. Thus, in the late sixteenth and
early seventeenth centuries the land was measured and the people on it

Epigraph: Saitō Yoshiyuki, "Kinsei shoki no nōmin tōsō," 53.

counted. This created two new public and universal (because divisible and exchangeable) values: land aggregates and populations. As value and data, the former had existed before, although in a different form, that is, less comprehensive and not measured in the equivalent of bushels of rice. Population data, however, were altogether new. In Tokugawa Japan everyone was to be accounted for.

The smallest unit for the collation, circulation, and exploitation of these values was the village as it emerged from the turmoil of a century of warfare. Further military conquests having become impossible, the victors turned their full attention to tribute, exacted now by decree rather than by the sword. The new rulers were not particularly interested in remote village affairs per se and, indeed, did not interfere beyond taking the minimal steps necessary to extract tribute and corvée.

This broad picture conveys the impression of an incorporation or cooptation of villages into the Tokugawa power structure with a minimal impact on them except for the new tribute system. In the past, agricultural surplus had flowed out of the villages in a number of different directions. Now it went only to a single class of beneficiaries. Such an interpretation is reminiscent of the conventional view of Tokugawa ideology, which assumes the appropriation of a ready-made doctrine, neo-Confucianism, that was just "waiting in the wings" to be mobilized for legitimating purposes by the new regime. Until recently, the Tokugawa village was also presumed to have been "already there," available for outside political exploitation. Scholarly historiographical exploitation in turn consisted in writing about this entity within a framework that, like that of the rulers, assumed stability.

More recently, however, historians have amended this view of the so-called Tokugawa village as a "natural community" typified by "village-level" tribute exaction, "consensual" decision making, and "autonomous" self-governance; they have historicized these qualifiers. This village, or more precisely, perhaps, because it is more image than anything else, the social reality that (mis)informed the above image, took six to twelve Tokugawa decades, depending on the region, to develop, and once established it continued to change, in unforeseen ways. In other words, the "Tokugawa village" (*mura*) should not be conceived of as a stable entity, but as an ever-changing Tokugawa village practice, a practice driven by external and internal forces that were closely interrelated. A projection backward (and forward) has often informed the discourse, often structural, about the Tokugawa village: the outcome of a long development *during* the Tokugawa period was assumed to have been there from the beginning (and to have remained throughout).

According to the perspective adopted here, one does not confront an entity only to record its history. Instead, one traces its genesis, which never ends, because, strictly speaking, time never produces lasting entities; they are produced only by administrative records, and the historians who read them, who often wind up in abstractions that relate only vaguely to practice.[1] Concretely this means that a "village" in the early seventeenth century, economically self-sufficient and consisting predominantly of, and ruled by, a few extended families, had little in common besides its name with the form it took two hundred and fifty years later, when it consisted predominantly of numerous small, often impoverished families tied into a wide regional administrative network and a national economy.

Of course, change has not been totally absent from historical discourse on Tokugawa village society. The changes that have been identified, however, have been mostly economic, generated by a commercial economy that developed during the eighteenth century. From this perspective, the village has been viewed as a stable social formation, and change as externally generated, economic in nature, and historically late rather than internal, political, and ongoing.

Historians and other scholars who look into the past who profess an interest in change often wind up missing it in their analyses. I have discussed this problem at some length with regard to Tokugawa ideology, arguing that many students fell victim to both that ideology itself and their own presumption that there is a universal need for all societies to have an ideology formulated as a doctrine.[2] What, then, one may ask, blurred historians' vision so often and for so long when they looked at Tokugawa villages, especially of the first half of the period? Why has

1. These reflections on writing a history versus tracing a genesis are inspired by Michel Foucault's "Nietzsche, Genealogy, History," in Michel Foucault, *Language, Counter-Memory, Practice: Selected Interviews and Essays,* ed. and trans. Donald F. Bouchard (Ithaca, N.Y.: Cornell University Press, 1977), 139–64; and by Claude Lévi-Strauss, *The Savage Mind* (Chicago: University of Chicago Press, 1966), 256–62.

2. See my *Tokugawa Ideology,* as well as my "Neo-Confucianism and the Formation of Early Tokugawa Ideology: Contours of a Problem," in *Confucianism and Tokugawa Culture,* ed. Peter Nosco (Princeton: Princeton University Press, 1984), 27–61.

the myth of stable, undiversified, harmonious Tokugawa rural communities persisted for so long?

DIVERSIFYING THE PICTURE OF EARLY TOKUGAWA RURAL SOCIETY

Some of the reasons are the same as the general reasons why "popular history" did not gain academic legitimacy until the 1960s. In a sense, while Japanese historians discussed at great length "the Tokugawa village," they did not see (into) the villages, because "real" history presumably was happening elsewhere.

In the West, Thomas C. Smith more than any other historian has been sensitive to the divisions and tensions (mainly, but not exclusively, economic ones) in seventeenth-century Japan. However, in 1958 he wrote that not much was known about the important political issue of allocating within the village "the tax bill among its individual holders."[3] In his *Agrarian Origins of Modern Japan,* he elaborated further but still had only his historical and sociological imagination, which he used with great skill, to rely on because of a lack of data.[4] Much research has taken place since the publication of Smith's classic study in 1959.

Mizumoto Kunihiko, whose lead I follow, has argued that postwar Japanese scholars remained stuck until the 1970s in the historiographical consequences of a Marxist structuralist interpretation of the rural policy that Toyotomi Hideyoshi (1536–98) established and the early Tokugawa bakufu continued.[5] This policy would have succeeded in dividing larger clan holdings into independent smaller ones.

---

3. Thomas C. Smith, "The Land Tax in the Tokugawa Period," in *Studies in the Institutional History of Early Modern Japan,* ed. John Whitney Hall and Marius Jansen (Princeton: Princeton University Press, 1968), 284, reprinted from *Journal of Asian Studies* 18 (1958): 1.

4. Thomas C. Smith, "Political Conflict in the Village," in his *Agrarian Origins,* 181–83. Most of that chapter, however, focuses on the last century of the Tokugawa period, especially on conflicts centered on *miyaza,* or shrine associations, which were most prevalent in the Kinai region.

5. Mizumoto Kunihiko, "Bakuhansei kōzōron kenkyū no saikentō—Asao, Sasaki-shi no shigoto o sozai ni," *Atarashii rekishigaku no tame ni* (Minka Kyoto shibu rekishibukai kikanshi) 131 (1973): 13–23. For a full historiographical survey, consult Kodama Kōta, Nagahara Keiji, et al., eds., *Kinsei, Nihon rekishi taikei,* 3 (Yamakawa shuppan, 1988), 385–407 (hereafter NRT 3). Mizumoto presents his argument in the form of a critical assessment of Asao

Asao Naohiro, for instance, emphasized the crucial role played by the local leadership of the *sō*-type villages, predominant in the Kinai region, around the capital, in the fifteenth and sixteenth centuries. Sō villages were autonomous corporate villages or groups of villages (of one *gō*, a medieval administrative district, or one *shōen*, or medieval estate) where part of the land was commonly cultivated and full administrative, judiciary, and often penal powers (including the death penalty) were held by an oligarchy of prominent peasants.[6] The overlords subcontracted many of these corporate villages via their elite as official units responsible for the total tribute due from their territory. This for-

---

Naohiro and Sasaki Junnosuke's work, but his critique reaches beyond them to Araki Moriaki, Miyagawa Mitsuru, and even the prewar scholarship of Furushima Toshio: Asao Naohiro, *Kinsei hōken shakai no kiso kōzō* (Ochanomizu shobō, 1967); Sasaki Junnosuke, "Kinsei nōson no seiritsu," *Iwanami kōza Nihon rekishi: Kinsei* (2) (Iwanami shoten, 1963), 165–221; Araki Moriaki, *Bakuhan taisei shakai no seiritsu to kōzō* (Ochanomizu shobō, 1959); Miyagawa Mitsuru, *Taikō kenchiron*, 3 vols. (Ochanomizu shobō, 1959–63); Furushima Toshio, *Nihon hōken nōgyōshi* (Shikai shobō, 1941). Many of these and other scholars formulated their interpretations of Tokugawa village society in essentialist Leninist terms, periodizing societies according to their dominant socioeconomic formation as determined by their particular mode of production. Lenin, in his *Development of Russian Capitalism,* used the Russian term *uklad* (literally, "structure") to refer to such socioeconomic formations. Many Japanese historians made a fetish of the term, using it as an explanatory device that obviated any need for further analysis. On the uklad theory, see also Mizumoto Kunihiko, "Bakuhanseika no nōmin keizai," *Nihon keizaishi o manabu: 2. Kinsei* (Yūhikaku, 1982), 66–70. A handy summary of the debate can be found under "ukurādo" in KDJ 2:56. According to this entry, the *locus classicus* is in Lenin's 1921 paper "On the Food Tax" and his earlier *Development of Capitalism in Russia.* Thus, the specific Tokugawa uklad was from the beginning one of independent, small landholders, created by Hideyoshi's national land survey, which presumably had the effect of a land reform. Asao and Sasaki later added a second uklad—of the extended patriarchal family—attaching differential values to the two uklads by arguing that local magnates, a negative historical force, were eventually overcome through struggles of small peasants aided by the bakufu (Mizumoto, "Bakuhansei kōzōron," 14–18).

6. An excellent brief summary of the history and operation of corporate villages can be found in KDJ, s.v. "sōson" (8:563–65); see also the entries "jigeuke" (6:721), "sōshō" (8:549), and "gōsonsei" (5:424–25). For a case study of the most well-known *sō* village (because best documented), see Tonomura Hitomi, *Community and Commerce in Late Medieval Japan: The Corporate Villages of Tokuchin-ho* (Stanford: Stanford University Press, 1992). On *jigeuke,* see also Fujiki Hisashi, "Ikōki sonrakuron," in *Nihon chūseishi kenkyū no kiseki,* ed. Nagahara Keiji et al. (Tōkyō Daigaku shuppan, 1988), 208–10.

mula of collecting tribute, then called *jigeuke* (perhaps best rendered as "land receivership"), was quite similar to the subsequent Tokugawa bakufu's policy of *murauke* ("village receivership"). The bakufu, Asao argued, was able to win this "corporate elite" to its own side and use it as the backbone of its local structure of domination. Thus, it would have been wealthy rather than small peasants who enjoyed bakufu support.

For Sasaki Junnosuke, the mura, or village, was a Tokugawa creation, headed by both the janus figure of the headman, or *shōya* (the link between village and supravillage authority), and village officials. Under a general rubric of establishing small, independent landholders, the bakufu would have implemented a differentiated policy toward local leaders, displacing some and supporting others. Sasaki's view was based on his interpretation of late Tokugawa *ikki*, or uprisings in which villages acted as a whole. He then applied this image of unified communities of small landholders fighting overlords in his discussion of the early period.

Mizumoto's critique is based upon a careful examination of early Tokugawa sō village disturbances in the Kinai region. Small landholders did not confront rural magnates, nor did solitary villages confront their overlords. Rather, these peasant struggles were against the arbitrary rule of their own village leaders, struggles unrelated to official land policies.[7]

The thesis of the bakufu's promotion of independent small landholders was based on an examination of land surveys and laws around the turn of the seventeenth century. Dissenting scholars, however, pointed out that the titled peasants officially established through these surveys were, *regardless of size, yakuya*, or corvée houses, selected by overlords to deliver village quotas of tribute and corvée (*yaku*),[8] a responsibility that also, because it was not shared by all villagers, functioned as a mark of local distinction and privilege. These titled peasants invariably not only controlled land but also had homesteads (*yashiki*) and were often land magnates and local bosses, sometimes with a semiwarrior background, in other words, the village economic elite.[9] Thus, the social picture of early Tokugawa rural Japan consisted of registered

7. Mizumoto, "Bakuhansei kōzōron," 18–21.
8. Mizumoto, "Bakuhanseika no nōmin keizai," 65.
9. Ibid., 63–64.

peasants/households, of whom some were singled out as accountable for tribute and others were not burdened with that responsibility. The former were "titled peasants" (not to be understood in the restrictive sense of title to land); the latter, although without homestead (*muyashiki*), often had some direct claim or perhaps merely a relationship of usufruct to land that was entered under their name.[10] The picture was further complicated by the fact that some of the titled units were large extended families, while others were small households.

MICRO STRUGGLES I: HEADMEN, ELDERS, AND SMALL PEASANTS IN CORPORATE VILLAGES (*SŌ*)

Mizumoto's discovery of internal tensions within early Tokugawa villages stimulated a reevaluation of the character of the *kyōdōtai,* or community, which historians assumed had been coopted by the new rulers. It was generally accepted that this incorporation had been achieved by the policy of extracting tribute on a village basis (murauke), the village being understood unproblematically as a "natural" community, its perimeters and internal composition reflected in the land and population surveys from around the turn of the seventeenth century. Yet these so-called *villages* (mura) that served as units of tribute exaction were not infrequently artificially established territorial units created by the surveys, and not preexisting functioning *communities* (kyōdōtai) merely recorded by them.[11]

The village cadasters did not include land residents held outside the village but did list the names and fields of nonresident landowners.[12] Some cadaster "villages," therefore, actually counted more outsiders than insiders. In Higashi-Tenkawa village, Settsu province (Hyōgo prefecture), for instance, insiders (89) were outnumbered by outsiders (133), residents in ten different villages.[13] At the time of the land surveys some communities were split up into several villages, some regrouped with neighboring ones to form a new unit based on the medi-

10. Naitō Jirō has stressed this point throughout his *Honbyakushō taisei no kenkyū* (Ochanomizu shobō, 1968); see, e.g., 28, 66, 178–79, 258–61, and 293.

11. Mizumoto drew new attention to this problematic in *Mura shakai,* pt. 2, chap. 2.

12. Mizumoto, "Bakuhanseika no nōmin keizai," 76–77.

13. Mizumoto, *Mura shakai,* 145.

eval gō, others simply moved to make room for castles, and many villages were brand-new, created on newly developed land (*shinden mura*) or as way stations on the highways.[14] These administrative interventions often triggered various forms of resistance, protest, and local maneuvering, if not to undo them, then at least to mitigate some of their negative consequences.[15]

Mizumoto's analysis of early Tokugawa disturbances in corporate villages of the Kinai problematizes the notion of these "natural communities."[16] "Early Tokugawa" has a very specific meaning here, referring to the decades between 1600 and the 1680s, a period further divided at the 1640s. Compared with the well-known peasant revolts of the mid and late Tokugawa, these early Tokugawa disturbances were distinguished by two characteristics. First, there were relatively few ikki, or large-scale uprisings, and they were almost all village affairs. Second, although similar to later intramural (or intra-mura) suits against abuses by village authorities concerning the calculation and allocation of tribute and corvée or their exemption thereof, the class identity of plaintiffs and defendants changed over time, roughly, in the 1640s and again in the 1680s. Before the 1640s, suits and petitions were signed only by the village elite, peasants who were from the same economic class as the headman but who directed their litigation at him. After the 1640s the suits targeted, besides the headman, that same elite, which now had gained power in village governance; the litigants now came from a new class of well-established landholders. Toward the end of the century the plaintiffs were predominantly peasants with very small holdings.[17]

14. For examples of split villages, see ibid., 139; for examples of several villages collapsed into one, see ibid., 146, and Mizubayashi Takeshi, *Hōkensei no saihen to Nihonteki shakai no kakuritsu*, Nihon tsūshi, 2 (Kinsei) (Yamakawa shuppansha, 1987), 136; for villages displaced for the building of Komoro castle in Kita-Saku district, Shinano, see NAK-T 4:188; for *shinden mura* in the same area, see Ōishi Shinzaburō, *Kinsei sonraku no kōzō*, chap. 3; for a recent work on such villages in the Kantō plain, see the first two articles under the heading "Shinden kaihatsu to minshū ishiki" in Chihōshi kenkyū kyōgikai, ed., *"Kaihatsu" to chiiki minshū: sono rekishizō o motomete* (Yūzankaku, 1991), 137–94.

15. Mizumoto, *Mura shakai*, 137–90.

16. Mizumoto, "Murakata sōdō," 289–307; idem, *Mura shakai*, chaps. 1 and 3.

17. Mizumoto, "Murakata sōdō," 289–94; idem, *Mura shakai*, 7–17.

The predominant complaint in pre-1640s suits of corporate villages was about the arbitrary exercise of power by headmen, who made important decisions without consulting the *sōbyakushō* ("all the peasants"). The inclusive nature of this formula is misleading, for it referred, not to all villagers, but only to the village elite and often to the core of that elite, the *toshiyori,* or elders. In pre-Tokugawa times that elite was not ruled by someone with special powers like those of a headman.[18] It is important to keep in mind that in these early decades of the seventeenth century the "elders" were *not* village officials in the eyes of the overlords, even though they continued to play traditional, key roles in community and intervillage disputes.[19] Headmen were established by the superordinate extramural (or extra-mura) powers in the 1590s and were picked from the ranks of the village elite. Thus, this elite came to direct its early suits against the member from its own circle who had been elevated to hold the new office of headman.

In the late 1640s, however, the character of these village disturbances changed in two ways: (1) the former plaintiffs were now made the targets of legal suits; and (2) these lawsuits became an integral part of efforts to shift the village basis of privilege and political power from pedigreed houses of titled peasants to households that were holders of *taka,* or tribute land. This new class of plaintiffs identified themselves no longer as sō-byakushō, "all peasants," but as *ko-byakushō,* "small peasants"[20] (a term I shall elucidate later; for now, let us stay with the defendants).

The complaints voiced by these "small peasants" concerned village heads *and* elders, who came to be officially incorporated into the structure of village governance around that time. On the yearly tribute rosters overlords sent to villages, they now appeared as a special category of addressees (besides the headman and "all the peasants") because they filled the new village offices of *kumigashira,* or kumi heads (of the five-household neighborhood groups created by the bakufu).[21]

---

18. Fujiki Hisashi disagrees with Mizumoto on this point and stresses a continuity of headmen from pre-Tokugawa to Tokugawa times in his "Ikōki sonrakuron," 208.

19. Mizumoto, *Mura shakai,* 19; see also Miyajima Keiichi, "Kinsei nōmin shihai no seiritsu ni tsuite: 1. Chūsei zaichihō no 'hitei' to 'naizai,'" *Chihōshi kenkyū,* no. 171 (1981), 1–11.

20. Mizumoto, "Murakata," 297; idem, *Mura shakai,* 7, 20–22.

21. Ibid., *Mura shakai,* 20.

The development of this institution clearly illustrates the transference of military organizational formulae to civil rule. In 1597 Hideyoshi introduced five- and ten-man units in his army to better check internal discipline. Tokugawa Ieyasu (1542–1616) used the idea to bring order to Kyoto in 1603, and his successor introduced the system in all bakufu territories. The five-household groups were adopted nationwide in the mid 1630s in order to establish multipurpose subvillage administrative units, which created new village power holders besides the village headman.[22] This tightening of control within the village via a paramilitary institution has usually been understood as part of the bakufu's strategy against hidden Christians and troublesome rōnin (masterless samurai). In light of Mizumoto's argument, however, other pressures were probably at work as well, because the creation of these political offices signaled a victory by the old elite over a former equal, the headman.

The overlords thus modified the intravillage power distribution in two significant ways. First, they undermined the traditional elite's oligarchic rule in corporate villages in matters of intravillage tribute and corvée allocation by appointing a headman. Then the overlords broke the headman's monopolistic power through the establishment of kumi heads. By specifying the elders' duties and prerogatives as kumi heads, the bakufu restored them to the political prominence they had all along believed to be rightfully theirs. Thus the power base in the village was broadened, even though the majority of the peasants were still left out.

This analysis modifies the standard picture of the relationship between village and state in the Kinai in important ways. Villages were not ready-made units that were simply subsumed by the new state structures. To a certain extent they were the creations of the warrior rulers, and not only because the surveys officially certified village borders. Yet these villages were not made once and for all either. They developed in ways unanticipated by their creators, because they constituted differential power fields whose members reacted to the new superordinate powers and forced those powers in turn to react to them.

Moreover, during the latter half of the seventeenth century village disputes in the Kinai region were political maneuvers by landholders for formal recognition as fully vested village members on a par with

22. For a brief sketch of this history of the goningumi, see KDJ 5:936, and *Kodansha Encyclopedia of Japan,* 9 vols. (Tokyo: Kodansha International, 1983), 3:45.

the titled peasants. As mentioned above, cadaster entries did not differentiate between peasants who held titles to land and others who did not, but between peasants with and without homesteads. The disputes of the second half of the century were new to the extent that they included attempts (with various degrees of success) by peasants, increasingly the small landowners, to shift the village political and status order from one based on privilege attached to some households (originally "homeowners") to one based on taka holding. I shall postpone the question why the new class of peasants could not simply argue that many of them now also had homesteads.

What were taka holders? *Taka* means "amount" and stands for *kokudaka*, "(rice) yield (measured) in koku," koku being equivalent to 4.96 bushels or 180 liters. *Kokudaka* refers, however, to assessed rather than actual yield. It was the official crop index, recorded in cadasters and yearly tax rosters and used to determine the yearly tribute (*nengu*). This index was calculated by assessing the grade of the arable (superior, medium, inferior; sometimes there were as many as thirteen grades)[23] and multiplying the assessed yield per square measure (e.g., per acre) by the actual size of the field. Dry fields and even the size of homesteads were also converted into koku equivalents. A taka holder was thus a peasant whose name was associated with some field listed on the cadasters, or more often, since few new surveys were made after the first ones, with some portion of the village tribute or corvée on the yearly tax registers. Thus, tenants without land of their own were not registered as taka holders, but their landlords were. It is of some importance to note that while taka has a close relation to plot size, it was not identical to it. The taka value—tribute or official value, which of course affected market value—of two plots equal in size differed if one plot had a higher assessed value than the other.

Village burdens could be allocated in a number of ways, depending on which constituent unit of the village—adults, households, "titled peasants," the taka value of holdings—was the basis of computation. The drive in the second half of the seventeenth century was for taka holders to be treated as titled peasants. More precisely, it was an attempt by newly established taka-holding households to join the ranks of the traditional "titled peasant" households, a struggle by a new class

23. Mizumoto, *Mura shakai*, 287.

and generation of peasants for fuller recognition by the old one. Implicit in this drive was the logic of the convertibility of economic power into political clout. The old guard's political importance was based on economic wealth; now, new landholders wanted the same for themselves.

The earliest recorded attempt, dating from 1649–51 in Kami-Kawarabayashi village, Settsu province, was not initiated by economically small holders (the number of similar disputes increased rapidly thereafter, peaking in the 1680s, when disputes clearly were led by members of the small peasantry).[24] This early request to distribute various yaku (corvée and other burdens) per assessed yield (see table 7) was one among a number of complaints against abuses by the headman and the elder. The socioeconomic status of the two men accused (Y and Z) and of the fourteen plaintiffs (A–N) *within the village* can be judged by the size of their individual holdings (kokudaka) and their ranking among the fifty-five taka holders of the village (all except L, an unclear case, owned houses).[25] Some of the peasants also held land in the neighboring village of Shimo-Kawarabayashi (see table 8).[26]

The plaintiffs were predominantly middle-ranking taka holders, A and B being exceptions as they rank even higher than the elder (Z) in terms of holdings and servants (the elder had no servants, while A had four), and the plaintiffs were all titled peasants. One may wonder why this drive for expanded political participation was led by titled peasants, who already held a monopoly on matters of village governance. Were they eager to share their power? Only twenty-one of the fifty-five taka holders were registered as titled peasants (here called *honyakunin*), and three more were listed as half-titled peasants (*hanyakunin*), and the request by about one-third of the titled peasants was to turn *all* taka holders into titled peasants. We do not know whether this request was ultimately granted, but in the 1670s L was listed as a titled peasant.

24. Ibid., 69–70.
25. Ibid., 72.
26. Peasants often held land in neighboring villages; thus, some of the involved parties's names also show up on Shimo-Kawarabayashi's tax roster. I recomputed and added data on the basis of the 1655 cadaster of Shimo-Kawarabayashi, in *Nishinomiya-shi shi*, vol. 4, *Shiryō-hen*, pt. 1 (Nishinomiya: Nishinomiya shiyakusho, 1962), 496–97. Kami-Kawarabayashi's cadaster can be found on 494–95, its population register of 1659 on 620–32. If we assume that some identical names on the two rosters refer to the same persons, Y of table 7 would have held an additional 9.2 koku in Shimo-Kawarabayashi; C, 4.6; H, 7.5; and K, 16.6.

Table 7. Plaintiffs and Defendants, Kami-Kawarabayashi, 1649–1651

| Peasants | Taka Holding | | Status |
	Koku	Rank	
Defendants			
Y	30.4	1	Headman
Z	15.0	10	Official elder
Plaintiffs			
A	22.2	3	Titled peasant
B	15.8	8	Titled peasant
C	14.7	11	Titled peasant
D	14.5	12	Titled peasant
E	14.3	13	Titled peasant
F	14.2	14	—
G	11.2	17	Titled peasant
H	9.0	22	—
I	8.4	23	—
J	6.7	26	Genin of B
K	5.9	29	Titled peasant
L	—	—	Retired head of B
M	—	—	—
N	—	—	—

SOURCE: Mizumoto, *Mura shakai*, table 1 (p. 72).

NOTE: The headman also has eleven co-resident and five separately housed bond servants (genin). Taka holdings are limited to land held *within the village*.

To answer the question why titled peasants might agitate to have their ranks opened to others, it is important to draw a distinction that may seem odd at first. In Tokugawa Japan, being accountable for tribute was not the same as contributing to it. Prior to these requests, the burden and privilege of *public accountability* for yaku (mainly tribute rice but also *buyaku*, corvée) was limited to "corvée households" (titled peasants). This title, as mentioned above, did not identify taka holders: although all villagers with some taka shared or *contributed* to the tax burden, only the titled peasants were accountable for it in the eyes of the overlords. This distinction simplified tribute extraction for the

Table 8. Taka Holders in the Neighboring Villages of
Kami- and Shimo-Kawarabayashi

| Koku | Taka Holders (number of known plaintiffs) | |
	In Kami-Kawarabayashi	In Shimo-Kawarabayashi
30+	1	0
25–30	1	1
20–25	4 (1)	3
15–20	4 (1)	5
10–15	7 (5)	5
5–10	14 (4)	8
1–5	13	11
–1	11	26
Total	55	59

SOURCE: *Nishinomiya-shi*, vol. 4, *Shiryō-hen*, pt. 1, 496–97.

overlords because it limited responsibility for it to the prominent villagers—a simplification of social space and also of social time, since it made no provisions for changes in village demographics.

When siblings or other dependents of titled peasants were established in separate quarters on a land parcel or when household heads retired on a separate plot, inkyo bunke (Kami-Kawarabayashi counted thirteen such cases in 1649, L being one of them), these branch houses did not automatically become titled peasants. The drive for taka-based access to the status of titled peasant was the result of the proliferation of new landholders. They shouldered tribute and corvée burdens without sharing the political privilege attached to the title. Given the large number of branch houses established by retiring titled peasants in Kami-Kawarabayashi—thirteen—the attempt to give these new households full political status as titled peasants may have been part of a strategy to increase the power of expanding lineages. It is important to remember that this is the first occurrence of such protest found to date and that it is somewhat unusual in that the initiative came from titled peasants. The number of such petitions, however, increased dramatically in the 1670s, when nontitled taka holders initiated them.

These petitions for entitlement, when granted, often signaled the end of the traditional *miyaza* in corporate villages, where a limited number of "shrine families" had succeeded in hanging on to their religiopolitical monopoly. Originally, in the fifteenth and sixteenth centuries, within the framework of corporate villages of a district or estate, the elders not only were secular leaders but also monopolized ceremonial life through the Shinto shrine associations, or miyaza. In the late sixteenth and seventeenth centuries, however, other peasants came to function as liturgical celebrants (*kannushi*) within the individual villages that emerged after the dissolution of the larger corporate units.[27] It should be noted, however, that miyaza continued to function as exclusive political clubs in a great many villages in the Kinai.

The Kawarabayashi area offers an example of such a dissolution of miyaza-based power. Its Hino shrine originally venerated the dominion lord Kawarabayashi as the *ujigami*, or tutelary deity. In the early 1600s he remained the patron god of only three villages, including the two Kawarabayashi's, and in the second half of the seventeenth century his sacred jurisdiction shrunk even further, comprising only Kami-Kawarabayashi and its branch village of new fields, Gorōemon-shinden. Ceremonial control was now in the hands of three families in the village. Toward the end of the century even they lost their status because villagers took turns presiding over religious ceremonies.[28]

Initially, as already mentioned, these struggles were led by traditional titled peasants against the headmen and the elders. They were followed in midcentury by demands from a different sector of the village population, namely, small taka holders who were not titled peasants. Although their motive may have been political, their professed aim was survival. They argued that their share of village expenses was disproportionately high since these were divided equally per household rather than calibrated according to holding size (taka).[29] As can be seen in table 7, many of the taka holders in Kami-Kawarabayashi were dangerously close to having no taka at all.

Around 1700, plaintiffs explicitly incorporated in their petitions the "landless" peasants (*mudaka*, "without *taka*," or *mizunomibyakushō*, "water-drinking peasants"). These terms, like "titled peasant," should

27. Mizubayashi, *Hōkensei*, 32–33.

28. Ibid., 223–24. Mizumoto presents another case where the struggle against entrenched religiopolitical power was waged at this level: Tateishi, in Yoshino district, Yamato province, in 1677–79 (*Mura shakai*, 74–76).

29. Mizumoto, *Mura shakai*, 76–80.

not always be taken literally, for many mizunomi peasants had some, if little, land of their own. In other words, they were not necessarily pure tenants. These suits were now directed explicitly not only against headmen and elders but also against great taka holders (*ōtakamochi*).[30] These plaintiffs perceived themselves as virtually landless and made common cause with those who actually were.

Various class fractions of the peasantry realigned themselves thus in their attempts to participate fully in decisions that touched their lives. Before the 1640s it was the traditional elite against headmen. In the second half of the century old titled peasants challenged headmen and elders. Then, in the 1670s all taka holders pressured the village leadership for widening decision-making participation. And finally, around 1700 the marginal peasants made common cause with the "landless" ones. At this last juncture, however, the argument changed because landless peasants could not be incorporated on the basis of their taka. They pleaded for corvée to again be computed per household rather than per taka.

This last point is hard to explain, as Mizumoto admits, because the request seems to work to the economic disadvantage of the poorer peasants.[31] Landless homeowners would be tax-exempt in a system where corvée and tribute were based on land holding but not in a system based on home ownership. This leaves one hypothesis, namely, that the poor peasants stood to gain politically from being recategorized closer to the status of full-fledged village members. It is important to note that the system they wanted, based on household, or *ie,* was different from that of the early Tokugawa period, because now it would include all households, not just a privileged few.

This drive did not succeed. As we shall see in chapter 3, political membership did not open up. On the other hand, many compromise solutions were reached in which burdens were computed in part on the basis of holding size, in part on the number of households. At the level of consciousness, however, things did change, as Mizumoto argues in his perceptive analysis of the term *kobyakushō,* "small peasants."[32] We are now in a position to clarify the uses and meanings of this term, for there are several.

30. Ibid., 80–85.
31. Ibid., 82.
32. Ibid., 85–102.

In the first four decades of the Tokugawa period petitioners signed collectively as "all the peasants," a phrase that in reality referred only to the village elite, who had always spoken for "all the peasants." "Small peasants" was the identity taken by all successive categories of later plaintiffs discussed above: first the heads of "corvée households," or titled peasants, then taka holders, followed by marginal peasants, and finally marginal and landless peasants together. As time went by, the term came to include, *for the people,* more and more sectors of the village population, all of them politically disenfranchised, and it gradually came to include the economically less well off.

For the bakufu, however, it was a different matter. There was stability of meaning over the same period. In its documents and legislation, the bakufu (and some domains) differentiated a specific large category of "small peasants" from other villagers. The term excluded village officials, bond servants (*nago* and genin), handicraft workers, and outcastes and referred only to taka holders, even very small ones. Small peasants were thus *tribute producers,* even if they themselves did not directly *pay* the tribute, for example, branch houses for whose tribute patron families or lineage heads were responsible.

These discrepancies between rulers and ruled in the referents for the term "small peasants" reveal that initially the bakufu defined it more broadly (all taka holders) than the commoners (titled peasants). Subsequently, the scope of both usages converged when the plaintiffs included all taka holders beyond the titled peasants. And finally, the peasants expanded the term's meaning beyond the bakufu's to include nonholders.

In the area of village practice other than suits, Mizumoto further documents the growing importance of taka holders in village affairs. His analysis of the identity of those who affixed their seals to tax rosters and village budgets in a couple of villages in the late seventeenth and early eighteenth centuries reveals a sudden expansion of those who endorsed these documents and participated in their composition. In one case, 45 percent of all taka holders signed the budget in 1676 but eleven years later 100 percent signed. In another, all taka holders signed the tax roster in 1706, while only 85 percent had signed four years earlier and only 54 percent had done so in 1680.[33]

33. Ibid., 95–101.

These various developments in consciousness and practice invite comments on interpretations of class in early Tokugawa rural society. Herbert Bix has attempted to document a rising peasant class consciousness and an expanding oppositional political practice against the ruling samurai starting in the eighteenth century, when according to his analysis class became important.[34] One weakness of his argument is that for the seventeenth century Bix worked basically with the official, legal, Tokugawa status definition of peasants and samurai and thus did not pay sufficient attention to economic and class divisions within the villages. The present analysis, however, reveals political action based on the recognition of the unbalanced relation between political and economic power, not between samurai and peasants, but within the peasantry. This configuration of practice, perception, and the reality of inequality was framed by the social and political structure established by the ruling samurai. Its setting was limited to the village, and the lines along which the confrontations took place were those that the rulers initially drew within the field of power—the village itself—lines subsequently redrawn when the population expanded.

The bakufu, as stressed earlier, was interested in villages only insofar as they were units of submissive tribute producers. Through legislation, it engaged in shaping the world of the village for that purpose. This "world-making" (to use Bourdieu's term) through legislation produced the headman, responsible for the village tribute, and titled peasants, the tribute payers.[35] Yet as the cadasters show, the rulers were also aware that various relations to the land existed at a level below that of the titled peasants, who often leased, granted, or gave parcels of their land to dependents. It appears that the rulers decided not to deal with these messy and shifting proprietary relations and instead chose the most cost-effective way to extract tribute: they assigned responsibility for *paying* it to the headman and the titled peasants. At the same time, however, they wanted to make sure that all agricultural (and hence, ultimately, tribute) producers, that is, all those who held some taka in one form or another (all small peasants) were notified of their share of

34. Herbert Bix, *Peasant Protest in Japan, 1590–1884* (New Haven: Yale University Press, 1986), xvii, 104.

35. Pierre Bourdieu, "The Force of Law: Toward a Sociology of the Juridical Field," *Hastings Law Journal* 38 (1987): 837–40, 846.

the tribute burden. Thus, the bakufu also created a new class of "small peasants," because it named them as such in official documents.

The bakufu thus reinscribed existing power relationships, a move welcomed by those whose interests were thus reinforced. Responsibility for the *delivery* of tribute was used for internal political purposes, first by the headman, then by the headman and the official elders, and finally by the titled peasants. The others, however, whose numbers increased dramatically through the division of property (widely practiced during the seventeenth century), leveraged their status as taka holders to increase their voice in village affairs. Mizumoto even surmises that only when some internal political unity was achieved, around the turn of the eighteenth century, did villages start to agitate in unison in the larger peasant disturbances directed against supravillage domination in the eighteenth century.[36] Be that as it may, this suggestion certainly reverses the standard picture of harmonious village communities in the early Tokugawa period, which would have begun to dissolve much later, when the peasantry fractured according to diverging class interests.[37]

MACRO POWER I: THE COLONIAL VARIETY

The dynamic relationship between Tokugawa villages and lordly power can be properly grasped only if one understands the specific nature of the political order established by the shogun and the daimyo. This new order was a regime of conquest like a colonial regime. Once the shogun and daimyo had taken over the country and eliminated or neutralized challengers from without (the court, religious establishments, commoner armies) as well as from within (rival daimyo or powerful vassals), they regrouped their troops in the towns and cities like a colonial army and faced the task of extracting tribute from the villages without direct use of coercive force. For this job they picked prominent natives (insiders) from among the local elite, backing them with their lordly military authority, and granted them privileges, mainly in the form of tribute exemptions. This policy created a new site of power in the villages and ample space for arbitrary local rule. The traditional elite

36. Mizumoto, *Mura shakai*, 101.
37. This is discussed in chapter 3, where the views of American scholars are presented.

rebelled, wrangling a share in the power from those thus selected from among its ranks. The lords accommodated this new power distribution because it eliminated a trouble spot at the site of tribute production.

Colonial powers profoundly affect the life of villages from a distance, if only through new ways of recording them or by their contacts with inside authorities. Similarly, the massive shifts in the field of macro power beyond the village during the decades around the turn of the seventeenth century affected village practice in the corporate villages of the Kinai—and other types elsewhere as well, as we shall see. The authority of powerful, albeit absent, rulers now loomed behind the local (partly new) leadership, thereby transforming its character, limiting its authority in some respects and enlarging it in others. Moreover, absentee rulership meant the exercise of coercive force through decrees, regulations, directives—rule by law and documents—which in itself transformed the nature of village governance.

In this context, let us return for a moment to the question of the purpose and social effect of the national land surveys, which constituted the first drastic intervention in village life in the period under study. Japanese scholars are divided on this question, although perhaps less than twenty years ago.[38] Mizubayashi Takeshi, in his brilliant synthesis

38. American scholars have taken the following positions on this question: John Whitney Hall, in the context of a discussion of the social effect of the land surveys, shifting the focus to village government, states that the "'landlord peasant' status was in fact protected and recognized by the structure of village self-government which relied on the wealthy peasant for positions of responsibility within the village" (*Government and Local Power in Japan, 500 to 1700: A Study Based on Bizen Province* [Princeton: Princeton University Press, 1966], 321). Thomas C. Smith shares this opinion in "The Japanese Village of the Seventeenth Century," in Hall and Jansen, *Studies,* 265–68, 280. Mary Elizabeth Berry mentions the two sides of the controversy, allowing some room for the equalizing theory, but ultimately seems to decide that Hideyoshi's surveys were not revolutionary with respect to landholding patterns (see her *Hideyoshi* [Cambridge: Harvard University Press, 1982], 118–21). Stephen Vlastos, on the other hand, speaks of "a new order in rural Japan characterized by a profound leveling of social and economic status" (*Peasant Protests and Uprisings in Tokugawa Japan* [Berkeley: University of California Press, 1986], 27). See also Philip C. Brown, "The Mismeasure of Land: Land Surveying in the Tokugawa Period," *Monumenta Nipponica* 42, no. 2 (1987): 115–55. Recently Brown has given the question the most extensive discussion available in English in his *Central Authority and Local Autonomy in the Formation of Early Modern Japan: The Case of Kaga Domain* (Stanford: Stanford University Press, 1993), 16–19, 54–88, a book that came to my attention as this manuscript was going to the publisher.

of Tokugawa history, offers cogent reasons why the cadasters did not establish a peasantry of small landholders and were never intended for that purpose. According to Mizubayashi, the three kinds of village-based data compiled under Hideyoshi had the combined effect of sanctioning existing land holding and land management patterns of small *and* large households (*ie*).[39]

The most well known of the registers is the land cadaster, or *kenchichō*, listing plots of land, of insiders and outsiders alike, in the order that the plots lined up geographically in each village. The *nayosechō*, or name register, listed these plots within each village per holder household (*ie*). Although compiled in the village, this name register was an official document since it was used to indicate the amount of tribute owed by the village.[40] A third register was the *iekazuchō* (literally, "register of the number of households"). It listed by and large the same households that were recorded on the other two registers. Here, however, the purpose was to identify those households that were responsible for corvée to the overlords. These documents not only established a tribute relationship between overlord daimyo and their subjects but also linked the village population of peasants as national subjects to the "state" at large under the shogun.

This relationship of national corvée for commoners was similar to that between the warriors and the state. For the warriors the unit for performance of service was each ie, as registered in the name rosters of the vassal bands; for the peasants it was the village as a collectivity of ie, recorded in the household register, another instance of a transfer of military organization techniques to the nonmilitary sector of society. The amount of tribute, corvée, or service was determined according to the size of the land listed in the cadaster, and thus, although it was channeled through the "titled" peasants (owners of homesteads), it was also produced by the nontitled (muyashiki) peasants. Some of the latter,

---

39. Mizubayashi, *Hōkensei*, 129–36. Brown (*Central Authority*, 75–76, 91) shares this opinion.

40. Shimadani Yuriko makes the same argument, but her research indicates that some of these name registers were compiled by intendants (see her "Kinsei 'honbyakushō' saikōsatsu no kokoromi," *Jinmin no rekishigaku*, no. 86 [1985]: 14). She also argues that lordly corvée in the early Tokugawa period, specifically for the battle of Osaka, was not levied only on elite *yakuya*, or service households, but was levied on all holders according to the size of their holding, taka, and that the land cadasters did not have lists of *yakunin*, service people, attached to them (ibid., 13, 21). This, she suggests, was not exceptional.

as outside owners of plots within the village, may have been titled peasants in their home villages.[41]

A comparison of entries in a name register with those in its corresponding cadaster reveals that the latter contains far more names, because it includes, besides the names of household heads, those of a number of dependents who worked the land.[42] This association of names with plots of land provides the basis for the argument that the cadasters reflect a policy by Hideyoshi to break down large holdings managed by extended families into smaller units and that the name registers compiled in the village were perhaps a means for the large holders, who listed only themselves there, to resist Hideyoshi's policy.

Mizubayashi questions the validity of this hypothesis because the cadasters did not focus on *land ownership;* if they had, their entries would have been identical to those on the list of household names. Instead, since one of the purposes of the cadasters was to make it possible to enlist manpower for service even at the national level, official cadasters recorded dependents working field parcels of extended families. If the overlords' intention had been to promote these dependents to economic independence, it is hard to imagine how this could have been achieved for people not even listed as owners in the household list simply by entering them on the cadasters as independent. The cadasters listed the manpower that worked the fields but could be put to other uses as well.

Dependents working identifiable plots were not necessarily fully independent owners. The two lists converge only much later, toward the end of the seventeenth century, when the number of owners increased and that of dependents on the cadasters decreased. The late-sixteenth-century cadasters simply reflect the composition of the various types of ie: the large, extended peasant households (what modern historians call *dogō*), single peasant families, and even nonpeasant families and mixed-economy units. The modern historiographical term *dogō* refers to wealthy landed villagers with local political clout, which in the sixteenth century could be, and often was, temporarily converted into military power. This class of landowners included "samurai of the soil" (*jizamurai*) and "men of the provinces" (*kokujin*), who enjoyed a more

41. This important point is made by Naitō, *Honbyakushō taisei,* 294.
42. For a comparison of the two registers of one village, see Mizubayashi, *Hōkensei,* 133.

official status of authority, at least nominally.[43] Villages ruled by dogō families were typified by pronounced internal economic (and concomitant political) discrepancies compared with sō villages, where such stratification was less severe.

Certain households were thus registered on the household registers, compiled nationwide in 1591 by order of Hideyoshi, as responsible for a wide range of corvée.[44] Takagi Shōsaku has drawn attention to the national character of some of this corvée that was earmarked as separate from that owed to the local overlord.[45] It included auxiliary noncombat corvée, needed by campaigning armies for transporting materiel and provisions (also provided by the villages) and building roads and dikes and was official corvée away from home ordered by the highest authority, the shogun (*kuniyaku*, or national corvée).[46] With the development of a system of way stations on the network of highways,

43. Ibid., 134. For definitions of these and similar medieval terms, see John Whitney Hall, "Terms and Concepts in Japanese Medieval History: An Inquiry into the Problems of Translation," *Journal of Japanese Studies* 9, no. 1 (1983): 1–32, esp. 23–32. For a case study of one such family, see Suzanne Gay, "The Kawashima: Warrior-Peasants of Medieval Japan," *Harvard Journal of Asiatic Studies* 46, no. 1 (1986): 81–119.

44. In the registers these households were variously referred to as honbyakushō, basic or titled peasant; *honke,* main house; *buyakunin,* corvée person; *kōgiyakunin,* official servant; or *kujiya,* official house. Modern Japanese scholars refer to them as yakuya, or "service households" (Mizubayashi, *Hōkensei,* 141–42).

45. The major findings of Takagi's research on the mobilization methods of late-sixteenth-century and early Tokugawa armies can be found in the following articles: " 'Kōgi' kenryoku no kakuritsu," in *Bakuhansei kokka no seiritsu,* ed. Fukaya Katsumi and Katō Eiichi, Kōza Nihon kinseishi, 1 (Yūhikaku, 1981), 151–210; " 'Hideyoshi no heiwa' to bushi no henshitsu: chūseiteki jiritsusei no kaitai katei," *Shisō,* no. 721 (1984): 1–19, translated as " 'Hideyoshi's Peace' and the Transformation of the *Bushi* Class: The Dissolution of the Autonomy of the Medieval *Bushi,*" *Acta Asiatica,* no. 49 (1985): 46–77; "Bakuhan taisei to yaku," *Ken'i to shihai,* Nihon no shakaishi, 3 (Iwanami, 1987), 309–41 (hereafter NNS 3). See also his lengthy contribution to NRT 3:160–223. For an answer to his critics, see his "Kinsei Nihon ni okeru mibun to yaku: Minegishi Kintarō-shi no hihan ni kotaeru," *Rekishi hyōron,* no. 446 (1987): 90–108. Minegishi argues that Takagi overstresses the effect of Hideyoshi's status laws at the expense of the economic underpinnings upon which they were based (see Minegishi Kintarō, *Kinsei mibunron* [Azekura shobō, 1989], 183–218).

46. KDJ distinguishes between *kokuyaku* (5:697–98) and *kuniyaku* (4:845–46). The former seems to be limited to extraordinary national or provincial levies of pre-Tokugawa times (1054–1546), ordered by the imperial or shogunal courts. The discussion of the latter is limited to the Tokugawa period and

portage duties, or *sukego,* were also assigned to surrounding villages by shogunal authority.

This mobilization of peasants by the highest national authority for noncombat military service affected local authority relationships in a number of ways. The villages, as identified on the rosters and registers, became production and support brigades for the "national," or shogunal, government in times of war. Thus, the whole country was, at least latently, a "garrison state," as Takagi put it.[47] When the daimyo received orders from the shogun to mobilize, many "natives" were assigned to serve in the "colonial" (samurai) army of daimyo, who were often transferred from elsewhere to rule them. This arrangement incorporated not only villages as a whole but also individual peasant households directly into a national organization, giving those selected for this service an enhanced local identity. Since there were virtually no national mobilizations during the Tokugawa period, however, the greatest effect of this system was not its practical use but the creation of an additional prestige value within the village, a form of symbolic capital, to borrow Pierre Bourdieu's famous simile, that was put to use to yield local political profit.[48]

This institution affected dogō magnates in two ways. On the one hand, it strengthened their hold over their dependents, since national authority added a surplus dimension to some aspects of their local power. On the other hand, this local power was now in certain respects shared with a higher authority, clearly stipulated, and hence limited. This limitation of dogō power was the result of a mobilization formula that was imposed on them via the kokudaka system of the cadasters,

to corvée by artisans. These volumes, published in 1984 and 1985, did not take into account Takagi's work, perhaps because it was too late to incorporate it or, less likely, because the authors of these entries disagree with it.

47. Takagi, "Hideyoshi's Peace," 46.

48. Pierre Bourdieu writes about the relationship between economic and symbolic capital as follows in his *In Other Words: Essays towards a Reflexive Sociology* (Stanford: Stanford University Press, 1990): "A capital (or power) becomes symbolic capital, that is, capital endowed with a specifically symbolic efficacy, only when it is *misrecognized* in its arbitrary truth as capital and *recognized* as legitimate and, on the other hand, ... this act of (false) knowledge and recognition is an act of *practical* knowledge which in no way implies that the object known and recognized be posited as object" (112, italics in the original; see also his *Logic of Practice,* 118).

and it differed from the one used by the warlord daimyo of the sixteenth century. When these daimyo mobilized, their orders pertained only to warrior retainers, and not to noncombatants. Specifications for these daimyo's retainers stipulated only the "kind and number of weapons and those wielding them";[49] support personnel were not listed. Each warrior provided his own followers through his personal authority as a local magnate, and he shouldered their expenses as well. The novelty of the Hideyoshi/Tokugawa system consisted in that now (1) the overlord's mobilization order reached commoners directly, over the heads of dogō/retainers, the local bosses; (2) the number of porters and other followers was specified; and (3) expenses were shouldered by the overlord. In other words, local magnates saw the autonomous nature of their authority undercut by a strengthened center.

Battle array charts (*jindatesho*) thus included a great number of noncombatants, mostly peasants. The original purpose of the kokudaka system was precisely to determine the number and duties of these noncombatants, who constituted the bulk of the armies. Takagi gives as an example the composition of the army of Sakai, daimyo of Maebashi (130,000 koku), toward the beginning of the eighteenth century. Only about one-third of the total number of men and horses of the main force were assigned combat duties: 2,000 men out of an army of 5,344. The vanguard consisted of a corps of "engineers" who built field camps for the troops; it included 10 carpenters, 50 porters (*ninsoku*), and 2 horses (see table 9).[50]

Since under the Tokugawa peace there were no national mobilizations after the Shimabara rebellion of 1637 (except in the two campaigns against Chōshū domain in the 1860s), one might wonder about the significance of the inclusion on paper of so many commoners in the armies of the daimyo and shogun. This mobilization formula, although not put into practice for over two centuries, contributed to the peasants' identity.

First of all, some of the national duties for which peasants were responsible were converted into permanent tribute categories in the second half of the seventeenth century. A portion of their tribute, cash (*busen*) as well as rice (*bumai*), was earmarked as military tax.

49. Takagi, "Hideyoshi's Peace," 54.
50. These figures are Takagi's, taken from NRT 3:191–92; they are more precise than those he gives in "Hideyoshi's Peace," 47.

Table 9. Composition of Sakai's Army, Early 1700s

Combatants	
Mounted samurai	347 (1)
Samurai on foot	87 (1)
Foot soldiers	1,129 (10)
Noncombatants	
Rear vassals attending mounted samurai	1,694 (0)
Lackeys, servants	306 (10)
Porters	1,179 (50)
Grooms	573 (10)
Artisans, doctors, cooks, etc.	29 (10)
Horses	
Riding horses	347 (1)
Pack horses	567 (10)

SOURCE: NRT 3:191, table 1.

NOTE: Figures in parentheses refer to the vanguard; a number of the rear vassals should be included among the combatants.

Furthermore, the grandiose shogunal progresses to Ieyasu's shrine in Nikkō, a total of fifteen, including those before its full-scale construction in 1636, also functioned as mobilization exercises, as did, on a smaller scale but more frequently, the daimyo's yearly marches between Edo and their domains, as required by the system of alternate attendance (*sankinkōtai*). In the progress of 1776, for instance, the shogun, escorted by his three collateral houses (*gosanke*) and twenty daimyo, was accompanied by no less than 620,000 low-ranking soldiers (*zōhyō*), 230,000 porters, and 305,000 horses. These processions took one week and were so large that, according to an eyewitness, they stretched the whole length of the road, which had twenty-one way stations, from Edo to Nikkō (145 km).[51] In the Chōshū wars of the 1860s, the peasants from the bakufu and some daimyo domains were effectively mobilized according to the formulae fixed over two hundred years earlier, readily accepting noncombat assignments as a "natural" part of their duties as subjects. By the same token, they resisted as "unconstitutional" the

51. Watanabe Hiroshi, "'Goikō' to shōchō: Tokugawa seiji taisei no ichi-sokumen," *Shisō*, no. 740 (1986): 138.

attempts to arm them for combat, insisting that if they were to bear arms they should be treated as samurai.[52]

Undoubtedly, the great division in Tokugawa Japan was between warriors and commoners. However, the peasants were essential even for the military organization of the country, and their public self-identity included noncombatant military service at a trans-domain, if not "national," level. To that extent, in addition to being subjects of their daimyo, they were also subjects, not of the emperor, but of the shogun, since he decided when mobilization was required.

MICRO STRUGGLES 2: PEASANTS VERSUS MAGNATE HEADMEN (DOGŌ)

Mizumoto's regional study of predominantly the corporate type of village left unexplained the relevance of its findings for the rest of Japan, especially the "less advanced" regions, where dogō households dominated village life. A typical example would be Toyota village in Izumi province (Osaka), where two dogō households (5 percent of the total number of households), each with an average of ten dependents, together controlled 30 percent of the arable.[53]

Saitō Yoshiyuki has looked into this question with regard to a number of villages of eastern Japan, in Niigata, Nagano, Akita, and other prefectures, and presents the following argument linking protests regarding the fair distribution of tribute throughout the village with the establishment of the village-based system of tribute levy (murauke).[54] In other words, he indirectly traces the genesis of yet another basic Tokugawa institution. Saitō starts by pointing out that this murauke system was not entirely a bakufu innovation. As mentioned earlier, a similar practice (jigeuke) was not uncommon on the old estates and in corporate villages.[55] Nevertheless, even there its implementation by the newly established headman caused problems. Saito discerns two issues related to headman governance: *abuse of authority* and *excessive privileges*, the latter an extension of their informal power as local magnates; and different responses to these problems by the bakufu before and after the

52. Kurushima Hiroshi, "Kinsei gun'yaku to hyakushō," *Futan to zōyo, Nihon no shakaishi*, 4 (Iwanami, 1986), 273–317 (hereafter NNS 4).
53. Mizubayashi, *Hōkensei*, 42.
54. Saitō Yoshiyuki, "Kinsei shoki no nōmin tōsō," 42–60.
55. Ibid., 43.

early 1640s, first *unambiguous support for the headmen,* then *an acknowledgment of the peasants's complaints.*

The issue of abuse of authority is illustrated by a case from Echigo, Ōtorisu village, where forty peasant households were ruled by two headmen (*kimoiri,* as they were called there). The headman of the East Kumi (possibly consisting of several neighborhood kumi), backed by all his peasants and some from the West Kumi as well, complained in 1662 to the intendant of Nagaoka domain that his colleague from the West Kumi had secretly overtaxed the new fields (shinden) of the East Kumi for the last eight years. The suit stressed that the accused headman had acted "without consulting the East Kumi's head and all the peasants." The case was settled out of court, the official yearly tax rosters (*nengumenjō*) were made public, and the head of the West Kumi was deposed. An apology from those West Kumi peasants who had not endorsed the suit from the beginning closed the affair. Like corporate (sō) villages, this was a village without great economic discrepancies between landholders. The issue was *abuse of authority by a headman.*

Other protests addressed the issue of the informal power of local magnates. The village of Shimo-Okamoto in Utsunomiya was ruled by a peasant magnate (dogō) with 166 koku, while the other fifty-three peasants together held 840 koku. Over a span of forty years (1637–78) at least six protests were lodged against the headman. The first was a complaint by all the peasants about the headman's exemption from his portion of corvée (proportionate to his 166 koku), which they had to shoulder. Headmen from neighboring villages mediated a settlement whereby the headman in question had to pay a fee in corvée rice (bumai) on half of his holdings. Seven years later, in 1644, fourteen peasants successfully petitioned the domain to form a separate village perhaps in order to escape shouldering the headman's exempt corvée burden, which now fell on only thirty-nine peasants. Ten years later they demanded the removal of the headman. Finally, in 1678, after a few other protests, they asked the intendant's approval for apportioning corvée not per household but according to each holding's assessed yield ("per taka"). These suits did not concern flagrant abuse of power by a headman; rather, they aimed at *changing the traditional patriarchal authority the headman, as a local magnate, wielded over small landholders,* who were very dependent on him.

The bakufu's response to these two types of protest shifted significantly after the Kan'ei period, which ended in 1643. Before that turning point the bakufu unambiguously protected its village-based tax agents by siding with the headmen, leaving their public authority unaffected, and by withstanding attempts to limit their privileges.

Two examples from Shinano province in 1621 illustrate how the bakufu backed its appointed headmen. In one, the intendant's representative, together with powerful figures from neighboring villages, saw to it that embezzled money, whose absence was discovered after the village account books were opened, was returned, but no further action was taken against the headman. In the other, the intendant refused two successive requests by the peasants to check the tax lists. Obviously, access to the records of intramural tribute allocation was not backed by bakufu authority.

The bakufu's protection of magnate power, not against accusations of abuse, but against attempts at limiting it can be seen in the bakufu's response to peasants who complained in Akita in 1617 that they were unable to shoulder the burden of more than 10 koku of the headman's total of 16 exempted koku. They wanted to cap the exemption at 10 koku. The intendant, however, ruled that headmen had a right to as much as 20 corvée-exempt koku even in villages of only 100 to 150 koku. With only 16 koku of the headman to take care of, he added, the petitioners should count themselves lucky. The same standard was upheld in 1620 in another bakufu case.

In the early 1640s the bakufu abandoned its unquestioning support of headman authority and privilege. By then embezzlement was clearly illegal and punished. Some headmen even wound up in prison.[56] To prevent abuses, the headman's monopolistic power was curtailed de jure. The first directives concerning intramural calculation and apportioning of tribute were issued in 1642 and 1644 as part of the bakufu's legislative response to the famines of the Kan'ei period. No doubt pressure had also been exerted by numerous petitions and suits— altogether a clear indication of the bakufu's initial reluctance or inability to regulate village affairs. The frequent settlement of these disputes without recourse to bakufu authority or through mediation of other headmen, as well as the protracted nature of some of them, further point to the same conclusion. The regulations of 1642 and 1644 stipulated that tribute allocations must be made public, and that all (taka

56. For examples dating from 1643 and 1648–50, see ibid., 50.

holding) peasants must participate in decision making.[57] This, Saitō concludes, amounted to the institutionalization of the famous murauke system, whereby the *whole* village, and not simply the headman, was in a way subcontracted as the legal agency for allocating tribute.

Two points should be made here. This is first of all a good illustration of Tokugawa legal expansion as a response to ad hoc problems. What James White argues with regard to peasant uprisings also applies to their petitions and protests. Peasants never succeeded or even wanted to overthrow the system, yet their petitions and protests were not without effect. Peasant agitation propelled legislative production, and insofar as the bakufu's legislative practice as such was never put into question its authority to rule was thereby legitimized in an indirect but significant and real way.[58] Moreover, as this shift in bakufu policy was the result of local struggles, it consolidated a new power distribution and political consciousness in the village and perhaps produced a new "civic" identity among certain sectors of the peasantry. This, at least, was the potential of this policy, even though it did not affect all community members; nor was it implemented in all communities at the same time. Much later, other peasants would agitate to participate in decisions regarding tax allocation.[59]

Some of the special powers and privileges of the dogō were being limited by other bakufu legal judgments. Thus, in the early 1650s in a village of a bannerman the question of corvée allocation to noncorvée households was raised; it was ruled that "privileges associated with past status are acknowledged, but times have changed (*jidai onaji de arazu*) and henceforward corvée [and other burdens] will be allocated equally according to assessed value (*taka: byōdō no takawari ni*)."[60]

The drive to apportion corvée and duties per assessed value rather than per household cut into the traditional power of dogō peasants. That these magnates resisted this as best as they could is illustrated by

57. The decisions are quoted in ibid., 51. For the text of these laws, see *Tokugawa kinreikō zenshū*, ed. Ishii Ryōsuke, 5 vols. (Sōbunsha, 1959–61), 5:155 (no. 2784, art. 11) (hereafter TKKz); and *Kinsei hōseishiryō sōsho*, also edited by Ishii Ryōsuke, 3 vols. (Sōbunsha, 1959), 2:156 (no. 280, arts. 9, 15).

58. James White, "State Growth and Popular Protest," *Journal of Japanese Studies* 14, no. 1 (1988): 7 n. 27, 17, 20–21.

59. Smith presents a dramatic example: in the town of Kurashiki some two thousand families broke the monopoly of thirteen titled peasants in 1790 (*Agrarian Origins*, 183–87, esp. 186).

60. Saitō Yoshiyuki, "Kinsei shoki no nōmin tōsō," 53.

two cases analyzed earlier. In the 1650 suit in Kami-Kawarabayashi village (see table 7) the headman capitulated, but only temporarily: shortly thereafter he reverted to the old system, a move that resulted in a new suit by the peasants. The series of suits and petitions spread over forty years in the village of Shimo-Okamoto in Utsunomiya, the second case cited in this section, started with the attempts to limit the headman's privilege in the form of exemption from corvée and wound up with a petition to switch to the taka-based system in 1678.

MACRO POWER 2: *DOGŌ* POWER AND THE DOMINANT CLASS

The mid seventeenth century was not the first time dogō struggled against extramural interference. Two generations earlier, around the turn of the century, they had even organized armed resistance against land surveys in a number of places. In Higo province (Kumamoto) they mobilized twenty thousand peasants in opposition to Sassa Narimasa, who was in charge of the land survey. Similar rebellions took place in the north, where dogō power was strongest. As Mizubayashi points out (and as I shall discuss shortly), this contrasts with the economically more developed Kinai region, where since the time of Oda Nobunaga (1534–82) this dogō class had spontaneously begun to split into those who sought fortune primarily in military campaigns and those who sought it on the land. In the "backward" areas, however, the rural magnates clearly felt threatened by the warriors and their land surveys.[61]

This struggle they lost. The rural magnates could stop neither the warriors nor the surveys, but they survived quite well the restructuring of political power that was taking place over their heads. It is important to clarify the changing structural position of this dogō class in order to understand how the dogō made the transition into the Tokugawa period, when they functioned as the overlords' local agents for over a century, until the bakufu dissolved their power in the first decades of the eighteenth century in part as a response to abuses.

Under warlords of the sixteenth century like the Rokkaku, the traditional control the dogō, as often semimilitary rural magnates and

---

61. Mizubayashi, *Hōkensei,* 145. On *dogō* uprisings, see Donald Burton, "Peasant Struggle in Japan, 1590–1760," *Journal of Peasant History* 5, no. 2 (1978): 144–47.

fief holders, had over their retainer/servants (*hikan*) and dependents remained firm. When they and their followers were called upon for military or other tasks by these warlords, they were recruited *in toto* as small coherent units. Oda Nobunaga, however, started to sever the dogō's ties to their subordinates when he used his formidable authority to bypass these local bosses by recruiting some of their dependents directly. Nobunaga presented projects such as the building of Azuchi castle in 1576, employing this labor force as kuniyaku, or "national service," and he indemnified the masters of these recruits with some tax exemption.

A second way in which the ties between dogō and their followers were dissolved was through transfers of warlords. When Nobunaga assigned a new territory to a daimyo, he ordered him to take his dogō along, as he did when he sent the Maeda to Noto.[62] These local magnates thus lost their power base of land and followers/servants and, as full-time retainers, became completely dependent upon their lords.

Many dogō were jizamurai, or landed men of arms; in the Kinai region, however, many of them had considerably reduced the portion of their holdings that they worked themselves. Thus loosening their ties to the land on their own initiative, many had joined Nobunaga's armies without giving up their landed property, expecting greater gains from military campaigns, in the form of increased holdings, than from working or managing the land they owned. Hideyoshi, as is well known, institutionalized this initial voluntary and incomplete removal of armed men from the land through his Sword Hunt Edict (1588) and his "Status Regulations" (1591).[63] Henceforward armed men would be clearly distinct from peasants. This had a profound effect on the social position of these landed samurai or armed rural magnates, splitting this class into two since it forced them to choose either to take the warrior road or to remain in their mini-dominions working the land. Under Nobunaga such a choice had been neither total nor final; under Hideyoshi it was both.

It is important to stress that either way, as new, full-fledged retainers

---

62. Mizubayashi, *Hōkensei*, 109. For a detailed discussion of Maeda's case, see Brown, *Central Authority*, chap. 5.

63. For the text of these decrees, see Tsunoda Ryusaku, William Theodore de Bary, and Donald Keene, comps., *Sources of Japanese Tradition*, 2 vols. (New York: Columbia University Press, 1964), 1: 319–22. The reason for quotation marks around *Status Regulations* will be explained later.

without land in the castle towns or as rural magnates without arms in the country, they did not become men without power in the new order. This class was reconstituted at the lower echelons of the ruling hierarchy, where it performed a number of essential functions with or without arms. The fact that some were now legally samurai and others were not should not obfuscate the fact that the new rulers encompassed nonsamurai and the ruled included peasants with a samurai background. Without a significant component of nonwarriors in the ruling cadres the system would have been unable to function, since almost all warriors were now separated from their subjects. Peasants were thus not only tribute producers, separated socially and geographically from the samurai; they were also essential to the operation of the system, in times of war, as we have seen, and in times of peace.

One can distinguish three ways in which the dogō were incorporated into the new power structure. Some became district intendants (*daikan*) or their assistants (*tedai*), others became village group headmen (*ōjōya*) in charge of a number of villages, and still others turned into a kind of contractor for "public works," especially land reclamation projects. We shall first take a look at the third group. Our example is from Kita-Saku district, a few kilometers east of Makibuse (see map 2).

As is well known, the seventeenth century witnessed the greatest boom in land reclamation in premodern Japan. Between 930 and 1450 Japan's arable increased by 10 percent. Another 70 percent was added by 1600. Equating the arable of 1450 with the value 100, it was 90 in 930, 100 in 1450, and 173 in 1600; then it almost doubled, to 314, by 1720 (and it was only 322 in 1874), as table 10 shows. Unlike the land reclamation of the eighteenth century, most of which was financed by merchant capital, the much larger projects of the seventeenth century were initiated and funded by the daimyo and the shogun. Often dogō and their bands of dependents were employed in these projects. This was the case with four such shinden (new paddies) projects in Kita-Saku.[64]

The most famous of the four shinden is Gorobe-shinden, the others being Mikage-, Shiosawa-, and Yaehara-shinden. They were developed between 1630 and 1662. The irrigation networks for the four projects, totaling some 175 km, took twenty years to build. The ducts that brought

64. Ōishi, *Kinsei sonraku no kōzō*, chap. 3.

Table 10. Total Acreage in Japan, 930–1874

	Acreage (chō)	Percentage of 1450 figure
930	862,000	91.1%
1450	946,000	100.0
1600	1,635,000	172.8
1720	2,970,000	313.9
1874	3,050,000	322.4

SOURCE: Mizubayashi, *Hōkensei*, table 17 (p. 301).
NOTE: 1 chō = 9,917 m².

the water to Gorobe-shinden alone were about 20 km long (including some 2 km hewn in rock, nine tunnels totaling 1 km, and a duct crossing a river) and passed through nine villages.[65] All four projects were undertaken by descendants of local vassal and subvassal houses of Takeda Shingen (1521–72). The warrior ancestors of these developers had continually sided with losing parties in the wars of the late sixteenth century. For instance, the Ichikawa house, to which Gorobe belonged, was first a subvassal of the Uesugi, then of Takeda Shingen, and subsequently of Oda Nobunaga and the Hōjō when its holdings were greatly reduced. The remaining Ichikawa property, mountain forest and some undeveloped grassland in the Kita-Saku plain, was finally divided among followers of the house (between fifty and one hundred). Gorobe, reluctant to leave the area, refused twice to enter Tokugawa Ieyasu's service; instead, he took the opportunity given by Ieyasu's decision to develop new arable. In return, Ieyasu acknowledged Gorobe's jurisdiction over his numerous hereditary vassal-servants (fudai and genin). In 1642, Gorobe received from the lord of Komoro domain 150 koku of the new fields as his "fief." Then the fifty or so fudai literally came out of the woodwork, writing to Gorobe, "We are sons of fudai

65. The calculations are based on data given by Saitō Yōichi in his *Gorobe-shinden to hisabetsu buraku* (San'ichi shobō, 1987), 1, 2, 56–57. The most detailed history of a shinden mura in English is the work of an anthropologist, Jennifer Robertson's *Native and Newcomer: Making and Remaking a Japanese City* (Berkeley: University of California Press, 1991), 76–103, 136–143. The remaining information on Gorobe-shinden and the developers of the other shinden that follows is again taken from Ōishi, *Kinsei sonraku no kōzō*, chap. 3.

who for generations have been in your family and fought together until your father's generation, but then we moved to the mountains not so long ago because there was no land left in the family. Now, however, that you have received 150 koku, we shall remain loyal in any battle that may lay ahead." They worked for Gorobe again, first as vassals, then for wages, and they were finally set free in 1713. Meanwhile, the Ichikawa had left the area in 1670 and become absentee landlords.

The founding families of the other new villages have similar histories. Kashiwagi Koemon, founder of Mikage-shinden, having also sided with losing lords, went to Suruga for a while to take an office under Tokugawa Ieyasu, but soon he was back in Kita-Saku in charge of bringing new land under cultivation. He eventually received eighty-three koku in tax-exempt new fields, enjoyed labor services from the new settlers, and wielded considerable power in the new village. He passed on to his descendants the right (exercised as late as 1819!) to veto any election of village officials by the titled peasants and the right to keep all the records, which he lent to the officials at his own discretion. For the first fifteen years there was not even a village headman; when one was finally appointed, in 1665, he came from a branch house, and the office remained in that family for half a century.

A second road taken by dogō in the seventeenth century, more frequently by dogō remaining on the land, led to the new rural office of ōjōya (village group headman). They thus became charged mainly with collecting tribute from a number of villages, their area of jurisdiction often coinciding with the pre-Tokugawa districts (gō).[66] In this way, they supplemented their economically based and informal patriarchal power as local magnates with a new official, administrative dimension. Just as the sixteenth-century warlords used "the state" (which they built) to continue furthering their interests, the landed dogō added the same surplus political value to their traditional authority.

It should be remembered that the purpose of Hideyoshi's land surveys, conducted and registered at the village level, was not tribute exaction but the mobilization of a national army. For taxation purposes, Hideyoshi relied on the old local administrative units (often the gō, encompassing a number of villages), which often became the juris-

66. For this paragraph and the following one, see Mizubayashi, *Hōkensei*, 136–37. Brown also stresses the indispensability of nonsamurai at the district and intendant level in Kaga domain (*Central Authority*, 114–41, 193, 205).

diction of a village group headman. Thus, one of the two dogō from Toyota village, mentioned earlier, filled the post of village group headman for thirteen villages.[67]

The village group headmen, as stipended agents for the city-bound warriors, were an integral part of the dominant class in not only structural but also economic terms, for in both status and privilege they were considerably removed from the ruled in the villages. Located administratively beyond the village and performing their corvée or service to the overlords as officeholders, in their village of residence they were exempt from the obligations shouldered by regular villagers.

As developers of new paddies, the dogō expanded the overlords' tribute base, and as village group headmen they channeled this tribute upward. In addition, they functioned at the next higher administrative level also, as district intendants or, more often, as their representatives or assistants. One usually thinks of intendants as samurai, but especially in the early decades of the Tokugawa period a good number of them were dogō. Why?

The indispensability of the disarmed fraction of the dogō class to the new military rulers was not only a consequence of the concentration of the samurai in urban centers. It was also the result, in some important cases, of massive daimyo transfers to new territories. After the Hōjō's defeat in 1590, Tokugawa Ieyasu was ordered by Hideyoshi to leave the five provinces he controlled and take charge of the eight provinces in the Kantō plain, most of which constituted the former Hōjō domain. This transfer affected the dogō of Ieyasu's old and new domains in different ways.

In his old domain, the transfer put into practice, in one stroke, the separation of warriors from peasants, splitting the dogō class into those who took their arms and followed Ieyasu to the Kantō and those who stayed behind. It was a move that also strengthened the integration of his vassal band, which, cut off from its economic base, now became totally dependent on its lord. In his new domain, however, the local dogō class became indispensable for ruling the countryside, since Ieyasu concentrated most of his army in and around Edo, granting many (but not all) rural administrative posts—hatamoto, or bannerman, fiefs in the "Tokugawa houseland" and daikan or *gundai* intendant offices for

67. For the system of village group headmen in the Ueda domain, see Bix, *Peasant Protest*, 62–64.

the remaining portion of the Tokugawa domain—to only a small fraction of the thirty-five thousand warriors under his direct command.[68]

The figures are quite striking. Forty percent of the Tokugawa domain was entrusted to some twenty-two hundred fief-holding bannermen, each with his own retainers, but the overwhelming majority of the latter were stationed in Edo, not in the fiefs themselves. For instance, the Sengoku bannerman, who in the 1790s held a fief of two thousand koku (in eight villages) in Shinano and an additional seven hundred koku in two other provinces, had thirty-two retainers in Edo but only four in Shinano. His Shinano office was headed by someone with a dogō background who also relied on locals: two *wariban* (the equivalent of village group headman) and the eight village headmen.[69] The remaining 60 percent of the Tokugawa domain was ruled by a mere forty intendants. They were assisted by helpers, whose total number in 1839 was less than a thousand, slightly over half of them based in Edo. Under Hideyoshi the intendants had been recruited from the ranks of vassals and dogō. In the early Tokugawa period they were former retainers from defeated daimyo (the Imagawa, the Takeda, the Hōjō) or local dogō who had served under them. This local entrenchment, perpetuated through heredity, led to numerous abuses that were further facilitated by the way these intendants were paid, namely, by allowances they themselves took from the tribute they collected. In the 1680s the majority of the intendants (thirty-five) were purged, and after 1725 intendants had to forward the total amount of tribute to the center, which substituted fixed stipends for their allowances. In addition, their posts were now increasingly being filled by staffers from

68. Mizubayashi, *Hōkensei,* 143. The figure 35,000 comes from Conrad Totman, *Politics in the Tokugawa Bakufu, 1600–1843* (Cambridge: Harvard University Press, 1967), 135. By the end of the eighteenth century only 44 percent, or 2,264, of the bannermen held fiefs, with a total kokudaka of 2.6 million koku (see KDJ 9:381, s.v. "chigyōseido"; for similar figures, see also Totman, *Politics,* 135), spread over forty provinces, and governed from 3,677 local offices because many fiefs consisted of separate territories, 43 percent of these fiefs having parcels in from two to six different provinces. The portion of the Tokugawa domain that was not parceled out in fiefs (each less than 10,000 koku) to bannermen (3.2 million to 4.2 million koku—the amount fluctuates over time) was Tokugawa "houseland" (tenryō), administered by intendants, called daikan (50,000 to 100,000 koku) or *gundai* (over 100,000 koku), whose number stabilized at around forty (KDJ 4:1040–44; see also Totman, *Politics,* 66–85).

69. Mizubayashi, *Hōkensei,* 268–69.

the bakufu's central Finance Commission. These purges and reforms signaled the end of those dogō who had survived as intendants.

Many of the intendants who were not dogō but samurai took up residence in Edo and, like the bannermen, maintained only skeletal staffs in their country and Edo offices. The two intendant offices in Shinano—Nakanojō (69,000 koku) and Nakano (54,000 koku)—had staffs of only three and four men, respectively, while their Edo offices had nine and eight. (Shinano also counted two branch offices, one in Mikage with a staff of three and one in the highway station of Oiwake with only one post.) Their small staffs consisted of helpers called *tedai* and *tetsuki*. The latter, shogunal retainers, were introduced only in the 1790s; the former were local peasants.[70] The situation was slightly different in the domains, for there the offices were often overstaffed. The small domain of Tanoguchi (12,000 koku) in Saku district, for instance, counted only twenty-five villages, yet there were three intendants.[71]

Given the sparse use of samurai for rural administrative purposes, these intendants and fief-holding bannermen had to be assisted by locals both in their small territorial offices and in the villages, where they were assisted by village group headmen and village headmen. Moreover, although one might expect responsibility for the expenses, if not for the personnel then at least for the upkeep of these offices, to have been assumed by the mighty bakufu, that was not the case. Routine maintenance expenses were shouldered by villagers, who were also charged with the corvée duties of cleaning, changing the paper of sliding doors, operating the hot bath, and so on. They also had to provide messengers to communicate between the rural and Edo offices of these administrators.[72]

---

70. This information on the daikan and gundai was taken from KDJ 4:1040–44; see also Mizubayashi, *Hōkensei*, 270–71, and Totman, *Politics*, 66–85. In 1853 the bakufu employed 640 *tedai* (291 of these in Edo) and only 225 *tetsuki* (146 in Edo). Thus, when in the 1790s the bakufu created the new post of tetsuki, to be filled by retainers, next to the identical post of tedai, filled by commoners, not only were its numbers significantly lower than that of the tedai but fewer than 100 retainers were deployed in the countryside (KDJ 9:885, s.v. "tedai").

71. NAK-KS2 (1): 486. One of these intendants, appointed in 1851, kept a detailed list of all incoming and outgoing presents for his first year in office: he himself gave gifts on 188 occasions, 4 times to headmen from five villages, and received gifts on 596 occasions! (Ichikawa Yūichirō, *Saku chihō*, 220–47).

72. KDJ 8:711, s.v. "daikansho"; 7:940, s.v. "jinya."

The system was extremely cost-effective and user-friendly for the samurai because the peasants, both elites and others, not only paid for it but ran it as well. The analogy of firing squad victims who first have to pay for the bullets and dig their own grave comes to mind. This analogy might seem far-fetched, but in Tokugawa times villages that for one reason or another had a member in prison had to pay the "boarding" costs.[73] Notwithstanding Confucian rhetoric about peasants' being "the basis of the country," the samurai were unwilling to dirty their hands through contact with peasants, not even for the purpose of levying tribute.

Samurai rural administrators, a rather rare breed in the first place, ranked low in the prestige and stipend hierarchy. Ogyū Sorai (1666–1728) wrote that "the intendants' sole preoccupation being to levy tribute, they appointed people just because they could write and count and they themselves were of low status ... which was the reason why no samurai with a pedigree became intendants, and this in turn was why no samurai, including the upper ranks of counselors, had any real sense of the people."[74] The fundamental division between manual and mental labor stressed by Karl Marx and Max Weber[75] is basic to the separation between warriors and peasants, although in Tokugawa Japan, as Andō Shōeki noted in the eighteenth century, it was more a question of manual versus no labor.[76]

The nonsamuraized fraction of the pre-Tokugawa dogō class was thus reconstituted as an essential lower fraction of the dominant class and maintained local power well into the eighteenth century. Its demise, however, is not to be attributed only to bakufu initiative against abuses that diminished the flow of tribute to the upper fractions of the domi-

73. Those confined to an intendant's jail whose provenance was known (i.e., those who were not vagrants, *mushuku*) had to arrange for their own food, make payments for their expenses to the prison guard, and provide even their own lamp oil. The situation was slightly different in Edo (see Hiramatsu, *Kinsei keiji soshōhō*, 936).

74. Ogyū Sorai, *Sorai sensei tōmonsho* (1727), in *Ogyū Sorai*, ed. Bitō Masahide, Nihon no meicho, 16 (Chūōkōronsha, 1983), 319, 320–21.

75. Karl Marx and Frederick Engels, *The German Ideology* (New York: International Publishers, 1970), 51; Max Weber, *Economy and Society*, ed. Guenter Roth and Claus Wittich, 2 vols. (Berkeley: University of California Press, 1978), 2:936.

76. Maruyama Masao, *Studies in the Intellectual History of Tokugawa Japan* (Princeton: Princeton University Press, 1974), 252–53.

nant class, a story of rationalization and bureaucratization; there was also a political side to this story.

Protests and petitions had led to limitations on headman authority in the first decades of the Tokugawa period. Then these dogō-headmen were forced to share power with a class of new landholders, often former dependents. Moreover, since the late seventeenth century their authority had been further checked by a representative from the other peasants, a *hyakushōdai* (a new village office to be discussed below). The position of village group headman was abolished in the bakufu domain in 1713 as a response to a violent peasant rebellion in the Murakami fief in Echigo. Similar rebellions against abuses by village group headmen followed in daimyo domains (Kanazawa, 1712; Hiroshima, 1718; Aizu, 1720; Kurume, 1754; Fukuyama, 1789), leading there also to the abolishment of the office. The bakufu and domains, however, could not long do without some conduit between their regional offices and the villages, hence the on-again, off-again status of the office of the village group headman (on again in the bakufu in 1734, on again in Fukuyama in 1791 and off again in 1823). In the bakufu the office was now staffed on a rotation basis by headmen from the villages under its jurisdiction.[77]

KNOWLEDGE AND POWER: THE STRUGGLE FOR INFORMATION

Data on land, population, and tribute were essential for the exercise of domination, which for Tokugawa Japan is a more accurate term than *administration*. Once established, power needed knowledge more than the sword to carry on. This information was organized around the kokudaka system, a thorough quantification of the country's economic potential established by Hideyoshi for military purposes of a national order. The daimyo who gathered these data for Hideyoshi benefited too, because the data gave them a more precise knowledge of their own power base, which was also expanded, since for the first time dry fields, commons, and even homesteads were rated and taxed. These data, while official because collected by and for those in power, was not public, precisely because of its link to power. Access to this information was

77. KDJ 2:613, s.v. "ōjōya."

obtained through struggle, that is to say, through the application of a kind of power that forced the authorities to yield it.

Village suits against headmen's abuses in tribute allocation were struggles for access to kokudaka data. The plaintiffs had in mind a specific use for these data, different from the one the overlords had in mind when they created them: they wanted the data as a leverage for justice, for a fair intravillage distribution of corvée and tribute. The logic behind the strategy to obtain it, however, was similar. Through their land surveys, Hideyoshi and the Tokugawa shogun after him made official and created for themselves knowledge that thus far had been the private (and less accurate) knowledge of the daimyo and thereby increased their power over them. They were able to force the daimyo to create and render this knowledge in part because they had converted their warlord superpower into public authority (*kōgi*) through a number of officializing strategies.[78] Hideyoshi and the shogun wielded a higher authority, which it was in the best interest of the daimyo not to resist. The peasants achieved the same result in a somewhat similar way by wresting privately held knowledge from their village superiors. For this the peasants needed a higher authority, which they gained when, after the 1640s, the bakufu supported the peasants in their demand for open village ledgers.

The story of the struggle for making official knowledge public does not end there, however, but the principle was established in the 1640s. I trace this struggle until the end of the eighteenth century in the following section. Here I shall first return briefly to the drive started in the mid seventeenth century to base village corvée allocation on a taka rather than a household basis. This was possible only because knowledge of each field's kokudaka was forced into the open, and resistance to it was strongest in dogō-ruled villages because there the plot discrepancies were the greatest. In such villages, if corvée were allocated according to holding size rather than divided evenly among all households, the elite would lose proportionately more than they would in places where economic discrepancies were less pronounced. Second, we shall examine the bakufu's endorsement of publicizing tax rates in the 1640s. Although implementation of the decrees to that effect was uneven, that

78. See my *Tokugawa Ideology*, chap. 2.

decade constitutes an important turning point with regard to the issue of accountability.

Knowledge of the kokudaka provided peasants with a standard of value they could use in various ways, depending on local circumstances, for quantifying things other than tribute. Sometimes complicated formulae that obviously were the outcome of protracted wranglings and negotiations, to which small landholders must have been partners, were worked out. Thus, in Kitasawa village (Kita-Saku) the following agreement using different measuring units for various items was reached in 1687, through the mediation of the local temple, it should be pointed out.[79] The preamble clearly states that the process involved "large and small peasants." The agreement covered both kinds of corvée, that owed to the bakufu and that due to the village, and stipulated the following:

> Tribute from the mountains: manpower to be assigned on the basis of horse ownership—one man per horse;
> Bakufu-ordered [extramural] corvée: labor and number of days to be assigned per taka; [bakufu-ordered] intramural corvée: labor and number of days to be assigned per household for both large and small peasants;
> Village fees: to be determined one-half per taka, one-half per household;
> Sake portion of village fees: two-thirds per taka, one-third per household.

Such a formula of corvée allocation necessitated knowledge of each holding's kokudaka. What did the peasants know about the share of the yearly village tribute they owed the overlord?

The amount of yearly tribute, determined by the overlords, was communicated to each village head by the intendant in a document most commonly called the *nenguwaritsukejō* (literally, "yearly tribute [*nengu*] rate letter"). From 1591 until around 1635, when they were standardized, in *most* bakufu territories *most* of these documents were very short, notes really.[80] They clearly reflect the sole concern of the

79. Saitō Yoshiyuki, "Kinsei shoki no nōmin tōsō," 56.
80. For the discussion that follows, see Arai Eiji, "Nengu waritsukejō no seiritsu," in *Kinsei no jikata-machikata monjo,* ed. Nihon komonjo gakkai, Nihon komonjogaku ronshū, 12 (Kinsei 2) (Yoshikawa kōbunkan, 1987), 228–55 (hereafter NKR 12).

overlords—tribute—in that they simply list the village taka, the assessment rate (not always), the amount of rice tribute in bushels (koku, sometimes in bales, *hyō,* one koku being the equivalent of 2.857 hyō), and the date the tribute was due. Adjustments for bad years were usually made by modifying these total figures.

This skeletal system worked because the headmen and the overlords had information that showed the further breakdown of the total village figure into amounts per holding, but this information was not to be found in most of these documents. The few exceptions list in detail and separately paddy fields, dry fields, and homesteads according to the grade of the arable; these were usually issued the year after a survey was taken. Why is it, then, that around 1635 in most areas of the bakufu territory and in the 1660s and 1670s in a few remaining pockets these forms became standardized, now always giving the detailed information that was only very rarely available earlier?

A tighter central control over intendants was not the only reason. Political pressure was also applied from below, not, obviously, from village headmen, who could thwart the system to their own advantage, but from the peasants. There were too many complaints about abuses that occurred because peasants were kept in the dark concerning the fairness of their share of village tribute.

As a first response to these political problems, starting around 1635 the intendants provided all the necessary detail in their yearly tribute letters, thereby binding headmen to extract such and such an amount from such and such a plot. This, of course, still did not make the headman accountable to the tribute payers, which led to numerous disputes. Indeed, the shogunal directives of the 1640s ordering intendants to make sure that headmen made the yearly tax list available to all the "small peasants" for their approval invariably mention that this was being required "in order to avoid quarrels in the villages."[81]

For the bakufu, as we have seen, "small peasants" included all taka holders below the titled peasants. These small landholders were thus granted new public political importance within the village: they yearly ratified the tax list. It is possible that the few regions that succeeded in postponing the implementation of these measures until the 1660s and 1670s (Sagami's Ōsumi and Musashi's Okutama) were areas where

81. TKKz, 4:122 (no. 2105, art. 14).

dogō power was stronger. In other words, this development indicates that the "small peasants" were not fully incorporated into the murauke system *as far as trans-village tribute was concerned* until the 1680s, that is, when villages as a whole, and not simply headmen, became responsible for the delivery of tribute.

The kokudaka system was thus manipulated as a standard of fairness by the people below in a class struggle, not against samurai, but against village leaders. This worked to the bakufu's benefit in two ways. Inasmuch as its *village tribute* system was widely used by the tribute producers as an ultimate scale for *communal fairness,* the system itself was safe from being subjected to other standards of justice; thus, intra-peasant practice legitimized overlord domination. Hints that appeals in petitions to a broader concept of Justice (which were common in pre-modern Europe) transcended the standard itself can only be found in vague references to notions of benevolent government or the need for peasants to reproduce themselves, to survive. These notions were marshaled in peasant protests, but they did not question the system as such.[82] Moreover, the bakufu, through its decision (under pressure) to widen access to the system for more and more peasants beyond the headman, first the kumi heads as village officials and then all the peasants as certifiers of the tribute allocation, created a new village practice that strengthened overlord legitimacy among a widening constituency of subjects.

The expanding political empowerment of villagers discussed thus far was limited to taka holders. Toward the end of the seventeenth century, however, the number of non–taka holders increased. They also had a stake in access to information first monopolized by headmen and then shared by the "small peasants," and this for two reasons. First of all, tenants were interested in knowing the breakdown of tribute allocation because the rent they paid to landlords included the amount of tribute due on the parcel they rented, tribute for which the landlord was responsible. Correct information about this tribute allowed tenant peasants to judge the fairness of their rent. Moreover, as we have seen, these peasants shared intramural corvée and fees, and they could use the taka system to argue for a fairer allocation of these duties.

In principle this information was made available by law, starting in

---

82. Stephen Vlastos discusses the arguments of these appeals in his *Peasant Protests,* 15–17.

the 1640s. A directive of 1642/8/10 stipulated that "for the calculation of the yearly tribute, etc. the intendant has to make village headmen meet with the small peasants and have them affix their seal to the tax roster of that year in order to avoid headmen's doing injustice to the small peasants."[83] In another directive, dated 1644/1/11, sent to the intendants of the Kinai and the Kantō, the bakufu reiterated that "every year the tax rates (*osamekatawaritsuke*) have to be shown to all the peasants without exception (*sōbyakushō nokorazu*) who have to affix their seal to it so that the quarrels of the past can be avoided."[84]

Now, empirically minded scholars invariably raise the question of practice: was not the fact that these laws were reissued again and again proof that they were a dead letter? Indeed, they were reissued, for example, in 1713/4 in a long directive overhauling intendant governance that admits to faltering practice in recent years, quoted in part here:

> The tribute roster that the intendant forwards every year to the village officials (*murakata*) has to be made known in detail to the peasants, small and large alike. This is a law from the past. In recent years, however, we have heard that nobody has seen them except the headman, and so on, and, moreover, that the headman, and so on, do not make the village budget available to the smallest peasants because there are unnecessary expenditures or illegal matters. Henceforward, as stipulated in past laws, not only the tribute roster, which goes without saying, but also the specific items of the village budget have to be made clearly known to the peasants large and small, who will affix their seal to the budget. And every year, the intendant will examine the budget document of each village and make inquiries of all the peasants of the village concerning details, this to avoid illegalities on the part of the headman, and so on, and unnecessary expenditures on the part of the large and small peasants.[85]

Documentary confirmation of actual compliance is, obviously, only sporadic, but as we saw earlier, seals of more and more peasants do appear on these documents, while they were absent at the beginning of the period. A more interesting question than that of the impact of legislation on practice is the reverse one, namely, what kind of practice prompted this legislation. It is clear that those who through these

---

83. TKKz 5:155 (no. 2784). For the discussion that follows, see Ōtsuka Eiji, "Nenguwaritsuke to mura nyūyō no kōkai ni tsuite," *Shinano* 43, no. 9 (1991): 1–24.

84. TKKz 4:122 (no. 2105).

85. Ibid., 134.

directives became, so to speak, politically more enfranchised were the ones who had exerted the pressure.

This continuing tug of war between those who wanted information made public, in principle officially backed by the bakufu, and those who resisted such requests resulted in more concrete legislation in 1745, 1750, and 1767. These directives required that a short version of the tax rosters, written by the intendant and listing the total amount of tribute and the precise amount due in each category of taxes, be posted on the public notice board or at the headman's gate. It was to remain there for the whole year and then be exchanged for the next year's one at the intendant's office.[86]

BUDGET CONTROL

Tokugawa villages were not only tribute units; they were also communities of people who did things together other than pay tribute, and communities have common expenses. Control over decisions concerning the size of the community budget, what it is to be used for, and how the burden is to be shared within the community translates into political power. And the degree to which such control lies within or outside the community largely determines the degree of community autonomy.

There are two opposing stereotypes concerning the autonomy of Tokugawa villages. One stresses their autonomy, because they were self-governing communities (kyōdōtai). The other stereotype maintains that villages were subject to overlord authority in so many important ways that self-governance was a sham. To maintain the distinction between these two interpretations in the discussion that follows, I use *communities* in reference to these social units insofar as they were autonomous and *villages* insofar as they were constituted by the overlords. Much of this controversy has been a matter of definitions and the political views that inform them or lessons one wishes to draw from them.[87] A discussion of local budgets may throw some light on this

86. Ōtsuka, "Nenguwaritsuke," 6–7. Ōtsuka's research suggests that these digests were posted, but most probably only for a few weeks.

87. For a good survey of the historiographical polemics surrounding this issue since the early twentieth century, see Uesugi Mitsuhiko, "Kinsei sonrakuron: kinsei sonraku to 'jiji,'" *Nihonshi kenkyū no shinshiten,* ed. Nihon rekishi gakkai (Yoshikawa kōbunkan, 1986), 175–93.

question of autonomy, which is usually argued from a legal and juridical angle, as we shall see in chapter 4.

The degree to which Tokugawa villages, sanctioned by the land surveys, were already also communities with communal economic interests
and expenditures varied widely. Whatever the case may have been, they
were certainly tribute units. And since tribute production and payment
loomed so large in the life of these villages, this undoubtedly furthered
their development into some sort of communities if they were not
already communities to begin with.

In Tokugawa Japan, decisions on sharing community expenses were
similar to those concerning tribute, because tribute was also a communal affair. To get a sense of the relative importance of community
and tribute expenses, let us consider briefly the main categories. Tribute
consisted of (1) tribute in kind, mostly rice (nengu), but also various
other contributions (*komononari*) and (2) corvée (yaku). Corvée for
overlords did not always take the form of labor: it could include cash
(busen) or rice payments (*kuchimai*, bumai); kuniyaku, "national" corvée or service the daimyo required for duties owed to the shogun;
buyaku, which daimyo or intendants requested on their own authority;
and a special category, sukego, or portage labor performed by groups
of villages attached to way stations on the highways. In addition,
there was corvée connected with the collection and transportation of
the rice tax. Many of these services included materiel needed to perform the labor. A number of other village expenses were indirectly
the result of overlord demands, including remuneration for village officials; their travel expenses on official trips; expenses for village meetings held in relation to the payment of taxes; and the cost of brushes,
ink, paper, and so on, to draw up official documents. All of these levies
ultimately had to do with the reproduction of the samurai ruling
class.

Community expenses proper, on the other hand, had to do with corvée and contributions of cash or materiel needed for the reproduction of
the peasants (the ruling class's reproducers), in all spheres of their communal life (economic, political, spiritual): roads, bridges, and irrigation
systems had to be maintained, festivals held, donations to temples
financed, and, occasionally, the expenses of suits (not lawyer costs but
travel expenses) shouldered, interest on loans paid, and so on. Aside
from the important political question—how this burden was spread

throughout the village—attention needs to be drawn to a number of other points.

First, the combined village and community expenses were high, and they increased considerably in the nineteenth century, when many financially strapped overlords, through sheer neglect, shifted infrastructural maintenance costs to the villages. For instance, for the village of Kichijōji, outside of Edo, which had no particularly heavy way station portage duties or irrigation systems to maintain, in 1845 these expenses amounted to 28 percent of its tribute (nengu). For Hara village (Saku district, Shinano), which had way-station and dike maintenance duties, between 1734 and 1841 the average expenses amounted to 44 percent; in some years it was 80 percent or even a full 100 percent.[88] Second, often only a tiny fraction of these total expenses were community expenses proper; in Hara village in 1734, expenses were virtually limited to festivals and religious occasions. Third, since the bulk of their expenses were direct or indirect overlord levies, the villagers had little control over the size and allocation of the expenses they had to share. Furthermore, overlords could and did increase these levies at will, while they were more reluctant to alter the yearly rice tribute. These structural constraints put severe limits on village autonomy.

Thus far I have avoided talking of budgets because Tokugawa villages did not have what we today understand by that term. Our notion of budget is forward-looking in that a budget is an itemized allocation of a known or projected amount of funds. Tokugawa village budgets were different, more like retrospective expense accounts drawn up at the end of the year, as itemized lists of expenses incurred during the year. An official copy of the budget was forwarded to the intendant at the beginning of the next year; the original draft, often at variance with the official version, remained in the village. The expenses were, of course, paid as they occurred; often, however, they were paid not by the villagers but by the headman or another better-off member of the com-

---

88. For Kichijōji, see NRT 3:441; the figure for Hara was calculated on the data provided by Kodama Kōta, "Kinsei ni okeru mura no zaisei," NKR 12:353. In 1840, Hara village (79 households, 72 of which belonged to titled peasants; total population 325; 470 koku) paid 155 koku tribute rice, and its village expenses, computed in koku at the then going price for rice, came to 131 koku, or the equivalent of 81 percent of the rice tribute; in 1845 the two amounts were equal (155.8 and 154.6, respectively, which Kodama wrongly reported as 44 percent instead of 99 percent) (ibid., 346, 353).

munity, who advanced the cash. Then at the end of the year, sometimes to the surprise of the villagers, the debt was divided up among them according to one formula or another, and each household paid its share to the moneylender, usually with interest and often at outrageous rates of 30–40 percent.[89] One of the reasons for this arrangement was the lack of independent village income from common property, which was the case in corporate villages especially in pre-Tokugawa times.

Villages and other communities have always had expenses, but written budgets like the ones described above, like so many other practices of rural administration, seem to have appeared only in the mid 1640s. This was the time when limits were being set to the headman's arbitrary powers. It was also the time when some of the corvée, such as the "national" corvée, was being converted into cash or rice contributions.[90] In other words, in earlier decades village expenses probably were predominantly in the form of labor. The headman, who was entitled to some of that corvée and as dogō also received corvée from a number of peasants as his dependents, did not always keep these two kinds of labor, official and private, apart.[91] Remunerations for village officials in the form of labor or tax allowances easily led to abuses and disputes. This explains the drive by villagers to substitute them with payments in rice and with salaries pegged to the total kokudaka of the village. In addition, the line between corvée ordered by the overlord and that generated locally could easily be blurred to the benefit of the decision makers in the village—and it was. Numerous complaints forced the bakufu to take action. The bakufu directive of 1713, quoted at length above, ordered that not only taxes but also village expenses be made public. This was not the first nor the last legislation on this subject.

In 1642/5, three months before the bakufu issued the directive with regard to "calculation of the yearly tax, etc.," it had identified this "etc." as "expenses related to the various corvées" in a similar way: the corvée was to be specified for the small peasants in writing; the headman and kumi heads were to affix their seal to it; and official approval

---

89. See KDJ 13:676, s.v. "murazaisei"; for village budgets in general, see also ibid., 683, s.v. "muranyūyōchō." In the Kinai region the interest rates were fixed at 15 percent in the late seventeenth century (see Fujiki Hisashi, "Ikōki sonrakuron," 214).

90. Kanzaki Akitoshi, "Muranyūyōchō ni tsuite," NKR 12:415.

91. In some places this practice persisted until the end of the seventeenth century. For three cases, of 1684, 1693, and 1694, see ibid., 419–20.

by seal of the intendant's helper (tedai) was to be secured.[92] A year later *all peasants'* seals were required.[93]

With such vague specifications, and with no sanctions provided for noncompliance, abuses at the intendant and village level continued, partly because tribute and corvée were not differentiated in these village budgets. In 1666/4 it was ordered that two lists be drawn up, one specifying each household's tribute, the other its corvée.[94] In 1694/1 the intendants themselves had to provide two copies of the list of items to be used for drawing up the budgets, one for the headman and one for the peasants.[95] During the Kyōhō Reforms of the 1730s the intendant's responsibility in this matter was stressed, but ultimately the burden of enforcement was put back on the village officials in 1744, when for the first time punishments were specified for not informing peasants of the amounts of tribute, corvée, and the village expenditures. Headmen would lose their office, and kumi heads would be fined. If there was blatant greed, the former was to be expelled and his property confiscated; the latter was to relinquish his office and be fined.[96] Village headmen had, of course, been punished in the past, but this was the first time that these punishments were determined as a specific category.

Also in 1744 the bakufu clarified the formulae for calculating tribute and village expenses:

> corvée for the shogun and the intendants plus village expenses and expenses related to suits and disputes, and so on, have to be computed per taka; this holds also for outsiders [with fields in the village];
> dwellers in the mountains, the wilds, bays or salt producing shores, and so on, or places with many households without taka or with

92. Sugawara Kenji, "Muranyūyōchō no seiritsu: Kinsei muranyūyō no kenkyū josetsu," NKR 12:386. The discussion of this legislation that follows relies on this article.

93. TKKz 5:158 (no. 2788, art. 14). The same article appears again in a directive of 1644/1 (ibid., 4:122 [no. 2105, art. 15]). In 1652 noncompliance was seen as a major source of administrative problems (ibid., 125 [no. 2108, art. 7]).

94. Ibid., 4:127 (no. 2110, art. 3).

95. Ibid., 5:140 (no. 2772, art. 4).

96. This stipulation is article 98 of Yoshimune's famous *Kujikata osadamegaki* (TKKk 4:210). For the additions to this text that specify the punishments, see John C. Hall, "Japanese Feudal Laws III," 788. The German translation also lists the punishments: Rudorff, "Tokugawa-Gesetz-Sammlung," 98–99.

small taka, have to compute by the number of persons and include dependent servants (excluding wives and children);

shares in the common use of mountain forests and moors have to be
computed per taka; this applies also to outsiders;

expenditures for festivals, donations for religious purposes, and so
on, can be decided in common agreement as one sees fit;

for all the above computations, however, prior custom can be followed in places that have been free from quarrels in the past.[97]

The bakufu's hesitant approach toward intravillage political matters
stands out clearly. Forced by circumstances to sanction a method with
its authority, the bakufu suggests the taka system as a safe guidepost
but then lists a number of exceptions and finally admits implicitly that
the taka system should be used (only) if everything else fails.

Thus, in the mid seventeenth century the bakufu insisted that official
"budgets" be drawn up to prevent village disputes about corvée distribution. A century later it gave minimal guidelines on how to achieve
fairness and prescribed serious penalties for negligent village officials.
In the late eighteenth and early nineteenth centuries legislation concerning village budgets was limited to efforts to shrink expenses through
sumptuary measures. Although the bakufu had repeatedly stipulated
since the early 1640s that "small peasants" should be involved in decisions concerning tribute and village expenses, it was only in 1744 that it
issued guidelines to deal with disputes and stipulated penalties. During
the century in between, peasants agitated around these issues on their
own and broadened their political base within the village. In this sense,
the stronger stance taken by the bakufu in 1744 sanctioned peasant
gains.

"REPRESENTING" THE PEASANTS

One of the most significant institutionalized intramural checks on village leadership, at least in principle, was the "peasant representative,"
or hyakushōdai. He was to keep an eye on village governance for all
the peasants, which in concrete terms meant foremost on decisions
made by the titled peasants with regard to tribute allocation and village expenses. This institution should have been of obvious interest

97. TKKk 2:67.

for scholars exploring the question of village self-governance. Yet they have not paid much attention to it, focusing instead on the question of village autonomy as reflected in village laws.

In an extended study of land ownership published some thirty-five years ago, Ōishi Shinzaburō discussed this position briefly as one of the three official village offices, *murakata sanyaku* (next to the headman and the kumi heads), the way it is described in the famous late-eighteenth-century handbook for local administration, the *Jikata hanreiroku*.[98] The earliest instance reported by Ōishi dates from 1714 (in Oiwake, Kita-Saku district). It is generally accepted that the office was institutionalized around that time, although not universally: not all villages had peasant representatives in the second half of the Tokugawa period.[99] "Institutionalization," therefore, depended on local conditions, that is, on whether or not overlords acknowledged such an office or whether villages established one on their own. *Villages* here stands, however, for titled peasants, who, for obvious reasons, were not eager to be monitored. Here again, therefore, the establishment of peasant representatives was often a response to a local crisis.

In 1724 in Gorobe-shinden (Kita-Saku district), for example, when the headman's retirement, officially for health reasons, caused strife, a peasant representative was installed.[100] Demands for creating peasant representative posts were quite numerous in the first decades of the eighteenth century. Once they were recognized by overlords, the peasant representative's seal was required on all official documents (including suits), next to that of the headman and the kumi heads.

Sakai Uji recently examined the history of this office in the Kanto provinces and concluded that its widespread "officialization" was nothing but the sanctioning by the bakufu and daimyo of a much older peasant practice.[101] According to Sakai, one has to distinguish between *sōbyakushōdai* ("all-peasant representative") and hyakushōdai ("peasant representative"). In general, the former is found in the records only

98. Ōishi Shinzaburō, *Hōkenteki tochi shoyū no kaitai katei: I. Kinsei jinushiteki tochi shoyū no keisei katei* (Ochanomizu shobō, 1958), 177–85, esp. 184–85; Ōishi Hisakata, *Jikata hanreiroku* 2:93.
99. KDJ 11:996, s.v. "hyakushōdai."
100. Ōishi, *Hōkenteki tochi shoyū*, 180–81.
101. Sakai Uji, "'Sōbyakushōdai' kara 'hyakushōdai' e: zenki hyakushōdai no seiritsu o megutte," in *Ronshū chū-kinsei no shiryō to hōhō*, ed. Takizawa Takeo (Tōkyōdō shuppan, 1991), 373–406.

between the 1660s and 1770s; the latter from the 1680s until the end of the Tokugawa period. Thus, "all-peasant representative" was the only title until the 1680s, when the second title started to appear, but it remained the predominant one until the 1720s, when it began gradually to lose ground, and it finally disappeared after the 1770s.[102] "All-peasant representative" was first used for a position that had sprung up within the villages, whereas "peasant representative" ultimately became the title used officially by the overlords and came to supersede the former. Sakai puts the official institutionalization of this office in the Kanto provinces in the 1690s.[103] This office thus developed within the context of the small landholders' struggle for access to information and power discussed earlier. Although the first written trace of "all-peasant representative" dates from the 1660s, the possibility or necessity of this village position is already contained in bakufu directives of the years 1641–43.[104] The second of two copies of the village budget the bakufu ordered made in those years was for the small peasants. This copy must have had a recipient. (The same goes for the tribute roster; see appendix 3, addendum to art. 35.) So it is very likely that, insofar as this directive was implemented, there must have been at least an informal peasant representative.

This "representative," however, was not necessarily a small peasant. It was more likely that he was a titled peasant and that if genuine peasant representation by a non-elite peasant was to occur, this had to be achieved by internal pressure, as the following case of Iribuse village (next to Ken's Makibuse) in Kita-Saku district indicates. There, the offices of kumi head and peasant representative had always been filled "since the ancient past" by some of the twenty-four titled peasants. The nontitled peasants, however, had agitated to have some say in who was elected, and they wanted to be candidates for office themselves. In 1760 an agreement was worked out, on bakufu orders, by two officials from villages in the area (see appendix 1 for the text). First, the rule that the kumi head always had to be a nontitled peasant was abolished. However, nontitled peasants *could* be elected, which must have been a con-

102. Ibid., 377, 380.
103. Ibid., 396.
104. Sakai refers to three directives in ibid., 397–98. One can be found in TKKz 5:153–54 (no. 2782, art. 10). The others are directives by the Kanto intendant (gundai) Ina Hanjūrō that Sakai found in the *Saitama-ken shi: Shiryō-hen,* vol. 7 (Saitama-ken, 1985), 46, 47.

cession, although the eventual transfer of power from a titled peasant to a nontitled one was still conditioned, it seems, by the willingness of the titled peasant to relinquish his post. Henceforward, however, the non-titled peasants would elect their own representative from among their own ranks.

Thus the genesis of the office of peasant representative was prompted partly by the movement from below whereby peasants insisted on access to crucial information on matters that profoundly affected their material well-being. In order to avoid trouble, the bakufu incorporated their demands by ordering the diffusion of information. Often, we surmise, this information came to be monopolized by the titled peasants. In a further move, then, the nontitled "small" peasants wanted a representative of their class to be the one who checked the village elite's governance.

That power remained with the powerful in the villages should perhaps come as no surprise. For a considerable time, however, the thesis that a small peasantry was established at the beginning of the Tokugawa period has prevented this view from gaining full acceptance. Even though the original stratum of village power holders split into two, some of them becoming salaried vassals, others remaining landed, the two new strata were able to make the transition into the seventeenth century quite successfully. Economic expansion, especially the development of new arable, and political agitation from within the villages, together with the overlords' responses to these developments, modified the traditional power of this old rural elite, which, however, succeeded in reproducing itself well into the eighteenth century and in some cases even until the end of the Tokugawa period.

Analytically speaking, one can refer to those who found themselves in this stratum as an objective class, because they monopolized either economic cum political power (in the beginning) or political power only (later on, when economically they became indistinguishable from "small peasants" in certain regions). When they lost their economic prominence, however, many were able to hold on to their social position by manipulating a special kind of power, namely, that of status. Within the villages, they closed ranks, forming a subjective class, to defend their privilege, a development taken up in the next chapter.

3
Status Power

Samurai fight with weapons, peasants with lawsuits.

Tanaka Kyūgū, 1721

American students of the sociopolitical or socioeconomic (as opposed to the purely demographic or purely economic) side of Tokugawa peasant society have, with the exception of Thomas C. Smith, framed their interpretations within a particular trajectory of peasant protest spanning the whole period. In the first century, overlord domination met resistance by solidary villages. By the nineteenth century, however, interclass confrontation had turned into intraclass struggle within the peasantry, its solidarity now fractured along lines of divergent economic interests.[1]

This picture of late Tokugawa peasant society is not to be questioned even if these scholars take different positions vis-à-vis class theory. Herbert Bix perceives a growing class struggle, while Stephen Vlastos works with a widened Marxian concept of oppression. William Kelley, on the other hand, does not discuss the early period and firmly rejects any notion of group solidarity to focus on shifting coalitions around temporary interests that cut across economic strata. That these scholars do not seriously engage the notion of social class as such is irrelevant

Epigraph: Tanaka Kyūgū, Minkan seiyō, 335.
1. Bix, Peasant Protest; Burton, "Peasant Struggle"; Irwin Scheiner, "Benevolent Lords and Honorable Peasants: Rebellion and Peasant Consciousness in Tokugawa Japan," in Japanese Thought in the Tokugawa Period, 1600–1868, ed. Tetsuo Najita and Irwin Scheiner (Chicago: University of Chicago Press, 1978), 39–62; Vlastos, Peasant Protests; James White, "Economic Development and Sociopolitical Unrest in Nineteenth-Century Japan," Economic Development and Cultural Change 37 (1989): 231–59. William Kelley limits his analysis to the nineteenth century in his Deference and Defiance in Nineteenth-Century Japan (Princeton: Princeton University Press, 1985).

for the point I want to make, namely, that they all posit in some way a
solidary village at the beginning of the Tokugawa period. Admittedly,
the seventeenth century is not the focus of any of these studies, yet one
still may raise the question whence and why this image of early village
solidarity.

This question is also relevant with regard to the research by Thomas
C. Smith, who stands alone in having highlighted, very early, the seventeenth century's great economic discrepancies.[2] For Smith, looking
for the agrarian origins of modern Japan, the seventeenth century as
origin of these origins was ultimately far removed from his interests.
Moreover, the modernization paradigm within which he was working,
although anti-Marxist in one way, shared with economistic Marxism a
slighting of political factors. Smith's research agenda led him away
from the questions taken up here.

These other scholars took as their subject the most salient features of
peasant protest, the ikki, or confrontations of supravillage authority by
whole villages or groups of villages. These confrontations occurred only
in mid and late Tokugawa. When Anne Walthall and Herbert Bix touch
upon intravillage protests, these are predominantly eighteenth-century
protests.[3]

STATUS AND CLASS—MUTUALLY EXCLUSIVE?

Perhaps a more fundamental question underlies the assumption that
economic discrepancies as source of class tensions developed only fully
in the eighteenth century, turning seventeenth-century villages into
communities that either were harmonious or harbored status conflicts,
which were considered to be less significant than class conflicts. This
question concerns the relationship between class and status and, ultimately, how economic and symbolic matters weigh in on one's scale of
reality.

We know that status in Tokugawa Japan was fixed by laws, starting
with Hideyoshi's famous Edict Restricting Change of Status and Residence of 1591, which thus created a "society of orders." Actually, that
edict did not aim at status as such: its immediate purpose was to secure

2. Smith, "Japanese Village."
3. See Anne Walthall, *Social Protest and Popular Culture in Eighteenth-
Century Japan* (Tucson: University of Arizona Press, 1986).

a stable, productive agricultural labor force at home while Japan was engaged in a war abroad. Nevertheless, in combination with the Sword Hunt Edict three years earlier, its sociopolitical effect was the great divide between rulers and ruled, samurai and (mainly) peasants. While this nationwide divide certainly was not without obvious economic underpinnings, namely, a division between producers and extractors of economic surplus, scholars have too readily assumed that it over-determined people's preoccupations and, hence, that all serious conflict centered around the opposition between dominators and dominated, or orders of rulers and commoners.[4] Status thus subsumed class before the two started to separate, that is, before class divisions as such appeared, which would have occurred only sometime in the eighteenth century.

According to Herbert Bix, "Generally throughout Japan from the 1760s onward, the division of peasants along economic lines was slowly beginning to override their unity along status lines.... One may reasonably hypothesize, therefore, that class and income stratification was starting to introduce distinctions between households, which, in turn, reduced the likelihood that mere status could continue to serve as a firm basis of solidarity."[5] And Nakane Chie writes that as a result of "the Tokugawa policy," "in theory there was no social differentiation among the households of a village community," but by "the eighteenth century ... differentiation in peasant statuses became common in most villages, resulting in titled farmers (owners) and dependants (tenants)."[6] Stephen Vlastos, who writes that "the juridically determined social order in which peasants were subsistence agriculturalists, as indeed they were in the early Tokugawa period, bore little relation to functional relationships within the market economy of late Tokugawa—circum-stances which profoundly affected conflict and collective action at the end of Tokugawa rule,"[7] evokes an image of an early peasant class unified by status that developed intraclass conflict only under the impact of a commercial economy.

4. Bix, *Peasant Protest,* xvi–xvii, xxvii; Vlastos, *Peasant Protests,* 11–14, 159, 166–67; Burton, "Peasant Struggle," 138, 151, 166; James White, "Rational Rioters: Leaders, Followers, and Popular Protest in Early Modern Japan," *Politics and Society* 16, no. 1 (1988): 46–47.

5. Bix, *Peasant Protest,* 103, 104; on p. xvii he writes that "the degree of peasant 'classness' tended to increase while their 'statusness' decreased."

6. Nakane, *Kinship,* 47, 49.

7. Vlastos, *Peasant Protests,* 7–8.

These interpretations contradict the argument presented in chapter 2 and have two points in common. One, they work within the framework of a legally defined status order, implying that legislation was the only source of status division (which effected class solidarity) and that no further status divisions existed in the village, because of the absence of legislation at that level, assuming, in addition, that villages did not generate status differentials on their own. Two, since the legally defined status of the peasantry gave way to internal class divisions, there were no internal class or social divisions worthy to be referred to as such prior to the development of a market in the eighteenth century.

Class and status are dichotomized historically here, to the point of occupying mutually exclusive sequential positions: status societies are succeeded by class societies.[8] A quick reading of Max Weber may give that impression, for he is quite explicit in saying that class situations are market situations, while status orders (*Stände*) are not, on this point approximating Karl Marx's historical view.[9]

Class societies are dominated by "functional" interests, the rational dictates of the market, which does not know personal distinction, and stratified through pure relations of property and production, generating classes that are unaware of their shared objective conditions unless they resort to social and political action. Status societies, in contrast, are organized in groups consciously distinguished from one another in terms of social honor, ascriptive privileges, lifestyles, and hence prescriptive modes of consumption that abhor and suppress the purely economic, which is typical of class societies.[10] In class societies, one may add, the ruling class owns the means of production (and its own means of consumption); in status societies, an elite also directly controls the means of consumption of others through extraeconomic means.

Status, which Weber defines as "an effective claim to social esteem in terms of positive or negative privileges," entails a clear social recognition of belonging, while property and social classes are constituted foremost by objectively shared interests, which may or may not lead to forms of associations. For the sake of completeness, I should further

---

8. For a similar dichotomy that has governed scholarship on seventeenth-century France (was it a "society of orders" or a "society of classes"?), see the discussion in Beik, *Absolutism*, 6–9.

9. Weber, *Economy and Society*, 2:927–28.

10. Ibid., 1:306–7; 2:929–30, 932, 936–38.

note that for Weber, property classes are "determined by property differences," while social classes are constituted by "the totality of those class situations within which individual and generational mobility is easy and typical," class situations being the "typical probability, within a given economic order, of procuring goods, gaining a position in life and finding inner satisfactions."[11]

Dichotomies, such as that of class and status, are put forth by Weber to construct ideal types that, although mutually exclusive, can serve as flexible, descriptive tools for analyzing social realities, which are always hybrids somewhere between the pure extremes. A closer reading of Weber, therefore, reveals that the ideal types are not essences functioning as monocausal explanations. His thought is more fluid; he thinks in more relational terms.[12] Weber suggests the following possible relationships between status and class: "Status *may* rest on class position of a distinct or an ambiguous kind. However, it is not solely determined by it.... Conversely, status may influence, if not completely determine, a class position without being identical with it." And "class distinctions are linked in the most variegated ways with status distinctions. Property as such is not always recognized as a status qualification, but in the long run it is, and with extraordinary regularity." On the relation between power and status, he writes: "Quite generally, 'mere economic' power, and especially 'naked' money power, is by no means a recognized basis of social honor. Nor is power the only basis of social honor. Indeed, social honor, or prestige, may even be the basis of economic power, and very frequently has been."[13]

Pierre Bourdieu, in his ongoing reflections on the theoretical implications of his own vast research, has spelled out more systematically the various ways in which class and status (in the modern sense rather than the historical sense of orders or estates) are linked and how power and honor can be the basis for each other. Bourdieu has thus developed notions of various types of capital (material, social, cultural, and symbolic) that can be converted into one another, which entails a critique of substantialist thinking and realist views of class. Hence the importance,

11. Ibid., 1:305, 302.
12. Pierre Bourdieu stresses the fundamental importance of thinking in terms of relationships rather than essences (see his *Logic of Practice*, 4; and *In Other Words*, 40, 126).
13. Weber, *Economy and Society*, 1:306; 2:932, 926.

as an analytic starting point for this relational approach, of the notions of *field* and social space, where people occupy certain positions, through which one "can understand the logic of their practices and determine, *inter alia,* how they will classify themselves and others and, should the case arise, think of themselves as members of a 'class.'"[14] Social spaces consist of differential power positions, determined intrinsically by material conditions and relationally by their distinctive distance from other positions. Agents thus identified as sharing common positions constitute only "theoretical classes" and not "groups which would exist as such in reality," unless they are actually organized politically.[15]

This objective truth of social classes has to be supplemented by considering what provides domination the surface of legitimacy that allows relations of exploitation to function as such. This "supplement" (from an objectivist standpoint) is provided by signs of distinction that effect a social misrecognition or, more precisely, at least a socially accepted misrepresentation of those relations. Such signs of distinction function as a rare symbolic capital whereby one distinguishes oneself foremost

14. Bourdieu, *In Other Words,* 50; see also 49 and 126. Japanese scholars' discussion concerning status, which centered around Minegishi Kentarō's articles, some of which he collected in his book *Kinsei mibunron,* has been hopelessly stuck in the kind of realist, reifying perspective Bourdieu criticizes. Bourdieu advises against "questions ... about limits and frontiers" when studying classes (*In Other Words,* 50), which is precisely what Japanese historians were preoccupied with in the 1980s, according to Minegishi (*Kinsei mibunron,* 56). In addition, Minegishi argues (13–21) against the Marxist views of two prominent medievalists: Kuroda Toshio's instrumentalist class interpretation of status as a means of "extra-economic coercion" and Ishimoda Shō's emphasis on the mediation of the state. Takagi Shōsaku (see chap. 2, n. 44) agrees with Minegishi's anticlass stance but emphasizes the role of the state (dissociated from class) in contrast to Minegishi, who argues that the origins of status were social. Recently, Asao Naohiro has pointed out that during the last decade a number of historians have avoided the substantialist dilemmas that framed the earlier debate and started to analyze the flexible and instrumental relationships between status and the evolving world of occupational diversification and competition, in other words, how public sanction of status served interest groups not readily identifiable as classes ("Kinsei no mibun," in MK, 35–38). Class has thus all but disappeared from the discussion of status among Japanese historians.

15. Bourdieu, *In Other Words,* 117, 118. The simple distinction between objective and subjective classes proposed by Bourdieu is none other than Marx's classes "in themselves" and "for themselves" or Berreman's "etic" categories and "emic" groups (see Gerald Berreman, "Social Inequality: A Cross-Cultural Analysis," in *Social Inequality: Comparative and Developmental Approaches,* ed. Berreman [New York: Academic Press, 1981], 18).

from those holding immediately lower positions, whose aspirations constitute a direct threat to one's social identity. "The logic of the symbolic," therefore, "makes absolute 'all or nothing' differences out of infinitesimal differences."[16] Thus, struggles within social fields will always also be at least (and exclusively, unless the objective conditions are clearly foregrounded) struggles for specific differences to thereby modify one's position within the established and accepted order of classification, an order of legally or customarily institutionalized "indices of consecrations."[17]

Bourdieu's reflections on class and status are the result of extensive sociological research in modern society, where, as he has noted himself, sumptuary laws do not set legal limits on the deployment of symbolic strategies, as they did in Tokugawa Japan. Nevertheless, what he has to say further about the relation between the two is very helpful for the present study. Status groups, Bourdieu argues, structure their strategies of distinction through a social logic of union and separation, seeking thereby "to make *de facto* differences permanent and quasi-natural, and therefore legitimate, by symbolically enhancing the effect of distinction associated with occupying a rare position in the social structure"; these strategies are therefore "the self-consciousness of the dominant class."[18] Hence Bourdieu's critique of Weber, to whom he acknowledges a great debt: "'Status groups' based on a 'life-style' and a 'stylization of life' are not, as Weber thought, a different kind of group from classes, but dominant classes that have denied or, so to speak, sublimated themselves and so legitimated themselves."[19]

THE GREAT STATUS DIVIDE

Bourdieu's insights are relevant for the study of the macrosocial space of Tokugawa society and most pointedly for the micro fields of power that

16. Bourdieu, *In Other Words*, 136–37; the quotation is from 137.

17. Ibid., 138. Bourdieu further elaborates on these "indices of consecration" as "objective marks of respect calling for marks of respect, a spectrum of honours which have the effect of manifesting not only social position but also the collective recognition that it is granted by the mere fact of authorizing such a display of its importance."

18. Ibid.

19. Ibid., 139. Bourdieu has mentioned and discussed his indebtedness to Weber on numerous occasions; see, for example, ibid., 21, 27–28, 46, 49, 106–7.

were the villages. From this perspective, Tokugawa feudalism's ever-multiplying status stratifications and hierarchies, literally embodied through codes of dress and address attached to hereditary households especially in the dominant class (thereby endlessly split into dominant and dominated fractions), can be seen as defense strategies of particular groups against the aspirations of neighboring groups. Although conceivable and indeed real because realistically possible in the turmoil of the sixteenth century, skipping several rungs on the hierarchy became gradually unthinkable, which strengthened domination in that the range of people's aspirations became more and more circumscribed. Those occupying the intermediary positions would certainly resist such ambitions by people below them.

Status legislation with regard to the peasant class developed over time and aimed mainly at reinforcing the distance between peasants and warriors. Peasants were not allowed to use surnames in public documents or to carry long swords, and they had to wear cotton, dismount when encountering samurai, use respectful forms of address, and so on.[20] Overlord authority, which through its land surveys had identified certain peasants as "titled peasants," did not differentiate further among this peasant elite except by lifting some of the prohibitions, allowing the use of surnames and the wearing of one sword by peasant officials such as village headmen and village group headmen.

It should be understood that the prohibition was not against *having* surnames but against using them in public, such as on official documents, and it was not a Tokugawa innovation, since it had existed already in the mid Muromachi period, as a prohibition of 1485 reveals.[21] And exceptions during the Tokugawa period were perhaps less frequent than one might think.

In the 1820s in Tsuyama domain (Mimasaka province), only 44 commoners from 266 villages were granted the privilege of using their surname; in Katsuyama domain (also in Mimasaka province) only 59 from 106 villages; and in Matsushiro domain (Shinano) only 2 out of 871 village officials were granted the privilege. Moreover, the prohibition on surnames was directed most specifically at peasants. Doctors

20. Minegishi reports such legislation for clothing in 1628 and for behavior in the 1640s in bakufu territories and in Chōshū domain (*Kinsei mibunron*, 114).
21. Kobayashi Kei'ichirō, "Shomin no myōji wa itsu goro kara tsukerareta ka," *Nagano*, no. 99 (1981): 1–2; see also Sekigawa Chiyomaru, "Shomin no myōji ni tsuite," ibid., no. 3 (1965): 14–15, 16.

and Shinto priests were exempt, and exceptions made for other commoners seem to have been far more numerous among townspeople than among peasants.[22]

Overlords identified peasants with the land, rather than the other way around. The peasants' generic (and public) identity was not related to their family, their household, or their lineage, but to the land, an identity that was sometimes inscribed in documents, next to their first name, where, in "sidescript," the size of their field was added, such as "Yohachi[2.785 koku]." That this prohibition spilled over, to various degrees at different points, into the "private" sphere is clear from the way documents of religious organizations for the management of festivals or membership lists of confraternities were signed. Only in the mid or late Tokugawa period did all the signatures on some membership lists analyzed by Kobayashi Kei'ichirō include surnames.[23] This is an indication that the status markers created by the overlords were being accepted by and large within peasant communities.

As we have seen, the political concerns of seventeenth-century peasants were intravillage divisions rather than the macro divide between samurai and peasants. In the villages the confrontations were between economically and socially neighboring groups, which is where such struggles always take place, as both Max Weber and Pierre Bourdieu have pointed out.[24] In premarket economies, according to Bourdieu, economic power must be partly converted into symbolic capital, "a

22. Sekigawa, "Shomin no myōji," 15.

23. One complete list, covering the years 1592–1902, of the organizers of a yearly festival at a Hachiman shrine reveals that until 1612 only first names were entered; a few surnames were included in some years between 1613 and 1669, when the list reverts back to first names for the next eighty years; and after 1748 all signatures include surnames. A Kōshin confraternity list (1693 to the present) includes the surnames of all its members starting in 1858 (Kobayashi, "Shomin no myōji," 3).

24. As Weber put it, "It is not the rentier, the share-holder, and the banker who suffer ill will of the worker, but almost exclusively the manufacturer and the business executives who are the direct opponents of workers in wage conflicts. This is so in spite of the fact that it is precisely the cash boxes of the rentier, the share-holder, and the banker into which the more or less unearned gains flow, rather than into the pockets of the manufacturers or of the business executives" (*Economy and Society*, 2:931). And Bourdieu writes that "minimum objective distance in social space can coincide with maximum subjective distance. This is partly because what is 'closest' presents the greatest threat to social identity, that is, differences (and also because the adjustment of expectations to real chances tend to limit subjective pretensions to the immediate neighborhood)" (*Logic of Practice*, 137).

legitimate possession grounded in the nature of its possessor," or symbolic power, "the power to secure recognition of power," before it is accepted as legitimate by those subjected to it.[25] In Tokugawa villages this symbolic capital, grounded in but not identical to material conditions, consisted of status and was largely generated and manipulated from within.[26]

"SHARED" COMMUNITIES

Several times in chapter 2 we came across various ways of dividing power, tribute, corvée, and so on, within the village. Households were corvée households (yakuya) or not, and some were only half so (hanyakunin). Official obligations could be distributed per household (*iewari, tsurawari*), per assessed yield (*takawari, tanwari*), or as combinations thereof. Every household (ie) had some share of privileges and burdens. A good part of village life was literally a matter of "shares," *kabu*. Tokugawa villages were "shared" communities to a very high degree, making them probably quite unique.

This term conveys well, through a concrete image, the concept behind this structure. *Kabu* literally means "stump" or "roots" of a tree or plant, and *kabuwake* means "dividing roots (shares)," as when one separates the roots of a plant into parts so that it can multiply and be divided further into share portions or recombined into bundles. *Kabu* is a quantitative and combining form that could also be, and was, applied to nonmaterial things such as status and power. (Modern stockholding companies, *kabushiki kaisha*, deal in shares or stocks, *kabushiki*.)

The concept of shares, while seemingly modern, is intimately related to the "refeudalized" setup of the early Tokugawa period, when over-

25. Bourdieu presents this argument in "Modes of Domination," chap. 8 of his *Logic of Practice* (122–34); the quotations are from 129 and 131.

26. Smith mentions both class and status when writing about the great contrasts in seventeenth-century villages, and he says that the documents leave "little doubt concerning the general picture of inequality among holdings.... Not infrequently we encounter *peasant* holdings that can only be described as estates." He goes on to say that it is "not surprising that such extremes of wealth and poverty among *hyakushō* of the village were accompanied by marked social distinctions." There were, he says, "two distinct economic classes among the peasantry," and "not infrequently the existence of distinct economic classes in the village was explicitly acknowledged" ("Japanese Village," 266, 268 and n. 28).

lords established villages as tribute units for a certain quota of produce, goods, and services based on the village kokudaka, or assessed yield. Although land cadasters and population registers recorded individual plots and the people on them, the yearly tribute expected by the overlords was the village quota. This relieved the rulers from keeping track of the ever-shifting land, population, and relations between the two within villages. They did not want to deal with the complex effects of time and change. Consequently, villages were left to deal with this reality on their own.

For the peasants, in other words, cadasters and registers were outdated almost as soon as they were compiled: households multiplied or died out, acquired or lost land; new fields were developed, others abandoned; changing weather conditions resulted in average or bumper crops, or total or partial crop failures. All these variations had to be juggled *locally* in a coordinated effort to produce the fixed quota (which only rarely was adjusted downward in bad years), in much the same way that factory workers have to adjust their schedules, breaks, sleeping, gestures, postures, and breathing to the set production quota at the fixed speed of the conveyer belt. A coordinated group effort is essential in such systems.

In the beginning, villages had to struggle with the discrepancy between real conditions and productivity expectations without any directives from above. Then, most of the nengumenjō, the yearly village tax bills, simply included the total amount due and the order that (1) all of it be forwarded after a meeting of "the headman, the elders, the small peasants, and outsiders who owned land in the village," and (2) "since the rate (*men*) is a global one for the whole village (*sōuke*) and it is natural that some peasants go bankrupt or abscond, the community make up the forfeited amount."[27] The question thus faced every year was how to effect an equalization (*domen, jinarashi*, literally, "land

27. Mizumoto discusses these intravillage adjustments in pt. 2, chap. 2, and pt. 3, chap. 2, of his *Mura shakai*. The following discussion, however, is based on Nishiwaki Yasushi's study of Niremata village, Anbachi district, Mino province (in what today is Gifu prefecture) (see "Kinsei zenki no nengu sanyō to 'mura' chitsujo: 'Narashi' sanyō o meguru murakata sōdō no bunseki o tōshite," *Shikan*, no. 106 [1982]: 19–39 [hereafter "Nengu sanyō"]; and "Kinsei zenki Mino Wajū chiiki no 'konō' to sonraku: Bakuryō Anbachi-gun Niremata-mura ni okeru kisoteki bunseki," *Gifu shigaku*, no. 76 [1982]: 41–82 [hereafter "Mino Wajū"]. The quotation, from a directive of 1621 by an intendant's assistant (tedai), is taken from idem, "Nengu sanyō," 20.

exemption," "land equalization") of this burden among all members of the village, which, if for no other reasons, thereby became a community with vital interests at stake, in other words, a matter of sharing.

There were two alternatives: either to apply a new rate to each plot according to its officially assessed grade to produce the supplementary tribute necessary for meeting the village quota or to check the actual harvest of each field and allocate tribute accordingly within or without the framework of graded fields. The latter practice, devised by the peasants, was ultimately sanctioned by law in the mid 1620s (in the district studied by Nishiwaki Yasushi, on whose research I rely). The tax bills ordered equalization based on the actual harvest and according to the grades of the arable.[28] The bakufu thus incorporated into its policy peasant practice that in fact was dealing with the shortcomings of the kokudaka system. This was one way in which the original system was supplemented by new directives to make adjustments for changes that inevitably occurred over time.

The amounts involved were sometimes considerable. In a village studied by Mizumoto, the village as a whole was 34 percent under par in 1623, but the individual fields' shortfalls varied greatly from a low of 9 percent to a high of 77 percent.[29] It is not hard to imagine the tensions this produced within the village, tensions between villagers and the headman (especially in the early period, when the headman monopolized both precise knowledge and decision-making powers) as well as between tenants and landowners (because landowners and not the tenants paid the tribute for rental parcels).[30] And yet, each year there was a deadline to be met.

28. Nishiwaki, "Nengu sanyō," 21–24. Besides the two alternatives mentioned in the Niremata documents, there actually existed a third one, which was practiced widely elsewhere: *jiwari*, or redistribution of the land (without changing the proportion of the total acreage held by each household). Often (but not only) applied when land was lost as a result of floods or other natural disasters, the land in the village was redistributed—sometimes by village initiative, sometimes by overlord order—only once or regularly at intervals of several decades. Unlike earlier scholars, Aono Shunsui considers this system an integral part of the Tokugawa *murauke* system (see his *Nihon kinsei warichiseishi no kenkyū* [Yūzankaku, 1982], 14–18). In some locales, this system operated until the 1950s (KDJ 7:769, s.v. "jiwariseido"). For the only discussion of the system in English, for Kaga domain, see Brown, *Central Authority*, 94–112.

29. Mizumoto, *Mura shakai*, 41–43.

30. Ibid., 52–63. In Saku district, Shinano province, tenants usually paid two-thirds of the harvest to their landlords, retaining one-third for themselves

Initially, the bakufu had a simple way of dealing with those peasants who fell in arrears: it took their land, gave it to someone who could pay the tribute share, and banished the culprits. We find such measures both in intendants' directives of 1640 ("transfer the land") and in bakufu rules for villages issued in 1642 ("banishment").[31] With the famines and crop failures of the 1640s threatening the very existence of many small landholders, however, the bakufu reversed course and instituted its famous policies to protect the "small peasants" from bankruptcy: it required, among other things, that all peasants approve the tax distribution by affixing their seal, instituted a system of receipts for payment of tribute, and forbade the sale of land.[32]

Mizumoto has heralded these equalizing village practices as victories by peasants for the causes of justice and equity, especially against the arbitrary rule of headmen, and they generally were.[33] In order to indicate, however, how local conditions made such struggles very complicated, and their immediate outcome at times less than an emancipation of small landholders, we shall follow in some detail Nishiwaki's case study of one such struggle in Niremata village, Mino province (Gifu prefecture).

FACTIOUS PEASANTS: NIREMATA, 1654

There are various overlapping dimensions to this case in Niremata village: struggles of elders to participate in village government, tensions resulting from the uneven impact of a drought on the harvest, a consolidation of lineage power, and an attempt to split the village into two. A partial apportioning of well water during the drought of 1654 had mixed results in Niremata. Upland fields could not be irrigated and thus

---

(Ichikawa Takeji, "Saku chihō ni okeru reizoku nōmin 'kakaebyakushō' no jittai," *Nagano*, no. 128 [1986]: 15).

31. Nishiwaki, "Nengu sanyō," 22. For the bakufu directive, see TKKz 5:155 (no. 2784, art. 8).

32. The famous prohibition on the sale of land was issued in 1643/3 (TKKz 4:121 [no. 2104, art. 3], 5:157 [no. 2786, art. 13]). For an English translation of this important law, see David John Lu, *Sources of Japanese History*, 2 vols. (New York: McGraw-Hill, 1974), 1:206–7. For a discussion of the law, see Ōishi, *Kyōhō kaikaku*, 9–43. The requirements of seals and receipts were legislated in 1644 (TKKz 4:122 [no. 2105, arts. 14, 15]).

33. Mizumoto, *Mura shakai*, 45, 56–60.

registered a serious crop loss. A denied request for a tax cut was followed by a request for an on-the-spot survey, addressed to the intendant's assistant (tedai) in charge of crop inspections. In this request the peasants promised either to accept and pay in full whatever lower amounts the inspector would set or, if the inspector did not act, to lower the tribute on the affected fields themselves and make up the deficit by additional levies from fields that had escaped damage from the drought. The inspector saw no reason to lower tribute rates, and so the trouble began.

A faction formed around Genzō (with 28 koku, only 5 less than the headman), the second largest landholder and one of the four kumi heads (there was also an elder). Niremata had a kokudaka of 526 koku and counted thirty-five resident landholders, eighteen of whom were independent tribute payers.[34] Genzō's faction held a total of some 120 koku. His followers tore up the agreement, insisting that tribute and corvée for the overlord be allocated across the board according to the regular rate regardless of losses. The other faction, led by the elder, the other three kumi heads, and the headman (the author of the agreement), was forced to borrow cash in various places to meet the village quota.

Around harvest time, in the tenth month, Genzō's faction wanted to split off from the village altogether and have its own headman, storehouse for tribute rice, runners, and so on. The intendant's assistant agreed only to partition the existing storehouse, providing two separate entrances, but Genzō rebelled: he destroyed the storehouse, scattered its instruments, stored the rice of his followers in his own granary, and again applied to secede. The headman argued that there was opposition from all the peasants because of the increase in administrative costs. Ultimately, the village split into two *Kumi* (not to be confused with the kumi of five-household groups) (see table 11).

Obviously, those who suffered losses beyond the village's average would benefit most from an adjustment of tribute amounts per field based on the actual condition of each field. These lowered amounts would be supplemented by others, who would pay above their normal share. We cannot know whether the secession drive was fueled by the uneven distribution of crop losses among the two factions, for we only have data on the headman's group (see fig. 3).

34. Nishiwaki, "Nengu sanyō," 24–38.

Table 11. Holdings of Niremata's Two Kumi, 1654

Headman's Kumi	Genzō's Kumi
33	
	28
24	
20	
19	
	15
14	14
13 13	13
12	
11	11 11
10 10	
9 9	9
8 8 8	8
7 7 7	7 7 7
5	5
4	
3 3	3
2 2	
	1

SOURCE: Computed from Nishiwaki, "Nengu sanyō," tables 2, 3, and 5 (pp. 28, 29, and 32).

NOTE: Each figure represents one household's kokudaka. The figures for the Genzō faction are approximate figures. For a different but very close set of figures, see Nishiwaki, "Mino Wajū," table 10 (p. 56).

It is worth noting, however, that all thirteen landholdings on Genzō's side were 15 koku (one) or less (the other twelve), while the headman's group included, besides some twenty-one peasants in that category, all four large holders of the village excluding Genzō (with 19, 20, 24, and 33 koku, the last one the headman's). Losses in the headman's faction

Fig. 3. Crop Loss per Holding Size in Niremata's Headman's Kumi, 1654

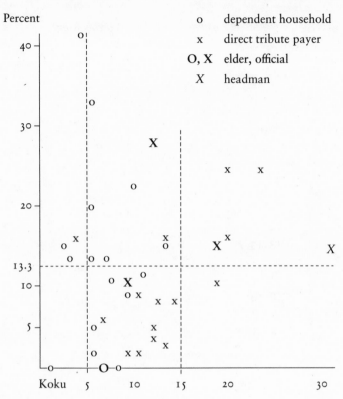

o   dependent household

x   direct tribute payer

O, X   elder, official

X   headman

SOURCE: Nishwaka, "Nengu sanyō," table 3 (p. 29).

averaged 13.3 percent of the quota.[35] As it turns out, sixteen house-holds (among whom there were nine dependents) had losses above the average, and nineteen households (including eight dependents, among whom were the only three that had no losses) had losses below the average. The bulk of the "small" peasants (seventeen out of twenty-two

35. Aono (*Warichiseishi*, 18, 51) estimates that if any adjustment of over 10 percent was needed to bring the actual yield in line with the putative yield, then a proportional distribution of the burden based on the land cadasters became irrational. Then villages had to resort to an equalization (based on an internal land survey they conducted themselves), or levy a fee per bale (*todai*, "a fee per *to* [one tenth of a koku or 18 liters]"), or, ultimately, perform a redistribution of land (jiwari).

households, with 5 to 15 koku) had less than average losses, but all six "very small" holders, of less than 5 koku (five of whom were dependents), lost more than the average (excluding one who had no losses).

What can we learn from this hard-to-follow detail? Its relevance has to do with the way tribute was paid: only independent landholders paid it, including the portion of their dependent holders' parcels if they had dependents. In the present case this applied mostly to landholders of over 15 koku, especially the larger landholders, among whom are the village officials. Six out of the seven such landholders in the headman's faction, it is worth noting, were also among those who suffered above average losses. While very small and small peasants undoubtedly could be ruined by a crop failure averaging only 13 percent (one holder of 1.9 koku registered a 52 percent loss; another of 4.4 koku, one of 42 percent), it was the large holders who lost most in absolute terms, since they also shouldered their dependents' tribute payments. Hence it was the large landholders who stood to gain most from a tax formula that supplemented their shortfalls with extra contributions from those with lesser losses, that is to say, from the "small peasants," who were mostly autonomous and without any dependents themselves. The loss of this stratum of small peasants alone constituted 38 percent of the headman's faction's total loss.

From a rational economic point of view, one may thus hypothesize that the wealthier peasants, led by the headman, sought to defend their interests through a tax formula that was most beneficial to themselves because it made the small independent peasants shoulder the burden. From this view also, Genzō would then represent the plight of the small peasants, which makes one wonder why more small peasants did not side with Genzō.

Before we turn to this question, a few observations are in order. This is a good illustration of how extramural authority affected village politics through the sheer mechanism of the village tribute quota. Weather conditions affected individual peasants unevenly, but the adjustment was communal, which in turn brought about a new unevenness, this one, however, the result of human decisions. While ultimately the overlords were the enemy, the immediate target of these struggles was within the village, where greater or lesser fairness could be achieved. And finally, the factions that formed were not mere collections of autonomous individuals differentiated only by holding size. The particular relation between dependents and their bosses in matters of tribute payments gave a special character to these factions.

Villages were structured by what one can call "lineages," although these were not exclusively blood lineages, since non-kin were among its members. Cognates were often set up as branch houses with various degrees of autonomy with regard to title to land. Even when they became independent, however, tribute-paying landholders remained tied to the main house through various obligations. Bond servants (nago, genin, and fudai, about which more will be said later) were even more dependent, even if they worked specific parcels of the main house land almost as if they owned them. This dependency related very concretely to the use of tools, equipment, and so on, but also to access to fertilizer, which in the early Tokugawa period was secured almost exclusively by cutting grass on the mountainsides. This access was not free. Not that extraordinary fees had to be paid—they were very modest—but this also was a matter of shares. And these shares were controlled by the lineages. Indeed, if one was not a member of a lineage, one could not have access to the mountains for fertilizer, wood, and so on. Outside the lineage there was no way to survive.

Genzō's village, Niremata, counted three lineages: the headman's, one headed by one of the kumi heads, and one headed by Genzō. Genzō's holding was second to the headman's and far larger than that of any of his lineage members. When Genzō decided to secede, he certainly had ambitions of becoming a headman in his own right, but his following was limited to his own lineage. The dispute over tribute allocation was thus used by Genzō as an occasion to play out lineage rivalries and increase his own power by adding to it the official dimension of a headmanship.[36]

Lineage cohesion was often reinforced ritually through ancestor worship, by members' belonging to the same ancestral Buddhist temple for annual or memorial rites for the dead. Niremata is an exemplary case of such practice. There were three temples in the village, one for each

36. One should recall that lineages were not sanctioned, either negatively or positively, by higher authority. For the overlords, the only official subdivision of the village was into kumi of five households, each with its own head. The authorities, however, may well have aimed at breaking lineage power indirectly, since intendants often required that kumi be organized strictly on a contiguous geographic basis; that is, they should not include just "kith and kin" (Ichikawa Yūichirō, *Saku chihō*, 25, 33. See also article 1 of the goningumi rules for Shimo-Sakurai village in Kita-Saku district [Shinano] of 1640 in appendix 2).

lineage: temple and lineage membership overlapped almost perfectly (only few households belonged to outside temples), even to the point that at the time of the split into two Kumi the two blood-related households of Genzō's group who shared the same temple as the head-man defected to the headman's Kumi.[37] This triggered a stern warning from Genzō that any further defections would result in the confiscation of the property by his Kumi! Effective or not, this threat illustrates the kind of power lineages presumed to wield even in matters of land-ownership.

Why did Genzō choose this moment to secede? The number and composition of Niremata's neighborhood kumi was not stable in the 1630s and 1640s: there were five in 1630, ten in 1634, and five again in 1641. It appears that while certain of these kumi were made up of lin-eage members only between 1638 and 1669, the smallest of the three lineages, Genzō's (who had been an elder and then kumi head all along), was dispersed over several kumi until 1649.[38] In that year, however, he was registered as head of a kumi in which all but one of the members of his lineage were gathered. The secession group that formed a separate Kumi five years later was thus nothing else but a single-lineage kumi. As in the case of Makibuse village in chapter 1, as well as in the case of Kodaira below, the bakufu rule concerning kumi formation seems to have been widely ignored, seriously affecting intra-village authority relationships.

The secession petition was signed not only by the five full members of Genzō's kumi: it bore sixteen signatures. Thus, within the secession move the voices of those without full political membership in the village suddenly became important, and to that extent the power of their leader and lineage head can be said to have been conditioned by their assent. It is clear, however, that such "emancipation" of dependents was cir-cumscribed by lineage control of the lives of its members. This is also evident if one compares the kumi membership list with the population register (shūmon aratamechō). Dependents do not figure at all on the first list, but they are marked as such on the second. On the latter their status as *kerai,* or vassals of their patron households, is clearly indi-cated. Thus the population registers, a neutral recording device in the eyes of the overlords, came to be used not only to record people but also to make their status official.

37. Nishiwaki, "Nengu sanyō," 34, 35.
38. Ibid., tables 7 and 8 (pp. 36, 37); idem, "Mino Wajū," 44.

FRACTIONED PEASANTS: NIREMATA, 1615–1680

A document of 1651 lists 33.7 titled peasants in Niremata. What could be the meaning of a fraction of a peasant? Here we face again the operation of shares, this time shares in the status of "titled peasant." Such a fractioned status, however, was not instituted by the higher authorities.

Niremata's household register (*iekazu aratamechō*) of 1635 reflects the overlords' perspective.[39] It lists 30 ie: 18 titled peasants and 12 "others," which include the headman, three temples, and a tobacco cutter, among others. This document, addressed by the headman to the intendant, is an *official report* of Niremata's corvée capacity. Another document, of 1651, lists a total of 42 ie (an increase of 40 percent over sixteen years), 33.7 of which owed corvée: 26 titled peasants and 16 others who held fractions (of 30, 50, 60, and 70 percent) of titled peasant shares with a total value of 7.7 shares, making a grand total of 33.7 titled peasants.[40] This document is an *internal village document* addressed by the five elders to the headman concerning the distribution of corvée due to the overlord. Some of these corvée-owing families were among those listed separately sixteen years earlier as "others." Many of the new full or fractional titled peasants were recently established branch families (with or without blood ties to their main families). The distribution of the required corvée among these ie reflects the village's adjustment to the establishment of new autonomous landholders.

The population registers (shūmon aratamechō) record this trend: between 1638 and 1646 all small landholders, even those of nonblood dependents (genin), are listed as independent units. From 1649 on, however, the genin are dropped, and we find only extended families listed. How does one make sense of these shifting ways of recording households, first as dependent (1635), then as independent (1638–46), and then again as dependent (1649)? This does not fit the pattern of gradual and progressive emancipation of dependents as a result of economic circumstances that Smith's description in his *Agrarian Origins of Modern Japan* leads one to expect.

39. Nishiwaki, "Mino Wajū," 43–44.
40. These figures are not computed from Nishiwaki's "Nengu sanyō," tables 2, 4, and 5 (pp. 28, 31, 32), which would lead to slightly different numbers; instead, they are taken from his "Mino Wajū," 43.

We get a first clue from two population registers from 1646 that differ in two major respects: none of the figures in the two documents are the same, and only one of the two bears a seal. This is an example of double bookkeeping. One register was destined for extramural *eyes,* namely, the intendant's, and was thus an official document; the other was for intramural *use,* reflecting genuine practice. The former lists 26 ie grouped in five kumi with a population of 224, the latter 41 real ie divided among eight kumi with a population of 267.

Nishiwaki explains the discrepancy as follows: the village underrepresented by fifteen the number of landholders in order to avoid an increase in tribute, especially corvée, which was assigned per ie, distributing this corvée among all the households, even those not registered as official tribute units. This created an ambivalent situation for newly established small holders. If they became full-blown titled peasants, their tax burden would increase, but with it would come full political membership. On the other hand, the titled peasants of old could only lessen their corvée burden by setting up small landholders to share this burden. The compromise was to limit the number of titled peasants but grant branch houses fractions of a "title," perhaps increasing the fraction as time went by and they became economically more secure, until they were "fully vested."

The bakufu was caught between two contradictory policies. On the one hand, especially after the famines and crop failures of the early 1640s, it had to help small landholders survive, which implied establishing them as autonomous tribute producers, as they were recorded on the land cadasters (the survey of 1623 showed fifty-two peasants, 30 percent of whom had holdings of less than five koku).[41] On the other hand, the real tribute payers were the wealthier peasants, those in the 10–30 koku bracket, to whom many of the smaller peasants were attached in some form of dependency. Nishiwaki's analysis of which bracket of holders held the highest percentage of taka (and hence produced the most tribute) in Niremata between 1637 and 1684 reveals an interesting pattern (see table 12). Before the 1630s the percentage of those with less than ten koku gradually increased to 13 percent. This trend was then interrupted during the crisis decade of the 1640s, when it dropped to between 3 and 7 percent. It picked up again in 1648, when it jumped to 35 percent, and it did not drop below 30 percent for

41. Nishiwaki, "Mino Wajū," table 7 (52).

Table 12. Categories of Holdings in Niremata, 1623–1684

	Taka Holdings (in koku)			
	0–10	10–20	20–30	30+
1623	10	25	55	8
1630	13	23	39	22
1642	3	32	26	37
1643	3	32	26	37
1644	5	8	38	47
1646	5	6	38	49
1647	7	16	33	42
1648	35	44	14	1
1651	39	36	18	6
1653	12	27	26	34
1657	29	55	6	9
1660	34	42	5	17
1669	39	39	11	9
1684	16	39	22	21

SOURCE: Adapted from Nishiwaki, "Mino Wajū," table 12 (pp. 61–62).

the next forty years, except in 1653, when it was 12 percent, and 1684, when it was 16 percent.

This curve seems to reflect the slow growth of small landholders, interrupted by the natural disasters of the 1640s, and their subsequent resurgence, perhaps as a result of bakufu policies. The question is, what happened to them during the half-decade or so when they disappeared from the statistics, and what was behind the sudden jump in 1648? The answer to the first question is simple: many of the small landholders were reabsorbed into their parent households. The larger members of the lineage tided them over during the bad years. This is one instance where one can observe, not an irreversible "emancipation" of dependents, but a circular movement whereby "independent" holders, in various ways still in need of the support of their parent households, returned to a position of full dependency.[42] It is important to note,

42. For instances of movement back and forth between the status of fully dependent bond servant (genin) and house-owning lifelong servant (fudai), and

however, that during this period far more non-kin than kin dependents were set up as independent branch houses. In other words, although non-kin dependents were "treated as kin," they seem to have been left to their own devices in times of crisis.[43]

This practice of absorbing small units into larger ones went directly counter to the intendant's policy of establishing small independent landholders. This is clear from the difference between two tax rosters (*menwarichō*) submitted to the intendant ten days apart, which explains the sudden jump in the numbers of small holders. The first roster, dated 1648/11/11, listing the names of twenty-nine tribute owners with their individual assessed values, was obviously returned by the intendant to be replaced by a second roster, dated 1648/11/21, which was almost twice as long, listing fifty-two names.[44] Although the total village-assessed value and the number of its tribute *payers* is the same on both lists, the second list certainly reflects the intendant's effort to identify, and thereby perhaps empower, the individual tribute *producers* and increase the number of households available for corvée.

The additional producers on the new list were overwhelmingly family members, especially direct descendants: thirteen sons and grandsons, two brothers, and two servants (genin). This does not mean that they were independent, because the original parent families continued to use their own seals for them on official documents. Neither were they all small owners: the headman's 72 koku of the first list was broken down on the second into 33 koku for himself, 23 for his son, 13 for his grandson, and 2 for a bond servant. It is among these new additions, however, that the "fractional peasants" appear. For example, the servant (incidentally, the younger brother of a 13-koku holder) is a 0.3 titled peasant; two others, with 8 and 10 koku, are both 0.7 titled peasants.[45]

---

between the status of fudai and yakunin and back to fudai over two generations, see Minegishi, *Kinsei mibunron,* 142–46.

43. In 1644 there were thirteen branch households in Niremata, eleven of which were not related by kinship to their main households (nine had no holdings). Smith (*Agrarian Origins,* 15 ff.), among others, stresses the fictional kin relationship that servants had with their masters' families and that they "were often maintained by virtue of an obligation to keep them rather than for strictly economic reasons" (29).

44. For the two lists, see Nishiwaki, "Mino Wajū," table 13 (64).

45. Data computed from ibid., table 15 (64); and idem, "Nengu sanyō," table 5 (32).

These gradations reflect to some degree holding size, although as many as nine fully titled peasants had smaller holdings than that of a 0.7 peasant, and also degrees of dependency to the main house as well as shares in political power. This status was not reflected on the tax rosters, but on the population rosters, where most of these peasants were also recorded as *heya-sumi,* or "living in a room" (of the main family).

Although the authorities recognized any taka holder as a peasant, they ultimately came to recognize, via the population registers, the lineage-based hierarchy among holders within the village. Here the trend was to cap the number of full-status peasants (eighteen in 1651; fifteen two years later; then fourteen; and finally thirteen in 1669), limit the number of official branch houses and restrict these to kin, and ultimately, in 1684, to absorb newcomers into the village (mainly craftsmen and nonpeasants) within the lineage framework explicitly as retainers. Only in the 1680s was the status of branch families as autonomous units acknowledged within the village.[46] By 1684 the heya-sumi category had disappeared, as had all extended families (see table 13).

The Niremata case illustrates the impact of population growth on village life in seventeenth-century Japan: how the village adjusted its internal social and political structure and how this adjustment had to take into account the overlord's own reactions to this growth and, in a feedback movement, to the village adjustments to his reactions. The political, social, and economic status of new households shifted several times over a sixty- to seventy-year period. Let us now closely follow an effort by some dependents to change their status.

FROM TRIBUTE PRODUCERS TO TRIBUTE PAYERS: SHIMO-KAIZE, 1687

Peasants were hierarchized according to degrees of autonomy, as Thomas C. Smith reported in the first chapters of his book. Titled peasants with extended households had a number of dependents aside from kin: lifelong servants (fudai), without separate living quarters and mostly single; and bond servants (genin), with or without separate living

46. Data are from Nishiwaki, "Mino Wajū," tables 10, 13, and 17 (56, 59, 78).

Table 13. Household Patterns and Branch Houses in
Niremata, 1669 and 1684

Types of Households	1669[a]	1684[b]
Linealogical composition		
Titled peasants	13	—
Kin branch houses	2	—
Non-kin branch houses	2	—
Total	17	34
Kin co-residents	22	0
Non-kin co-residents	2	0
Total	24	0
Nuclear family		
Main family	5	17
Kin branch houses	4	9
Non-kin branch houses	0	4
[unclear]	[2]	[9]
Total	11	39
Extended family		
Main family	7	0
Kin branch houses	0	0
Non-kin branch houses	2	0
[unclear]	[0]	[0]
Total	9	0

[a] Headman's Kumi only.
[b] Both Kumi.
SOURCE: Compiled from data in Nishiwaki, "Mino Wajū,"
tables 10 and 17 (pp. 56 and 78).

quarters, single or married, with or without a plot more or less their
own. One step above them were semiautonomous branch houses
(kadoya), which were servants set up in a separate "dwelling," or
shack. These structures, often located at the entrance to the compound,
quite commonly were no more than hole dwellings with a pointed,
thatched umbrella roof reaching to the ground, identical to prehistoric
Yayoi dwellings. Also considered as dependents were indentured servants, who were almost always unmarried. Extended families set up

branch households (bunke or kakae) as titled peasants or not. They all remained incorporated into a lineage structure.

The ladder of emancipation and prestige extended through the various ranks of bond servants to semi- and fully established branch houses, titled peasants, and eventually patron household if one established one's own branch family within the old lineage, or beyond if one broke off from it to establish a separate one. Much of this classification was based on ownership of house and land, but ownership was a very fuzzy notion, as we shall see. Additional factors intervened. One was status, which was not unambiguously connected with economic wealth. A second factor was political power in the village as lodged in the village council and the lineages. A third was whether or not one paid one's tribute portion of the village quota directly or not.

All these factors interacted, and there were no strict rules that applied automatically. Moreover, if tradition or custom were invoked, the question often became whether or not the particular norm applied, as Wittgenstein has acutely observed. Hence, disputes led frequently to suits settled either through conciliation, often by Buddhist priests and elders from neighboring villages, or by an intendant. The supporting data in these suits were official documents. Composed for the lordly purposes of controlling population and extracting economic surpluses, these documents were used politically within the villages in status disputes.

Disputes concerning status, position, and hence power in the village as expressed in these documents often had a certain degree of urgency added to them when one party refused to sign the population register that was just about to be turned over to the intendant (as we saw in Ken's case, in chapter 1). The refusal to sign under one's entry because of the status attached to it drew the higher authorities into these disputes. The examples of this strategy that follow are from the eastern part of Shinano province, mostly from the Kita-Saku district.

The first case is a lawsuit from Shimo-Kaize (1687–88) submitted to the intendant by three plaintiffs, Tokubei, Kichibei, and Hikozaemon, against their patron, Hanbei, concerning their disputed status as fully established branch houses (kakaeya) or semiautonomous branch houses (kadoya). There are six documents: the original suit; an official written response, which the defendant was invited to submit to the intendant according to custom; and four additional recorded testimonies (*kuchi-*

gaki) by the headman, the titled peasants, and other witnesses, the last three dated eight months after the suit was initiated.[47] The texts that follow are edited translations, modified for clarity.

1. Tokubei, Kichibei, and Hikozaemon's suit (1687/11)

1. In past years, we were recorded every year in the population and kumi register as Hanbei's fully established branch houses (*kakaeya*), but this year Hanbei registered us according to a new procedure as [only] semiestablished branch houses (*kadoya*). We had a conference with Hanbei and told him that we would not affix our seal to the registers unless we were entered as kakaeya as in the past. Then the headman and the village council urged us to affix our seal; otherwise if the entries were changed, the rosters could not be presented to the shogunal authorities [in time]. Since we did not wish to go as far as to cause trouble to the authorities, we affixed our seals.

Twice we went to the higher officials about our registration in the population roster as kadoya, and we explained our ancestry to them. They suggested that Hanbei change the entries back to kakaeya. Now, because of the selfish (*wagamama*) behavior of Hanbei, we request to change kumi away from Hanbei. Please summon him and communicate our request.

2. The three plaintiffs and the defendant share a common "ancestor" three generations back through their "great-grandfather," Umanosuke [the three plaintiffs were related through Umanosuke's adopted son, originally the son of an uncle (see fig. 4)]. When Umanosuke retired, he gave half of his 44 koku to his son Goemon, keeping the other half for himself. At his death in 1645, this latter portion was divided into three between Tokuzaemon (Goemon's son), Shige'emon (Umanosuke's adopted son), and Shin'emon (Umanosuke's son by a woman other than his wife). This was witnessed by two villagers (Daitokuin and Chūemon) and a peasant from the new branch village (Jirōemon).

3. Shirōemon and Bun'emon were at Umanosuke's funeral, but all memorial services down to the thirty-third year were conducted by the three inheritors (Shige'emon, Tokuzaemon, and Shin'emon), to which people in the village can testify. Now, Hanbei, in his selfish manner, maintains that because we are within the (undivided) 44 kokudaka, we are only kadoya. But Bun'emon, Shirōemon, Shige'emon, Shin'emon, and Tokuzaemon, all five of them (individually), have a part of this 44 koku and have contributed the yearly tribute and corvée separately according to their taka.

47. The six documents of this case can be found in NAK-KS2 (1): 946–52 (no. 476). The first three are also reprinted in Aoki Kōji, *Hennen hyakushō ikki shiryō shūsei*, 17 vols. (San'ichi shobō, 1979–93), 1:568–71.

Fig. 4. Umanosuke's Lineage, Shimo-Kaize, 1630s–1680s

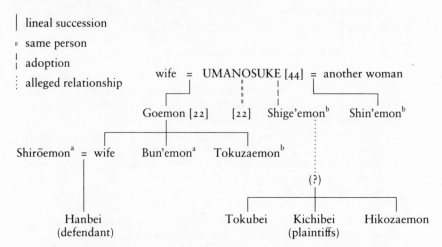

| lineal succession
‖ same person
¦ adoption
⋮ alleged relationship

wife = UMANOSUKE [44] = another woman

Goemon [22] [22] Shige'emon[b] Shin'emon[b]

Shirōemon[a] = wife Bun'emon[a] Tokuzaemon[b]

(?)

Hanbei
(defendant)

Tokubei Kichibei Hikozaemon
(plaintiffs)

[a] present at Umanosuke's funeral in 1645

[b] inheritors of Umanosuke's 22 koku and sponsors of all memorial services

NOTE: Based on the plaintiffs' argument in paragraphs 2 and 3 of their suit. Some data in this chart, especially the relationship of the plaintiffs to the lineage, were challenged later in the suit. Moreover, Shin'emon had a son by the same name. Bracketed numbers represent koku.

We testify to the truth of the above and request that Shin'emon and Tokuzaemon be summoned and that you inquire with them about this matter, and that you summon Hanbei and reach a decision.

1687/11
Shige'emon's children from Kami-Kaize,
Tokubei
Kichibei
Hikozaemon

The plaintiffs build their argument about their status as full-fledged branch houses on genealogy, or more properly *linealogy* (as we shall see via Shige'emon), and on the performance of memorial services. They maintain (against Hanbei) that the original estate was divided into separate tribute units. Thus, as "children" of one of the owners (Shige'emon), they cannot be considered Hanbei's dependents (kadoya). As full branch houses, they would not be on an equal footing with Hanbei, their patron, but as such they certainly would be full lineage members in their own right.

Hanbei's counterargument in the reply requested by the intendant follows. He opens with an attack on the alleged linealogy and responds to the allegations one by one in great detail. Without the necessary local knowledge of the kin and power relations, which constituted an invisible subtext, the detail must have been as confusing for the intendant as it is for us. Reading Hanbei's reply, one can thus put oneself without much effort into the sandals of the intendant; reader positions are always distant ones, though not always equidistant.

2. Hanbei's Response to the Intendant (1687/12/4)

1. *Re:* The reasons why the three plaintiffs are [only] kadoya. Their grandfather was Bunzō [and not Umanosuke], who had an older brother, Bunshirō. My great-grandfather Umanosuke bought them as lifelong bond servants (*fudai*), and hence they were supposed to serve him forever. However, because they had served since their youth, they sued for their freedom, which was granted them, and so they were established under Umanosuke as his kadoya. In addition Umanosuke gave them the land they had brought under cultivation during their service years. Bunshirō's corvée obligation as kadoya was twenty days of labor every month; Bunzō's was fifteen. Bunshirō married Tsuru, one of Umanosuke's bond servants [*gejo*, the term for a female genin], having two daughters by her: Miya, who left Umanosuke's household to work in a temple when Umanosuke's wife died, and Musu, who bought her freedom with cash and married someone from another place. When Bunshirō died, he gave his land to Bunzō, who became a kadoya.

2. This year, at the transplanting of the rice seedlings (*taue*), only Kisaburō's [another recalcitrant kadoya, who was not one of the three plaintiffs] and Tokubei's wives showed up, while they themselves did not come and help [as they should have as kadoya]. So I went to Chūemon, the headman, to officially request that he inform the higher authorities and seek a decision, to which Chūemon replied to wait until he got more information about the matter. After some postponement, Chūemon, Zenzaemon, and Heizaemon [the headman and two village officials, presumably] communicated that the men in question offered their apologies for not showing up at the transplanting of the rice. The same three officials also offered some sake with their own apologies, which I accepted, and I was asked to forget the whole thing, which I did.

3. To record them as kadoya is not a new practice. In 1644, under intendant X [named], the population registers and household rosters recorded Yaemon [?] as Umanosuke's kadoya and Shige'emon as Shirōemon's. [Here Shige'emon, of crucial importance to the plaintiffs, is argued by Hanbei to have been a kadoya, certainly not on an equal footing with the other four inheritors of the estate.] These documents, written by Daitokuin with all seals of the village attached after a full

meeting, list the division of fields. The following year, Umanosuke passed away, but because Shiroemon was a grandson-in-law, he could not inherit the kadoya [Shige'emon, who had been his kadoya thus far].

Subsequently, under three different intendants [named], the entries are still kadoya, but as headman [Hanbei had been headman, as Umanosuke had been] I had difficulties with that. In the current population register submitted to the intendant, there are also kakaeya entries. However, given the fact that these persons are in that situation [of dependency toward me] and cannot but obey me, ultimately it does not matter how they are registered.

Now, you may ask, why [after just saying that the label does not matter] I registered them, nevertheless, on this year's registers as kadoya. The reason is as follows. A decision was made in the village council to [upgrade and] register as kakaeya relatives (uncles, brothers, etc.) of full kumi members [only titled peasants were full kumi members]. So we registered them all equally as kakaeya. The above persons, however, have been kadoya for generations, and they are therefore not like the others and should not be registered as if they were their equals; hence their registration as kadoya.

4. *Re:* The signing of the goningumi register by these three as kadoya. This whole thing was triggered by Kisaburō's refusal to sign as kadoya, and the dispute was brought before the headman, who came to me. I stressed to him again and again that I could in no way remove the kadoya entry from Kisaburō's name, and I also gave him reasons why the others, Kichibei, Hikozaemon, Tokubei, and so on, should remain registered as kadoya and told him that each of them should affix their seals in the presence of the others. So the headman called them all and explained to them in detail why they should be registered as kadoya, to which they all agreed, and thus they affixed their seals to the goningumi roster. This is the truth, which you can verify with the headman and the titled peasants of the village.

5. *Re:* The adoption. The 22 koku of the retired Umanosuke were inherited by Tokuzaemon, Shin'emon, and Shige'emon. The land division was witnessed by Jiroemon, Chūemon, and Daitokuin. You can ask the latter two and have them testify.

6. *Re:* The funeral and memorial services. Because there was no unhulled rice for the funeral, my father, Shiroemon, who was employed by the intendant's assistant (*tedai*), Ichikawa Gohei [from Gorobe-shinden?], borrowed six bales from the storehouse. All other expenses were divided into two by Tokuzaemon and Shin'emon, and they were also responsible for the memorial services from the first through the seventh year and did not collect any contributions from Shige'emon. [However,] after that, Shin'emon (Umanosuke's son by a woman other than his wife) and my uncle Bun'emon did *not* set them [Bunzō and Bun-shirō] free. Their only proof that they were set free is that they, as life-

long bond servants, made a request to be set free, but what they said [about this] to the authorities is a lie, which has been the cause for a longstanding grudge and quarrels between us.

As for the remaining memorial services, I do not know about Shin'emon, but as far as my uncle Tokuzaemon is concerned, because he was only four when Umanosuke died [he did not contribute], my father, Shirōemon, took care of all the services.

7. *Re:* The holdings of Kichibei, Hikozaemon, and Tokubei. On the cadasters of the 1629 land survey, Bunshirō and Bunzō were recorded as Umanosuke's dependents [co-residents?] (*uchi*). Next, on the cadasters of the 1676 land survey, Shigehei, Hikozaemon, and Kisaburō were recorded as Shirōemon's dependents (*uchi*).

8. *Re:* The rewriting as kakae on the new population register. There was a dispute concerning signing the new register under the heading of kadoya. The matter was brought before the two intendants [named], and their opinion was that if I by all means insisted on their being kadoya, this would lead to an endless dispute and prevent the registry from being submitted in due time. Therefore, the headman and the titled peasants consulted with each other, and they said that it did not matter what was entered as long as the registers were submitted in time, and so I changed the entry and submitted it with my seal.

1687/12
Hanbei

Hanbei's argument is very complex, but I shall limit myself to the main points. The hierarchical relationship between fudai, genin, and kadoya is clearly stated. Fudai are bought, usually at a very young age from outside the village. Prices for fudai are rarely mentioned in documents, but in Hirabara, a few kilometers to the north, a ten-year-old boy was bought for three *bu* (worth about 1.5 koku of rice on the market), and a four-year-old girl for six bales (about 3.6 koku of unhulled rice) in the 1650s.[48] They were virtually house slaves for life unless their

48. The prices are from Ichikawa Yūichirō, *Saku chihō,* 119; the equivalent in rice for the gold price is calculated from Ono Takeo, *Edo bukka jiten,* Edo fūzoku zushi, 6 (Tenbōsha, 1989), 451; the bales of unhulled rice are calculated at the rate of one bale per 0.6 koku (NAK-T 5, "Furoku," 4). Brutal as this practice may seem, these children were seen, perhaps all too euphemistically, as rescued (quite a few of them had the name Kaisuke, "bought and rescued" [Ichikawa Yūichirō, *Saku chihō,* 119]). They were certainly given a better livelihood than children who are recruited into prostitution for foreigners in Southeast Asia; nowadays recruiters exchange television sets for children, or they buy them still in the womb (Murray Kempton, "A New Colonialism," *New York Review of Books* 30, no. 19 [1992]: 39).

freedom was purchased, as in the case of the two female genin. "Freedom," the transition from fudai to kadoya, meant that they were "given" the land they themselves had brought under cultivation, but most of their labor was still for their former owner, who also paid the necessary tribute on their land. The refusal by some of the kadoya to help out with transplanting the rice seedlings at Hanbei's signaled that they did not consider themselves kadoya owing labor to a boss. In addition, Hanbei's case rests on documents that testify to their kadoya status. As in the Niremata case, a clear line was drawn between dependents who were relatives of titled peasants and those who were not (most kadoya).

Another source provides social background data on the stratified minisociety of Shimo-Kaize village. In 1643 Shimo-Kaize's population of 218 lived in thirty-one main homesteads, three kado dwellings, and eleven long houses. Three households each had 1 "dependent," and thirteen houses had a total of 30 servants (male and female).[49] Eleven of these servants were recorded as *hikan* (a rather pejorative term for "serf," common in pre-Tokugawa times). The village kokudaka was 336 koku, averaging 10.8 per household; the largest holding was 22 koku, the smallest 2.3. Thus we know that Umanosuke was the largest holder of the village, since he had 22 koku after he retired. He also had a rather large house, because his must have been one of the three houses of 27 *tsubo* (930 square feet, or 90 square meters). The kadoya, on the other hand, were housed in buildings that varied from 425 square feet, to half that size. Most of the long houses measured only some 210 square feet.[50] By the time this suit was filed, however, many of the kadoya must have already been promoted to kakae as a result of the gradual breakup of the larger holdings.

Next, the defendant Hanbei submits a recorded testimony that is certified as true by the headman.

3. Hanbei's Recorded Testimony, Certified by the Headman (1687/12)

1. *Re:* The question that the three were kadoya for generations but now claim that they are kakae. They filed a suit concerning this dispute. In my response, I claim that my great-grandfather Umanosuke bought Bunshirō and Bunzō, that they should have worked for him forever, but that they were set free[, etc.]. Now, when I investigated who received this land that they had developed and what Bunjirō and Bunzō were in rela-

49. These data are from Ichikawa Yūichirō, *Saku chihō*, tables 2, 8, and 9 (77, 100, 101).
50. Ibid., 78, 79, 119, 124.

tion to the three plaintiffs, I found that the two cadasters had entries as I claimed and that Bunzō was Tokubei's *oyabun* [real or relational parent or patron], Hikozaemon's father-in-law, and Kichibei's grandfather; and that this Bunzō was the one whom the three suitors claim to be Shige'emon. Bunshirō is Bunzō's elder brother. Now, who bought Bunzō and Bunshirō as fudai, and is there proof that the two performed service for the indicated days per month? They were bought by Umanosuke from X [named]; there is no proof that they performed the alleged service, but everybody in the village knows that they did.

2. *Re:* The yashiki [homestead and compound] of the three plaintiffs. Is it in my yashiki or is it separate [an important question to determine their degree of autonomy]? Until forty-three years ago, Bunzō and Bunjirō were put up on Goemon's yashiki, which was part of the inheritance of 22 koku he received from Umanosuke. But there were difficulties with building a [new] residence for them. Luckily, there was an empty building in a separate yashiki, which is where they were put up, and that is where the three plaintiffs live now. As far as the yearly tribute is concerned, until twelve years ago, the 44 koku were recorded as one registered holding, but they had informally (*naisho ni*) divided it among themselves, and each individually paid tribute as allocated by me. Because this was difficult, the headman divided the yearly tribute as well as the corvée into separate parts.

1687/12
Hanbei
I certify that the above is true
Yahei, Headman

Yahei, the new headman who replaced Chūemon, vouches for Hanbei's version of the three plaintiffs' ancestry: they are mutually related and tied to a kadoya. Equally important are the location of their living quarters (whether they are within or outside someone's compound—he confirms that they now live in Hanbei's grandfather's compound) and their independent tax status. The latter seems to indicate that the village headman had treated them as independent tribute payers.

These three documents were apparently insufficient for the intendant to make up his mind on this question of status, because seven months later three additional recorded testimonies were produced, the first one by the headman and the thirteen titled peasants.

4. Recorded Testimony by the Headman and the Thirteen Titled Peasants (1688/7/11)

1. We have been asked whether the three plaintiffs in question are Hanbei's kakaeya or his kadoya. Since we are unaware of circumstances long past, we do not know whether they are one or the other. They were listed separately and they paid tribute and corvée separately.

2. The three allege that their grandfather Shige'emon had been adopted by Hanbei's great-grandfather Umanosuke and that they were attached to the portion of the land on which Umanosuke retired and which he passed on to Shige'emon. Now, is there certainty that Shige'emon was Umanosuke's adopted son? It is hard to tell whether he was his adopted son or his kadoya because it is too long ago and the situation is not clear. Of course, as far as the division of Umanosuke's 44 koku is concerned, the three plaintiffs have today a portion thereof, but on what basis this was divided, that we do not know.

3. Now the question: Did the three plaintiffs pay their tribute and corvée separately and have they been listed separately on the name registers since Shige'emon's generation or not; and if not, then since when and for how many years have they been paying taxes separately? Afterwards [after Shige'emon's time] they made all their contributions, tax and corvée included, together with Hanbei, but they delivered separately the taxes and corvée of 1676, twelve years ago. Now, if further asked on what grounds this separate payment of twelve years ago took place or how the division of land occurred, we do not know, but Hanbei was headman then.

4. Hanbei alleges that the three plaintiffs are without a doubt kadoya because every year since his great-grandfather's generation down to his own they performed kadoya corvée and the villagers all know that. When investigating the truth of Hanbei's allegation, we found that although we do not know what will happen now, every year at the time of the transplanting of the rice seedlings, the three, including their wives, without exception helped on Hanbei's paddies. This is what Kichizaemon said. As for others who may have helped on that occasion, there were others, although we do not know their number.

5. Hanbei alleges that forty-four years ago, Shige'emon was recorded as kadoya on the population and house registers, documents certified by Daitokuin and separately by the whole village with the seals of the peasants. Because this was so long ago, we were not there when these documents were written, but [when we checked them] we found that it was Daitokuin's writing and that all the peasants certified those documents with their seals.

6. Hanbei alleges that "under the next three intendants, the three plaintiffs were always listed as kadoya; but that under the last intendant they were also sometimes registered as kakae; ultimately, it did not matter how they were registered since they were his dependents, who had to obey him." Is this true? In those days population registers were compiled only every five or ten years. Hanbei in the end could not remember for sure, and he and Zenzaemon admitted not knowing whether it was kakae or kadoya.

1688/7/11
Yahei, Headman
Thirteen titled peasants

The village leaders are unwilling to pronounce on the status of the plaintiffs. They state, however, that the trio was attached to Shige'emon's land (and not Goemon's). Thus they corroborate the plaintiff's alleged filiation to Umanosuke via Shige'emon. The question then became whether Shige'emon was an adopted son or a kadoya. They say that they do not know because it was too long ago but that documents exist that could verify this. What is puzzling is that the plaintiffs seem to have become independent tribute payers, at least informally, when Hanbei was headman. His argument, however, clearly rests on his assumption that no matter how they were registered, they were his dependents.

Next is a recorded testimony (with the headman's certification) by Shin'emon, whose father, of the same name, was Umanosuke's son by a woman other than his wife.

5. Shin'emon's Recorded Testimony, Certified by the Headman (1688/7/11)

1. My father, Shin'emon, is Umanosuke's son by another woman. Of Umanosuke's 44 koku, 22 went to Goemon, son by his wife; the other 22 went to Shige'emon, Tokuzaemon, and myself. Shige'emon, Tokuzaemon, and I attended Umanosuke's funeral. Furthermore, Umanosuke's 44 koku are now in the hands of Bun'emon, Shirōemon, Shige'emon, Tokuzaemon, and myself; we pay tribute and corvée separately according to our taka. I looked into this; also into what the three plaintiffs said. My father, Shin'emon, died ten years ago, and because he was *non compos mentis (fuchōhō)*, he did not tell me anything. As to the division of the 22 koku, I do not know of a document to that effect, but Shige'emon, the *oya* [parent or boss, patron] of the three plaintiffs, received 5 *shō* [0.05 koku] of paddies and 5 shō of buckwheat dry fields from Umanosuke when the latter died. At the funeral were Tokuzaemon and myself. The three plaintiffs did not help. Tribute and corvée were paid separately.

2. This is my pedigree. Hence I have been asked whether the three plaintiffs are Hanbei's kadoya, and since I line up in the lineage at the same [generational] level as the three plaintiffs, I was requested to talk about the times since Hanbei's great-grandfather Umanosuke, on the supposition that I was knowledgeable about them. But as mentioned earlier, since my father was *non compos mentis,* he did not transmit to me any details. However, in Umanosuke's generation, the three plaintiffs' oya, Shige'emon, worked for Umanosuke fifteen days a month.

1688/7/11
Shin'emon
Certified as true by Yahei, Headman

Everyone is evasive; collective memory seems blocked, this time through the state of *non compos mentis* of a conveniently dead man who while still alive might have casually provided his son with the right information. But he did not. A certain labor dependency of Shige'emon vis-à-vis Umanosuke is acknowledged, but this dependency is not spelled out as one typical of a kadoya. Everybody seems to sympathize with the plaintiffs by not providing the crucial information that would otherwise nail them.

Finally, there is a recorded testimony by two of the three men who arranged Umanosuke's inheritance: Daitokuin (a Buddhist priest, judging by his name) and Chūemon.

6. Recorded Testimony by Chūemon and Daitokuin (1688/7/11)

1. This concerns the three plaintiffs' allegations that: they are not kadoya; their oya, Shige'emon, is Umanosuke's adopted son; the 22 koku of the retired Umanosuke were divided into three and given to Tokuzaemon (son of Goemon, Umanosuke's son by his wife), Shin'emon (son by another woman), and his adopted son Shige'emon; this division is well known to Daitokuin and Chūemon from this village and Jirōemon from the branch village. We were summoned and asked to investigate.

Forty-four years ago, still alive, Umanosuke told us that he wanted the 5 shō of paddies and dry fields each to go to Shige'emon. He died that year. In the spring of the following year the three of us got together and made the transfer to Shige'emon, but the talk about dividing the 22 koku into three is a lie. As to the adopted status of Shige'emon, the three plaintiffs alleged that we knew that well, but we do not know whether he had been adopted or not. We have not heard rumors that he was adopted or that he was a kadoya.

1688/7/11
Chūemon
Daitokuin

Almost a year after the suit began, in a testimony by men who knew Umanosuke, it turns out that Umanosuke's property was not divided into three as alleged all along. But at the same time, they are ignorant of Shige'emon's adoption or his kadoya status! It is striking how just about everything is a matter of dispute: the status of kadoya or kakae, the relationship of adoption, the question of inheritance, the meaning of joint versus separate tribute payments.

We do not know the outcome of this suit, but it seems likely that the result somehow favored the plaintiffs. This absence of a clear settlement, which would result in one side's admitting defeat, is rather typical, as we shall see. One also senses the lineage tensions between Hanbei's side and Shin'emon's; village politics were often lineage politics. Overall, one also has the impression of a status system in transition.

FROM TRIBUTE PAYERS TO FULL PEASANTS: KODAIRA, 1629–1849

Titled peasants are often understood to be descendants of peasants entered on the early land surveys as landowners and tribute payers. Ancestry and ownership would thus be necessary to qualify for the title of "titled peasant." Accordingly, one would expect that as the population grew (especially during the seventeenth century, when the growth rate was 50 percent) and the number of kin-related small landholders that branched off from the original households increased, the number of titled peasants also increased. On the other hand, if many new peasants came from the ranks of non-kin dependents (who were not descendants from original titled peasants) and ancestry was more important than landownership, one might expect nontitled peasants to outnumber titled peasants. *Honbyakushō,* "titled peasant," is specifically a title, and its rarity points to privilege and limited access. Ancestry, however, was only one way to anchor and preserve this privilege against other claimants, and it was not an absolute criterion: it was only one strategy among others to secure distinction and status.

Thus, a number of questions have to be answered with regard to the status of titled peasant. Why did the number of titled peasants tend to become limited? Whence the rarefaction? What criteria controlled entry to this status group—ancestry, ownership, wealth? And did the overlords or the village council control these criteria? How did lineage power intersect with the power or prestige individuals derived from the title? Was this symbolic capital—which within the village was political capital—immune to devaluation (could one lose one's status as a titled peasant) or marketable (could one sell or buy the status as such)? Could one transfer the title independently from the land, or were the two inseparable? I touched upon some of these questions in chapter 1. Here I shall discuss them more fully.

In discussing the original titled peasants, identified as homestead owners in the early registers, I have described their function in rather vague terminology: they were accountable for the tribute, responsible for it, and they channeled it. This language is intentional, because nontitled peasants also produced and contributed to tribute and corvée. The original titled peasants were clearly the economically wealthier peasants, if for no other reason than that they had homesteads. The basis for the title was thus economic and rested on ownership not simply of land but of homesteads as well. By the same token, it was also political, since it was the local elite that became titled. The term "titled peasant" thus has two sides, an extramural and an intramural one, the former having to do with responsibility for tribute and corvée, the latter (both reinforced by and the basis for the former) with local status and power.

The early titled peasants managed land, not uncommonly estates of more than one hundred koku, and a number of dependents co-residing on the homestead as well. Gradually these estates were divided and parceled out to dependents, who thereby became economically independent to some degree from the original owner, who nevertheless retained his preeminent position within the expanding lineage by registering the various households (ie) and their land as being part of (buntsuke) or within (uchizuke) the main holding. Often, but not always, the former referred to kin (affines, descendants, and relatives), the latter to non-kin.[51] Genealogically, or perhaps more precisely, *linealogically*, these new units were branch houses of the main house.

In Shimo-Kaize, as we have just seen, there was a great difference between kadoya and kakae, which I referred to as semi-established and fully established branch houses, respectively; and the trend was "emancipatory" from kadoya to kakae. The evolving relationship of these kakae to the titled peasants can be described as follows. The number of titled peasants increased until the last decades of the seventeenth century, when they appear to have reached a quota in most villages that was maintained for about a hundred years. During that century the number of kakae grew, but then it decreased and by the end of the period, in the 1860s, they had virtually disappeared, having become titled peasants.[52] These turning points in the trajectory of the relationship between kakae and titled peasants need explanation. Why a growth in the numbers first of titled peasants, then of kakae, and then once again of titled peasants?

To follow this trajectory, the struggles that determined it have to be analyzed and the question of status that constitutes their center

51. Ichikawa Takeji, "Kakaebyakushō," 6.
52. For instance, in Ozawa village of Saku district in 1704, 33 percent of the peasants were kakae, but in 1864 all kakae had disappeared. The same drastic drop occurred in nineteen out of the twenty-five villages that constituted the Tanoguchi bakufu fief, of which Ozawa was a part (ibid., tables 3 and 4 [7, 8]).

addressed. With this in mind, we shall follow in some detail the history of Kodaira village (presently part of the town of Mochizuki in Kita-Saku district) as presented to us by Ozaki Yukiya.[53] In 1647 its assessed yield was 175 koku, making it a small village.

In 1629 Kodaira counted thirteen peasant owners of residences (yashiki), making them "titled peasants" (see table 14). In 1643 there were twenty: the original thirteen plus two branch houses, all holders of between 8 and 21 koku, and five others with holdings between 4 and 8 koku as yet without homesteads. Since the latter five were entitled to a *yashikibiki,* an exemption of tribute owed on their residence, they must have been titled peasants as well.[54] In addition, there were two other peasants with less than 1 koku who differed from the other twenty in that they did not enjoy the exemption; they were nontitled peasants.[55] The number of titled peasants thus increased from thirteen to twenty in about a dozen years.[56] Two hundred years later, in 1849, there were twenty-one Kodaira peasants marked in the registers as *osabyakushō* ("head peasant"), a variant of *honbyakushō.* Nothing seems to have changed, yet this *longue durée* is filled with colorful events.

The 1677 population roster shows clear status divisions. The peasant population, aside from one outcaste, then comprised twenty titled peasants (including seven patrons), thirteen clients (including three kadoya), and a number of bond servants (fudai and genin). Economically, however, the members of the two main groups are not always distinguishable. Although all holders of more than eight koku are titled peasants, some clients have equally large or even larger holdings and bond servants as well. The three clients and the one outcaste have holdings larger than that of the smallest titled peasant (under 1 koku). Nine of the clients, however, have no holdings at all (mudaka).

Over the next twenty years two great shifts occurred. In 1694 one titled peasant, a sake brewer (whose descendant is still in business

53. Ozaki Yukiya, "Kinsei sonraku naibu no mibun kaisō ni tsuite: Shinano-kuni Saku-gun Kodaira-mura kakaebyakushō mondai o chūshin ni," *Nagano* 29, no. 8 (1977): 752–68, no. 9 (1977): 815–30.

54. In Matsumoto domain this amount was 1 koku (Naitō, *Honbyakushō taisei,* 85).

55. Although the five holders of 4 to 8 koku had no *yashiki,* they were nevertheless granted the *yashikibiki,* which means that they must have been (new) titled peasants (Ozaki, "Kinsei sonraku," 755).

56. Ibid., table 1 (755).

Table 14. Kokudaka and Peasant Status, Kodaira, 1629–1849

Koku	1629		1643		1677		1694		1698		1731			1765			1849			
	H	K	H	K	H	K	H	K	H	K	H	K	M	H	K	M	H	b	K	M
120																				
98											1			1						
80							1													
54																	1			
25							1													
24					1															
23					1															
22					1															
21			1																	
20											1									
19																				
18			1																	
17					1															
16			1														1			
15																				

(koku)	1	2	3	4	5	6	7	8	9	10	11	12	13	14	15
14	2	3													
13	1	2													
12	3														
11	1			1								1			
10	3	1													
9	1	1		1	1			1		1		1		1	
8	2	2		1	2							1		1	
7		1	1	1		1	1	1		1					
6	1	2		1			1	1		1		4			
5	3	1		2	1	1	1	1	1	1	1	2	1	3	1
4		2		1	2	1	1	1	1	1	1	1	1	2	
3		2		2	1	2	1	1	2	1	1	1	3	4	
2		1		1	1	1			3			8	2	11	
1		1		1	1	1			1	4	4	8	4	6	
0.5			2	1					1	3	2	7	2	11	1
0.1				4				3		11		16		8	1
0		9						5	27	1	15		10	3	1
Total	13	20	2	20	13	20	21	47	21	40	21	45	21	48	2

SOURCE: Compiled from Ozaki, "Sonraku mibunsei," tables 1, 2, 4, 7, and 9 (pp. 755, 758, 763, 822, and 830).

NOTE: H = Honbyakushō; K = Kakae; M = Mizunomi; h = hyakushō.

today) had become very successful, for he had 80 koku, which put him far ahead of the next two holders, with 25 and 13 koku. The situations of some of the kakae had also improved: the nine taka holders, the largest with 11 koku, each had more land than sixteen of the twenty titled peasants, but there were now also twenty-seven landless clients. The total number of clients now stood at thirty-six. By 1731 the picture has changed again. The sake brewer, had nineteen servants and had acquired another 28 koku, bringing his holding to almost 100 koku. But twelve of the now twenty-one titled peasants had only 1 koku or less. Now, there were forty clients, of whom all but one had land. This does not mean, however, that there were no landless peasants (mizunomibyakushō): there were eighteen of them, one of whom was a client.

Ozaki does not detail the composition of the goningumi, but it is likely that the kumi were structured along lineage lines. It is important to note as well that membership in the goningumi was limited to titled peasants, twenty-one households out of a total of seventy-eight.[57] As we shall see, lineages played an overwhelming role in village politics, one that has not received much scholarly attention. As lineages grew, the number of temples grew from one temple of 2 koku to three, one with less than half a koku, the other two with 5 and 16 koku. It is likely that these temples serviced not simply "the village" but the lineages.

We should take a closer look at who the titled peasants and clients were. A comparison of three population registers (shūmon aratamechō), for the years 1694, 1695, and 1698, reveals numerous and frequent changes in the identity of titled peasants and clients. Between 1694 and 1695 the number of titled peasants increased by one (to twenty-one); however, this new titled peasant, who had been promoted from the status of client, became a client again three years later, but under a different patron. In another case, a patron changed places with his client, the latter now assuming the position of lineage patron and titled peasant. Another titled peasant went into service outside the village for

57. This was also the case in Tenjinbayashi, a neighboring village. In 1699 there were nine goningumi in Tenjinbayashi, each counting exactly five members (titled peasants), except for one group that had only four members. Together with the headman, this adds up to forty-five titled peasants; nineteen of them were patrons for a total of thirty-two kakae. In addition, there were six servants and four outcastes (see Ozaki Yukiya, "Mochizuki-machi no buraku no rekishi [1]," *Mochizuki no burakushi* 1 [1975]: 53).

several years and gave up his title. Other cases in 1698 show a similar instability in the membership of both ranks. One titled peasant passed his title on to his client when he left the village on a service stint. One Jihei who in 1695 was a client turned up three years later as not only a titled peasant but also a patron of three clients: one was Jihei's former fellow client; one was Sajihei, a titled peasant who had two clients in 1694 but only one in 1695 and was himself Jihei's client by 1698; and the third was the successor to Sajihei's former client.

The situations of a number of titled peasants were precarious, and their clients stood ready to take their place. (By now the titled peasants constituted a *numerus clausus*.) These clients were often second and third sons and in some rare cases bond servants. The fiction that they were all born within the village, however, was maintained; although most bond servants came from the outside, when they were promoted to client status they were recorded as "born in the village." Also, as we saw in chapter 1 to be the case in Makibuse, none of Kodaira's approximately thirty bond and indentured servants were married. Either they could not afford a family (a very widespread phenomenon beyond Japan also)[58] or they were not allowed to have one (they needed their patron's approval to take a spouse).[59]

In the 1702 population rosters of the neighboring village of Kasuga, one looks in vain for clients. Instead, there are a good number of mudaka, peasants without taka, recorded as doing "internal work" (*naisaku*) for their parents or brothers. They had families and lived in separate quarters and were thus kin, established as branch families who officially had not been granted land by their main family.

What qualified one to be a titled peasant, and why was their number restricted at a time when more and more branch houses were being created? Economic power obviously was not the decisive factor: quite a number of clients held larger holdings than most of the titled peasants. There was no upper kokudaka threshold that automatically made one a titled peasant or a lower one whereby one lost one's title. At the same time, all of the clients who were promoted held at least close to

<hr />

58. I referred earlier to Pierre Bourdieu's study of the Béarn region in France. I still remember the live-in stable hands on the farms of the village in Belgium where I was born, all bachelors who were never taken seriously and bore the brunt of many jokes and pranks.

59. Minegishi, *Kinsei mibunron*, 140–42.

five koku. Unlike the holding, the title usually could not be divided (although in Niremata it was). Hierarchical lineage structure seems to have determined all important relationships within the village. In society at large the great divide was between samurai and nonsamurai, in the village between titled and nontitled peasants; both the nonsamurai and the nontitled peasants were subjects of governance. The nature of status in samurai society differed from that in peasant society. Whereas samurai status adhered to all descendants of samurai, for long periods of time during the Tokugawa period the number of titled peasants was limited; only one of a titled peasant's sons could inherit the title—which was also the case with samurai *offices*. The title of "titled peasant" thus seems to have functioned not simply as a marker of status but also as a title of office. And initially this was the case, since titled peasants were created and set up as such to provide the overlords with the goods and services they expected from their subjects. But why its scarcity, given that many nontitled peasants obviously provided the same function? Were there also extramural influences at work in the limitation of the number of titled peasants?

Naitō Jirō's answer to this question, which is perhaps too one-sided, is that the titled peasants were those who had a *hyakushō kabu*, or "peasant share."[60] In the beginning only the "titled peasants" (homestead owners) had such a share. While this may sound tautological (titled peasants are those who have a share in the status of peasant as opposed to those who do not), the term *share,* as we shall see shortly, was used very early on to refer to title holders.

In accounting for the nearly universal phenomenon of the continued restriction of the number of title owners, Naitō concentrates on extramural factors, thus ignoring the increase in the number of titled peasants in roughly the first half of the seventeenth century. He cites two cases where daimyo legislated explicitly against an increase in the number of "peasant shares," one of them using the term *kabu*.[61] In bakufu legislation there is no explicit reference to limiting the number of titled peasants, but many bakufu-initiated village laws (goningu-

---

60. Naitō, *Honbyakushō taisei*, 28.

61. The two cases involve the Kaga domain and the village law of Iwamoto village in Echizen (ibid., 94–95). The latter mentions the term *kabu* and is a document that dates from between 1601 and 1607. For the full text of this document, see Miyagawa, *Taikō kenchi-ron*, 2:304. Another case is Ueda domain (see NAK-T 4:464).

michō zensho) mention the need to provide successors to bankrupt peasant houses.[62] Naitō's interpretation of this injunction seems plausible. He argues that if shogunal policy had simply aimed at establishing small landholders, there would have been no need for such encouragement: there were plenty of small landholders with lands and homesteads who could have succeeded to bankrupt titled peasant houses. This injunction makes sense only in a context of limited access to the status of titled peasant.

Another extraneous influence was undoubtedly the bakufu's 1673 prohibition against dividing land below a certain size: For peasants the minimum size was ten koku, and for headmen, twice that amount.[63] This law was issued around the time that the great riparian works of the seventeenth century were coming to an end. In many regions the acreage had been increased, so that an expanding population could be absorbed. Thus the further creation of branch houses would result in smaller holdings, and often, for example, in small mountain villages, even in a reduction of acreage of arable by the amount of land taken up for new homesteads. In many areas the branch houses established during this period of expansion became titled peasants.

In the registers in Ueda domain, a few kilometers to the north of Kodaira, one finds clients until around 1624, when they begin to be entered on the name rosters as equal to the titled peasants, and by 1654 they are all registered as such on the cadasters; that was when the number of titled peasants was frozen. And this seems to have been in response to orders from the overlord. Subsequently, in the 1670s, clients reappear on the kumi rosters under various labels—"kakae," "elder brother kakae," "younger brother kakae," "nephew kakae," and so on—as dependents of titled peasants and yet as owners of homesteads and lands.[64]

The same thing happened in Gorobe-shinden (discussed in chapter 2), a few kilometers to the east of Kodaira, with the large development of new fields by a dogō. When all the available flat land was brought under cultivation by the late 1660s, the number of titled peasants froze at forty-five households, and kakae were entered on the population registers (shūmon aratamechō and *goningumichō*) as dependents of

62. Naitō, *Honbyakushō taisei,* 95–98.
63. For an English translation of this law, see Lu, *Sources,* 1:207.
64. NAK-T 4:463–64.

titled peasants, hence not as full community members. Half a century later, in 1712, the number of titled peasants in Gorobe-shinden was still forty-five, but thirty-four of them had a total of eighty-three kakae.[65]

Naitō points out that if there was a limitation on the number of titled peasants set by overlord power, as was sometimes the case, and if, by bakufu order, it had become difficult to establish branch houses (and if, one may add, certain sectional intravillage interests were served by such restrictions), then new branch houses, even if they were economically independent and as well off as their parent families, had officially to be registered as still part of, or dependent on, their parent families. In other words, this limitation maintained hierarchical relations between main and branch families and the importance of lineage structures.[66]

This arrangement looks very much like another tatemae reconciliation of the contradictions between legal principle (making branching a virtual impossibility for the majority of peasants) and actual practice (it was not admitted to on paper, but it happened nevertheless). A tatemae approach to law can perhaps best be rendered as a "nod and wink" approach—the Italians' perception of their own relationship to law. The authorities had documents showing compliance with the law (the stable number of titled peasants), and the peasants had a practice they could live with—an eminent illustration of what Pierre Bourdieu calls a misrecognition of reality that fools nobody.[67]

Thus, the lineages used bakufu restrictions on partitioning holdings to structure themselves and were at the same time structured by it. In and of itself, however, lineage economic power was not effective if it could not be translated into political power, which meant acquiring for its members the title "titled peasant." Since the number of titled peasants was restricted, however, they had to wait for the moment that a titled peasant, for one reason or another, had to give up his share. Another bakufu institution leveraged by lineages was the kumi system. Kumi organizations were used to strengthen lineage filiations, because

65. Ibid., 464.
66. Naitō, *Honbyakushō taisei*, 50, 175–79.
67. Bourdieu, *Outline of a Theory of Practice* (Cambridge: Cambridge University Press, 1977), 133, 171. The Japanese categories *tatemae* (face, façade) and *honne* (real intention), which John O. Haley skillfully uses in his discussion of "law as *tatemae*" (*Authority without Power: Law and the Japanese Paradox* [New York: Oxford University Press, 1991], 186–90), fit perfectly Bourdieu's analytic notion of misrecognition.

all heads of the five-household neighborhood groups were patron houses. Intravillage lineage hierarchies and administrative structures, the latter ordered by overlord authority, thus overlapped.

Let us return now to Kodaira village. By 1731 forty landholding kakae and seventeen landless peasants, all incorporated into hierarchical lineage relationships, were ruled by twenty titled peasants, half of them virtually landless (i.e., having less than one koku). The situation was unavoidably wrought with tensions. Some tatemae, or cosmetic, as opposed to substantial, changes had been made in the entries of the population registers a few years earlier, changes that reduced somewhat the difference in status between titled and nontitled peasants. The former were no longer entered as having been titled peasants *daidai*, "for generations and generations," and to the latter's name was no longer added *onbyakushō tsukamatsuri makari ari*, "deferentially in service of titled peasants."[68] But how could these nontitled peasants go about effecting substantial changes? Some overlords (in Ueda domain at one point) had legislated against such changes; others (often in bakufu territories) were not interested in such matters.

In 1769 a number of kakae in Kodaira organized themselves as spokesmen for their class, although they did not form a majority, and raised an issue that was of some interest to the authorities, namely, the structure of the neighborhood kumi. That year eighteen (out of fifty-eight) kakae filed a suit requesting that the kakae system be abolished. They argued that patrons should not also function as kumi heads because this constituted a repressive, overlapping authority structure. On 2/29, however, before the suit was even filed, sixteen of the twenty-one titled peasants of Kodaira submitted a written rebuttal to the five village officials (the other titled peasants). They argued that there had been twenty-one titled peasants in the village "since ancient times"; that they, together with the kumi heads and the representative of the peasants (hyakushōdai), made all the important decisions; and that issues of kumi membership were always discussed by all the peasants. The next day the remaining forty kakae wrote to the village officials that they disapproved of the suit by their eighteen status mates.

This attempt at staving off the suit failed, and the officials filed a recorded testimony with the bakufu's intendant at Mikage-shinden,

68. Ozaki, "Kinsei sonraku," 767.

stating that the overlapping system was according to longtime village law and that at a meeting of 2/8 "all" the peasants had decided not to change the entries in the new population rosters that were due within a few weeks. Moreover, they reminded the authorities that prior to this suit of the eighteen, three among them had gone directly to the office in Mikage-shinden about this matter and that that office had shown little interest, ordering a private settlement (*naisai*). The plaintiffs, however, had ignored the decision that was subsequently reached in the village. Finally, a few days later, in the third month, the suit was filed together with a rebuttal signed by the village officials and the titled peasants.

The plaintiffs obviously wanted to use the institution of the neighborhood kumi as leverage to break the power of their bosses, while the defendants stated that the overlapping system was village law and did not cause problems to the plaintiffs. The latter, however, argued that while Tokugawa law required that kumi be established by neighborhood and that a head then be designated, in Kodaira only patrons were kumi heads. The plaintiffs made it clear that they believed the village officials had been maneuvering to prevent kakae from becoming kumi heads. (The case of nearby Iribuse, discussed in chapter 2, was very similar.) The defendants, conceding this point somewhat, proposed a compromise whereby the titled peasants would constitute three separate kumi and the other peasants would be grouped in genuine neighborhood associations and would choose their own heads. This compromise solution was rejected. The eighteen were intransigent and wanted to negotiate only if the entry "patron" (kakaeoya) were taken off the population register. They cited the precedent of neighboring Makibuse, where the overlapping system had been abolished. But the village officials were unimpressed, arguing that Kodaira had its own village law and that it did not matter what was practiced elsewhere.

This suit describes concretely the trouble patrons caused their clients; some complaints are about the symbolic distancing of the village officials from the peasants. In the third month the new population register had to be signed. The custom had been for peasants to drop by the headman's home to certify their entries with their seals, but now they were all summoned to assemble in the headman's yard, with the officials inside and the representative of the peasants acting as a go-between. The officials gave three reasons for this hierarchical arrangement. First, since the village had become part of the bakufu domain (in

1765) the village law had to be read to the peasants once a year, which was why they were gathered together to hear the reading and sign the register at the same time. Second, the headman's house was too small for a gathering of all the peasants. And third, since the weather was fine, it seemed like a good idea to use the outdoors. The last two reasons sound spurious: it is doubtful that the headman's house was too small, and in the mountains of Nagano in the third month the weather is still bitterly cold. Obviously, the kakae interpreted this setup as arbitrarily emphasizing the differences in status between the officials, or patrons, on the one hand, and the peasants, or kakae, in general, on the other.

The eighteen had set out for the bakufu office at Mikage-shinden (some sixteen kilometers away) with their suit once before, but the village officials had gone after them and persuaded them to return by promising a private settlement. The negotiations had faltered, however, over the abolition of the patron system, and the eighteen had reintroduced their suit. Then the issue of a conflict of interests was raised, the plaintiffs expressing their concern that the decision by the titled peasants to have the village shoulder the officials' travel expenses might have had something to do with the overlapping responsibilities of patrons and kumi heads. The titled peasants simply denied the allegations and asserted that the decision about shouldering the defendants' costs had been made not only by the twenty-one titled peasants but by all the peasants. Costs had also been a factor in postponing the suit of the eighteen for over four years. They had submitted their suit to the peasant representative several times, but the village officials had ordered prepayment of the costs of the suit. The titled peasants' view of this was that all these earlier attempts had constituted only informal talks, not formal proposals for a full-fledged suit.

The plaintiffs, conscious of their economic independence, also requested that any household that could not be self-sufficient be excluded from the kumi. The officials responded by arguing that economics had nothing to do with full kumi membership: lack of economic self-sufficiency was no reason, they said, to lose one's status as titled peasant and patron. Only if one became a servant in *another* village did one lose one's status. But this was not the case with Kyūzaemon, whom the plaintiffs cited as an example. Kyūzaemon, patron and kumi head with a meager holding of 0.085 koku, was working as a servant (*hōkōnin*) in another household. He had in his kumi one successor house and one *dōshin* (a Buddhist priest without a temple). When one of these two disappeared the field had to be taken over by another peasant, who had himself only 0.15 koku but never lifted a finger to cultivate the minuscule plot.

The suit contains yet another reference to a previous suit, this one involving a kumi head (0.4 koku) who had expelled one of his kakae "because not only had he always been insolent but he had also ignored advice from the village and he was selfish (*wagamama*)." The village officials had then told the kakae that because he now had no patron he could no longer live in the village. This kakae also had brought a suit to the Mikage-shinden office. The case had been stopped, however, through mediators brought in from another village. The same expelled kakae, together with his three co-kakae, were among the eighteen plaintiffs.

By the time of the suit, the titled and nontitled peasants were economically virtually undistinguishable. Only five titled peasants had holdings of more than 2 koku (the sake brewer, with 120; the headman, with 14; and three others, with 5, 4, and 3 koku), four more had 1 koku, and the remaining twelve had holdings below 1 koku. On the other hand, nineteen kakae had more than 1 koku. Both plaintiffs and their ten patrons were spread evenly on both sides of the 1-koku divide. Four patrons found all their kakae united on the side of the plaintiffs, and eight had succeeded in rallying all theirs in opposition, while the kakae of the remaining eight were divided between plaintiffs and opponents to the suit.

The outcome of the suit, mediated at the wealthy temple Fukuōji, appeared to be largely a victory for the plaintiffs: reference to kakae and mizunomi in the kumi membership lists was to be dropped, kumi would now be arranged geographically, and kumi leaders were to be elected from within the kumi every other year. But it was a hollow victory, because after four years, in 1773 and 1774 three separate but identical suits were submitted (by twenty plaintiffs, thirteen of them new ones) about the problem of overlapping jurisdictions. This time, however, the plaintiffs' demands were on a smaller scale: they wanted to be freed from their status as kakae and to be "recognized in the population roster as born in this village." There was no critique of the kakae system as such, no insistence on abolishing it. This obviously was not a "class suit," for all kakae. Moreover, all petitions were also co-signed by the officials and the patrons in question. What was the rationale behind this new drive, coopted, it seems, by all those with any power? Who among the kakae signed, and why not all of them now that the drive enjoyed official sanction? (There is secondary evidence of an additional petition, now lost, by another ten kakae, bringing the total kakae supporters to thirty, still just above half of the total kakae population of fifty-six.)

The petitioners made a distinction between kakae that were related by kinship and those that were not. What four years earlier had appeared to be a united front as far as claims were concerned had broken down along kinship lines. Fictional kinship was fine, the petitioners seemed to say, but it was not the real thing and should not be treated as such. Distinctions were introduced, or made stronger, in order to separate the two and to produce distinction that was acceptable to the authorities.

It annoyed the thirty kin branch houses that they would have the same status as the twenty-six non-kin branch houses, and they wanted not simply to have their kakae status removed but to be acknowledged as *hyakushō,* "peasants." (A similar distinction between kin and non-kin kakae had been made in Shimo-Kaize.) The result, however, was not equality with the old titled peasants, here called *onbyakushō,* or "honorable peasants," but a further splitting of this status whereby the kin kakae became second-class onbyakushō, while the non-kin kakae became simply *hyakushō,* peasants—but the term no longer simply described an occupation: it now was a title designating their status within a finely graded hierarchy.

The population register of 1780 includes the following seven ranks of peasants (the number of peasant households in each rank is given in parentheses):

   1. "onbyakushō [honorable, i.e., titled peasant] living in this village since ancient times" (18)

   2. "onbyakushō born in this village" (29)

   3. "hyakushō born in this village" (18)

   4. "hōkō [in service] at X with Y (born as onbyakushō in this village)" (5)

   5. "X's kakae, born in this village" (3)

6. "X's mizunomi ['landless' (tenant)]" (3)

7. "mizunomi born in this village (onbyakushō since ancient times but now mizunomi)" (1)

This new status stratification was an ingenious device to accommodate some of the demands while preserving distinction and the distinctions that constitute the symbolic capital—they had hardly any other—of the dominant fraction of the village. The demands of the kakae, both kin and non-kin, were met: in ranks 2 and 3 they were now recorded as "born in the village" and no longer as kakae but as peasants, hyakushō. The special demand of the kin kakae was also met, for they were now distinguished from the non-kin by the "honorable" prefix *on*. And former titled peasants (onbyakushō) were recognized as such: in rank 4, for those who had to give up their title because they went into service outside the village while retaining some land, and also in the lowest rank, because they had lost all their land (below the mizunomi of rank 6, who had some land). There are, however, a few kakae left, in rank 5.

Later population rosters tell the continuing story of wranglings over status promotion and maneuvers against status pollution. All non-kin hyakushō of rank 3 became absorbed as onbyakushō into rank 2, and all dependent mizunomi of rank 6 were promoted to dependent kakae of rank 5, who later were gradually incorporated into rank 2. On the 1849 roster only the names of peasants are listed, without any prefixes. Had equality been achieved? Not quite, because there are "sidescript" entries next to the names. On this roster, twenty-one peasants are marked as osabyakushō, "head peasants" (three of them mizunomi), forty-eight as hyakushō, "peasants" (among whom are three mizunomi), and two as kakae (one mizunomi). Finally, after some two hundred and fifty years all but two in this peasant village had become "peasants." Had status been superseded by class at the end of the Tokugawa period, as the historians mentioned at the beginning of this chapter argue? Not quite. *Mizunomi* is a clear economic marker for landless peasants. Yet three mizunomi are among the elite twenty-one.

Similar struggles concerning the status of titled and nontitled peasants took place in the area around Kodaira at roughly the same time. We shall look briefly at two additional cases that involved "mass" decisions, one involving promotion to, the other demotion from, the status of titled peasant. A group promotion of kakae to titled peasants should not be interpreted too readily as a final step toward equality. Often, subtle or even explicit social distinctions were maintained between the old elite and arrivés.

In 1780 in Nagatoro (in today's Saku city, some fifteen kilometers east of Kodaira) thirty-five clients were set free by twenty-five patrons, and they became full members of the neighborhood kumi (resulting in the creation of seven new kumi); but all of them had to be given permission by their former patrons, who thus became their guarantors.[69] The reasons these guarantors gave for setting their clients free included the following: "he has his own holding"; "he has a separate house but no land yet, but he will cause no trouble"; "I shall give him land, and he will cause no trouble"; "he is my relative, and I shall give him 1.44 koku."

Having a clear title to some land (even one koku or less) was a basic condition for becoming a titled peasant in Nagatoro. It is ironic, however, that these amounts of land were insufficient to maintain even a small peasant household. These peasants, now nominally "full peasants," must have supplemented their income through nonagricultural pursuits. Economically, the term "titled peasant" was an empty title; its significance was purely political and social.

The "independence" thus gained was conditional upon good behavior; the guarantorship certainly suggests as much. Sometimes the difference between old and new titled peasants was codified and expressed in public signs. In Tanoguchi village (also in Kita-Saku district) the village laws of 1681 stipulated that clients promoted to the status of titled peasant were not allowed to wear haori coats, *hakama* ceremonial aprons, or *ashida* (high rain geta, or wooden clogs) or to use umbrellas, and the pillars of their houses could not exceed eight *shaku* (2.40 meter); nor could they use tatami mats, and they were not allowed to enter homes of "real" titled peasants, but had always to stay in the entrance way. (As we shall see in chapter 5, prohibitions identical to these were issued against outcastes.) Such distinctions within the ranks of titled peasants could be maintained for a long time. In one case, someone whose household had been promoted to titled peasant in the 1780s was reminded in writing two generations later, in 1844, that he could not wear a *kamishimo* ceremonial over-

69. Ichikawa Takeji, "Kakaebyakushō," 12–13.

coat except when he was the main mourner at a funeral or the groom at a marriage (an allowance made because of relaxing standards, it was stated). If these things were disregarded, he was warned, his house would return to its former kakae status.[70]

The group demotion case, a rare occurrence, is from Kasuga-shinden (a few kilometers south of Kodaira), which, with only 145 koku, was a rather small village.[71] In 1767 the headman in one stroke demoted twenty-five titled peasants to kakae status. The result was a suit (in the third month, as was so often the case) brought by the demoted to the headman. The headman, however, single-handedly, and without any further endorsement by village officials, passed the suit on to the bakufu authorities in Mikage-shinden—in an effort to doom it.

It should be noted in passing that this circumstance throws some light on the process of lodging suits. Dan Fenno Henderson has argued that villagers' suits had to be approved by the village headman and could be initiated only after conciliation efforts had failed.[72] Japanese scholars have disputed this point. According to Ishii Ryōsuke, no conciliation efforts were needed; the headman had simply to provide an accompanying letter, which the headman failed to do in this case.

All four kumi heads (the only ones among the twenty-two patrons who had not been consulted, "because this would have led to a dispute") immediately wrote to the same authorities, explaining the case and requesting an investigation. The headman had put the twenty-five former titled peasants as kakae under their relatives (brothers or parents), who thus became their patrons. His reason for this drastic step was that there were too many tiny peasants in the village with holdings of "0.02, 0.03, 0.05, 0.08, 0.2, 0.3, 1 and 2 koku, and too many irregularities, making it difficult to apportion expenses to each and every peasant; it was much easier to rechannel this through patrons." The intendant investigated the case and returned the original petition to the village, noting that he would attend to the matter if the request was forwarded properly, via all the village officials. In the second month of the following year the kakae were reinstated as titled peasants.

70. Ibid., 8–9.

71. For a summary statement of the case and some of the documents, see ibid., 10–12. All full documents for this case can be found in NAK-KS2 (1): 964–68 (nos. 490–93); for the village kokudaka, see ibid., 724.

72. See Henderson, *Conciliation* 1:136; and Ishii Ryōsuke's critique in his long review of this work in *Law in Japan* 2 (1968): 216–17.

LINEAGES, *GONINGUMI*, AND VILLAGE POLITICS:
ŌASHI, 1840s

Lineages were left untouched by the kumi organizations established by order of the overlords. As the suit by the Kodaira kakae makes clear, lineages are not unalterable biological networks. The plaintiffs wanted to do away with the social construct of patron and client, with the inscription of dependency onto relations between main and branch houses. As Naitō suggested, the maintenance of hierarchical relationships between households along lineage lines may have been prompted by the kabu structure of the title "titled peasant."

In the following case study, we shall take a close look at how lineage politics were structured by the institutions of titled peasants and kumi membership. The location is Ōashi village (presently part of the town of Akashina in central Nagano prefecture). A number of kumi rosters from that village dating between 1731 and 1872 examined by Ozaki Yukiya give one a good sense of the composition of the kumi.[73] What is striking, but certainly not exceptional, is that in every case village offices and kumi headships were passed to members of the same families.[74] That this was a privilege is clear from the fact that when the number of kumi had to be reduced by one, and hence one family would lose its leadership position, it was decided that the two former kumi leaders would hold the position in alternate years.[75] This tightly knit group had turned this privilege into a monopoly by devising ways to prevent any member from losing his status and hence to prevent others from joining.

---

73. Ozaki Yukiya, "Chikuma-gun bakufuryō ni okeru goningumichō to goningumi no jittai: Chikuma-gun Ōashi-mura no baai," *Shinano,* 16, no. 2 (1964): 45–60.

74. Ozaki has documented this in detail for the period between the 1750s and the 1820s (ibid., table 7 [559]). Dan Henderson presents an agreement from 1867 between the six titled peasants of one village as evidence for a collusion to rotate the headmanship every five years among themselves and thus keep control of the land cadasters (see his *Village "Contracts,"* 164–66): "If outsiders raise objections, the six as a group would come forward strongly, and try to settle the matter.... If besides our six some outsiders become the headman or group chief [kumi head], some one of the six of us will carefully keep custody of the survey records, and we will make sure to agree on all issues. Hereafter, besides agreeing within the six-house group, we would definitely work together in harmony no matter what the problem is and help each other to the greatest extent" (164).

75. Ozaki, "Chikuma-gun," 54.

Scarcity and access had to be controlled in order to maintain the value of this political and social capital.

In 1848, however, five households wanted to split off from a nine-household kumi to form a separate kumi with their own elected head because "the kumi was too big." Yet a nine-household kumi was not unusually large: the largest kumi counted eleven households, and the smallest, three. The officials consulted the higher authorities, who gave permission for a new kumi; however, "in consultation with the village officials" it was decided that the current head of the kumi would move with the five petitioners as their new head, a strategy to maintain a monopoly on political power against the threat of a newcomer. The five did not agree to this condition and so refused to sign the population register. They also rejected another peasant whom the officials tried to impose upon them as head in a failed attempt at compromise. The result was a suit and a new compromise: the village officials would be in charge of the new kumi for three years, and then they would decide on another head.

Tarōshichi, the leader of the secession quintet, had been a trouble-maker in the village before this incident. Nine years earlier, in 1839, he and his son had been involved in a suit against two other peasants, also a father and a son, about collecting firewood. The Buddhist priest and officials from a neighboring village, however, had worked out a settlement. In 1844 another member of the secession group, Risaemon, had been involved in a quarrel at a wedding in his home. The quarrel arose after Risaemon announced that he was going to change the name of his younger brother to Heijirō, which he claimed was the name of one of his forbears, and one of the guests made it clear that he found this ludicrous. The quarrel had simmered down, but soon thereafter Risaemon and Tarōshichi had sued the guest for slandering them and causing not only trouble at the wedding but also hardship by criticizing their family pedigree. They had proof, they said, that about two hundred years before, in the 1650s, a Heijirō had been recorded in the cadasters as a titled peasant. Thus, for at least ten years before the secession incident Risaemon and Tarōshichi seemed to have been buddies prone to causing trouble.

The issue of the new kumi headship flared up again when, after the three-year interim, the five requested the promised appointment of a kumi head and the village officials postponed it for another seven years!

To the new suit the five filed, the officials answered that the five in question had not changed their behavior, so none of them could be chosen as head because "in our village, heads have to come from households with a long pedigree (*senrei nagatachi ni kagiri*, limited to [houses] with longstanding precedent)." The five argued that headships should have nothing to do with pedigree (*iegara*) or status (*mibun*), that it was unreasonable to bring these things to bear on matters of village governance. Risaemon had used the public occasion of the wedding to stake out his claim to a long pedigree. Given the political importance of pedigree, undoubtedly his declaration was a political move and was perceived as such by the guest who ridiculed it.

Eight years later, in 1859, a new compromise was reached. The officials' requirement for headships was now *hitogara*, or character, rather than pedigree. But, the officials added, since none of the five in question had the necessary character, they had to wait until someone with the proper character emerged in the group who could be appointed as head. Therefore, each year one of the five would function, not as *hangashira* (the local term for kumi head), but as *hangashira-dai*, a proxy head.

This is another example of an ingenious solution by "splitting." It provided face-saving compromises that allowed both parties to claim victory. The village officials defended their turf: they stuck to *principle* by not capitulating to the demands of the five. The latter, in turn, gained self-governance, which *in practice* put them on an equal footing with the other kumi heads. The real solution would come about with time, which was on the side of the secessionists. It was inevitable that they would eventually get what they wanted, perhaps in the next generation, when these fine distinctions had become, for everyone, a dead letter. And this was indeed what happened. What was the nature of this "inevitability"? Why could five peasants hold out for so long?

This protracted conflict, of which we know only the peaks, points to social fault lines in the village that are invisible in the texts of the suits. It turns out that Tarōshichi and Risaemon and the other three members of their kumi were related (see fig. 5). The fault lines demarcate divisions of lineage power. Over time, the five had come to constitute an economically powerful lineage. The conflict over these several decades was one between old and new lineages, the former trying to block

Fig. 5. Lineage of Risaemon's Secessionist Kumi, Ōashi, 1725–1869

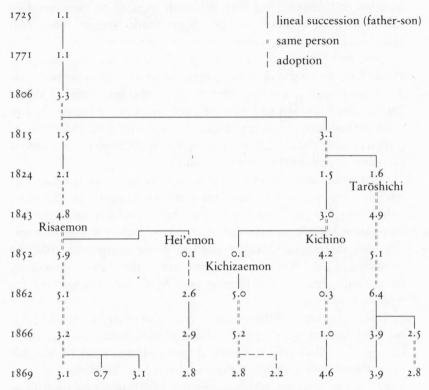

SOURCE: Adapted from Ozaki, "Chikuma-gun," table 8 (p. 58).
NOTE: Names are of secessionists. The numbers are of kokudaka.

the translation of the latter's economic power into political clout by appealing to family pedigree, social standing, and personal character.[76]

Pedigree was at issue in the quarrel over names (when Risaemon and Tarōshichi claimed a two-hundred-year-old ancestry) and in the disagreement about kumi leadership. Since both disputes developed into suits, it is not surprising that the village appears to have conducted a pedigree check. On the tribute list of 1725, under the ancestor Matsuemon (the holder of 1.1 koku in fig. 5), the officials noted that the

76. Writing these lines in October 1992, I was struck by how the suppression of the economic in the name of "character" during the debates preceding the U.S. presidential election was similar to the strategy employed by the village officials discussed here.

older records had been lost in a fire. Needless to say, there is no guarantee that this was an impartial investigation. Since the name Heijirō, which Risaemon intended to give his younger brother (Hei'emon), does not appear in subsequent village records, it seems likely that his claim of titled ancestry going back to 1650 was not recognized.

In the 1700s, during the first two generations of the lineage as we know it, the household's holdings remained at the low kokudaka level of 1.1. Around 1800, however, the holdings tripled, which allowed the household to create a branch house in 1815. This trend continued during the following decades, leading in 1848 to the attempt to consolidate the economic power of the lineage (which now totaled 15.4 koku) by giving it a political dimension. The lineage continued to grow, and by 1869 it counted nine households and a total of 26 koku. Ultimately, in 1872, the lineage split into two separate goningumi, headed by Tarō-shichi's two sons.

In order to acquire political power commensurate with their economic strength, lineages had to do more than simply create ever more branch houses. Either they could consolidate their power within the village (and thereby strengthening intralineage authority) by setting up a separate goningumi or they could acquire for some of their branch houses titled status when such a share came on the market through the bankruptcy, abscondence, or venality of some shareholder. Whichever route they decided to take, they needed foremost the approval of the local decision makers, and various factors determined the ease or difficulty with which that was given. The careers of a few titled peasants from Gorobe-shinden illustrate the process.[77]

Gorobe-shinden, as the name indicates, was a village of newly developed fields. In the first two generations, since there was little competition for land, social mobility was not very restricted. In 1695 three villagers from Gorobe-shinden wanted a relative of theirs to move into the village as a tenant. They promised to take responsibility for him and establish him as a kakae; eighteen years later this newcomer became a titled peasant with 1.6 koku. One couple came as servants (hōkōnin) in the 1640s, bought some land, rented a house, became kakae, borrowed money to buy a house, then bought land in other villages. In 1713 the household gained titled peasant status with 12 koku, two bond servants, and one horse. Another peasant also started his career as a

77. Ōishi, *Kinsei sonraku,* 125–27.

servant, in 1673. In 1687 he was able to buy land, build a house, and take the place as titled peasant of one who had died. Later, however, he sold the house and title, became a kakae again, and finally ended up landless (mizunomi).

Where land was scarce—a general problem toward the end of the seventeenth century—social mobility by means of upper-status "shares" became restricted. Shares became available when a shareholder died without offspring or successor, left the village, went bankrupt, or decided to sell his share. Symbolic capital, originally an expression of real capital, could be converted back to it: in 1760 a share in Kasuga village (a few kilometers east of Gorobe-shinden) went for the outrageous price of twenty *ryō*;[78] two years later in Gorobe-shinden itself someone paid only one ryō.[79]

The market for the title of titled peasant was restricted in three ways. First, it was a village market, limited to the actual residents. A peasant could be titled only in his own village (even if he had additional fields in other villages) because the status entailed a position of village leadership. Second, the price for the title was set within the village, not on an intervillage "market for titles." Third, cash alone was insufficient. Since the title was essentially a social one, its acquisition had to be sanctioned socially. Beyond cash, symbolic capital consisting of social esteem and communal "harmony" was needed. There were specified procedures for obtaining a title, as an incident of 1812, also from Gorobe-shinden, illustrates.[80]

That year someone's client bought the title of titled peasant from a third peasant. At the time of the yearly registration of the population, he asked his former patron to erase his client status. The patron, however, insisted on a formal written request, which met the objection that "things were never done that way before." "*Au contraire*," the patron returned, "you have to go through the village council." Inevitably, the intendant was presented with a suit.

78. Ichikawa Takeji, "Kakaebyakushō," 10. Kobayashi Daiji lists prices for symbols of elevated social status in the second half of the Tokugawa period (without giving place or date or citing sources): 5 ryō for a *kamishimo* ceremonial outfit, 10 for village headman's rank, 15 to use a surname, 20 for the rank of village group headman, and so on, all the way up to 100 ryō (see his *Sabetsu kaimyō no rekishi* [Yūzankaku, 1987], 193).

79. Ōishi, *Kinsei sonraku*, 132.

80. Ibid., 134–35.

The officials, fearing trouble if the suit came to a judgment, decided on the following course. The plaintiff, they said, was a diligent peasant and deserved to be a titled peasant but should have notified his patron before buying the title—or certainly immediately after buying it—instead of waiting until the next population registration: he had to admit to wrongdoing. The patron, on the other hand, should be honored to have cultivated such a qualified peasant, with a sizable holding, who had contributed diligently to a government request for funds: such a peasant deserved to be set free.

Both were reprimanded, and both were satisfied. This is an example of a typical solution, with a balanced interplay of apologies, shared blame and praise, and thus no clearcut winner or loser. The aftermath of this solution is also instructive. Soon thereafter, three more clients of the same patron asked to become clients of the new titled peasant. The trio circulated secret memos bad-mouthing their patron, but this tactic led nowhere: their status remained unchanged.

COOPERATIVE VILLAGES

The villages discussed in this chapter were mainly dogō villages with tightly structured lineages. In contrast to the corporate sō villages, predominant in the Kinai, they were characterized by strong hierarchical arrangements, their origins in large extended families. Political equality always lay just beyond the horizon, always one more status distinction away. Both sō and dogō villages had their roots in pre-Tokugawa formations.

A third type, one that has not received much attention even in Japanese literature, goes by the convoluted name *shozokudanteki kyōgyō-tai,* literally, "small, family-type occupational cooperative village."[81] Harada Seiji compared the structures of twelve villages of Fukuyama domain (Bingo province, Hiroshima prefecture) as they appear in a document from 1647 and found what he calls patriarchal-type villages and cooperatives.[82] Traditional patriarchal villages were to be found in

81. An excellent bibliography of the few articles and books on this type of village can be found in Harada Seiji, "Kinsei zenki sonraku no shoruikei: Fukuyama hanryō o chūshin ni shite," *Shigaku kenkyū,* no. 193 (1991): 26 n. 3.

82. Harada rejects the term *dogō* because most of the large landholdings had disappeared in the warfare at the end of the sixteenth century, but his "patriarchal" villages look very much like villages other scholars refer to as being controlled by dogō.

the hills and mountains and typically engaged almost exclusively in wet rice cultivation. Cooperative villages dominated by small peasants were mostly in the coastal areas, with only dry fields, or on inland flat terrain, with a balanced economy of wet and dry fields. The latter two regions are characterized by open terrain, making expansion possible and reducing competition for land, which is in great contrast to conditions in the hills and mountains.

Harada's hypothesis linking in a general way ecological conditions with certain types of village organization is suggestive but certainly far from conclusive, given his small sample. Nevertheless, his structural comparisons put in sharp relief different village structures and can serve to conclude this part of our study. Harada divided the peasantry into the following categories: (1) titled peasants without bond servants (genin): small, independent cultivators with holdings usually between 5 and 15 koku; (2) titled peasants with genin, broken down further into peasants with 15 or more koku, that is, typical patriarchal families, and peasants with less than 15 koku; (3) genin; and (4) *mawaki,* or kin branch houses.

Table 15 contrasts two such villages. In Futamori, with a kokudaka of 165 koku, the titled peasants were clearly divided between those with genin (more than 20 koku) and those without; all genin belonged to the wealthier peasants. Harada argues, however, that this top-heavy hierarchy (approximately 72 percent of the arable was owned by the five peasants with holdings of 15 or more koku; 22 percent by those with 5 to 15 koku; the remaining 6 percent by peasants with below 5 koku) is not a leftover from medieval times: in 1601 the respective percentages were approximately 26, 55, and 19. Pre-Tokugawa villages would have been characterized by small holdings like those of Mizunomi village (466 koku). Typically, here only one holder had more than 20 koku, while most titled peasants, both those without and those with genin, had 3 to 10 koku, as did a large number of the genin. Of these twenty-three genin only eight were attached to the top three titled peasants; all the others were genin of small peasants with holdings hardly larger than theirs. The smallest titled peasant (with between 1 and 3 koku) had four genin, as did the titled peasant just above him.

Many small holders had genin who were taka holders; in some cases the combined kokudaka of the genin was almost twice that of their host family (see tables 16 and 17). These "bond servants" obviously were

Table 15. Patriarchal and Cooperative Villages in Fukuyama Domain, 1647

Koku	Total Ie	Titled Peasant Without Genin	Titled Peasant With Genin	Genin	Mawaki
		Futamori Village (Patriarchal Type)			
30–40	1		1		
20–30	2		2		
15–20	2	1			
10–15	1	1			
7–10	2			2	
5–7	1			1	
3–5	2			2	
1–3	1			1	
0–1	10			3	
Total	22	2	3	9	
		Mizunomi Village (Cooperative Type)			
30–40					
20–30	1		1		
15–20	2		2		
10–15					
7–10	6	3	3		
5–7	13	10	2		1
3–5	38	27	1	1	6
1–3	57	15	1	9	13
0–1	65			13	
Total	182	55	10	23	20

SOURCE: Adapted from Harada, "Shoruikei," foldout table 9 (between pp. 14 and 15).

NOTE: Total number of ie (households) includes 7 muyashiki (those without a residence) for Futamori and 66 for Mizunomi.

Table 16. Titled Peasants and Genin, Uchitsuneishi Village, Fukuyama Domain, 1647

Koku	Titled Peasants	Genin
10–15	2	7
7–10	2	4
5–7	2	3
3–5	4	5
1–3	2	3

SOURCE: Harada, "Shoruikei," table 11 (p. 16).

Table 17. Holdings of Host House and Genin, Kurome Village, Fukuyama Domain, 1647

	Koku
Host House	
Kichi'emon	11.964
Genin	
Sakejūrō	6.028
Jinshirō	5.823
Fujisaemon	3.045
Jinshichi	2.312
Sōshirō	1.728
Yoshichirō	1.253
Total	20.189

SOURCE: Harada, "Shoruikei," table 13 (p. 17).

situated quite differently both socially and economically from those of Futamori, and they look more like the clients (kakae) we have encountered elsewhere. Mizunomi was a typical "cooperative" village with large numbers of almost equal holdings among mawaki as well, the result of the division of property through equal inheritance. This was a village with high status mobility. In a relatively short time, these mawaki became fully titled peasants, and the genin seem to have had no difficulty following the same route. Part of the reason may have been the availability of additional space: between 1619 and 1647 Futamori added only 6 koku to its arable, while Mizunomi added 55.

The reason these families organized themselves as a cooperative on a more or less equal basis was, according to Harada, to meet the overlord's extraordinarily high extraction quota, which set a premium on rice, a crop that was not produced here, or if it was, the yield was far less than in the hills and mountains. There is certainly room for debate and further research on an argument that so categorically relates geographic location and type of agriculture with social organization and, further, links the cooperative villages, through their type of agriculture, with extraction policies. What is clear, however, is that Japanese rural society offered a number of organizational patterns and that status rigidity seems to have been linked with the availability of space, a phenomenon we encountered in the case of Gorobe-shinden.

To conclude, then, status distinctions and status-generated distinction were part of village life throughout the Tokugawa period. As the frequent appearance of virtually landless titled peasants in the records shows, status was not replaced as a differentiating mechanism by economic class as such. The *sources* of status distinctions were intravillage economic factors and extravillage political realities, which reinforced the former: the stature of traditional, established peasants, undoubtedly the decision makers in the villages, was enhanced by their being assigned the communal responsibility for tribute and services owed to the overlords. This official duty somehow made them the only ones who were real peasants.

Some overlord measures contributed either directly or indirectly, but not uniformly and universally, to limiting the number of titled peasants. After the 1673 prohibition against partitioning holdings below a certain size, the villages seem to have resorted to fixing the number of titled peasants while in reality putting very few, if any, constraints on actual practice. This necessarily resulted in recording economically independent peasants as dependents, which solidified lineage formation, strengthened status divisions, and limited political power to small segments of the village population.

Within these institutional constraints, resistance to status mobility depended on lineage expansion and the availability of additional arable. In extended families, the hierarchical relations among members were unambiguously inscribed in their economic and social positions, for it was clear who controlled the means of production and reproduction.

Although this material reality was misrepresented symbolically through familial and paternalistic terms of kinship address and on ritual occasions,[83] the symbolic had less autonomous determining power than it would have later. The head of the family had a clear title to the land, owned the buildings and agricultural tools, and had the final word concerning which members could set up their own families. With partitioning, control over these means was transferred to branch houses. The preeminence of the main family came then to rely increasingly on symbolic means, status distinctions being one of the most important. The availability of additional arable worked against the maintenance of rigid status hierarchies and promoted status mobility.

When Japan reached an ecological barrier in the early eighteenth century, status again came to play a greater role in village life (contrary to the opinions of many American scholars). It seems that status production, the generation of ever finer status distinctions, was a powerful tool for offsetting the politically negative implications of economic decline. Economic development affected eighteenth-century villages in two ways. Some peasants succeeded in accumulating more land, or economic capital, which they sought to translate into political capital, but they encountered status barriers. More often, however, a great economic leveling downward took place for most of the peasants, turning them into very small holders (and an "objective" class), which is also contrary to prevailing interpretations. Either way, economic development brought pressure to rearrange the structure of the political field in the villages.

This pressure could take a number of forms. Peasants could simply become nonplayers in the status game by removing themselves from it and migrating to the urban centers. They could become part-time players by seeking employment (hōkōnin) elsewhere for a period of time, as many did starting in the late seventeenth century, although this negatively affected their position, standing, and status in the village.

---

83. Smith astutely observes with regard to "ceremonial services" that "the participants themselves made no consistent distinction between ceremonial and labor services, often calling both by the same name. It would seem—one cannot speak with certainty in such cases—that the two services were thought of as being essentially the same. This is not because people failed to observe that one had economic value and the other not, but because this difference though evident was insignificant in view of the fact that the two had the same social character" (*Agrarian Origins,* 30). On kinship terminology, see ibid., 15 ff.

They could also try to change the rules of the game, yet with the notable exception (in the present study) of the first of the two drives in Kodaira to abolish the system of kakae altogether, this did not occur. Most of the demands were efforts, not to change the rules of the game, but to change one's position within the field where the game was played, which ensured its longevity.

4

Village Autonomy

In effect, the village had the security of the administrative state along
with the freedom of the outlaw.

John Owen Haley

Village autonomy has two major components: financial and juridical.
Japanese historians have given little consideration to the former, analyzed in chapter 2, in their debate about whether or not (more often
than the degree to which) Tokugawa villages were autonomous. Their
discussion has centered on the juridical aspect of village powers, judicial
and prosecutorial, as found in village regulations.[1] Between roughly
1900 and 1950 a number of village laws were made available in about
half a dozen compilations, mainly the work of legal scholars. Then,
starting in the 1960s some historians began using these documents to
examine the relationship between village and state, questioning the legal
scholars' assumption of village autonomy.

Hozumi Nobushige, one of the drafters of the Civil Code, and Miura
Kaneyuki pioneered the study of the goningumi system around 1900,
no doubt inspired by the same concern that made the late Meiji (and
Taisho) government promote "local self-government." This research
produced several volumes of goningumi regulations, edited by Hozumi
Nobushige and Shigetō, father and son, in 1921 and 1944, and Nomura
Kanetarō, also in 1944. To these works should be added Maeda
Masaharu's studies, especially his 1952 analysis and compilation of
village *codes,* which were different from the goningumi *laws* because,

Epigraph: Haley, *Authority without Power,* 61.
1. For an overview of this historiography, see Kadomae Hiroyuki, "Kinsei
no mura to kinseishi kenkyū," *Rekishi kōron,* no. 95 (1983): 94–101; Uesugi
Mitsuhiko, "Kinsei sonpō no seikaku ni tsuite," *Minshūshi kenkyū,* no. 7
(1969): 80–106, esp. 80–81; and idem, "Kinsei sonrakuron." See also NRT
3:401–5.

according to Maeda, they developed mostly independently from the laws ordered by the extravillage authorities.[2]

This first phase of research has made available some six hundred village laws and two hundred village codes. In the multivolume histories published by every prefecture for the last twenty years and in the innumerable local histories promoted by the even more recent *furusato būmu,* or boom of hometown-ism, hundreds of additional village regulations, as well as statistical analyses of them by region, can be found.[3]

The first generation of scholars, with the exception of Maeda, were legal scholars trained in the German formalist tradition. For them the mere existence of these village laws constituted proof of a tradition of self-government. But while such an interpretation was of service to the Japanese state's attempt to revitalize local self-government in the interwar decades, it conveniently overlooked the fact that goningumi laws had undeniably been an important instrument of central control over local life during the Tokugawa period.

Maeda, on the other hand, subscribed to the autonomy thesis in perhaps less radical terms but for opposite reasons. Village *codes* or rules *(okite),* he argued, locating their origin and archetype in the famous codes of Nakano, Sugaura, Imabori, and other corporate vil-

2. Scholarly attention was drawn to village laws as soon as historical interest in the Tokugawa village as such was developed with Fukuda Tokuzō's *Die gesellschaftliche und wirtschaftliche Entwickelung in Japan,* Munchener volkswirtschaftliche Studien (Stuttgart: J. G. Cotta, 1900), an economic history of Japan published in German before it was published in Japanese. These works on village laws are: Hozumi Nobushige, *Goningumi seido* (Yūhikaku, 1902); idem, *Goningumi seidoron* (Yūhikaku, 1921); idem, comp., *Goningumi hōkishū* (Yūhikaku, 1921); Hozumi Shigetō, comp., *Goningumi hōkishū zokuhen,* 2 vols. (Yūhikaku, 1944); Nomura Kentarō, *Goningumichō no kenkyū* (Yūhikaku, 1944). The compilation by Nobushige contains the documents he used for his first two books. Shigetō, Nobushige's son, compiled two more volumes, to which he added indexes for all 477 laws contained in both father's and son's compilations. Nomura's study contains another 121 laws. Maeda Masaharu studied 216 village codes in his *Nihon kinsei sonpō no kenkyū* (Yūhikaku, 1952) and "Hō to sonraku kyōdōtai: Edo jidai ni okeru sonpō o chūshin ni," in *Hōken shakai to kyōdōtai,* ed. Shimizu Morimitsu and Aida Yūji (Sōbunsha, 1959), 169–214.

3. Kanzaki Naomi, for instance, recently analyzed 143 village laws of the old Musashi province (today's Gunma prefecture) in "Musashino-kuni no sonpō," *Tama no ayumi,* no. 65 (1991). Examples of similar studies are idem, "Kōzuke kuni no sonpō," *Gunma bunka,* no. 225 (1991): 39–55; Yokota, "Kinsei sonraku"; and Uesugi, "Kinsei sonpō."

lages from Ōmi province, some of which dated back to the mid fifteenth century,[4] constituted an independent tradition. The overlord-generated goningumi regulations (the goningumichō zensho, "preamble to the goningumi roster"), called here village *laws,* adopted many items from these customary codes (especially from the end of the seventeenth century), which in turn took on many formal and substantial features of these laws over time.[5] Maeda's rather tenuously argued thesis of village autonomy and its postwar critique by scholars such as Kodama Kōta,[6] mostly in the form of polemical counterassertions, made clear the need to examine closely how these two kinds of village regulations were related to each other and to extravillage authority. Two scholars addressed these questions in the 1960s: Uesugi Mitsuhiko, who compared laws and codes for content and form, and Ōide Yukiko, who focused on the juridical status of the codes.[7]

VILLAGE LAWS AND VILLAGE CODES

Using fifteen categories, Uesugi compared the content of all of Maeda's village codes with a good number of Hozumi's village laws and concluded that, given an overwhelming similarity, the village codes functioned to *supplement* overlord law as expressed in the village laws of the goningumi rosters.[8] He pointed out that no village code contradicted any overlord stipulation (to which we shall return), but he also warned, following Maeda, that neither these codes nor the laws covered all aspects of village life; the more extensive laws reflected village life

4. Ten of the twelve pre-Tokugawa village codes Maeda looked at are from Ōmi province (*Nihon kinsei sonpō,* "Sonpōshū-hen," 1–15); for a translation of some of the Imabori codes, see Tonomura, *Community and Commerce,* 198–207 passim.

5. Maeda, *Nihon kinsei sonpō,* 7–9, 18.

6. For some critiques, see Uesugi, "Kinsei sonrakuron," 176; and idem, "Kinsei sonpō," 81 n. 6.

7. Uesugi, "Kinsei sonrakuron"; Nanba Nobuo, "Hyakushō ikki no hōishiki," in *Seikatsu, bunka, shisō,* ed. Aoki Michio et al., Ikki, 4 (Tokyo Daigaku, 1981), 43–88; Ōide Yukiko, "Kinsei sonpō to ryōshuken," *(Nagoya Daigaku) Hōsei ronshū,* nos. 18 (1961): 1–31 and 19 (1962): 73–128; Mizumoto, "Kōgi no saiban," 283–316; Mizubayashi Takeshi, "Kinsei no hō to saiban," in *Chūsei no hō to kenryoku,* Chūseishi kōza, 4 (Gakuseisha, 1985), 144–71.

8. Uesugi, "Kinsei sonpō," 86–87. The village codes were more detailed in certain areas, for example, rules to implement attendance at village council meetings, tribute collection, sharing of commons (use of mountains and water), regulations of festivals, and penal matters.

only as it related to overlord interests.[9] After the 1720s the codes' form and language conform closely to the overlord laws, and a good number of them stress the need to obey the laws.[10] According to Uesugi, if there was resistance against overlord power as Maeda argues, there are no signs of it in the texts of the village codes.[11] Over time, village codes came to look more like the lords' laws in form and content, growing longer in response to lordly expectations, especially in sumptuary matters. Ōide presents a more detailed picture of the relationship between village codes and laws, using as her basic data Maeda's and Hozumi's compilations. She first addressed the question of origins and saw an increasing trend of lordly influence in the codification of village codes, especially in the second half of the Tokugawa period.[12]

The overlord's interference took various forms. It was most pronounced when the codes were a direct response to an order from above. A striking example of such lordly initiative is the drafting in 1827 of a lengthy village code for the Kanto villages that were grouped into leagues, *kumiai*. Regional village leagues, linking dozens of villages, developed in the last decades of the eighteenth century.[13] Sometimes a third party outside the village (usually a headman from a neighboring village) was made to participate in the process. This occurred frequently in Mino province in the late Tokugawa period on the occasion of recalls of headmen.[14] More often, villages proceeded to draft codes on their own with regard to a specific overlordly regulation. Other villages presented their codes to the lord on their own initiative. Thus, the "officialization" of village codes was not simply the result of explicit coercive power from above. It was just as often sought from below by local officials adopting a submissive posture, wanting to ingratiate themselves with the authorities by delivering voluntary proof that they were "within the law."

9. Ibid., 88; Maeda, *Nihon kinsei sonpō*, 59.

10. Uesugi, "Kinsei sonpō," 88–90.

11. According to Uesugi (ibid., 88), Maeda argues that village codes reflected villagers' resistance ("Hō to sonraku kyōdōtai," 211–13), although Maeda speaks only of areas of autonomy, especially in matters of justice.

12. Ōide, "Kinsei sonpō," 11–19.

13. For the text of the 1827 code, see Maeda, *Nihon kinsei sonpō*, no. 128 (159–66). On these village leagues, see Anne Walthall, "Village Networks: Sōdai and the Sale of Edo Nightsoil," *Monumenta Nipponica* 43, no. 3 (1988): 279–303.

14. Ōide, "Kinsei sonpō," 112–23.

What was the legal status of these village codes? Officially, the bakufu acknowledged *shikitari yaburi,* the breaking of custom, as a legal ground for suits, but in several lists of "civil" court cases compiled during the Tokugawa period, Ōide could find only a single case based on that claim and one other case that explicitly argued a breach of a village code.[15] Obviously, infractions of village codes were almost never brought before the overlords. In other court cases, overlords acknowledged village codes if these supplemented their own laws without contradiction. The greatest claims for autonomy, however, have to do with village policing and penal powers, which received detailed attention in many codes.[16] What was the bakufu's attitude toward village justice?

In a rare explicit statement on the matter, a response to a query of 1829 on whether a village could impose fines for gambling beyond those stipulated by bakufu law, the superintendent of finances (*kanjō-bugyō*), who also functioned as the overseer of litigation, revealed that the bakufu did not forbid village justice but silently acknowledged it as a *secondary and separate form of justice,* not as the lowest echelon of its own judicial machinery. In practice, village justice was allowed in matters the bakufu did not or could not handle. Local administrators, however, could deal with village disputes *kokoro jidai,* "as they saw fit."[17]

From this we can conclude a general tendency on the part of the bakufu as well as the locals to keep things within the village,[18] often through the mechanism of conciliation and apologies. This tendency created room for potential conflict, because certain serious crimes *had* to be reported upward, for example, manslaughter, arson, even theft and gambling. Obviously not all thefts were reported, although bakufu, domain, and village laws all stipulated that they be reported.[19] When

15. Ibid., 24. This is case no. 58 (dated 1781) from the 160 cases collected in what was left after the Tokyo earthquake (1923) of the *Saikyodome* (Record of judgments), cases that came before the bakufu's supreme court, the Tribunal, or *Hyōjōsho*. The other two collections perused were the *Mokuhi* (Private articles) and the *Kujiroku* (Record of suits).

16. Maeda, *Nihon kinsei sonpō,* 93–149; Uesugi, "Kinsei sonpō," 93–94.

17. Ōide, "Kinsei sonpō," 75–76.

18. Maeda, *Nihon kinsei sonpō,* 31, 116.

19. For the bakufu's general law, see article 56 of the *Kujikata osadamegaki* of 1742, in TKKk 3:189; for an English translation, see Hall, "Japanese Feudal Laws III," 755. For reference to domain laws and village laws, see Ōide, "Kinsei sonpō," 78–79.

gambling became a serious problem in the second half of the period, the bakufu explicitly allowed local punishment: in 1723 the bakufu proclaimed that it was no longer necessary to report gambling in bakufu and daimyo domains of the Kanto area, and the law was extended to the whole country in 1788.[20]

That villages had certain penal powers did not mean that they were free to apply any kind of punishment. Death penalties were strictly forbidden, although Mizumoto has found village codes in Echigo that listed the death penalty among possible punishments for about fifty years in the second half of the eighteenth century, an extremely rare case according to Mizumoto.[21] Maeda reports one village law in 1621 that prescribed the death penalty for gambling "after obtaining the opinion of the overlord."[22] And we shall soon see that the village codes of Hozu stipulated that (village) samurai could cut down peasants who offended them.

Banishment, or *tsuihō*, was allowed when its application was not "private" or arbitrary: permission had to be secured in advance from intendants; sometimes, however, reporting it after the fact made it legal.[23] There was one way of banishing people that was not labeled *tsuihō*: a person could be legally taken "off the [population] roster" (*chōgai*) in response to a request by village officials or relatives, which resulted in loss of residence and legal status for the person in question. Banishment might also consist in expelling a person to a location just beyond the village border and letting him or her live (or die) there in a makeshift shelter. Shinzō in chapter 1 was a victim of both removal from the roster and expulsion beyond the village. Perhaps the most well known form of village punishment is ostracism (*murahachibu*), whereby a person was cut off from social interaction and most mutual help. This particular form was generated by the village itself. It is found only in village codes, not in village laws.

Throughout the period, village codes relied on overlord authority— "borrowed" its power, so to speak—by stipulating that any infringement of the codes would be reported to the lord. Ōide sees a gradual

20. Ōide, "Kinsei sonpō," 82.
21. Mizumoto, "Kōgi no saiban," 295.
22. Maeda, *Nihon kinsei sonpō:* "Kenkyū," 103; "Furoku," 16.
23. Ōide, "Kinsei sonpō," 85–87. See also article 26 of the goningumi rules of 1662 from Shimo-Sakurai, Kita-Saku district, Shinano, in appendix 3.

merging of the two kinds of justice, lordly and village justice. Punishments became lighter; physical punishments (banishment or mutilation) tended to become rarer from the middle of the period onward and were replaced by fines; increasingly, crimes were reported beyond the village. With the rural crisis of the nineteenth century, the village leadership was no longer able to handle village affairs and came to rely on the overlords to resolve conflicts, thereby increasing considerably the time and energy intendants spent adjudicating disputes.

CLASS AND STATUS CODIFICATIONS

I mentioned earlier that the bakufu's main status codification related to the separation of warrior rulers from commoner subjects. It did not legislate status differences among peasants aside from setting the village officials (*murakata*, "village persons") apart from the rest of the peasantry, from amongst whom those responsible for the tribute were singled out as titled peasants. This legislation, however, is not to be found in the bakufu's best-known (but secret) code of 1742, the *Kujikata osadamegaki,* or in the famous rural administrative regulations for intendants from the Kan'ei period (the 1640s), but in the goningumi laws. That is where the overlords' expectations were made clear to the mass of commoners.

Many of the stipulations concerning tribute payment, open information about each peasant's share of the tribute, and the village budget (which was discussed earlier and for which I referred to bakufu legislation addressed mainly to intendants) were incorporated into village laws very early on. This can be seen, for instance, in the expansion of successive versions of goningumi regulations for the same village. Appendix 2 offers the translation of one of the earliest village laws in bakufu territories (twenty-one articles), from Shimo-Sakurai, in Kita-Saku, dated 1640. The second extant version, from ten years later, consists of forty-seven articles, twenty of them from the bakufu's nation-wide directions for villages, issued twelve months earlier, in 1649/2 (see appendix 4).[24] By 1662 this village law, now comprising fifty-six articles, had acquired the form it would have for the next two hundred years (see appendix 3).

24. See Hozumi Shigetō, *Goningumi hōkishū zokuhen,* 1:28–36; cf. TKKz 5:159–64 (no. 2789, arts. 28–47). On the controversy concerning the historical status of this famous edict, see appendix 4.

Before turning to these village laws, however, we shall examine perhaps the most famous of the shogunal Keian edicts, the one of 1649, which was issued for all villages in the realm. Status is hardly an issue in the edict. Only article 16 deals with it by prescribing cotton as the only fabric to be used by peasants (see appendix 4), a typical sumptuary regulation that under the guise of ethics (frugality) pretends to regulate economics (consumption) but in fact targets politics by codifying status.[25] Economic production and well-being per se are given far more emphasis. A basic concern is the maintenance and reproduction of the means of production, that is, the peasants: they should be fed more when labor is more demanding (art. 10), keep in good health (art. 22), maintain collective productivity through mutual help (art. 29), and so on. Much advice is given about ways to increase productivity and wealth. Among the items included are how to select grains (art. 6); injunctions to sharpen hoes and sickles once a year (art. 7); how to build toilets to collect manure (art. 8); the necessity of supervising the labor force, planning around the weather (arts. 11, 12), and disposing of surplus children (art. 18); encouragement to make a profit (arts. 5, 21) and raise one's standard of living by being business-minded (*shōshin, akinagokoro*) (art. 17).These were all things peasants did of their own accord, one would assume, but here they become the object of bakufu "national" legislation.

Economic well-being (*shinshō*), its improvement, and its social reward in the form of respect (art. 30), as well as the scorn that can be a product of its absence, are major themes of the edict (arts. 2, 17, 30, 35). Economic well-being is seen as the basis of morality, because poverty leads to crime, a process described as an alarming cascade of worsening conditions: "poverty may cause illness, warp the mind, cause one to steal, violate the law, wind up in prison, receive the death penalty, be crucified," to which is added an ominous "etc." (art. 32). This is an interesting "economization" of virtue in the same alarmist terms the Confucian scholar Yamazaki Ansai (1618–82) used to characterize the inevitable fall from one evil thought into the abomination of abominations, the killing of the lord.[26]

25. During the seventeenth century in Kishū domain, village group headmen were allowed to wear pongee; headmen and elders could use silk only in collars; and peasant dress was limited to cotton (see Hirayama Kōzō, *Kishū-han nōsonpō no kenkyū* [Yoshikawa kōbunkan, 1972], 185).

26. Ooms, *Tokugawa Ideology*, 220, 223, 247.

In some sixteenth-century writings virtue was quantified and externalized through its identification with calculation and foresight in the management of people by lords.[27] In Ansai's neo-Confucianism, virtue was politicized and internalized in terms of the values of respect and silent loyalty.[28] In these village regulations, it was given an economic and social slant. Article 31 looks very much like a transposition into an economic key of the famous passage in the *Great Learning* that describes the expansion of the ruler's virtue throughout the realm. Here, however, the source is not the ruler but any subject whose creation of wealth will be imitated within the village, in neighboring villages, in the province, and in neighboring provinces. Another crucial virtue, filial piety, is transformed in a similar way: "No matter how devoted one may be to one's parents, it is difficult to be filial when one is in misery (*fuben*)" (art. 32). This was one way that Confucianism reached the masses. Buddhism and even folk belief in curses are marshaled in the Kita-Saku version of this edict to enjoin peasants to take great care of their horses and bulls (art. 14).

Social status and standing are unambiguously linked to economic well-being: people will start to respect you, be nice to you, and even promote your official status from a lower seat (in shrine associations and councils) to an upper seat if you improve your material conditions (art. 30). We know from chapter 3, however, that village practice was altogether a different matter: status was used to hold off competitors for political power who were agitating on the basis of their economic achievements.

Status issues were far more prominent in village laws and village codes than in the Keian edicts. The prohibition on wearing anything but cotton appeared in Shimo-Sakurai's village law (art. 10 [see appendix 2]) in 1640, a year after it was proscribed by the bakufu in its Kan'ei edict. In the next extant edition of that law (1662 [see appendix 3]), a sartorial status distinction is made between headmen and peasants (art. 10), and it is stressed that one should not exceed the bounds of one's status on ceremonial, that is public, occasions (art. 12). Moreover, the first article presents a hierarchized list of people, from house owners to servants, and so on, down to outcastes and nonhumans. Elsewhere too

27. Ibid., 24–25.
28. Ibid., 219–20, 247–48.

(arts. 2, 9, 22) the religious types are lumped together with the outcastes and criminal elements.

In numerous other village *laws,* similar concerns with status are expressed beginning around the mid seventeenth century. Rules stress the forms of greeting and behavior that peasants (even former samurai) should use in the presence of samurai.[29] Small peasants were to observe a specific etiquette in their dealings with the village leaders.[30] Interestingly, the latter stipulation dates from the end of the century, when the small peasants, who had come into their own economically, were agitating for higher status within the village.

Status maintenance, however, is threatened not only by disrespect. Self-assertive behavior can be an expression of economic security: many elements of material culture—specifically, as Weber notes, modes of consumption—function as status signifiers. Hence, regulations in this area reveal where threats to status distinctions developed. "In the building of houses, at weddings, funerals, regular village council meetings, behavior and dress should be according to previous regulations and one should not make light of status in anything" (1684, 1697). Permission was needed to build new-style houses (1698). Umbrellas and geta might keep one dry when it rained, but peasants could not use them; instead they had to make do with straw hats and, presumably, straw sandals (1828, 1838). "Only taka-holding peasants entered on the land surveys can build structures with gates, walled fences, and eaves; branch houses of kin that have such features may keep them, but from now on this will not be allowed" (1767).[31] Similar status-related prohibitions can be found also in village *codes.* To cite one rather late example from 1832, cotton was prescribed for all seasons, and silk was forbidden, as were haori coats; umbrellas were only for officials; geta and leather-soled sandals were forbidden; and sake consumption was to be limited to one or two shō, that is, two to three liters.[32]

These regulations, whether generated from within the village as codes or without as laws, were normative attempts to protect social and

29. Hozumi Shigetō, *Goningumi hōkishū zokuhen,* 1:33 (1650), 68 (1679).
30. Ibid., 1:235–36 (1698).
31. Ibid., 1:129 (1684), 222 (1697), 236 (1698); 2:1159 (1828), 1193 (1838); 1:407 (1767).
32. Maeda, *Nihon kinsei sonpō,* no. 137 (177–78).

economic positions via status signs whose symbolic power rested on their being relatively rare. Such regulations were, perhaps, less necessary in the early period, when extended families prevailed and hierarchy was so obviously tied to gradations of economic dependency that proper behavior was instilled through a socialization that could dispense with written codes. However, the obvious leveling effects of the commercialization of the peasant economy necessitated codification that generated differences.

When it was dissociated from the status holders' shrinking economic base (landless titled peasants), status ceased to function as an obvious sign of class value (except as a déclassé one). The draining of the economic, however, revealed (and created) the political, now the shrunken signified of status. Hence the struggle between, on the one hand, status holders (old titled peasants) revalidating their now purely symbolic capital by reference to ancestry (when this status value was certified in land survey records) and, on the other, challengers (new economically autonomous peasants) appealing to the same logic that had created status as an expression of economic autonomy, which they now possessed, and had given political voice, which they were now being denied.

Since village codes were drafted by the village elite, it is not surprising that from the beginning some of them quite explicitly reveal a clearly defensive "class" effort to preserve privilege, status, and power, as well as their economic base. Such strategic class-based linkages, however, are hard to demonstrate if one limits oneself to the textual study of codes. Links can best be established by focusing one's research on a village or region whose socioeconomic structure can be identified. Very few historians have engaged in this kind of research, but there are at least two such studies on which we can rely: Igeta Ryōji's, for the village of Hozu in Tanba (near Kyoto), and Ōide Yukiko's, for the Mino region (Gifu).[33] They reveal a village structure different from the three studied so far (the corporate village, the village dominated by dogō, and the cooperative village).

33. Igeta Ryōji, "Hōkenteki sonraku kyōdōtai to mura okite: Tamba-kuni Hozu-mura gomyō shūdan no sonraku shihai," *Dōshisha hōgaku* (1960–62): 58 (1960): 52–78, 61 (1960): 80–109, 62 (1960): 27–56, 65 (1961): 23–45, 70 (1962): 66–98, 75 (1962): 87–108; idem, *Kinsei sonraku no mibun kōzō* (Kokusho kankōkai, 1984); Ōide, "Kinsei sonpō."

STRATEGIES FOR ELITE REPRODUCTION: HOZU
VILLAGE, 1500s–1900

The Hozu locale (in Kameyama domain, Tanba province, which today
is part of the township of Kameoka, some fifteen kilometers, across the
mountains, west of Kyoto) consisted administratively, at least from the
1580s, of two villages, a northern (Kita-) and a southern (Minami-)
Hozu, which together constituted a large community. In 1749 it numbered 376 households with 2,068 koku. Kita-Hozu's 125 households
formed one kumi, while Minami-Hozu's 251 were divided into three
regional kumi. In addition, there was a fifth kumi, a *gomyō* ("five
names [shoots]"), that was not regional, but comprised a number of
households in both villages. The gomyō households (24 in 1616; 53 in
1669; 61 in 1801; 83 in 1872)[34] each bore the family name of one of
the five village founders, and they called themselves samurai throughout the Tokugawa period.[35] Officially, in the eyes of the overlord in
Kameoka (less than two kilometers away), they were titled peasants
(*otonabyakushō*). In addition to and separate from these five kumi there
was a community of outcastes concentrated mainly (in 1872, 69 of the
74 households) in Minami-Hozu.[36]

In Tanba there were many groups like the gomyō, samurai of the
soil who maintained their family identity well into the Tokugawa period.[37] What was unusual about the gomyō was that, at some point
in the sixteenth century or perhaps later, these families had consolidated into an organization that maintained itself until the Meiji period

34. Igeta, "Hōkenteki sonraku," 58:59–60. Hayashi Motoi has a different
reading for gomyō, namely, gobyō (see Hayashi Motoi, *Kyōhō to Kansei*,
Kokumin no rekishi, 16 [Bun'eidō, 1971], 395). I am following Igeta, who did
the original research, and he confirmed the reading gomyō.
35. Igeta, "Hōkenteki sonraku," 58:55–56.
36. For data on the outcaste population of Hozu, see Igeta Ryōji, "Kinsei
kōki no buraku sabetsu seisaku," *Dōshisha hōgaku* 110 (1969): 28–49 and
111 (1969): 53–84, esp. 54 and 66 for the population data; idem, "Mikaihō
burakumin no iriaiken," *Minshōhō zasshi* 78, suppl. no. 1 (1979): 201–16;
and idem, "Mikaihō buraku to iriaiken: Kyōtō-fu Kameoka-shi Hozu-mura no
baai," *Dōshisha hōgaku* 136 (1975): 101–44.
37. For instance, neighboring Umaji was ruled by two such families called
ryōmyō ("two names") (see Igeta, *Kinsei sonraku*, esp. chap. 2; see also Igeta
Ryōji, *Hō o miru Kurio no me: rekishi to gendai* [Kyoto: Hōritsu bunkasha,
1987], 89–101).

Plate 3. Hozu Village. From the bank of Hozu River, facing north, midway between Hozu and the castle town of Kameoka. Photograph by author.

when they formally incorporated. The gomyō was clearly an institution set up to defend class interests against other classes of villagers, such as the bond servants (genin) employed by these households and the small peasants, who were kept small for over two hundred years. The threat against the reproduction of this local upper class came from social change that took three successive forms. First, as landed samurai these families lost institutional support from the overlords, who did not recognize village samurai. Second, economic growth enriched the small peasants and led to the emancipation of many bond servants. Finally, the gomyō's own reproduction, if not checked, would weaken their economic base if with each generation holdings were divided among new branch families. This class succeeded in meeting these challenges until the nineteenth century. Because these families ruled the two Hozu villages, their strategies inform the village codes, which reveal where normative defenses had to be erected.

The 1636 "village" code, eleven short, one-line articles, was explicitly called "Rules for the Genin Peasants of Minami-Hozu" (the ones for Kita-Hozu are not extant).[38] All the articles are prohibitions to prevent status pollution: genin peasants cannot wear swords or leather-soled sandals, use umbrellas, or go by samurai names; children should not address their parents as *toto* (dad) and *kaka* (mom); a genin peasant cannot refer to himself or herself as *midomo* or to others as *ore;* anyone rude in the company of samurai shall be cut down.

The last three rules need some explanation. *Toto* and *kaka* are children's terms, obviously devoid of reverential connotations. One can only guess why they constituted a problem in the eyes of these village samurai. Perhaps these samurai sensed that, as Bourdieu has remarked, "concessions of politeness ... always contain political concessions"[39] and thus felt that they needed to dictate intrafamily behavior—the personal is political. *Midomo* and *ore* are status- and rank-marking personal pronouns, the former used by samurai to refer to themselves, the latter used for inferiors.[40] Thus, genin peasants were not to speak or behave as equals to "samurai," a privilege the gomyō, who perceived themselves as samurai, preserved for themselves. This contrasts sharply with articles one finds in numerous village laws expressing the overlord's point of view that former samurai, which legally the gomyō were, are to be treated as peasants.[41]

The article affirming the samurai's right to cut down peasants encourages the swift action that had become outlawed by Ieyasu's rule of 1603 that "the killing of peasants for no reason (*muza to*) should be stopped, but if [a peasant] is guilty, he should be caught, arrested, and punished in accordance with a verdict by shogunal officers (*bugyōjo*)."[42] The samurai of Hozu village, one presumes, were not only going by a pre-Tokugawa practice: they were codifying it explicitly in 1636, an unusual example of a code contradicting lordly law.

38. Igeta, "Hōkenteki sonraku," 58:58.
39. Bourdieu, *Logic of Practice,* 69.
40. Nowadays, *ore* is used only as first-person pronoun; in Tokugawa times, however, it was also used as the third-person pronoun for inferiors. For *midomo,* see the entry in *Kōjien* (Iwanami shoten, 1955); for *ore,* see the entry in *Daijiten,* 13 vols. (Heibonsha, 1934).
41. Hozumi Shigetō, *Goningumi hōkishū zokuhen,* 1:33 (1650), 68 (1679).
42. The rule outlawing the killing of peasants "for no reason" was the last article of a seven-article decree issued by Tokugawa Ieyasu (the only one he issued about local governance) (see Kodama Kōta and Ōishi Shinzaburō, eds., *Kinsei nōsei shiryōshū,* vol. 1, *Edo bakufu hōrei 1* [Yoshikawa kōbunkan, 1966], 1).

Slow economic growth made genin potential buyers of land. In order to control the transfer of land out of gomyō hands, "village" rules were issued in 1691 (and again in 1731 and 1746) prohibiting the sale of paddies and fields to genin; they could acquire only homesteads with garden plots of dry fields. Similar economic restrictions were instituted against the outcastes elsewhere. Other sartorial regulations in Hozu, such as the prohibition against wearing leather-soled sandals, are also identical to those imposed on outcastes. In Hozu, therefore, which also had an outcaste community, small peasants, even taka holders, were treated like outcastes in a number of respects.[43]

There were no restrictions on land sales among peasants. A samurai unable to find a samurai buyer and wanting to sell to a peasant had first to report the price to the samurai council, whose directions for the sale had to be followed; that is, the council set the price. In 1759 a new regulation forbade others than samurai to fish with nets in the Hozu River. The river was also the source of additional wealth through the rafting of logs, but the village samurai had a monopoly on this business too.[44] Although by the mid Tokugawa period they lost to the overlord their control over the use of the mountain, they still had a monopoly on the use of the commercially very valuable standing trees.[45] These "samurai" clearly constituted an economic class, both objectively, since they were the important landowners and entrepreneurs of sorts, and subjectively, because they were very conscious of the interests that bound them together, which they defended through status and commercial legislation that denied the small peasants economic opportunities.

In the eighteenth century, class differentiation occurred slowly within both the dominant and the dominated class in the two Hozu villages: the greatest holdings—between 1596 and 1636 two samurai had increased their holdings from 56 and 65 koku to 75 and 104 koku, respectively—leveled off to 50 koku, and peasants came to hold land. Yet the two groups remained distinct economically: the gomyō holdings clustered in the 5–20-koku bracket. In the 1720s and 1730s a number of peasants became very small owners (see table 18 for Kita-Hozu),

43. Igeta also makes this point in his "Kuchi-Tanba chihō no hisabetsu shūraku," in *Zenkindai Kyoto no burakushi,* ed. Buraku mondai kenkyujo, Kyoto no buraku mondai, 1 (Kyoto: Buraku mondai kenkyujo, 1987), 122.
44. Igeta, "Hōkenteki sonraku," 58:60–61, 65:44, 24–25.
45. Igeta, "Mikaihō buraku," 104–5.

Table 18. Kita-Hozu Holdings, 1723–1872

	1723		1740		1763		1820		1872	
Koku	G	P	G	P	G	P	G	P	G	P
50+	1						1			
30–50	6		5		1				2	
20–30	2		1		2		3		3	
10–20	2	2	4	4	6		2		5	
5–10	3	2	3	2	4	1	1		3	5
1–5	6	9	5	9	2	10	9		2	7
−1	3	33	5	32	1	31	1	17	4	40
0	1	33	3	35	3	42	2	69	4	23 [5]
Total	24	79	26	79	19	87	19	86	23	75 [5]
Total G + P	103		105		106		105		103	

SOURCE: Igeta, *Kinsei sonraku*, tables III-17, III-37, and III-44 (pp. 191, 308, and 335).

NOTE: G = gomyō; P = non-gomyō small peasants (fudai and genin houses not included); numbers in square brackets refer to outcaste households; Igeta gives no earlier figures for outcastes.

but they clustered in the category of less than 1 koku. In the following decades, however, many became landless again, although the overall number of peasant owners remained at a higher level than before the 1720s. In striking contrast to Kodaira village (analyzed in chapter 3), where titled peasants became economically indistinguishable from nontitled peasants, the gomyō in Hozu succeeded extraordinarily well in maintaining economic supremacy. Socially too the two groups remained distinct. There was no intermarriage between the village samurai and the rest of the village population, although there were numerous intermarriages between peasant owners and genin and fudai.[46]

Gomyō strategically regulated landownership, so that the nongomyō peasant population (genin and small peasants) consisted only of very tiny holders, who thus had to become servants and tenants to the gomyō as a group. The restrictions on land sales were only one part of this overall strategy. In 1748 rules forbade villagers to become tenants

46. Igeta, "Hōkenteki sonraku," 58:65, 61:92, 101.

or seek employment elsewhere. The gomyō thus kept wages for servants low and rents for tenant farmers high. In 1781–82 all this was challenged by demands that the wages of women servants and of rafters employed in the logging business be increased, that the prohibition against service in other locales be lifted, that land rents be lowered, and, aiming at the heart of the system, that treating peasants as hereditary vassals be stopped.[47] We shall return to this crisis shortly.

In order to prevent the downsizing of their holdings, the village samurai started practicing single inheritance by one son around 1700. The other siblings, to whom the prohibition against outside employment obviously did not apply (the "village" rules were for the non-gomyō), left the village to seek employment as servants or engage in trade in Kyoto or Osaka and eventually return with their own assets.[48] This is interesting because the survival of older patterns of authority and power is usually considered characteristic of "backward" areas; in the Kinai region these patterns are usually said to have disappeared rather early. In the present case, however (which was not exceptional in southern Tanba), the proximity to Kyoto and Osaka was an important factor in making the reproduction of these relations possible.

The small peasants responded to this class organization of the village samurai or landlords by forming their own, as a religious (*nenbutsu*) sodality. The first documented trace of its existence dates from 1733, but it may have been formed earlier. Although it was divided geographically into several kumi, this organization spanned the two villages and functioned as an official institution to defend the small peasants in their confrontations, physical or legal, with the gomyō. The village authorities, that is, the gomyō, acknowledged the peasants' organization as a semipublic institution, since they corresponded with it and allowed its representatives to testify in suits involving peasants. Other villages in the area, such as Umaji, had similar organizations, which, although structured "horizontally" as fellowships, nevertheless had their own hierarchy.[49]

47. Igeta, "Kinsei kōki seisaku," 111:71. The "label" *fudai*, as opposed to the "reality"—a contrast perhaps best understood again as tatemae versus honne—had disappeared from records after the 1750s; these were mainly newcomers from outside who had been living with gomyō households since the 1720s (idem, "Kuchi-Tanba," 120).

48. Igeta, "Hōkenteki sonraku," 62:35–36.

49. Ibid., 61:105–9.

In 1781/6 an incident among a few villagers soon developed into a confrontation between the two classes.[50] One day a few young peasants walked through the village wearing leather-soled straw sandals. A couple of gomyō members from Kita-Hozu berated the young men for breaking village regulations by wearing rain gear and beat them up. The angry victims rallied the support of the nenbutsu sodality and went to the house of one of the assailants, where they were denied an audience. Then the peasants decided to boycott the gomyō by refusing to work for them in the fields and in a business of fruit products owned by one of the gomyō.

The gomyō ordered an end to the boycott because it interfered with their livelihood, but the peasants refused because the whole affair, they argued, was the result of the other side's unreasonable behavior. The assailants admitted to having beaten up the young men but thought their behavior had been justified because the latter had broken the rule forbidding peasants to wear leather-soled straw sandals. Such incidents obviously were symptoms of other economic and social tensions and signaled the start of the various demands mentioned earlier. In the 1780s Hozu and the Tanba region, like much of the rest of the country, witnessed peasant disturbances.[51]

Although they had maintained their economic dominance (see table 19), by 1800 the gomyō were under considerable pressure from the peasants, who for over a decade had been challenging their authority in the various ways described. At the same time, the financially strapped domain lord came to rely on the gomyō for "loans." The gomyō exploited this situation to enhance their members' status within the village in the following way.

The domain had a number of schemes (five of which were implemented within the domain) to borrow money from the peasants and from other sources of revenue in Kyoto and Osaka.[52] Two of those schemes are relevant for the present discussion. The first one consisted in obtaining individual loans from wealthy peasants. Thus, in 1764 and 1800 the daimyo borrowed a total of 45 *kanme* (copper currency equal to 1,000 *mon*) from three wealthy Hozu villagers (with combined hold-

---

50. Ibid., 70:67–68.
51. Anne Walthall discusses the unrest in Hozu following this "sandal incident" (*Social Protest*, 109–11).
52. Igeta, "Hōkenteki sonraku," 75:89–97.

Table 19. Gomyō Holdings, Minami- and Kita-Hozu, 1801

Koku	No. of Households	Koku
100+	1	
50–100	9	
30–50	7	
20–30	9 (17)	(928.5)
10–20	9	
5–10	7	
1–5	11	
–1	8	(436.1)
Total	61	1,364.6

SOURCE: Igeta, *Kinsei sonraku*, table III-36 (p. 308).

NOTE: The total number of households was 376: 61 (16%) gomyō and 315 (84%) peasants. The total kokudaka was 2,068: 1,364 (66%) gomyō, with an average of 22.3 koku each; and 703 (34%) peasants, with an average of 2.2 koku each. It is unlikely that the kokudaka includes plots owned by outsiders. Also, most of the fields listed under peasants were held under tenancy, so that most of the peasants had less than 1 koku, which amounted to some vegetable plots around their homesteads.

ings of 227 koku). In addition, loans were obtained from whole villages in the form of advance tribute payments. As always, repayment was a problem, redemption was postponed, interest rates were lowered, and so on.

The bulk of these loans, private and communal, were shouldered by the large landowners. Unlike the other villages in the area, which were receiving interest payments with return of the principal postponed, "Hozu village" generously forfeited its principal (and thus also the interest payments). But the gomyō samurai-landowners wanted something in return from the lord for the real capital they had provided him: symbolic capital. They requested official recognition of their samurai pedigree as *gōshi* (landed samurai), which of course they had always considered themselves to be, this no doubt in order to shore up their position within the village. A hundred years earlier decrees had explicitly forbidden the wearing of swords by peasants and adopting the title gōshi.[53]

53. Igeta, "Kuchi-Tanba," 124.

The lord, however, aware of the frictions and tensions between this group and the common peasants, was wary of further accentuating class differences by making them official; he therefore proposed allowing thirty non-gomyō village notables, like the leadership of the nenbutsu confraternity, to wear haori (ceremonial coats, a status marker). The gomyō objected strenuously and got their way. For the lord, there were only titled and common peasants; ancestry did not play a part, since membership in these groups normally shifted over time. Moreover, the gomyō would not be genuine landed samurai, but cash samurai who had bought their status. The gomyō, however, wanted the peasants to be officially their vassals (kerai).

Another point of friction with the lord developed when he "discovered" that all gomyō households formed one single separate kumi, while all other peasants were grouped in their own kumi. (Since Hozu was only a fifteen-minute walk from the castle, this "discovery" two hundred years into the Tokugawa period is not to be taken too literally.)[54] The gomyō were supposed to form the leadership of each kumi; otherwise some peasant households would acquire a semihereditary position as kumi heads, resulting in a new status next to that of the titled peasants. From the lord's point of view, village government consisted of village officials, kumi heads, and peasants, and the status system contained only titled and small peasants. The lord, however, was in no position to follow through on the principles he had announced in the negotiations with the gomyō, and he wound up recognizing for thirty-nine members of the gomyō a venerable samurai pedigree going back over three hundred years to Hosokawa Takakuni (1484–1531). Similarly, in neighboring Umaji, under a bannerman, thirty-nine of its "titled peasants" became landed samurai in 1807, and two years later the remaining twenty-two were also promoted, for reasons not unlike those in Hozu.[55]

Within a year of their promotion as officially certified landed samurai, the gomyō had to deal with a consequence of a scheme they had resorted to in order to control their peasant tenants, who had been agitating for lower rents. For some time, possibly since the agitation in 1781–82, the

54. This is not to suggest that Hozu was governed by the same house throughout the entire Tokugawa period. Hozu had six different overlords during the seventeenth century. In 1702 the Aoyama daimyo and finally, in 1748, a Matsudaira house came to rule the fifty-thousand-koku domain of Kameyama (from the castle town by that name, now Kameoka).

55. Igeta, "Kuchi-Tanba," 124.

gomyō had been renting land to the outcastes as a countermove against some small peasants who had gone on a rent strike in order to press their demand for lower rents. These renters had refused to continue renting some low-quality fields. The gomyō had simply replaced them with outcaste tenants. In Umaji, which had had no outcaste community, the *ryōmyō* ("two names"), a group like the gomyō but consisting of two lineages, imported thirty-three outcaste households in 1808 for similar reasons. These were pure peasants, who did not engage in the removal of dead cattle, a job that was taken care of in the area by five other outcaste communities, one of which was Hozu's.[56]

This heightened the tension between the outcastes, who were now also strikebreakers, and the peasants, who had seen their boycott come to naught. The tension erupted into violence when, in 1802, peasants repeatedly destroyed the grass and firewood that the outcastes had gleaned from the commons, which the outcastes needed for their fields.[57] The disputants were reconciled, but violence erupted some six times in the summer of 1808, forcing the outcastes to take legal action first with the Hozu leadership, then with the domain. In 1811 this led to a settlement that favored the outcastes by increasing their portion of the commons, and this was followed by an additional increase in 1815. But the peasants had already scored against the outcastes in 1809: "in order to avoid trouble in this time of tension," the outcastes were not to deliver their rice tribute on the same day that the peasants delivered theirs.

In this conflict with the peasants, the outcastes found allies in the village leadership, that is, the gomyō, and the overlord. It is clear, however, that the gomyō played the outcastes off against the peasants in order to keep rents high and that the lord supported this policy because the solidity of his tribute base, namely, the gomyō's economic well-being, depended on it.

This outcastes' increased access to mountain land was strictly limited to foraging for agricultural use: none of the collected material could be sold, and no (commercially valuable) standing trees could be cut down. Moreover, based on the Meiji data (see table 20), it appears that the

56. Ibid., 97.
57. The following information is culled from Igeta, "Kinsei kōki seisaku," 111:55, 61–65, 71–72, 77, 81; and idem, "Mikaihō burakumin," 209–12. See also his "Kuchi-Tanba."

Table 20. Minami- and Kita-Hozu Holdings, 1872

| Koku | Gomyō | | | Peasants | | | Outcastes | | | Total |
	M	K	Total	M	K	Total	M	K	Total	
80+	1		1							1
50–80	3		3							3
30–50	6	2	8							8
20–30	12	3	15							15
10–20	16	5	21							21
5–10	7	3	10	1	5	6				16
1–5	6	2	8	16	7	23				31
−1	4	4	8	66	40	106	2		2	116
0	5	4	9	110	23	133	67	5	72	214
Total	60	23	83	193	75	268	69	5	74	425

SOURCE: Igeta, *Kinsei sonraku*, table III-44 (p. 335).
NOTE: M = Minami-Hozu; K = Kita-Hozu.

share of the area of mountain land available per household was heavily slanted in favor of the peasants, in a ratio of 100 to 28, or roughly 4 to 1, a ratio that remained unchanged throughout the nineteenth century. In 1909, as a result of activism by the burakumin descendants of the outcastes, this ratio was changed, to 4 to 3. But it was only in 1961 that equality was achieved, at least in terms of land. Igeta suggests, however, that in terms of quality of mountain land, discrimination continued to persist.[58] Although Igeta does not mention this, it may very well be that some of the disproportion in the common land available for use to

58. "Mikaihō buraku," 108. A famous case for the clear right of access to commons by *burakumin* was settled in the Niboku court (Nagano) as late as 1973, when it was decided that, contrary to earlier arguments, burakumin were indeed full members of rural communities, with equal rights, and did not constitute separate, nonagricultural communities. Hozu outcastes were involved in litigation for over a century and a half (see Igeta Ryōji, "Meiji kōki no kenri tōsō no ichi jirei: Mikaihō burakumin no byōdō iriai yōkyū," in *Nihon kindai kokka no hō kōzō*, ed. Nihon Kindai Hōseishi Kenkyūkai [Bokutakusha, 1983], 482–514. On the Niboku case, see Igeta, "Mikaihō buraku," 101–6; and Aoki Takahisa, "Niboku iriaiken jiken to hanketsu no igi," *Buraku mondai kenkyū* 40 [1973]: 34–70). Frank Upham kindly alerted me to the existence of these modern cases.

peasants and to outcastes is to be explained by the fact that shares may have been calculated by holding size rather than per household.

Through a number of devices and strategies, a clearly identifiable class of samurai-landowners succeeded in securing its survival as a class for some three centuries. In part these village samurai resisted overlord authority by maintaining a posture of samurai vis-à-vis the peasants whom they continued to rule as vassals. On the other hand, they also relied on the overlord, who acknowledged their dominant position as titled peasants, and they succeeded in forcing him to officialize their position further by granting them the title of landed samurai, which they had coveted for some two hundred years. Village regulations were an important means to preserve this class's economic preeminence, and status was an effective weapon to maintain class difference.

Village legislation was put into the service of similar overt class interests in Mino province, as Ōide Yukiko has demonstrated. There the peasants were divided between *kashirabyakushō* ("head peasants," i.e., titled peasants) and *wakibyakushō* ("side," or regular, perhaps marginal, peasants). The former held a monopoly on village power and relied on a variety of customs that set them apart from the others: they had their own protective deities (ujigami) and wedding ceremonies, and they did not marry across class lines. Such an upper-class peasantry, with its marks of distinction, was found throughout the province, whatever the jurisdictional character of the overlords—daimyo domains, Tokugawa houseland, or intendant territories.[59] The familiar scenario of economic growth threatening the preeminent position of the dominant fraction of the peasant class also played itself out here. The village codes of this entire region were almost exclusively concerned, not with cultivation, but with maintaining the relationship of domination between the two classes.

Who were these titled peasants? They defined themselves either as families who were registered on Hideyoshi's survey; or as landed samurai "since the ancient past" privileged to have surnames, wear swords, and have their own protective deities; or quite straightforwardly as large property owners. Descent and ownership, however, were not sufficient to defend them against the economic threats that would eventually erode their distinction as a class. Hence the reliance on sumptuary vil-

59. Ōide, "Kinsei sonpō," 111–14. The next several paragraphs are based on ibid., 113–22.

lage codes controlling consumption, specifically its most visible form: houses. Almost universally there were detailed building codes prohibiting regular peasants from having gates at their residences or entranceways, roofs with eaves, or rooms with ceilings.

To these were often added other limitations, for example, on public display of wealth: stone tombstones were prohibited, as were cremation huts and the use of palanquins. None of this legislation regulating status came from the overlords, although they generally acquiesced in it. As in Hozu village and the Tanba region, this system did not meet any serious challenge until the first decades of the nineteenth century (1800–1840), although related incidents occurred sporadically from the 1630s.

Increasingly, with the rising number of infringements, class and status conflicts were less likely to find a solution in the divided villages. The overlords distanced themselves as much as they could from these problems and insisted on in situ conciliation. For this purpose they relied more and more on the mediation of the leaders from surrounding villages. They also began to inquire into the content of the village codes, and they even had these same leaders from other villages preside over the drafting of new codes for problem villages. Needless to say, such village regulations are hard to reconcile with the standard image of Tokugawa villages as consensual and autonomous communities. Even from the beginning these regulations were not based on communal consensus, and they lost their autonomous character as well when they were redrafted by nonvillage members.

In the (very) long run, the struggle to maintain status regardless of economic reality was lost. Ultimately, regular peasants bought their privileges from the lord: six of them offered to pay three hundred ryō to be reclassified as titled peasants; in Ōgaki domain (100,000 koku) the lord even decreed that all peasants be promoted to that status in 1867.

Igeta sees the Hozu pattern of status manipulation as distinct from the more familiar dogō and corporate villages; and it should be added that they were also different from the cooperative villages of Fukuyama. Without the pyramidal, paternalistic structure of villages tying individual households to individual magnate landlords, a whole "incorporated" class of large landholders kept another class of very small landholders dependent as a group; many tenants had multiple "landlords," with whom they interacted as a group. This, Igeta suggests, was typical of the mountainous parts of the larger Kinai region (including South

Tanba, Yamato's Yoshino district, Ōmi, Kii, Settsu, Wakasa, and Mino).[60] However, historians have traditionally contrasted villages in Kinai to dogō villages, which were typical of the central regions, the Kanto and the northeast, as corporate villages having more fraternity-like miyaza organizations in which the hierarchy of large and small landholders was not directly related to patterns of domination. Igeta surmises that this may have been typical only of the plains around the capital. Elsewhere, in the mountainous parts, old village elites were able to neutralize the pressure for change prompted by economic growth: the mechanism of status legislation was directed at a small peasantry, to whom the elite were not necessarily linked in a one-to-one landlord-tenant relationship.

OSTRACISM (*MURAHACHIBU*)

Murahachibu, perhaps the best-known village-specific penal measure, was absent from lordly legislation. There were multiple ways of getting rid of undesirable community members—banishment, disinheritance, stripping of "civic status," and so on—all of which had to be sanctioned by supravillage authorities in the form of prior requests or at least post factum reporting. Ostracism, however, was purely a village affair. It was the result of a decision made "by the community" to sever all social intercourse with a member and cut the household off from almost all mutual assistance. According to one popular interpretation of the term (which literally means "eight parts [out of ten]"), those ostracized could count on community assistance only for two "parts" of community life, namely, fire and funerals, but not for the other eight: coming-of-age ceremonies, weddings, memorial services, births, sickness, floods, travel, building and repairs (e.g., roof thatching).[61] In addition, ostracized members would not be greeted and were not allowed to participate in meetings or festivals. In other words, it meant social and economic ruination.

In the following case we shall look at the process of ostracism and glimpse the tensions that crisscrossed village life. This case is unusual and of special interest because the victim initiated a suit with the bakufu

60. Igeta, *Hō o miru*, 95.
61. Akutsu Muneji, "Mura gitei ni tsuite no ichi kōsatsu: toku ni seisai sadame no shojirei," *Gunma-kenshi kenkyū* 25 (1986): 99.

Plate 4. Rethatching a Roof, Mera Village, Minami-Izu, Shizuoka Prefecture, 1964. Community assistance was needed for the work but was denied when the household was ostracized. Photograph by Haga Hideo, courtesy of the Haga Library, Tokyo.

authorities and the case was settled in court.[62] This incident took place in Sasaemon village in Musashi province, a medium-sized village of 1,000 koku with some seventy households (now part of the town of Sugito in the eastern part of Saitama prefecture), located along the highway to Nikkō in a large bakufu territory of over 110,000 koku, which an intendant administered from Edo. The incident started at the end of 1827/2 and was resolved with surprising speed—in just two months' time—at the intendant's office in Edo.

The plaintiff was one Chōjirō, who because of ill health was allowed to be represented by his son Kichitarō. There were nineteen defendants, including the headman, kumi heads, and titled and nontitled peasants. Chōjirō was probably a well-established peasant; he even had a branch house, which was headed by Takejirō, a kumi head in another village. Chōjirō belonged to the Terabori kumi but was closely related both

---

62. Fuse Yaheiji, "Shiryō: Mura hachibu no soshō," *Nihon hōgaku* 23, no. 3 (1957): 96–109.

geographically and socially to two other kumi. The defendants were spread over Chōjirō's own kumi and a fourth one, the Tosho kumi, a sign that the community was probably divided.

At noon on 1827/2/23 three village members—Kyūjirō, Shigeshichi, and Seijirō—visited Chōjirō at his home and insisted that he immediately repay them loans totaling more than five ryō. Kyūjirō and Shigeshichi lived in Chōjirō's kumi, while Seijirō lived in the Tosho kumi. Kyūjirō was "homeless" (mushuku) or not registered anywhere. He had been punished with medium banishment for some crime, which meant that his home and land had been confiscated and that he was not allowed to travel to or reside in any of a number of provinces, including the one where Sasaemon village was located. He was an illegal resident, an offense punishable by maximum banishment.[63] He lived with and worked for Shigeshichi's father. Seijirō, who was registered in a village of another district, was married to Sen, daughter of the Tosho kumi's head. He and his wife had gone to live with his in-laws after causing some trouble with his own parents in his native village.

When he was confronted by the trio, Chōjirō expressed great surprise and did not recall anything about the loans. A quarrel ensued, and the three alleged creditors decided to help themselves to some bales of rice and other things. A fight broke out, and they started destroying tools and farming implements. One of Chōjirō's sons ran off to the branch house to alert Takejirō. Soon after Takejirō arrived on the scene, about a dozen peasants from Chōjirō's kumi appeared, led by the kumi head. Now negotiations started. Chōjirō was ready to pay off two of the three claimants, leaving the "homeless" out of the bargain. The headman, however, was adamant that Kyūjirō be part of the settlement negotiated by the whole gang of villagers. Thus Chōjirō was forced to pay over three ryō, rather than the claimed full debt of five ryō, a debt he never acknowledged. It was Takejirō, from the branch house, who put up the money.

That was not the end, though. Two days later a gang of twelve young men from Chōjirō's kumi appeared at his doorway and shouted that he had been ostracized. When Chōjirō asked why, they did not

63. Light banishment was accompanied by confiscation of land; medium banishment by confiscation of land and homestead; maximum banishment by confiscation of land, homestead, and household effects (see Tsukada Takashi, "Kinsei no keibatsu," NNS 5:97).

answer, but turned and left, hurling insults at him as they went out. Then the Tosho kumi head, Seijirō's father-in-law, and three other members of that kumi came, and they also declared him ostracized. Chōjirō, now outlawed by two of the four village kumi, including his own, looked for mediation to the headman, one of whose main tasks was to settle intramural disputes before they became lawsuits. Once again, the headman stubbornly refused to intervene, which left Chōjirō only one recourse, namely, to lodge a suit with the intendant, even though his chances of receiving any response other than an order to settle the matter internally were slim.

The suit was drawn up according to the required format and presented a clever argument, which is why Fuse Yaheiji, the scholar who discovered it, thinks that Chōjirō may have relied on the legal expertise of a suit inn (*kujiyado*) in Edo. The suit document acknowledged that matters such as these were usually settled out of court in order to avoid lawsuits but stated that the present issue was not a frivolous one, because the intendant's immediate interests were at stake. The main argument was that ostracism would prevent Chōjirō from producing tribute or from performing horse corvée on the Nikkō road (which was of particular importance to the bakufu, since it led to Ieyasu's shrine). The result was a quick summons for the defendants to appear by 10:00 A.M. on 3/28 at the intendant's office in Edo. They were to bring a written reply to the accusations (which would be read to the plaintiff) for a confrontation with the plaintiff; otherwise they would be found guilty and fined accordingly.

From the settlement document drafted a month later, we can reconstruct what happened at the hearing. First of all, the illegal "*mura*lien," Kyūjirō, was not included. There were a total of sixteen defendants with an unrelated village headman as their spokesman. Another village headman functioned as mediator between the defendants and the sole plaintiff, Chōjirō's son Kichitarō. Kichitarō maintained that the money dispute and the ostracism were related. The defendants not only denied such a link but also denied that any declaration of ostracism had ever taken place! Typically, the mediator forced both parties to acknowledge that they each were in the wrong. The mediator considered the money matter to have been resolved before the trial, since the debt had already been paid off, although not to the complete satisfaction of the three claimants. Therefore, the plaintiff withdrew his accusation of a linkage. The defendants admitted to the declarations of ostracism and agreed to write an apology and reinstate the plaintiff as a fully privileged community member. As was customary at such settlements, both parties agreed that the suit had been settled and that no new suits would follow.

The affair had split the village into two camps, illustrating, perhaps, Ōide's thesis that while there were many instances of intravillage settlements made by extravillage authorities in the early period, toward the end of the Tokugawa period village divisions often ran so deep that recourse to outside authority became increasingly necessary.[64] That village ostracism was open to abuse is obvious, but it was not until the year after the case just discussed that the bakufu began to regulate it, forbidding young people to initiate it.[65] An indication, perhaps, of increased village strife, other cases must have drawn the bakufu's attention at the time. Ostracism, like banishment, was a solution that created more problems, producing bankrupt peasants, "homeless" types, and vagrants, which had been a serious concern of the authorities since the eighteenth century.

As far as the details of the above case are concerned, there are obscure areas that raise unanswerable questions. Chōjirō denied liability, and yet his branch house was willing to pay off the alleged debt. We do not know the reason for this turnabout or the nature of the pressure Chōjirō put on Takejirō to forward the money. There are also overtones of gang behavior and extortion, perhaps fueled by the marginal members of the village, who seem to have received protection. Yet it is also unlikely that the three so-called creditors would have wholly fabricated their claims. They and their young supporters may have created an atmosphere of opportunity for Chōjirō's enemies within the village to settle old scores; the headman does not appear to figure among his friends.

Indeed, the headman deliberately allowed things to escalate, first by refusing to allow the illegal resident Kyūjirō to be excluded from the settlement negotiated at Chōjirō's doorstep and then by letting the ostracism stand. He did this even though he apparently lacked the support of half the village and he might get into trouble during the course

64. See, e.g., Yamamoto Yukitoshi, "Kinsei shoki no ronsho to saikyo: Aizu-han o chūshin ni," *Kinsei no shihai taisei to shakai kōzō,* ed. Kitajima Masamoto (Yoshikawa kōbunkan, 1983), 79–127.

65. Fuse, "Murahachibu," 107–9.

of the interrogations if the matter of Kyūjirō's status were to surface. He may have been responsible for the fact that no mention was made regarding Kyūjirō that might alert the intendant, which makes one wonder what he held over Chōjirō that kept the latter from playing that card: could it have been the threat to force payment of the remaining two ryō?

Ostracism was different from banishment (tsuihō), whereby one was expelled from the village; however, the two were similar in that ostracism was in effect intravillage banishment. Extravillage banishment could be triggered by a vote whereby someone was declared, without any material proof, to be the perpetrator of some crime. One case will illustrate this point.[66]

In Iwaya village (Tanba province), a certain Shōhyōe reported the theft of some of his belongings to the village officials, who decided to take a vote in the village on who the thief might be. The ballot pointed to Rokuzaemon, who lived across the street from the victim; Rokuzaemon, however, had absconded before he could be punished. He was sentenced *in absentia* to banishment of five *ri* (20 km) beyond the village, with the proviso that if he returned home and was reported, the father of the fugitive would not resist his whole family's banishment. Three years later the son returned secretly. When he was discovered and reported, a powerful village elder interceded with the village council on the man's behalf and succeeded in having the entire family's banishment suspended. The son, however, had to leave again.

After her son's second expulsion, the mother started slandering Shōhyōe, who, although a victim of a theft, had been the source of the family's suffering for a crime that had not even been proven. Again the family was reported to the village officials; an "investigation" was launched, and it was decided that the woman had become deranged and was thus not accountable for what she had been saying. A year and a half later (1717/5), however, Shōhyōe and his wife, finding life unbearable, moved to the other part of the village, which since 1664 had been divided between two jurisdictions. This example introduces another form of village justice, one based on the results of the ballot box.

66. Taoka Kōitsu, "Murahachibu to tsuihō ni tsuite," *Chihōshi kenkyū* 12 (1954): 4–6.

FIGHTING CRIME BY POPULAR VOTE (*IREFUDA*)

Tokugawa villages, so the generalization goes, were ruled by consensus, not by the democratic principle of majority rule. In his study of Japanese law, published in 1991, Carl Steenstrup is quite categorical about what he calls "the *Japanese* custom" in this regard: "Decision by *majority* was only known among monks in monasteries. It is an *Indo-European* custom, the basis of 'democracy'; and in Japan only became *temple* practice, because of the import of the monks' rules (*vinaya*) from India. The *Japanese* custom is to discuss, until agreement is reached. And if no agreement, no decision."[67] Kodama Kōta, however, who wrote the entry "irefuda" for the first volume of the *Kokushi daijiten* (1979), mentions that election of certain officers by vote was practiced in various sectors of society: for certain positions at the imperial court, in Katō Kiyomasa's domain (1562–1611), in the Pure Land sect, and often for the election of village officials but also for the allocation of newly developed paddy, the assignment of village corvée in connection with the alternate attendance system or public works, and the setting of prices for goods.[68]

Consensus in Tokugawa villages was not a universal, communal consensus. Many historians of peasant societies have romanticized it by taking at face value a decision making that presents itself as consensual agreement. Others, pointing to its representational function, understand consensus to be a ploy to consolidate elite power by making dissension within that elite seemingly less real (because not publicly voiced).[69]

---

67. Carl Steenstrup, *A History of Law in Japan until 1868* (Leiden: E. J. Brill, 1991), 132; the emphasis is in the original, and Steenstrup cites no sources.

68. KDJ 1:828. Anne Walthall mentions an occasion in a village when six women signed ballots used for voting upon village officials ("The Life Cycle of Farm Women in Tokugawa Japan," in *Recreating Japanese Women, 1600–1945*, ed. Gail Lee Bernstein [Berkeley: University of California Press, 1991], 68–69).

69. James Scott's *Moral Economy of the Peasant* (New Haven: Yale University Press, 1976) is representative of this romantic view of village politics in general, which Irokawa Daiichi shares in regard to the Tokugawa peasantry (see his "Survival Struggle of the Japanese Community," *Authority and the Individual in Japan: Citizen Protest in Historical Perspective*, ed. Victor Koschmann [Tokyo: University of Tokyo Press, 1978], 257–58). Samuel Popkin, in *The Rational Peasant* (Berkeley: University of California Press, 1979), is specifically skeptical of "consensus decision making" (58–59). Carol Gluck,

Whatever the interpretation of "consensual" decision making, one important area of life was decided on by vote in many villages, the fight against crime. Upon the recurrence of some crime such as arson or theft, a vote could be taken on the identity of the putative offender. The person who received the majority of votes (together with his kin and neighborhood presumably) would then be incriminated, as would anyone who did not participate in the vote.[70] A number of village codes refer to the procedure as *irefuda* (also read *nyūsatsu*), or "putting a tag [ballot] in [a box]."[71] Recently Ochiai Nobutaka has looked into this practice in northeastern Japan more systematically.[72]

Villages were not allowed to punish crimes of arson and theft, but they were empowered to search for the criminals and apprehend them. With regard to arson, Ochiai reports the following case from Higashi-Kami-Isobe village (Kōzuke province, in present-day Gunma prefecture). After several instances of arson over the span of a year, the following decision was made at the end of 1777 by six headmen of the fief, six kumi heads, and nine peasant representatives. A vote would be taken concerning the possible perpetrator and the "winner" would be thrown in jail; his daily ration of five gō (0.9 liter) of rice was to be provided at village expense. If the fires continued, however, a second vote was to be taken and the new "winner" jailed. If the real arsonist were caught, he was to be handed over to the authorities, and the suspect already in custody would be freed by the decision of the village officials.

A certain hapless Seigorō was thus voted into jail, though not without the protest of his family and kin. One of the six headmen consulted with his colleagues and the lord of the fief and then filed a petition with the fief's commissioner of finance for an investigation into the damage suffered by the village, since this had hindered the performance of their highway portage corvée. A number of officials from other villages and

---

who emphasizes the practical local exploitation of ideology in her *Japan's Modern Myths: Ideology in the Late Meiji Period* (Princeton: Princeton University Press, 1985), shares Popkin's perspective in this respect but winds up refracting ideology through the play of very localized interests to the point that its specific power evaporates; yet trees can have a forest effect.

70. For a case in Imabori that probably dates from 1639, see Tonomura, *Community and Commerce*, 206 (no. 290).

71. Maeda, *Nihon kinsei sonpō,* 43–46.

72. Ochiai Nobutaka, "Kinsei sonraku ni okeru kaji, nusumi no kendanken to shinpan no kinō," *Rekishi hyōron,* no. 442 (1987): 63–84.

Buddhist priests were involved as go-betweens; the case went to Edo and was settled out of court a year later in 1778/3. Nevertheless, the lord's authority upheld the decision already made by the village.

Crimes like arson and theft, especially when they recurred, in small lineage-based communities might easily lead to feuds between groups of families. To prevent such intravillage vendettas, it was foremost necessary to remove any possible justification for retaliation against putative criminals. This logic may explain the recourse to balloting, which provided at least the semblance of a restoration of order, an effect that may also have been obtained by the mere talk of resorting to a ballot, or by postponing the counting of ballots. Moreover, the victim of the ballot was most likely to be someone with few allies in the village, who would thus divert and diffuse more serious interlineage tensions.

While in principle arson and theft had to be reported and the suspect punished by the overlords, and villages certainly in principle had no power to impose the death penalty, unlike some corporate villages in pre-Tokugawa times, historians are finding more and more exceptions. As already mentioned, Mizumoto reported the only cases he knew: some villages that had the death penalty in their codes for a few decades in the late eighteenth century. Ochiai reports several codes stipulating the stoning of arsonists, followed by the burning of the arsonist's house and the expulsion of his or her family or, if the arsonist fled, the stoning to death of a family member.[73]

The village of Higashi-Kami-Isobe also had to deal with thieves. In 1786, a group of 132 peasants in Higashi-Kami-Isobe asked its six village headmen and seven kumi heads to consider allowing searches of homes for stolen goods. This option was weighed but postponed until a new theft took place, when a request for a search would be submitted to the village officials. If the culprit were found, he would be fined or put to death; if he were not caught, a vote would be taken and the highest vote getter fined. Here again we have the assumption of the right to impose the death penalty. This clause also appears in a village code of 1723 in Mino province. Following the theft of rice a half-year later, a house search was approved by the village officials; the suspected thief was caught and fined 15 *kanmon,* but he was not reported to the authorities. Such searches could be made by the victim himself, the vil-

73. Ibid., 67.

lage officials, or the whole village and were sometimes conducted over several villages, depending on the local custom or the nature of the case.

As mentioned by Kodama, voting was practiced also for the election of village officials. In such cases, however, ballots were signed! It is not difficult to imagine what this meant in terms of village power alliances, but *sōdanfuda* ("consultation balloting") or collusion was forbidden. The same prohibition held for crime voting, although it seems that in that case the ballots were not signed; scratching the ballot was sufficient according to some village regulations. Sometimes swearing oaths before the gods and drinking holy water (a practice also followed at the beginning of ikki, or uprisings) were required prior to balloting, the peasants swearing that they would not be swayed by "favoritism or prejudice." The setting at a Shinto shrine, the taking of an oath, and drinking of holy water were by no means common, but point to a religious origin. And indeed, anonymous voting has ancient roots and was widely practiced in antiquity and medieval Japan, as the medieval historian Seta Katsuya has demonstrated.[74]

Rakushogishō ("dropped written oaths [before the gods]"), as they were then called, were also used to anonymously identify a criminal. Some of these "oracles" were not votes but single anonymous accusations dropped in front of shrines. Since these were viewed as signs from the gods having no link to the profane world, if one was picked up, the finder was obliged to implement it.

Anonymous accusations were frequently posted on walls and were a means to openly denounce corruption at temples or to reveal plots. Nevertheless, posted denunciations were outlawed in antiquity and also by the pre-Tokugawa bakufu authorities,[75] who preferred to pursue criminals through their own courts, where, incidentally, they also relied on oracles to solve unclear cases. The Tokugawa village practice of irefuda (which Seta does not mention) undoubtedly has its origins in these rakushogishō. In Tokugawa times, however, the "election" of criminals (in contrast to that of officials) was not only initiated by the village but also ratified and even ordered by the overlords.

On 1696/12/27 three bales of tribute rice were stolen from the village storehouse in Fuse village, Shimōsa province (Chiba prefecture). Two days later 131 peasants and the village headman and kumi leaders

74. Seta Katsuya, "Shinpan to kendan," NNS 5:58–86, esp. 65 ff.
75. Ibid., 59, 61–62.

decided to resort to a vote; the winner would be banished. Guards were stationed throughout the village to prevent collusion, and oaths were required. After the ballots were counted, two peasants were banished, and three others, who received only one or two votes, were condemned to house arrest. Two of the latter fled to a temple, the Buddhist priest interceded on their behalf, and their sentence was suspended. The fields of the two who were banished became village property, and their houses, horses, tools, firewood, and other belongings were distributed among the family members. All this for the theft of three bales of rice. But this was no ordinary rice: it was the lord's tribute rice. The results were reported to the lord, who may very well have put pressure on the village to find a culprit.

There were numerous variations on the ways penalties were calibrated to the ranked outcome of the ballot or the number of votes received. In descending order, those who received the highest number of votes might be fined five kanmon plus ambulatory exposure, and those who received the second and third highest number might be fined three and one kanmon, respectively. Or those with fewer than five votes might be declared not guilty, and so on. This system had the additional effect of putting on notice those community members whom "public opinion" judged to be of somewhat questionable character.

In the early period, punishments for thefts were very harsh, banishment without mutilation, which rendered a person a hinin, or registered beggar, being among the lightest. But even in 1711 there were villages where the criminal would be expelled after his ears and nose were first cut off, marking him forever, in a most visible way, as a criminal. It seems to have been the custom, at least in the early period and in some locales, not to physically mutilate female offenders but to strip them and parade them through the village, subjecting them to what one could call gaze mutilation.[76] Of course another possibility was ostracism; or making convicted thieves wear red caps, or ring bells at weddings and funerals (very public occasions) until the next thief was caught (which could be weeks, months, or years), or treat the village to three shō (5.4 liters) of sake every year on a particular date; or even assigning them field guard duty until the next thief was arrested. These measures ingeniously mobilized time to protract indefinitely the effect of public exposure (yet another form of punishment, usually limited to three days).

76. Tsukada Takashi, "Kinsei no keibatsu," 96.

Plate 5.   Exposure of a Thief. This form of village punishment usually lasted
three days. Stolen bamboo shoots lie next to culprit. Woodblock print, c. 1745,
from Miyatake Gaikotsu, *Shikei ruisan,* Miyatake Gaikotsu chosakushū, 4
(1985). Reprinted with permission from Kawade shobō shinsha.

If theft was a crime, so was not reporting it, perhaps according to the same logic that informed crime voting: it neutralized reasons for private intravillage vendettas by moving them into the public sphere. In some villages, if a theft came to light that had gone unreported, the victim received the same treatment as the thief: banishment. And many village codes specified rewards for reporting thieves to the village authorities, which leads one to believe that although nonreporting was a serious problem for the officials, it was looked upon positively by the common peasant. And there was often opposition to the practice of irefuda. Otherwise why would some village rules stipulate that those who argued against it be treated as if they were guilty of the crime itself?

That crime voting often only created new problems was well understood by the peasants, hence their maneuvering to postpone the vote and perhaps increase their efforts to find a criminal. To accommodate such concerns, some villages decided not to open the ballots after the first vote, but to resort to a second vote after a new occurrence and then combine the results of both ballots. It was often the village officials who favored the voting procedure and the common peasants who resisted it. The latter often saw in it a weapon officials wielded as a means of control over the ordinary peasants. After all, the voting occurred in the presence of the officials, who were immune to the result because the victim was never an official.[77]

In 1769 in Tomikura village (Shinano) there was a rash of thefts, and the village officials conducted investigations in several neighboring villages. Then a rumor was started, most likely by these other villagers, that the thief was in Tomikura itself. Thus a decision was made by "all the village officials" and "all" the peasants to proceed with a vote, apprehend the largest vote getter as the thief, and confiscate his homestead and fields. In order to thwart possible opposition, it was also decided that if the designated criminal did not abide by the rules (one assumes by fleeing or suing), then the village officials would take their suit against the seventy-six peasants of the village for obstructing village justice to the shogunal authorities.

This was hardly the much-heralded self-determining practice of autonomous villages: the officials invoked the specter of a suit to enforce their will. And there are other instances of the village leadership's in-

77. Ochiai, "Kaji, nusumi no kendanken," 79.

voking the mobilization of shogunal authority (including the possibility of torture) to confront the rest of the peasants with crime voting. While the village leadership allied itself thus with the overlords, the peasants often fled to temples for asylum or sought to stop suits brought against them by the leadership and the overlords.

Just as Ōide saw the increasing convergence of village laws and lordly laws throughout the second half of the Tokugawa period, Ochiai has documented a similar trend in the practice of village justice. One example of this trend is yet another case from Higashi-Kami-Isobe village. In the aforementioned arson case of 1771 extramural authorities became involved mainly because of the protests leading to a suit by relatives of the jailed Seigorō. In the far less serious case of theft in 1786, the matter was resolved intramurally, and the voting was postponed as a last resort, the village exercising its right to conduct house searches instead. When the culprit was found in this instance, he was fined, but he was not reported to the authorities. In a new village regulation from 1838, however, the only solution set forth for theft was the most extreme one: if the village authorities heard rumors (*fūbun*) about thefts from fields, they would immediately proceed to a vote, the result would be reported to the bakufu, and the "guilty" would be banished from the village.

The reform of the village leagues instituted in the 1820s in the Kanto area strengthened further this convergence of village and lordly justice. In such village leagues, after the 1820s, voting no longer took place in a single village, but was conducted throughout the village league as a whole. Thus, when a theft occurred in one village, a vote would be taken in all the villages and the winner would be reported to the bakufu.[78]

It seems that at this point the village had abandoned any claims for self-governance in the area of penal jurisdiction. Confronted with increased social problems, the village leadership increasingly functioned in reality, if not in principle, as an executive branch of the overlords. This may suggest an answer to a question Anne Walthall raised in her article on village leagues.[79] Walthall represents the leadership of these village leagues as supporting "peasant interests," although some peasants must have been served better than others, since historians have

78. Ibid., 81.
79. Walthall, "Village Networks," 286.

stressed fractional divisions among the peasantry. She then raises the question why, unlike in earlier cases of village protests, no league leadership was ever punished by the bakufu. If the above practice in penal matters is any indication, the answer may well be that the bakufu had no reason to doubt that the village leadership was doing its bidding.

Another aspect of penal jurisdiction that should be mentioned is the categories of people who were not subject to village justice, even if they were residents. Registered blind people, registered beggars, and outcastes were status marginals who were not attached juridically to villages, districts, domains, or townships. They were subject to regional (e.g., the Kanto, with its center in Edo, or the Kinai around Kyoto) or national jurisdictions of their status organization. Intrastatus civil and criminal matters of these groups were handled by Danzaemon in Edo, for beggars and outcastes of most of eastern Japan, and by Kengyō in Kyoto, for all the registered blind.[80]

JUSTICE BY ORDEAL

Pinning down a criminal by voting after taking an oath before the gods gave the outcome the character of a divine verdict—one whose numinous power suffered serious entropy later in the period, as we have seen. Genuine ordeals, however, were still used on a number of occa-

---

80. Henderson, *Conciliation*, 1:91; Tsukada, "Kinsei no keibatsu," 102–4. Danzaemon and Kengyō, originally names of persons, became hereditary title names attached to the respective leadership positions. Although Kengyō meted out the death penalty as late as 1696, his powers seem to have gradually weakened in the second half of the Tokugawa period. In the *Goshioki saikyo chō*, a list of 974 cases of punishments of prisoners (divided into 231 categories) between 1657 and 1699, Tsukada Takashi has found two clear instances in which the Kengyō decided in favor of the death penalty (Tsukada, "Kinsei no keibatsu," 103–4). The first instance, in Edo in 1683, involved an accomplice in an affair another man was having with the wife of a blind man. The blind husband had killed the accomplice and wounded the adulterer. Although the law permitted a husband to kill his wife and her lover if he caught them in the act (Hiramatsu, *Kinsei keiji soshōhō*, 581), the blind man was nevertheless entrusted to his *zatō nakama* guild (the guild for the registered blind), perhaps because he had killed the accomplice and not the adulterer. The guild asked Kengyō in Kyoto to have him wrapped up in a mat (*sumaki*) and drowned. He was handed over to Kengyō, who had him executed that way. (This punishment, absent from the bakufu's quite elaborate penal code, seems to have been used often by yakuza as a private death sentence [KDJ 8:141].) The second case, in 1696, concerned a blind arsonist from Echigo (Niigata) who was sentenced to be burned at the stake in Edo.

sions in the first half of the seventeenth century, precisely when overlords were trying to monopolize the exercise of violence, wresting away penal powers for serious crimes from local power holders, whose practice they declared a "private" and illegal justice. Since ordeals were still practiced well into the Tokugawa period, one might assume that they were local "illegal" affairs. Yamamoto Yukitoshi, however, has presented a number of incidents from Aizu domain that clearly show that this was not the case.[81] The overlords often permitted trial by ordeal, sometimes ordered such trials, and even adjusted their own verdicts according to the results of subsequent ordeals. It should be noted that all of Yamamoto's cases concern conflicts between villages and that many of these intervillage disputes revolved around new borders drawn as a result of the murauke system. In some cases, common forage land was divided among five villages each belonging to a different overlord.

The first case concerns a dispute of 1619 between two villages, Tsunazawa and Matsuo, about the use of a mountain area commons. The conflict had escalated into an armed confrontation that resulted in one death. The domain took several depositions, made arraignments, and dispatched investigators, but the facts could not be established. This was in the middle of the winter. In midsummer, with tensions at a peak, the two villages were ordered to resort to a fire ordeal in the presence of a domain official and villagers from the area.

As it turned out, the lord, unable to determine the common border on the mountain, had arbitrarily decided on one. The villages, however, had refused to accept his decision, and it was they who had requested the ordeal, which took place at the Shinto shrine of a neighboring village. No one from Tsunazawa dared volunteer to hold the red-hot iron, so that it was up to the headman to step forward after making a short farewell speech, as if he did not expect to survive the ordeal, as the saying goes. His opponent was a burly fellow who had no qualms about volunteering. Both donned ceremonial dress, received the *kumanogoōhōin* (a talismanic document from the Kumano shrine used for oaths), with which to grasp the iron, and approached the fire (see pl. 6). The domain official lifted the red-hot iron out of the fire (with tongs, one presumes) and handed it over to the contestants. The headman grabbed it three times and then put it aside. The burly representative of

81. Yamamoto, "Kinsei shoki no ronsho," 107–21. The next several paragraphs of this section are based on ibid.

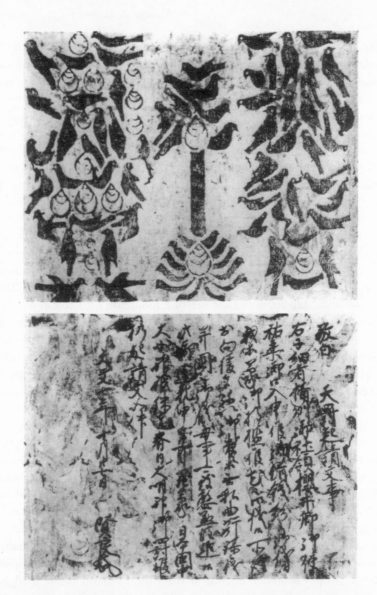

Plate 6. *Kumanogoōhōin*. A talisman dated 1538/10/27 from the Kumano shrine, used for oaths. The image on the front (*top*) represents five Sanskrit letters formed by the shapes of seventy-five birds, messengers from the Kumano *gongen*, centered around a pearl bearing the stamp of the Cattle King (*goō*), a reincarnation of the life-giving (*ubusuna*) gods. The oath was written on the back. From Miyaji Naokazu, *Kumano sanzan no shiteki kenkyū*, Miyaji Naokazu ronshū, 3 (Sōyōsha, 1985). Reprinted with permission from Miyaji Harukuni, Tokyo.

Matsuo, on the other hand, dropped it in the fire, having been burned by the talisman, which had instantly burst into flames. He lost, and what happened next explains the headman volunteer's initial reluctance and his swan song before submitting to the ordeal: the loser's hands and feet were cut off, and he was buried, his tomb serving to mark the new border between the two villages. These are the details Yamamoto found in the Aizu gazetteer account written two hundred years after the event, in the early nineteenth century. The colorful details aside, the lord, his own solution having been rejected, granted the petition for an ordeal.

The most recent ordeal discovered by Yamamoto dates from 1653 and took place in Echigo (Niigata) to settle a mountain-use dispute between two groups of villages, numbering four and three villages, respectively. A suit had been filed, but the dispute continued. A couple of months after the suit was filed, the two village group headmen decided to seek the advice of the gods. An agreement was drafted on the back of a kumanogoōhōin and was signed with the names and blood seals of the ten representatives who would take the test. The talisman was burned, its ashes mixed with dirt from each border claimed by the two parties, and the mixture then swallowed by the ten representatives. The agreement was that whoever got sick after seven days and seven nights would lose the match. This was probably unlikely to happen, hence the Solomonic proviso that if no one became sick the new border would be midway between those claimed by the two parties. During a tense week of observation the contestants showed no symptoms. The new border was fixed as agreed upon and ratified by the domain authorities. Yet thirteen days later the results of the ordeal were reconfigured by the two village group headmen, who declared one side the loser. The shogunal authorities reversed the original decision, and a new map was drawn up according to the final results of the ordeal.

Settling otherwise unresolvable village disputes by ordeal was quite common prior to the Tokugawa period. Yet enthusiasm for decisions by ordeal may have been on the wane. In a village in Ōmi, for instance, rules drawn up in 1606 and 1607 rewarding volunteers for the red-hot iron ordeal handsomely with a land grant of twenty koku, tax-exempt in perpetuity, point to the need of incentives to recruit volunteers. Moreover, given the formidable presence of overlord authority after 1600, we see how gradually this way of local dispute resolution lost ground. Nevertheless, to perceive ordeals as irrational survivals from medieval times that were fundamentally incompatible with Tokugawa practice, would be too simple.

Admittedly, the outcome of an ordeal has more in common with a court verdict—both produce a winner and loser—than with the prevailing Tokugawa solution of punishing both parties in violent quarrels (*kenka ryōseibai*), a form of martial justice, or with its peacetime equivalent of conciliation, in which both sides usually shared the blame. In this sense, ordeals are of the same order as medieval court practice. On the other hand, ordeals also signal abdication of worldly authorities in juridical decisions about right or wrong; they restore order by diffusing tensions through the mechanism of scapegoating. In the above two examples, the bakufu each time reversed its decision; the merits of the cases did not matter as long as peace was restored in one way or another, a stance typically taken by the courts throughout the Tokugawa period. At the village level also, a similar practical logic prevailed when balloting produced a scapegoat.

LOOPHOLES AND LEGAL MANEUVERING

Thefts had to be reported to village authorities, but the very codification of this expectation and the penalties for failing to follow it point to peasant reluctance. Village authorities in turn, had to report thefts to the overlords, as virtually all village laws required, but often this did not happen. The death penalty was supposed to be a prerogative of overlords, yet historians continue to discover village codes, and not only from the beginning of the period, that recorded it as a dreaded possibility.

Laws are not always observed, and it is not uncommon to judge the significance of laws by how often they are used. It is argued that since Tokugawa edicts were issued again and again, they were ineffective and thus insignificant. Other legal historians who have studied the codes, however, hold the opposite view, assuming that the norms of the codes reflect practice. Rather than refute these views by argument, it is perhaps best to counter them by looking at actual practice. Thus the question is not whether villagers circumvented some laws—they did, hence the need to reiterate them—but how. Evidence of such circumvention will provide some access to the level of villagers' law consciousness. At least it will reveal some points of resistance to lordly law, which is relevant in relation to the question of village "autonomy." We shall proceed again by looking at some cases.

The murauke system of subcontracting the village for purposes of tribute and internal governance created a setting in which under certain circumstances the village, which was set up to do the overlord's bidding, could instead rally around its own interests. When villages did so openly, the issue was likely to receive a hearing from the overlords. When something else was envisioned, however, secrecy was important. Such cases most likely left few documentary trails. The first traceable examples of such secrecy are from corporate villages that from pre-Tokugawa times had a high degree of independent governance.

In 1591, while the land survey was in progress in Imabori (Ōmi province), the village members signed a double pledge: (1) that they would pay the full tribute, and if any household absconded, the five neighboring households would shoulder the arrears; and (2) that if their tax petition was not accepted, "we the villagers, will flee and we are all of one mind to do so; if anyone acts against these decisions, we will dissociate from him or her as pledged."[82] Another document, from Nakano corporate village in the same area, dated 1638, is a combination of a pledge and a village rule, recording a measure taken by the villagers against a possible reassessment adding new fields to the cadasters. It stipulates that none of the 107 signatories would reveal hidden paddies, not even to their wives or children.[83]

By Tokugawa times, villages had to officially acknowledge in writing that they had received overlord directives, a requirement that seems not to have existed in medieval times.[84] How could this acknowledgment and practical consequence be circumvented, since *ukeru* ("to receive") implied that ignorance of the law was no valid excuse?

The ninth stipulation of an overlord directive, dated 1658/10/9, to

82. Tonomura, *Community and Commerce*, 167, 205. For a similar measure, taken in the context of a tax appeal, see ibid., 203 (no. 468); and Ishio Yoshihisa, *Nihon kinseihō no kenkyū* (Bokutakusha, 1975), 12.

83. Tonomura, *Community and Commerce*, 180; Yokota, "Kinsei sonraku," 144, 155. Henderson reports a case from 1832 in which six villages in Mino province jointly agreed to protect their grassland against conversion into fields, resisting all such applications no matter where the proposed reclamation might be located (Henderson, *Village "Contracts,"* 179–82).

84. Yokota, "Kinsei sonraku," 155; the example that follows is from 155–57. See also Tonomura, *Community and Commerce*, 185–86.

the same Nakano corporate village ordered the abrogation of village credit unions (*tanomoshikō*). The directive was acknowledged as received by the village kumi's signatures as well as by a separate letter of receipt by the headman, dated 11/10. A corroborating letter of receipt by the kumi, dated 11/16, was addressed to the headman. However, two weeks later, on 12/2, the kumi addressed another document to the headman in which they stated that since compliance with the overlord's order would cause financial hardship (even for paying tribute), they had decided to continue the operation of the credit union secretly. If, however, this leaked out and the village leaders were summoned by the lord, the whole village would go to the lord, explain that it was not their fault, and apologize.

The reason the lord gave for his abolition decree was that there was too much eating and drinking at credit union meetings. In the document of the kumi, vowing the secret continuation of the credit union, it was stipulated that henceforward self-restraint would be exercised in this matter. Thus, they selectively decided to interpret the law's intent by complying with the lord's reason and otherwise disregarding the order. It is interesting not only that the kumi resisted the lord's order but that the kumi did not think that it would be possible to negotiate openly with the lord over a point that on the surface seems quite reasonable. The sense must have been strong that one could not force authority to acknowledge mistakes. For this reason, the shogunal courts never issued a verdict of innocence in criminal cases. So that this outcome would be assured, before the court hearing proper a "preliminary investigation" with or without torture produced a written admission of guilt from the suspect.[85]

In 1659/10 the prohibition was reissued, but that was the last time the overlord legislated on the matter; he seems to have tacitly accepted the credit union's existence after that. Yokota, the scholar who researched this case, based this conclusion on the fact that in 1677, when

---

85. In contemporary Japan, with only one lawyer per 9,300 people, in contrast to one lawyer per 360 people in the United States, police investigations continue to play a far greater role in the process of convicting suspects than prosecution lawyers do. Prosecution proceeds only after the police have gathered enough evidence to ensure a conviction, so that the conviction rate is more than 98 percent (Leslie Helm, "A Long Haul for Japan's Plaintiffs," *Los Angeles Times,* January 14, 1991, A12; Teresa Watanabe, "Japan Casts Envious Look at U.S. Crisis Management," ibid., May 7, 1995, A10–A11).

a dispute between two groups of villages from two different districts broke out concerning credit union funds, one party considered bringing a suit before the authorities.

Vicarious responsibility was a cornerstone of overlord law. That this caused resentment, jealousies, and complicated human relations at the village level is not difficult to imagine. It is surprising, however, to find a village code that flatly states that everyone will be held responsible for his own portion of the tribute and that no help will be forthcoming from the rest of the village. This is what one historian found in the 1759 edition of the code of Ichijōji village (Yamashiro province).[86] The relatives, the kumi, and the village were supposed to take over fields of households of orphaned minors, as clearly spelled out in standard village laws (see appendix 3, art. 40). In Mochizuki (Kita-Saku, Shinano) the intendant got involved in such a case in the late 1680s.[87] A certain Sōtarō died, leaving a son too young to work the fields, but relatives were reluctant to step in. The village officials, unable to find a solution, queried the intendant, who ordered the obvious: the son should be raised by some relative, and the fields taken care of collectively by all the relatives. But that was precisely the problem. Upon receiving the order, the relatives got together to decide whether to comply. Two of the half-dozen relatives refused to affix their seal to the order and were summoned to the intendant's office for a good scolding. Even so, one of the two recalcitrants held out and refused to affix his seal. There are no further data to allow one to pinpoint the problem or know what happened to the one relative who held out. He may have had good reasons for refusing to be part of the solution, and the intendant may have felt that five relatives out of six were sufficient to take care of the fields. It is interesting, however, to find peasants pondering whether to follow an intendant's order, some of them categorically refusing to comply.

This sort of resistance is of a different order than the uprisings (ikki) on which American historians have so often focused; nevertheless, it illustrates the disregard with which peasants could treat lordly authority. In large-scale confrontations, according to admittedly romanticized

86. Katada Seiji, "Kinsei sonpō no henshitsu ni tsuite: Yamashiro-kuni Atago-gun Ichijōji mura no baai," *Chihōshi kenkyū*, no. 34 (1958): 33.

87. Ozaki Yukiya, "Shinshū no nōmin to buraku," *Mochizuki no bura-kushi*, no. 4 (1978): 41–42.

and heroicized accounts, the peasants spoke their mind quite bluntly.[88]
Such uprisings were condemned by the rulers as illegal conspiracies
(*totō*). When, during the ikki of 1754 in Kurume domain, the daimyo's
officials tried to tell the peasants that the prohibition of "conspiracies"
was the foremost law of the realm (*tenka dai ichi no gohatto*), the
peasants who heard this, the record tells us, "burst out laughing, asked
why the officials appeared today, beaming with authority and full of
contempt for the people, reading to us orders high up from horseback,
to us who are waiting here holding authority in high esteem and
observing the laws. We know that the prohibition of conspiracies is the
foremost law of the land. But the lord indulges in debauchery...."[89]

Banishment was a punishment that sometimes needed to be concealed. Banishment itself was not completely forbidden, but its arbitrary application was (for a village law, see appendix 3, art. 26).
However, since banishment resulted in the disappearance of a name
from the population register, the effect of its application was hard to
hide. From headmen's notes or diaries we learn how this could be
done.[90]

In 1757 a village guard caught a woman stealing rice from a field.
The village decided to follow precedent and sent her into exile. According to the principle of vicarious responsibility (*enza*), her husband deserved the same punishment, but since he was absent (being in service
elsewhere) he was forgiven. The house, however, was put up as collateral for the yearly tribute, and its effects were given to the guard. The
woman's banishment was handled as follows. She was kept on the
population rosters until she had settled somewhere else. Then she was
handed a certificate of leave, and her brothers had to sign a sworn
agreement never to allow her in the village again. Thus, on record it
appeared as if she had moved. Obviously, such tricks worked only as

88. Herbert Bix (*Peasant Protest*) cites sarcastic statements peasants allegedly addressed to samurai, such as the following: "Since they [inspection offi-
cials] are so skilled in local affairs, we wish to learn from them how to grow
rice" (79); "Since you officials think that 'peasants' are particularly useful
beings, we wanted to let the samurai do the hard work of peasants and see for
themselves how profitable we are" (94); "We don't need your kind to look after
us" (179).

89. Nanba, "Hyakushō ikki no hōishiki," 76. This is an important article
on the people's consciousness of the law related to the *ikki,* which is beyond the
scope of the present study.

90. The following examples are from Mizumoto, "Kōgi no saiban," 306–8.

long as nobody in the village reported them—which would have been done at the risk of all sorts of informal reprisals.

A diary from 1826 reveals the following strategy to hide a banishment by making it appear as if the person in question had absconded. A culprit had been caught by guards from a different village, and his village council had decided to kick him out but instead reported him as missing. As was usual in such a case, the domain ordered a search for the fugitive, which the village feigned to conduct, and then reported the culprit as still missing. After a second search (usually lasting thirty days) was conducted, he was again declared missing and was then officially declared *nagatazune* (literally, "long search"), that is, homeless (mushuku, or nonregistered). As it turned out, the man returned to the village five years later gravely ill, died soon thereafter, and was quietly buried at the local temple.

As we saw in Ken's case in chapter 1, local officials could collude with district magistrates or intendants, who tried as far as possible to avoid becoming involved in dispensing justice. If "private consultation" (*naibun nite*) among themselves led to the conclusion that "village justice" might reestablish order, then both parties would benefit from adopting it even if the solution might bend official policy. Why would overlords so readily relinquish their authority? What was the logic of such practice?

LAW AS *TATEMAE*

Mizumoto has found a document from 1751 that may shed light on these questions.[91] It is a memo (*kōjō no oboe*) from a village group headman to an intendant's assistant from Takada domain (Echigo province, Niigata prefecture). It seems to be an exchange of opinion between two local intermediary officials from the village and the district intendant office.

On 1751/7/17 a peasant had been seen returning from the fields with stolen rice. An investigation had followed, and a confession that included four other thefts as well had made the situation serious enough to report to the village group headman. Thus it had become a matter for the domain's court (*gosahō*). The village group headman, however, had his own ideas about how to proceed. Thinking it might be better to get

91. Ibid., 309–10.

rid of this habitual troublemaker altogether, he wanted to change the village headman's report into a request for banishment. Hence, the village group headman's request for the private opinion (*gonai-i*) of the intendant's assistant on this course of action.

The document implies that although in principle only the court should deal with thefts, the village group headman suggested a solution that would spare the court the trouble of dealing with the particulars of the case, leaving the actual legal process up to the village. Mizumoto finds further support for this interpretation by quoting Hiramatsu Yoshirō, the great authority on the Tokugawa penal system:

> Private and public law were mixed together in the following sense. The principle governing punishment and pleading by defendants in civil lawsuits, which not only aims at solving the disputes between litigants but at the same time is satisfied with establishing "shogunal authority" (*goikō*), permeated not only criminal trials but also the execution of the penalty. And this is sometimes the case also for minor misdemeanors and especially for criminal cases involving private interests.[92]

Officially (tatemae), the shogun and daimyo proclaimed a monopoly on juridical matters, but their primary concern certainly was not social justice nor even the maintenance of overall public order as such. They were preoccupied foremost with safeguarding their authority. Therefore, they silently tolerated "private justice," as long as it was not publicized and did not openly challenge that authority. This two-sided stance affected the status of village codes and village justice.

THE LAWLESS VILLAGE

According to John Haley, the Tokugawa village was "an institutional structure that in allowing evasion of official legal controls also promoted external deference and internal cohesion"; it had "the security of the administrative state along with the freedom of the outlaw."[93] The application of the outlaw metaphor to Tokugawa villages may at first

92. The quote is from Hiramatsu, *Kinsei keiji soshōhō*, 837.
93. Haley, *Authority without Power*, 61. Haley further develops the thesis that the Tokugawa village pattern of justice and the peculiar relationship between communities, on the one hand, and the authorities and the law, on the other, discussed as "law as *tatemae*," still govern life in modern Japan (187–190). Mizumoto also discusses the tatemae aspect of Tokugawa law in his "Kōgi no saiban," 308–12.

seem problematic. Haley uses it only to convey a strong sense of the weakness of centrally controlled mechanisms of law enforcement in the village. The metaphor is appropriate in another way as well, however. Although all villages had laws and codes, village life as it is revealed by the various cases studied often appears to have taken place in an outlaw world, or at least in a world in which the world of Kurosawa's *Yōjimbō* was a possibility.

The general propensity on the part of both extra- and intravillage authorities to keep things within the village, and the structural setup that made this possible, is perhaps the main reason for the impression of the "lawless village." This mutual avoidance had two results. On the one hand, the semblance (tatemae) of internal harmony had to be maintained so that overlords would feel content to leave villages alone. On the other hand, this left the exercise of power unchecked. The gomyō in Hozu and similar groups elsewhere had a free hand in securing their lasting domination by putting themselves "outside the law" that they wrote for fellow villagers and imposed on them.

The main concern of local wielders of power was that conflicts might develop to the point of alarming the overlords. As a preventive gesture to keep the overlords out, the local power holders often deferentially submitted to the lords the codes they had written to demonstrate that they were "within the law" of the lord. In a prophylactic move to keep the villagers contained, the village authorities discouraged them from initiating lawsuits by painting those who did as troublemakers in village regulations (compare the negative tone regarding lawsuits in appendix 3, arts. 16 and 54, with the earlier, neutral stance in appendix 2, art. 19). Obviously, individuals seeking access to overlord authority did not use it only as the only means for contesting local powers through suits and petitions. Local authorities invoked the image of overlord intervention as a last resort, "borrowing" extramural power to avoid actually activating it, to keep (themselves) on top of things. Aside from actual collusion (in Ken's case), the local authorities sometimes threatened lawsuits or presented the specter of torture in the lord's court.

If one keeps in mind that villages were informal power fields where the competition was often between lineages, one may perhaps start to perceive in a new light some of the practices discussed in this chapter—ostracism, crime voting, and the measures taken against collusion in casting ballots. As Chōjirō's lawsuit illustrates, ostracism was not always initiated by a "unanimous village," but often by intravillage factions, to the point that the bakufu limited its use in the nineteenth century. In villagers' minds, solutions to unresolved crimes often tended to be structured along lines of splits in the community. Crime voting may have been a solution to prevent such situations from being used for settling old scores. The posting of guards throughout the village to prevent "consultation balloting" suggests that such a scenario is not far-fetched. Similarly, unreported crimes might lead to retaliations or vendettas against one's enemies as the putative perpetrators; hence the pressure to make the nonreporting of crimes a crime.

From this perspective, villages no longer resemble autonomous, harmonious, egalitarian communities. Rather, like social formations anywhere, they constitute spaces where groups of people, households, or lineages vie for positions hierarchized by class, status, and law using the weapons of class, status, and law.

5

Status and State Racism

From *Kawata* to *Eta*

The animality of man, in man and against man (whence the systematic "bestialization" of racialized individuals and human groups) is the particular method that theoretical racism adopts in thinking about human historicity.

Etienne Balibar

In the preceding chapters, an argument is made for the pervasive functional importance of social and political status in village life throughout the Tokugawa period. High social status, buttressed by bakufu measures as well as village codes, was the single most significant source of local authority and power. Moreover, with the development of a commercial economy in the eighteenth century, political status was not displaced by economic status, even though titles became available for purchase on a restricted village market. Instead, officialized status (originally in part a by-product of the overlords' assignment for tribute responsibilities to local magnates) took on an independent, symbolic value, having the potential to politically offset the loss of material assets. Status, however, retained important links to a material base. Economically successful peasants frequently tried, sometimes effectively, to use recently acquired wealth to secure access to, or even displace, the old village "status aristocracy." Ultimately, economic status, whether past or present, was always at issue in claims of political and social status.

The existence of a "nonstatus" category, however, forced certain people to exist apart from and outside of the status system described above: the outcastes, as we have referred to them thus far, or the so-called *eta*. These people did not refer to themselves by that derogatory term meaning "plentiful dirt," or polluted. Instead, they called themselves *kawata*, literally, "leather workers," after their principal occupa-

Epigraph: Etienne Balibar, "Paradoxes of Universality," in *Anatomy of Racism*, ed. David Theo Goldberg (Minneapolis: University of Minnesota Press, 1990), 283.

tional profession, a practice I shall follow here. The history of discrimination against the kawata as a function of status in Tokugawa society directs attention to the early modern relationship between sociopolitical status, legislative practice, and a form of racism—a term that may cause surprise but is not used lightly. Like other social groups, for example, the samurai, merchants, and peasants, the kawata were legally restricted to their birth-ascribed status. Registered beggars, or hinin ("nonhumans"), also constituted a "nonstatus" group, but one that was not hereditary: a person could become a hinin, be sentenced to that status, or be allowed to leave it, but once a kawata, one died a kawata.

In his work on systems of social stratification, the anthropologist Gerald Berreman argues that all status systems assign people a "differential intrinsic worth" according to their position in the social hierarchy.[1] In the case of the kawata this intrinsic worth was negative to the extreme, for they were marked as existentially and unredeemably polluted, defiled, impure. In Japan, where notions of purity and pollution have historically functioned as powerful categories of ritual classification, the kawata suffered the worst consequences of the social application of these values. Even though the status system, with specific regard to the kawata, was legally abolished in 1871, their descendants are the only persons in Japanese society today who continue to suffer discrimination because of their ancestors' status during the Tokugawa period.

Today the kawata's descendants are referred to officially as *burakumin,* or "hamlet people," after dropping the Meiji era's qualifying prefix *tokubetsu,* "special." Estimated as numbering as many as 3 million people, the burakumin are Japan's largest "Japanese minority."[2] There are still some six thousand segregated communities throughout Japan, where most of them live. Many burakumin try to "pass" into Japanese society; some succeed, to the point that their descendants are

1. Berreman, "Social Inequality," 14.

2. I have adopted the (perhaps) high figures provided by the Buraku Liberation Movement. For a discussion of these figures, see *Nihon shomin seikatsu shiryō shūsei,* vol. 14, *Buraku,* ed. Harada Tomohiko (San'ichi shobō, 1971), 1 (hereafter NSSS 14). See also George De Vos and Hiroshi Wagatsuma, *Japan's Invisible Race: Caste in Culture and Personality* (Berkeley: University of California Press, 1966), 114–18; and Ninomiya Shigeaki, "An Inquiry concerning the Origin, Development, and Present Situation of the *Eta* in Relation to the History of Social Classes in Japan," *Transactions of the Asiatic Society of Japan.* 2d ser., 10 (1933): 113.

not aware of their own burakumin background. The 1871 Emancipation Decree did not make private or even public discrimination illegal (although article 14 of the postwar constitution prohibits discrimination by the state). The Emancipation Decree simply repealed the legally sanctioned status distinctions in the realm of occupations and social status: "The appellation eta/hinin shall be abolished; henceforward they shall be treated as common people in social status and occupation." Frank Upham writes that legal emancipation "meant little. The government was at best indifferent to significant change.... In fact, government policy directly contributed to continued discrimination by registering Burakumin as 'new commoners.'"[3] Their situation is not dissimilar to that of blacks after the abolition of slavery in the United States, which did not eliminate racial inequality and discrimination.

In attempting to account for this discrimination against the kawata/burakumin, we need to address the role of Japanese cultural beliefs about purity and pollution. Undoubtedly, pollution was the idiom of discrimination that turned kawata into eta. Moreover, insofar as they constituted a status group, it may be that they not only shared assigned universal characteristics of status differentiation but revealed in its purest form the function of status as socially sanctioned disrespect for a particular group of people. How the ascriptive logic of status systems works is thus a second question that needs to be considered. Closely related to this question is a third one, that of racism. There are several reasons why this term can be considered appropriate in a discussion of the kawata/burakumin.

Berreman makes a good pedagogical case for using analogical terms —*caste* and *race*—that by definition are alike only in certain (but sufficient) respects.[4] To make the notion of caste and its effect on people's lives understandable to Americans, Berreman encourages speaking of a caste system as a form of racism, because Americans are familiar with that reality. (He would encourage the reverse in attempting to explain racism to Hindus.) He writes that burakumin "comprise a 'race' in the

---

3. Frank K. Upham, *Law and Social Change in Postwar Japan* (Cambridge: Harvard University Press, 1987), 80. For the text of this brief decree, see *Burakushi yōgo jiten,* ed. Kobayashi Shigeru et al. (Kashiwa shobo, 1985), s.v. "kaihōrei" (56).

4. Gerald Berreman, *Caste and Other Inequities: Essays on Inequality* (Meerut, India: Folklore Institute, 1979), 190.

sociological sense of Western racism, but an 'invisible' (i.e., not genetic or phenotypic) one."[5]

The kawata/burakumin are more than a sociologically "invisible" race. In the course of his research on caste and race, Berreman found that "*all* systems of birth-ascribed stratification seem to include a claim that the social distinctions are reflected in biological (i.e. "racial") differences."[6] This observation, while not true for all status groups in Tokugawa Japan, certainly applies to the kawata. Although the kawata are indistinguishable from other Japanese, explicitly *racial* theories, which *differentiate,* and *racist* theories, which *discriminate,* have developed since the Tokugawa period to explain the origin of the kawata in order to justify discriminatory practices against them.

The absence of physical properties to distinguish them from "majority" Japanese (hence "invisible" differences) and the construction of a racial theory (hence a different "race") have combined to produce a particular kind of intra-race racism, one based exclusively on descent. Genealogies, however, are known only to those who literally know the record. Without that knowledge, discrimination against burakumin would be impossible. This is where the state plays a crucial role. As mentioned above, the 1871 Emancipation Decree did not outlaw discrimination per se. Indeed, all former kawata were entered on the population registers as "new citizens" (*shinshimin*), so that state records perpetuate the kawata's separate identity, making it possible today for anyone sufficiently interested to consult the old population registers to discriminate against burakumin.[7] Without active complicity by majority Japanese, discrimination would disappear; some, however, still care enough about racialized status to check these records.

Revulsion and defilement, the cultural idiom and social disposition through which discrimination against the kawata is commonly expressed, are often correlated to the high valuation of purity in the Shinto tradi-

5. Ibid., 188. This invisibility can have peculiar effects; thus, unaware of their own descent, some Japanese may share prejudices against burakumin until the day when their own burakumin background is revealed and they are shocked to discover that they have been discriminating against their own (Sam Jameson, "Japan's 'Untouchables' Suffer Invisible Stain," *Los Angeles Times,* January 2, 1993, A24).

6. Berreman, "Social Inequality," 14.

7. The ineffectiveness of recent restrictions of access to these records is discussed below.

tion. Yet, the first laws to identify categories of Japanese associated with specific occupations as *senmin,* literally, "despised, mean (*iyashii*) people," were laws adopted *in toto* from China in 645, during the Taika Reform. Scholars often trace the development of discriminatory practice in Japan to that point.[8] However, the composition of these "despised" social groups, their position in society, and the nature of prejudice against them has changed considerably over time. Legal discrimination decreased greatly during the early Heian period (ninth century) and became insignificant in medieval times. For example, a law of 789 declared children from mixed marriages between "good" (*ryō-min*) and "low" people (senmin) to be ryōmin, whereas previously they had been marked as senmin. Moreover, whole subclasses of senmin were simply set free when government offices to which they had been attached as dependents were dismantled and slavery was abolished in 907.[9] Although many nonagricultural occupations were socially devalued in medieval times, the first reference to some of them as "plentifully polluted" (*eta* written with the characters still used today) appears only in the 1450s.[10]

It is often said that the Buddhist reverence for life, as well as Shinto notions of pollution associated with death and blood, played an important role in targeting butchers and tanners as particularly defiled, and indeed a few *late* texts confirm this. Thus one finds a clear reference in a Buddhist monk's diary of 1446 to "those who carve up dead cattle and horses for consumption" as "the lowest kind of people,"[11] although the source of abomination seems to be more the eating of meat than the butchering. Nowhere does one find reference to hereditary pollution dissociated from occupational succession.

Medieval concepts of despised occupations and human defilement were social and occupational (hence functional in a sense), loosely defined and applied, and formulated neither by law nor as a hereditary condition. In 1871 a law had to be enacted to abolish the *official* status "eta-hinin," which points to a legal dimension for discrimination during the Tokugawa period that was missing in medieval times. In Toku-

8. For one such example in English, see Ninomiya, "Inquiry."
9. Teraki Nobuaki, *Kinsei buraku no seiritsu to tenkai* (Osaka: Kaihō shuppansha, 1986), 22.
10. Ibid., 26.
11. Watanabe Hiroshi, *Mikaihō buraku no keisei to tenkai* (Yoshikawa kōbunkan, 1977), 70.

gawa Japan lie the origins of the state's role in the ongoing discrimination against the kawata/burakumin. Some scholars estimate that more than one-third of today's approximately six thousand buraku communities originated in the eighteenth century,[12] when we begin to find discriminatory and segregationist laws, racist in their effect, being enacted throughout Japan against the kawata.

Today one can see how cultural notions of pollution and racism conspire with bureaucratic practices to perpetuate discrimination against burakumin. But how can the introduction of the new status for kawata in the Tokugawa period, and the new laws, practices, and ideologies that developed along with it, be explained? What role did bakufu legislation play in this?

I shall start by discussing a number of episodic events, legal cases, and incidents involving kawata. The need for such an approach stems from the paucity of microhistorical narratives of the burakumin's Tokugawa past in English. Emiko Ohnuki-Tierney's symbolic functional analysis posits the kawata ahistorically, as a necessary prop for Japanese culture to construct a counterimage of itself.[13] Historical and cultural distance easily robs past agents of their subjectivity even for well-intentioned scholars, who nevertheless tend to assume that ideological representations were internalized by those who suffered the most from them. Thus Ian Neary, in his book about the modern liberation struggle of burakumin (to which he is obviously sympathetic), writes quite confidently: "The *eta:hinin* regarded themselves as impure, not quite human, not deserving equal treatment."[14] He conflates what Bourdieu calls an objective, socially assigned position and a subjective relation to that position on the part of those who occupy it.[15] The kawata did not

12. Teraki, *Kinsei buraku*, 111.

13. Emiko Ohnuki-Tierney, *The Monkey as Mirror: Symbolic Transformations in Japanese History and Ritual* (Princeton: Princeton University Press, 1987).

14. This sentence is preceded by the following imperious passage: "All that existed within the *eta:hinin* groups was simply a deviant reflection of the majority culture of the locality. With neither leadership nor culture there was no sense of identity. Indeed the development of a set of religious beliefs which supported the regulations systematically imposed from the eighteenth century, effectively prevented the emergence of any kind of self-esteem which would provide a basis from which to challenge superior bodies" (Ian Neary, *Political Protest and Social Control in Prewar Japan: The Origins of Buraku Liberation* [Manchester: Manchester University Press, 1989], 26).

15. Bourdieu, *Logic of Practice*, 27.

even call themselves eta. When, for instance, a bakufu intendant in Harima province inquired at a certain village whether there were any eta, the answer was that there were some kawata, yes, but no eta.[16] To my knowledge, the *political* situation of the kawata during the Tokugawa period has mostly been ignored by Western scholars.[17] The events to be discussed will expand our understanding of the position, treatment, and self-perception of the kawata first through an analysis of social and political practice. They will supplement the macrocultural or microindividual and ideological explanations that are often invoked in discussions of the kawata/burakumin.

EPISODES

"In Service of the Shogun," 1743

The date is 1743/11, the place Kami-Hosoya village in Yokomi-gun of Musashino province (Saitama prefecture).[18] A few weeks before, a local criminal had been sent to Edo to be executed. Now his head was being returned for a three-day public exposure. To manage the event, the headman called upon the chief of the kawata hamlet attached to Shimo-Wana village.

In many ways the kawata were not under the rule of the regular village headman. Hence, instead of contacting his colleague in Shimo-Wana, Kami-Hosoya's headman communicated directly with the head (*etagashira*) of the kawata/hinin community associated with Shimo-Wana village. Moreover, the headman had no authority over the head

16. Wakita Osamu, *Kawaramakimono no sekai* (Tokyo Daigaku shuppan-kai, 1991), 5. Hatanaka Toshiyuki reports that in Kinai the eta called themselves *kawata* ("'Kawata' mibun to wa nani ka," MK, 307). In Hozu village, discussed in chapter 4, the kawata, referred to officially as *egō*, literally, "polluted district (the e of eta plus gō)," referred to themselves with a homonym, substituting the e of Edo ("inlet," "bay"), perhaps because their community was the "capital" of the five kawata communities in south Tanba (see Igeta, "Mikaihō buraku," 110; and idem, "Kuchi-Tanba," 95, 111).

17. One notable exception is Frank Upham, who shows an acute awareness of the various political aspects concerning the kawata as they have been dealt with by Japanese scholars (*Law and Social Change*, 79–80). Most of the studies of the burakumin deal with the modern liberation movements. De Vos and Wagatsuma (*Japan's Invisible Race*) provide no more than a general background for the Tokugawa period.

18. Tsukada Takashi, "Kinsei no keibatsu," 119–23.

of the kawata and could not give him direct orders; rather the Kami-Hosoya headman invited him to take charge of the situation.

Why Shimo-Wana and not some other kawata community? The headman had no choice in the matter. Kami-Hosoya was part of a specific geographical area that included a number of kawata hamlets operating under their own leadership in Shimo-Wana. These territorial divisions went by various names, the most common being *kusaba* or *dannaba*. The kawata performed prescribed duties for the area: skinning and disposing of dead cattle and horses and reworking the hides into leather goods (footgear, drum skins, armor, bow strings, etc.), catching fugitives and lawbreakers, guarding prisoners and executing criminals, patrolling the villages, and policing festivals and markets. Such duties or rights were divided among the kawata/hinin as shares (*dannaba kabu*). The Shimo-Wana dannaba comprised twenty-five villages and was one of five such dannaba in Yokomi district.[19]

After the job was done, the two kawata heads in charge handed the implements used (*gokōgisama godōgu*, "the honorable tools of the honorable public authority [the shogun]") back to the headman, who drafted a receipt properly addressed to "Mister (*dono*) Jin'emon and Mister Genzaemon from Shimo-Wana village." During their three days on duty, all twelve kawata and two hinin were served meals in a room at the headman's, as were a number of kawata heads from other hamlets who had come to take in the scene.

This was a rare occasion for the kawata/hinin to function with pride and authority at an extraordinary event as full-fledged officials. Four of the higher-ranked kawata wore long swords, the eight others short ones. Swords, a professional attitude, polite addresses, and being entertained at the home of the village headman, apparently without much concern about "pollution," were all marks of public respect. Their authority was manifested in other ways as well.

At noon on 11/15 an intendant's representative arrived to prepare for the display of the head he had brought from Edo. That evening he conferred with Jin'emon and two other kawata leaders about, among

19. Tsukada Takashi, *Kinsei Nihon mibunsei no kenkyū* (Kōbe: Hyōgo buraku mondai kenkyūjo, 1987), 18–20. In the Kanto area, shares were time allotments of certain days to certain households; in the Kinai, the shares were territorial segments that were given to households for their operations (Igeta, "Kuchi-Tanba," 102).

other things, how much to charge onlookers for viewing the spectacle, since it was "the custom in the countryside to charge eight *mon* for a crucifixion and nine for a beheading." According to the kawata's reconstruction of the event, Jin'emon replied, "We do not take money as executioners; besides, if you charge fees in the countryside, people will not come near but crowd the roads and look from afar and this would be of no service to the shogun." As it turned out, a fee was charged, and forty-six people came from eleven villages and had a jolly, drunken time.

In Edo at least, executions were not grand public spectacles, but took place in the prison courtyard. Perhaps the authorities were aware of the dysfunctional crowd behavior executions provoked, as described by Michel Foucault in *Discipline and Punish.* However, other aspects of penal practice, such as parading the criminal or exposing the corpse or head, were meant to have a salutary effect. The kawata understood this deterrent effect, for they wanted people to "come near" and see. More people would show up if no fee were charged; they protested that if executions were staged and money paid to view them, dignity and honor would be lost—the shogun's as well as their own.

In their meeting with the intendant's emissary the kawata leaders also argued about protocol. The official announced that it was a "national law" that ten guards be used on an occasion like this. The kawata heads countered that in Edo twelve kawata and a great number of hinin were used for an ambulatory exposure, but if there were to be no ambulation, then two hinin in addition to twelve kawata would suffice; in other words, a total of fourteen guards, and not ten, were needed. Moreover, they said, they had no orders from Danzaemon in Edo to lower the numbers. The official nevertheless ordered them to limit the number of guards to ten. The kawata leaders agreed, with the proviso that they would check with Danzaemon on what to do on such occasions in the future.

Satisfied that all preparations had been made, the official left the next day at noon, having handed over the display item. The three-day event began the following morning with fourteen rather than ten guards on active duty. The official did not get the last word after all. Clearly, the kawata had followed their own professional judgment and the procedures as proscribed by their (semi-)national leader Danzaemon, who received a written report from them a week later.

Almost a hundred years after this event, a crucifixion took place in the same village. Again local kawata were mobilized to stand guard for the three days the corpse was to be exposed. The crucifixion proper, however, was performed by a team of two of Danzaemon's underlings, whom he had dispatched with fifteen helpers from Edo.

Shimo-Wana's dannaba was located within the territory of one bakufu intendant. This was not always the case, for in practice, if not in principle, dannaba often cut across a number of jurisdictions and even domains. Therefore, the kawata's social and political topography was different from that of the peasants. They lived in their own hamlets under a separate local and regional jurisdiction in fairly close contact with their leader Danzaemon in Edo. They were often required to, or simply did, cross into social and geographical areas generally forbidden to them while performing their duties. This was especially true during the late Tokugawa period, as the following example illustrates.

Catching Thieves, Arresting Vagrants, 1848

In 1848/3 three prisoners escaped from the bakufu intendant's rural office (*jinya*) in Mikage-shinden (in the center of the Kita-Saku plain, Shinano).[20] They headed south but were caught some fourteen kilometers away, at the village of Kutsusawa, just as they were about to disappear into the mountains. They were escorted back to prison by a team of kawata and a lower official from the Mikage-shinden office. The official had difficulties enforcing his authority over the kawata.

First of all, the kawata disobeyed his orders concerning the size of the escort. Because many men from different hamlets had joined the party, their number was well beyond that prescribed for such an occasion. Moreover, when the noisy troupe arrived at the Nakasendō way station of Shionada at midday, they protested the official's decision to feed them the same riceballs (*nigirimeshi*) the prisoners were being fed: while performing official business, they said, they deserved a full meal served on a platter. The group became angry, forced their way into two inns, and proceeded to eat and drink their fill.

Afterwards an investigation was launched by the kawata head of Mikage-shinden. Twelve kawata were summoned, but none of them had been part of the escort from Kutsusawa; they had joined later. All in all, seventeen kawata from nine villages (representing a bakufu fief

20. Saitō Yōichi, *Gorobe-shinden,* 251–60.

and three domains—Tanoguchi, Iwamurata, and Komoro—within a radius of some fifteen kilometers) were said to have feasted at the inns. Ultimately, the headmen from the parent villages of the hamlets of the kawata in question wrote a joint request for pardon. One kawata from Gorobe-shinden was finally jailed.

Strictly speaking, the Mikage-shinden kawata head's jurisdiction was limited to kawata in that bakufu territory. However, in an area like Kita-Saku, where the fertile plateau had been carved up by half a dozen overlords, he often found it necessary to coordinate activities, such as the catching of thieves, in regions beyond his jurisdiction. The foregoing investigation concerned two issues: a false initial report of the identity of all participants in the event; and the forced entry into the inns under the rubric of official business. Almost everywhere in eighteenth-century Japan laws were issued forbidding kawata from entering the homes of ordinary commoners "even if it rains." In Kita-Saku such laws suddenly appeared in the domains of Komoro, Iwamurata, Okudono, and Tano-guchi, all in 1738.[21] The second issue thus involved the breaking of laws ordering segregation between kawata and commoners.

In 1855 four vagrants (mushuku) wearing long swords were reported at an inn at Kodai. Dispatched from Mikage-shinden to apprehend them were two kawata armed with sticks—which was unusual, since they customarily wore one sword when on official business, although some regulations seem to have prohibited swords for kawata (see art. 3 of the regulations for outcastes in Okudono domain, Kita-Saku, in appendix 5). The vagrants resisted arrest, assaulted the two kawata, and escaped, leaving each kawata with deep cuts (some eighteen centimeters long) across the face and forearm. When peasant uprisings escalated to armed confrontations, kawata were mobilized along with samurai retainers to quell the peasants. Such incidents involving kawata police have been documented for Fukuyama domain (1787), Shinano's districts of Aida (1869) and Kita-Saku (1782), and a number of other places.[22]

21. Ozaki Yukiya, *Shinshū hisabetsu buraku no shiteki kenkyū* (Kashiwa shobō, 1982), 17.

22. On Fukuyama and Aida, see Bix, *Peasant Protest*, 124 and 202; on Kita-Saku, Banba Masatomo, "Mibunsei no teppai e: Shinshū ni okeru burakushi sobyō (4)," *Shinano* 16, no. 12 (1964): 36. For another example from 1755, see Teraki, *Kinsei buraku*, 63. John B. Cornell mentions kawata being called upon in 1871 to defend the castle of Takasaki (Gunma prefecture) and the mobilization of more than five hundred kawata to garrison a fortress during an

When kawata were used against rioting peasants, they were not looked upon as officials to whom respect was due. For example, when three kawata hamlets were mobilized in the Fukuyama riot of 1787, the peasants apparently voiced their anger and indignation by shouting things like "If you dare insult us by turning the likes of abominable eta on us, we'll kill them and feed them to the dogs!"[23]

At other times kawata joined in rebellions, apparently without objections from the other peasants.[24] Such was the case with Ōshio Heihachirō's uprising in Osaka in 1836. It sometimes happened that kawata communities were split between those who were mobilized to suppress the unrest and those who actively participated in it. In 1823 four kawata were among the twenty-six people punished as ringleaders of a large rebellion in northern Kii.[25]

When peasants rioted, kawata were mobilized to suppress them, but when kawata rioted, a rare occurrence, peasants, not other kawata, were mobilized to bring them under control. The authorities deployed commoners against commoners to keep the peace, playing off the emotionally loaded status antagonisms between them. The next incident involves villagers who mobilized such hostile sentiments when they discredited a fellow peasant by defaming his pedigree as polluted by low-status elements.

---

uprising of some seventy thousand peasants in northern Kii ("From Caste Patron to Entrepreneur and Political Ideologue: Transformation in Nineteenth and Twentieth Century Outcaste Leadership Elites," in *Modern Japanese Leadership: Transition and Change,* ed. Bernard Silberman and H. Harootunian [Tucson: University of Arizona Press, 1966], 63).

23. Teraki, *Kinsei buraku,* 64.

24. Hatanaka ("'Kawata' mibun," 327) lists seven riots between 1748 and 1866 in which kawata participated.

25. Teraki, *Kinsei buraku,* 64. Some historians have raised the question whether kawata were actually ringleaders in all instances where they were punished as such. They may have been the victims of lower officials' eagerness to demonstrate results of their mopping-up operations (see Kobayashi Shigeru's remarks in Kobayashi Shigeru et al., "Zadankai: Kinsei hisabetsu buraku ni kansuru hōrei o megutte," in *Kinsei hisabetsu buraku kankei hōreishū: Tenryō o chūshin to shite,* ed. Kobayashi Shigeru [Akashi shoten, 1981], 498). In the Chihara riot of 1782, described and analyzed by Anne Walthall (*Social Protest,* 21–23, 151–55, esp. 154), the kawata community of Minami-Ōji was singled out for special punishment (see Hatanaka, "'Kawata' mibun," 321–24).

The Bonboku *Incident, 1777–1780*

In Kita-Saku in 1777/3 a certain Yōjirō was excluded from a young men's dance at the village festival in Ōzawa.[26] The village officials had concurred with this expulsion, because Yōjirō was someone "with a bad pedigree." This claim did not go unchallenged by Yōjirō and his father Chūemon, and led to a lawsuit two years later. At issue was whether the officials had slurred Chūemon's ancestry, and if so, on what grounds.

The intendant in charge tried to take an easy way out. Avoiding the central issue, he cited Chūemon's violent behavior during the present quarrel and sentenced him to be handcuffed for a time. This triggered a number of personal appeals, not to the intendant, but directly to the domain's investigators in Edo. In 1779/9 one of Chūemon's relatives went to Edo. Chūemon himself was joined in an appeal to Edo by two of his sons in the third and sixth months of 1780. Domain authorities were thus forced to address the substance of the dispute and come forth with a decision regarding Chūemon's status, which is why we know the arguments on both sides.

Chūemon's rebuttal consisted of several points. First, one of his ancestors had been entered as a titled peasant on the land survey of 1629, one hundred and fifty years earlier. Second, another ancestor had served as a local guide to land surveyors in the 1650s and 1660s. And third, he had commended land to the village shrine. This, in his eyes, entitled him to treatment as a regular community member.

Of these three points, the village officials accepted as valid only the first one, even though they acknowledged Chūemon as a tribute-paying peasant. Yet ancestry and tax status notwithstanding, the village officials believed that their discriminatory stance was justified. Their reasons were also threefold: Chūemon's family had not married local people; he acted as if he were on equal terms with the blind; and he did not relate to kawata the way the other peasants did. Through circumstantial evidence and innuendo it was argued that the social behavior of this otherwise legally certified peasant justified discriminatory treatment. The absence of local marriage alliances suggested that Chūemon had family ties with "others." The blind associates referred to here were

26. Ozaki, *Shinshū hisabetsu buraku,* 101–2, 259–60.

zatō, not just people with impaired vision (*mōjin*) but members of an official organization for storytellers, musicians (*biwahōshi*), masseurs, and so on, all of whom were blind individuals who earned an independent living in their occupations.[27] As such, *zatō* were a subcategory of senmin, lower people, just as the kawata were. Thus the statement that Chūemon was on a level with them suggested that he too was of a lower status.

The same suggestion was made with regard to Chūemon's association with the kawata. He was even accused of not paying the "sheaf" (*ichiwa*), which every peasant household was required to pay the kawata for the services they performed for the village. Moreover, it was claimed that one of Chūemon's ancestors, a certain Saemon, had made his living as a *bonboku,* a local name for entertainers who performed the lion dance (*shishimai*).

Entertainers were yet another category of senmin; they were eventually put under the jurisdiction of the kawata chief Danzaemon in Edo during the eighteenth century. Like other holders of low occupations, they were usually housed in separate quarters. For example, in the land register of Azumi district in Shinano circa 1650, *yamabushi yashiki* (compounds for mountain ascetics), *dōshin yashiki* (Buddhist priests without temples), and a yashiki for shishimai performers are listed. In 1687, in a village of the same district, officials had to intervene in a dispute between kawata, *Ebisu* (Ainu), and shishimai dancers regarding group rank, a dispute that was settled in favor of the kawata.[28] Throughout the seventeenth century the authorities had often settled disputes among various classes or occupations of "lower people," sometimes by consigning them, as they did the hinin and entertainers, to the jurisdiction of the kawata.[29]

In the case of Chūemon the local temple mediated a conciliation. The domain meted out punishments to both parties, differentially but graded according to status, for having caused so much trouble. Chūemon was

27. The penal code distinguishes between *mōjin* and *biwahōshi* (see TKKk, 4:234). Internally, the *zatō* were organized hierarchically into dozens of ranks at a national level under the jurisdiction of Kengyō in Kyoto (see KDJ 6:406, s.v. "Kengyō").

28. Banba Masatomo, "'Buraku' no seiritsu ni tsuite: Shinshū ni okeru burakushi sobyō (2)," *Shinano* 12, no. 9 (1960): 49, 59.

29. See Tsukada Takashi, "Kasōmin no sekai: 'Mibunteki shūen' no shiten kara," in MK, 225–67.

sentenced to domiciliary confinement (*oshikome*) for ten days and was manacled for between fifteen and thirty days. The village officials received a lighter sentence: domiciliary confinement (*enryo*) for between ten and thirty days.[30] The authorities did not settle the question of Chūemon's status.

As a very peculiar genealogical reckoning, genealogy was invoked as the ultimate proof of Chūemon's low status. One entertainer ancestor erased his long and venerable peasant lineage. "Genealogical descent," like occupation, language, or skin color (here as in other times and places), becomes the arbitrary, socially defined basis for a particular form of discrimination—one of Tokugawa Japan's unique ("early modern") contributions to Japanese cultural and social practice that is not yet part of the past even today. It did not exist as such in the early Tokugawa period, nor was it a legacy from the Middle Ages; rather, it was a product of eighteenth-century Tokugawa society and culture. Another important point is that the verdict could have been different. Aside from local public opinion, manipulating "genealogy" and association, official legal "world-making" had also to do with whether one was a kawata or not.

The Kidnapping of a Hinin Woman, 1781

Kawata exercised policing functions in numerous villages far from the locale of their residence. They lived together, often only a couple of families, especially in Shinano, which lacked the large kawata communities that were common to the Kinai—not in, but next to, villages,

---

30. There were various degrees of domiciliary confinement. For commoners only there was *tojime* (door closure), which entailed nailing a bar across the door to prevent contact with the outside world; having only some effect in the close quarters of city neighborhoods, it was replaced by reprimands and fines in 1740. *Oshikome* (shutting up) was not limited to commoners and forbade social intercourse for twenty to one hundred days, but the doors were not locked. For warriors and priests, there were three other kinds of confinement. In *heimon* (gate closure), the most serious penalty of the three, all gates and windows were closed, though they were not nailed shut, and contact with the outside world was forbidden for a period of fifty to one hundred days. In *hissoku* (forced closure), the gates were closed for thirty to fifty days, but the prisoner was allowed to sneak discretely through the wicket in the main gate or through a side entrance at night. In *enryo* (restraint), the lightest form of domiciliary confinement for elites, the gates were closed, but the wicket or side door was left unlatched (*hikiyosete oku*), allowing similar goings and comings at night (see TKKk, 4:231–32, and the relevant entries in KDJ).

outside the gates, at the borders, or near the entrances or exits of way stations.[31] Although they were segregated from the other villagers, they nevertheless were considered part of the village in some ways, especially when it came to confrontations with other villages, as the following example, also from Okudono domain, shows.

This incident, in 1781, involved Mon, the daughter of Kanesuke, a hinin from Kami-Kaize village (Minami-Saku district). Kanesuke had lived there for several decades without having been properly registered: he was an illegal resident. He made a living working for two kawata who had shares in the dannaba where Kami-Kaize was located. One of these, Magoichi, was from the kawata hamlet of Tanoguchi; the other, Tahee, was from Kaetsu (both villages were located seven kilometers north of Kami-Kaize).[32] Hinin often worked for kawata, but in this area there were no hinin communities. Kanesuke, not registered and without the support of a network of peers, had a client-patron relation with Magoichi and Tahee.

Mon had been involved with a certain Heizō, a registered peasant from Shiga village (seventeen kilometers to the north, in bakufu territory), for over a year when, on 1781/5/26, she disappeared. Suspicion fell immediately upon Heizō, who had visited her that day. Kanesuke alerted his patron Magoichi, who notified Yata, the prison guard at Tanoguchi and probably the head of Tanoguchi domain's kawata.

Heizō was found in Oiwake station on the Nakasendō, close to Karuizawa (thirty kilometers from Kami-Kaize and eighteen kilometers from Shiga). Yata tied him up and took him into custody in his own house. After learning from Heizō that he had taken Mon along and entrusted her to an inn in Oiwake, Yata handed him over to Magoichi on the third day of the following month (the intercalary fifth month). The next thing to do was to get Mon back to her father, Kanesuke. Until then they would keep Heizō with the kawata community in Tanoguchi. The matter became complicated, however.

On the seventh, the village officials of Kami-Kaize became involved and pressed more details from Heizō. Mon and Heizō had known each other for one year and had plans to get married. They had eloped (or he

31. Ozaki, *Shishū hisabetsu buraku*, 30, 32.

32. Ozaki Yukiya, "Shinano kuni Saku-gun ni okeru buraku no shiteki kōsatsu," *Buraku mondai kenkyū* 18 (1964): 93–98; a short version of this incident can be found in Ozaki, *Shinshū hisabetsu buraku*, 261–62.

had taken her), but since he could not marry her soon, he had thought of putting her into service for four or five years at an inn at Oiwake. Why did the village officials become involved in a matter of an illegal resident?

The kawata had originally hoped to solve this case by themselves, without recourse to the authorities, in part, no doubt because of Mon's and her father's nonregistered status. Their plan was to quietly arrange an exchange of Heizō for Mon without much further ado. They had expected Heizō's village of Shiga to find Mon and bring her home. Shiga village, however, had no intention of looking for Mon, but assumed, nevertheless, that Heizō would be allowed to return without a problem. On the fifth day of the month, they had even refused to negotiate the matter with the kawata. That was when Yata and Magoichi handed the affair over to the village officials of Kami-Kaize. Heizō was transferred there on the seventh, and negotiations with Shiga started.

As before, the Shiga officials showed no interest in helping search for Mon. In addition, they were lukewarm about Heizō's return, because they found it "difficult to accept that Heizō had been imprisoned by kawata from Tanoguchi." The assumption may have been that it was the kawata's job to catch criminals, but they had no business locking them up, for we know that the representatives from Kami-Kaize objected to this way of putting it. They argued that what they had done to Heizō was something altogether different from throwing him in jail. Shiga village complained also that "the apprehension and jailing by a kawata would cause Heizō to lose his status."

Legally speaking, this was nonsense. The mere fact of being caught for a misdemeanor or felony did not automatically result in loss of status. When commoners were sentenced to become hinin, this was the result of a specific verdict. The allegation here, however, is that close contact with a kawata would lower Heizō's status (the same argument as in the Bonboku Incident), or at least cause the loss of his good name, although the term used was *mibun,* "status." After learning either that Heizō had intended to marry a hinin (which toward the end of the eighteenth century would result in loss of commoner status) or that he had kidnapped a woman who had then disappeared, his own villagers thought that perhaps Heizō had become a liability and therefore already considered him not to be one of them.

In the negotiations on the eleventh between the two headmen, Shiga indeed refused to take Heizō back and insisted that Kami-Kaize help with the search for Mon. Kami-Kaize had lost its leverage for forcing Mon's return now that Shiga, for the most spurious and insulting reasons, did not want Heizō back. The infuriated officials of Kami-kaize decided to lodge a formal suit, risking even more trouble because of Kanesuke's illegal situation. They even threatened to carry their case to Edo if the local intendant's office did not agree that Heizō should be handed over only after Mon had been returned.

Shiga's insult by way of status pollution pushed the confrontation to new heights by exploiting to the extreme the shared popular notions about kawata. Initially the kawata had aimed for an informal solution, without drawing official attention. As the village authorities became involved, Kami-Kaize identified increasingly with the kawata and hinin that served the village. Local pride took over, and Kami-Kaize declared itself to stand by them all the way.

The respective intendants of each village, notified of the lawsuit, were still eager to settle out of court. They chose new intermediaries, who succeeded in having both sides agree to Heizō's return to Shiga without any reference to the problem of Mon's return to Kami-Kaize. The reason given was that neither the innkeeper to whom Mon had been entrusted nor Mon herself could be found. It is likely that the officials from Shiga had known this all along and had already abandoned any hope of getting Heizō back, since they could not offer Mon in exchange. Shiga's professed reasons had driven the Kami-Kaize officials to initiate the suit, but after they found out that Mon's whereabouts were not known they could not comply with the mediators' insistence that Heizō be allowed to return to his village. This, however, was what the intendants ultimately ordered.

The intendants judged the case closed after Heizō had returned to the village where he was registered. They do not seem to have further investigated Mon's disappearance or even her alleged service contract. After all, she was a woman, daughter of a hinin, and unregistered, far less valuable than a registered peasant and his return to his village. While the village authorities of Kami-Kaize rallied around one of their subjects, the "law" as represented by the intendants shared the popular discriminatory views. We are left in the dark about Mon's fate.

Anyone who knows anything about Oiwake at that time, however, would probably share Ozaki Yukiya's supposition that Mon was sold into prostitution there and was whisked away as soon as the affair came to light. Oiwake, with approximately two hundred prostitutes, was one of the largest pleasure stops on the Nakasendō. Many of these women came from the ranks of kawata and hinin. Therefore, it is likely that the intendants did not think Mon was worth the trouble it would take to find her.

This incident illustrates how the notion of status pollution or illegal residency could be played up or ignored, how values could be strategically modified in a power game in which pollution was not the issue but a weapon. A village (Kami-Kaize) could decide, at some risk, (1) to treat an illegal hinin as one of its own, (2) to back efforts by kawata to right a wrong, and (3) to threaten with a lawsuit even if it meant going to Edo. Or a village (Shiga) could write off one of its own registered peasants under the pretext that his status had been polluted through contact with kawata. The outcome suggests that the authorities beyond the village shared prejudicial views against kawata and hinin, favoring the peasant.

The Clog Thongs Riot, 1843

The law sometimes was slanted significantly in favor of the peasants. Most famous in this respect is the outcome of a riot of peasants against kawata known as the Clog Thongs Riot.[33] The production of footgear was one of the common occupations of kawata.[34] On 1843/7/22 Tatsugorō, from the kawata hamlet of Nagase village in Iruma district (Musashino province), went to sell thongs (*hanao*) for wooden clogs (*geta*) at the market of Ogoseimaichi village. At the end of the day, Tatsugorō still had eighteen pairs of thongs, which he tried to sell to a certain Hinoya Kiee, who did not show much interest in them. A number of people gathered to watch the two men haggle over the price. They soon joined in, hurling insults at Tatsugorō, and eventually forced him to sell his thongs at a price far below what he considered fair.

33. The four documents concerning this incident, two of which are court records, are available in NSSS 14:569–96. I rely heavily on the introductory summary of the incident (569–70) rather than on the brief sketch, inaccurate in some detail, given in Teraki, *Kinsei buraku,* 64–65.

34. Watanabe village in Settsu province employed four hundred people making various kinds of footgear, which they were allowed to sell on fixed dates at nine designated locations in Osaka (Teraki, *Kinsei buraku,* 51). On the economics of the leather trade in nearby Minami-Ōji, see Hatanaka, "'Kawata' mibun," 308–21.

Angry, he protested vociferously, but the hinin market guard forced him to return home.

That evening Tatsugorō talked things over with the members of his hamlet, and a fairly large number of them set out for Hinoya Kiee's house in Ogoseimaichi, yelling and shouting. The next day they forced their way into his compound. At that point someone from the neighboring village of Ueno, acting as mediator, quieted the crowd down, listened to both sides, and put the blame squarely on Kiee. The people from Ogoseimaichi, in accord with neighboring villages, filed a suit with the Kanto Bureau of Investigations. The kawata, in turn, filed one with Danzaemon in Edo. Meanwhile, following the incident, Ogoseimaichi decided to bar kawata from their market in the future. The devastating effect this would have on the livelihood of the kawata may help explain the massive response that followed.

Twenty-nine peasants from Ogoseimaichi forced their way into the Nagase kawata community on 8/5 with the intention of capturing Tatsugorō, allegedly with the approval of the Kanto investigating officer. The kawata, however, were prepared. With the help of some "500 kawata" from the area armed with bamboo spears, they instead rounded up the 29 intruders and locked them in a shed. Two days later, on the seventh, an officer from the Kanto bureau arrived and succeeded in getting the captives released on a promise that both sides would get a fair hearing. Then an investigating officer arrived from Edo, but with quite a different agenda. The two officials conferred on the tenth, and the higher-up from Edo decided on a policy of forceful suppression.

The next day he mobilized over 300 peasants from the surrounding villages, 34 of them armed with rifles, and ordered a roundup that yielded 252 kawata from twenty-three villages in three days. On the fifteenth, yet another officer arrived from Edo to mobilize 830 peasants and 101 riflemen as a show of force and to prevent any retaliation. One week later, on the twenty-fourth, 97 of the kawata arrested were accompanied by over 700 peasant guards on a three-day journey to Edo. The investigations and trial lasted two years, perhaps because of the sheer number of suspects, perhaps because of the bakufu's determination to emphasize the gravity of the case. The long duration was also a form of punishment, since the kawata were being detained during that time at considerable cost to their families, their communities, and their health.

The "verdict" clearly favored the peasants. As is so often the case with "verdicts," the blame and punishment were shared, although very unevenly. The tendency to punish both parties of a dispute seems to have been part of the concept, or façade (tatemae), of "justice" meted out by the authorities. The kawata from Nagase village were severely reprimanded, and 102 received the following sentences: gibbetting of the head after decapitation (1 case); simple beheading (1); major deportation (4); medium deportation after flogging (3, including Tatsugorō); banishment from Edo (1); expulsion from the community (1); flogging and banishment beyond ten miles from Edo (1); flogging (1); manacles (85); house confinement (2); and demotion from kawata head, *kogashira* (2). In addition, Danzaemon was condemned to house arrest (heimon) in Edo. In stark contrast, only a few peasants were found guilty. None of them had been detained, and their punishments were not physical, but limited to manacles (5) and fines: Nagase's headman was fined three kanmon, and the kumi heads were severely reprimanded; in Ogoseimaichi, the headman was fined five kanmon, and the kumi heads three.

The imbalance between the two verdicts becomes staggering when one discovers that in the course of their two-year presentencing detainment, sixteen kawata died from "unspecified illness," including Tatsugorō and all of those condemned to death and deportation. It appears that the most serious sentences, following rather than preceding the punishment, ratified *faits accomplis*.

The details of this event are known to us through four documents: two separate court records and two private narratives by the same writer. In the latter are two memorable quotes that reveal kawata sentiments, if not those of the participants then at least those of the narrator. According to Nagayoshi, one of the kawata who was condemned to maximum deportation but who died while still in prison, "This uprising is the first since the beginning of Edo and is unique in Japan (*Nihon ichi*). To have come to stand out as those who started the riot is for us, precious instruments, the fulfillment of a divine promise (*senryō dōgu warewaretomo myōga ni kanashi tokoro nari*); if you die once, you do not have to die again; to sacrifice one's life [for this cause] is our deepest wish." Sadaemon, who shared a similar punishment and fate, threatened revenge after death: "We are wild gods (*arakamisama*) even though we are of vulgar and low status (*gesugerō no mibun*); if even an ant's wish rises to Heaven, wouldn't our resentment reach there too?"[35]

Toward the end of the Tokugawa period, minor incidents could escalate and trigger persecution of kawata by peasants and authorities that popular prejudice alone fails to explain. It is perhaps significant that the so-called Clog Thongs Riot originated at a market. The kawata's policing work in their dannaba and in prisons was a performance of official duties by a minority of the kawata. As vendors, which most of them were, they vied for profit. Official documents often contain complaints that kawata harassed commoners while trying to sell their wares (see arts. 2 and 5 of Komoro domain's regulations for outcastes and art. 3 of those of Netsu village, in appendix 5). Ordinary peasants and merchants may have begun to resent the competition and success of kawata in the market. It is certainly striking that while the local mediator at Hinoya Kiee's house found Tatsugorō innocent and put the blame squarely on Kiee, Ogoseimaichi village reacted by closing its market to all kawata. Furthermore, the kawata reacted as a group when one of their own was wronged. The discussion that took place after Tatsugorō returned home points to a shared consciousness of injustice to themselves as a class and a sense of presumed rights that needed defending. After the protest at Kiee's had become a massive and successful resistance against an attacking group of peasants—for it was the peasants who rioted—it was this class action that led to a severe reaction by the authorities, who blamed the victims, the kawata, for defending themselves. Had this been a matter of one peasant village locking up a mob of peasants from elsewhere who were seeking to settle a score, the authorities probably would not have reacted in this way.

Resisting Repression at the Village Level, 1856

Small incidents could lead to sweeping discriminatory measures, but sometimes it was the other way around: sometimes official discrimination triggered resistance. In the following two instances, the kawata confronted the authorities directly and voiced a reasoned critique of discrimination.

35. NSSS 14:582. The same proverb about an ant's wish rising to Heaven is also applied to the suffering of horses and bulls, in article 13 of the Regulations for the Villages of All Provinces of 1649, as adapted by an intendant in Kita-Saku in 1665 (see appendix 4).

In early 1856/4 five kawata from Mure village (under the intendant of Nakanojo in Shinano) were caught gambling in Naganuma village.[36] Within days this led not only to a new prohibition against gambling but also to a series of repressive regulations, to which the kawata responded immediately in a carefully argued written plaint. They listed the prohibitions and their responses to them one by one. In particular, the prohibition against the use of regular or high wooden clogs, umbrellas, or parasols even in snow- or rainstorms (only straw coats were allowed) and the wearing of leather-soled clogs and tabi socks was countered with the argument that "even among people of [low] status, there is not one who does not experience the four seasons' hot and cold weather conditions."[37] In other words, they argued that they were humans too.

This was an appeal for fair treatment based on a human commonality rather than on institutional status divisions. The ultimate victims of status distinctions, the kawata, raised a protest to an unsympathetic audience, reminiscent of Plato's unmasking of ideology in the *Gorgias* (523e), where he speaks of the same kind of judges who "have placed in front of their souls a veil made of their eyes and ears and their whole bodies."[38]

Another prohibition made the kawata aliens in their own country, for it forbade certain cultural practices, namely, the use of banners and high lanterns at festivals. The kawata argued that these were "symbols of gratitude for the benevolence of the Great Peace and the radiance of the grace bestowed by the country" and such a policy was alien to "our national tradition." In other words, they argued that they also were Japanese. They continued, "Although the order to slight gods and

36. Ozaki, *Shinshū hisabetsu buraku*, 163–69.

37. Ibid., 165. Komachi Yūhachi, a Shingaku teacher, voiced a similar sentiment in 1828 when he advocated empathy for the despised classes by pointing out that when one feels cold or hunger, others will feel the same (see Komachi Yūhachi, *Jishūhen*, in *Nihon keizai sōsho*, ed. Takimoto Sei'ichi, vol. 19 [Nihon keizai sōsho kankōkai, 1915], 445).

38. Plato, quoted in *The Levinas Reader*, ed. Séan Hand (Oxford: Basil Blackwell, 1989), 243. Levinas writes that "Plato sets forth a *beyond* of institutional justice, like that of the dead judging the dead (*Gorgias* 523e), as if the justice of the living could not pass beyond the clothing of men, that is could not penetrate the attributes that in others, offer themselves to knowing, to knowledge, as if that justice could not pass beyond the qualities that mask men.... In the social community, the community of clothed beings, the privileges of rank obstruct justice."

Buddhas may very well happen in some regimes under heaven, such things are [only] typical of foreign, 'ruined' countries."

In addition to asserting their right to be treated fairly as human beings and as Japanese, the kawata argued that, as subjects, they were no different from the rest of the population. When they were accused of disregarding prescribed segregation by "passing" as regular commoners, they retorted that the breach had actually occurred from the other side: "In recent years, peasants have behaved like kawata when eating the meat of cows and horses." To the prohibition against the hanging of signboards, they replied that such a regulation would depress business, making it difficult to feed their families, especially since they received no compensation for their police work. Noting that they performed national corvée (kuniyaku) just as everyone else did, the kawata also protested discriminatory regulations regarding the style of their homes. They concluded with a political critique, redefining as injustice what was being officially represented as a reform (*kaikaku*). By arguing that reforms were rare, they implied that this was not a proper occasion for one. Moreover, to institute a "reform" in addition to punishing the gamblers constituted double, and therefore unjust, punishment. They understood the bias of the punishment, for they pointed out that the peasants in the village had heard nothing about an order for a "reform": "only we, kawata, have been targeted for such treatment."

The village officials responded to this written protest the next day (the fifteenth) by initiating an investigation into the kawata involved and by lodging a suit with the intendant because their orders had "met with scorn and were not obeyed." On the sixteenth, three kawata were summoned to appear before the intendant. They set out the next day but got only as far as the village of Nakano, where, after calling upon fellow kawata, they disappeared. On the eighteenth a new summons arrived for other kawata, but when the village officials from Mure went to the kawata hamlet to deliver the summons, there were no men to be found there. Allegedly, they had all left the night before for an unknown destination. Under pressure, however, it came out that two nights earlier they had made plans to disappear with other kawata of the area.

Absconding kawata trying to "pass" as regular commoners came to be defined as a major social problem in the late eighteenth century.[39]

39. See, e.g., laws issued in 1778, 1795, 1796, and 1799 (Kobayashi, *Kinsei hōreishū*, 151, 215, 217, 238–39).

Yet, the detailed criminal records of Nagasaki indicate that quite a number of them returned to their original communities. Unable to overcome the numerous obstacles to entering society, such as the need for sponsors (lineages in many villages and individuals in towns), the requirement to present identification certificates when settling in a new locale, and so on, they returned.[40] *A fortiori,* this was the case with group exodus such as the one in Mure, for the fugitive males returned a couple of weeks later. Some of them were jailed, others reprimanded, and the local temple petitioned a pardon with unknown (to us) results.

Toward the end of the Tokugawa period some kawata protested and resisted what they explicitly identified as groundless, unjust, and cruel treatment, not just by other Japanese but by officials as well. The kawata argued not only that they were human beings and Japanese but that they were full members of the realm even though the state did not acknowledge their "citizenship." Contrary to what Neary writes, they did not think of themselves as "impure, not quite human, not deserving equal treatment," and they said so, not only among themselves but in an eloquent written protest.

Resisting Repression at the Domain Level, 1856

The most famous instance of defiance took place in Okayama domain in 1856.[41] The context here also concerns a "reform." As a result of the political and economic repercussions following Commodore Perry's opening of Japan in 1853, Okayama domain in 1855/11 initiated a series of social reforms that included a decree on frugality. The last five of this decree's twenty-nine articles came to be known as a special decree (*betsudan ofuregaki*) because they applied only to kawata. Among the stipulations were the following: Clothing must be plain, without designs or crests, and either yellowish-brown, persimmon, or indigo blue in color. Kawata had to remove their wooden clogs whenever they met peasants, and they could not wear them at all when they went to other villages. These regulations were typical of discrim-

---

40. See Harada Tomohiko's remarks in Kobayashi Shigeru et al., "Zadankai," 494.
41. KDJ 11:912, s.v. "Bizen no kuni Okayama hanryō Ansei sannen shibuzome ikki"; Teraki, *Kinsei buraku,* 67–69. The current name, Shibuzome ikki (Persimmon Dye Riot), was given at the occasion of its centennial anniversary, in 1956 (see also Cornell, "Caste Patron," 60–62).

inatory laws against kawata, but they also applied to genin and small landholders (in Hozu) and even new titled peasants (in Tanoguchi) (see chapter 3). This "reform" was to be enforced by the beginning of 1856. On 1855/12/27–28 the village headmen informed the respective kawata heads of the new regulations and requested their seals of approval.

Shocked by the stepped-up discrimination, the kawata heads insisted on postponing ratification to allow time for prior discussion in their communities. The hamlet assemblies all opposed ratification, which led to a number of regional meetings of kawata heads. First the leaders of five urban hamlets convened at the Jōfukuji (in Shimo-Ifuku village, Mino district), the head temple for all the kawata of Bizen province, under the pretext of paying the customary New Year's visit to their temple. There they decided to mobilize all the kawata communities of the domain at a general meeting in order to press for the repeal of the discriminatory laws. Seventeen heads of rural hamlets, however, had already agreed at a separate meeting to first ratify the laws and then press for a repeal. On 1856/1/15 the heads of fifty-three communities held a stormy meeting at the Jōfukuji in which the leaders from the countryside resisted the more radical plan of their urban colleagues. After several sessions the radicals prevailed and drafted a formal petition to withdraw the laws.

The kawata's arguments against the discriminatory regulations were clearly spelled out: (1) kawata were cultivators, paid tribute, and were thus "honorable," that is, titled peasants who should be treated like other peasants and not singled out for separate treatment in a time of crisis;[42] (2) many of their fields were of low quality, increased discrimination would squelch the incentive for young people to work them, and therefore the fields would lie fallow and produce no tribute; and (3)

---

42. In other incidents also the kawata expressed their self-image as *onbyakushō*, that is, honorable, or titled, peasants (see Mae Kei'ichi, "Kinsei chū-kōki ni okeru 'kawata' no keizai seikatsu," in *Burakushi no kenkyū: Zenkindai-hen*, ed. Buraku mondai kenkyūjo [Kyoto: Buraku mondai kenkyūjo, 1984], 266–70). We saw in chapter 2 how a whole new community of exclusively peasant kawata was created in Umaji in 1808 (Igeta, "Kuchi-Tanba," 97); Kisaki village, in Tanba, counted twenty landholding kawata, some of them extremely wealthy (owning thirty-six koku, some of it in neighboring villages) (see Igeta Ryōji, "Iriai sabetsu to buraku mondai," *Kindai Kyoto no burakushi*, ed. Buraku mondai kenkyūjo, Kyoto no buraku mondai, 2 [Kyoto: Buraku mondai kenkyūjo, 1986], 171).

when they could not meet the tax quota, many kawata obtained the remaining cash by pawning clothes, which would now become impossible if the proposed restrictions on the kinds of clothes they could wear were imposed. This also would negatively affect their ability to pay tribute. It should be noted that this last point implies that peasants were engaged in economic exchange with the kawata and accepted kawata clothing for pawn without much fear of pollution.

The domain denied the petition on 4/6. The intendant (gundai) charged with seeing that the regulations were ratified pressured the village group headmen to secure the signatures of all the kawata heads. One by one the kawata heads capitulated (some under torture) and signed the documents. On 4/15, however, another general assembly (the fifteenth) was convened. In the tense atmosphere something unexpected happened. The kawata leadership had thus far remained within the law by taking the petition route, but now they were criticized by the rank and file, who raised the possibility of making an illegal, direct appeal (*gōso*). In subsequent strategy deliberations it was decided not to surprise the domain lord by going to him directly but instead to approach a certain elder who had a "liberal" reputation. The elder headed a rural office in Mushiage, in Oku district (some twenty kilometers from Okayama castle), which geographically was perhaps a safer place to stage a mass protest.

The domain officials, aware of what was brewing, on 6/9 ordered a village group headman to "investigate" the Kōnoshita hamlet, which had taken the lead in recommending the direct appeal. This immediately triggered the decision to proceed with the illegal protest. Mobilization instructions were hurried to all males between the ages of fifteen and sixty of all fifty-three kawata communities. In the early morning of 6/13, disregarding pleas and threats from the village group headmen and village headmen, some fifteen hundred to two thousand kawata gathered in a dry riverbed in Yōkaichi village (Oku district). The next afternoon they started their march in the direction of Mushiage. By night they had arrived at Sayama village, where they put up camp and made preparations for the next day's trek to their destination.

The elder, of course, had been informed about this small army on the march and had prepared troops armed with cannon to welcome the protesters. He met them at Sayama the following day, however, and participated in negotiations that ended in a promise that he would forward their petition to the domain's council of elder retainers, who would then review the discriminatory laws. When they had received this promise, the kawata disbanded. The domain council, while appreciative of the compassion shown to the protesters, felt that the honor and authority of the village headmen were at stake and ordered the immediate ratification by the kawata leadership, which now had no choice but to comply.

Punishments followed betrayal. Twelve of the ringleaders were arrested and jailed; by the time they were sentenced, three years later (in 1859/6), half of them had died. The entire populations of the communities that had participated in the protest were sentenced to one to two weeks' domiciliary confinement. A few of the officials—the village group headmen, the village headmen, and the Oku district commissioner and inspector—were held responsible for the mismanagement of the situation, and they also were punished with domiciliary confinement. This incident of protest, resistance, and reprisal has inspired the struggles of burakumin against continued discrimination in the twentieth century.[43]

The Tag Incident: Gorobe-shinden, 1978

Today the burakumin conduct their antidiscrimination drive on many fronts: in the workplace, in the courts, in the media, in religious organizations, and throughout the education system. Reclamation of their history is as vital to the burakumin as ethnic studies are to minorities in the United States and elsewhere. An incident in Mimayose, near Gorobe-shinden, led quite unexpectedly to such a historiographical effort.[44]

On March 10, 1978, a resident of a public housing complex in the village of Mimayose found a small note (7 cm²) tacked to his front door. On it was scribbled: "In Mimayose [this word is written in katakana] there is not even one tsubo [3.3 square meters] of land occupied by a *chorippo* [derogatory local slang for burakumin]. Get your face

---

43. For examples of discrimination in the twentieth century, see Ninomiya, "Inquiry," 115–25; and Hane Mikiso, *Peasants, Rebels, and Outcastes: The Underside of Modern Japan* (New York: Pantheon Books, 1982), 139–71.

44. In Tokugawa times, Mimayose (which was located five kilometers east of Ken's Makibuse and was the place where Ken lived with her first husband) was a small village. It bordered on the Nakasendō and the fields of Gorobe-shinden, which we have come across several times already (see map 2; see also Saitō Yōichi, *Gorobe-shinden*, 16 ff., 151–58).

out of here. [Signed:] The people of the community (*chorippo no sumu tochi wa, Mimayose ni wa hito tsubo mo nai; hayaku dete ike. Kumin ichidō*)." The victim was not a burakumin, but his older sister, it seems, had married one, a genealogical pollution of the sort in the Bonboku Incident two hundred years earlier in Ōzawa village, less than ten kilometers to the southeast. Although Mimayose had no buraku, there were three in the administrative village of Asashina, of which Mimayose was a part. When the burakumin heard of this incident—the fifth in five years—they decided to take action. The burakumin in Asashina collected garbage, disposed of hazardous materials, and emptied latrines. When they went on a strike lasting twenty-nine days, the community was forced to publicly address the problem of discrimination in a number of meetings with the burakumin's representatives, while its garbage went uncollected.

The burakumin, incensed by the allegation that "there is not a single burakumin in this community," decided to reclaim their past, which brought them into confrontation with the elite Gakushūin University in Tokyo. During the Tokugawa period, the three buraku of what is today Asashina village were part of Gorobe-shinden, a village whose history has been studied by a number of scholars, among them Ōishi Shinzaburō,[45] because of the extraordinary technology involved in the building of the irrigation system when Gorobe-shinden was developed in the 1620s. Some twenty thousand documents preserved in the Yanagisawa house of Gorobe-shinden's hereditary headman had been transferred to Gakushūin University; an additional ten thousand had remained at various locations in the area.[46]

Now the garbage collectors of Asashina started a drive for the return of these documents, which was complicated by legal issues of ownership and custody. They eventually won their battle, and all thirty thousand documents are now in a memorial building, the Gorobe Kinenkan, in Asashina. The reclamation of their past has just begun.[47]

45. Ōishi, *Kinsei sonraku*, chap. 3.

46. For a photo of the successor to the Yanagisawa house standing next to a small stone shrine built by his ancestor in 1643, as well as a photo of the wooden water duct (part of a canal that was twenty kilometers long) crossing a river, see ibid., frontispiece.

47. Saitō Yōichi's *Gorobe-shinden* is an early product of this research.

DIMENSIONS AND DEVELOPMENTS

These episodes provide a sense of the complexity of the status question surrounding the Tokugawa ancestors of today's burakumin. The kawata were part of the administrative apparatus: they were state functionaries, but polluted ones. Pollution, however, was not only *discriminatory* and prejudicial but also *discriminating* and selective: in certain areas of daily intercourse, in certain circumstances, it was suspended in practice; in others, it could be activated. And there is clear evidence that the kawata's self-perception diverged from the perceptions others had of them, that they related to their position differently than the non-kawata did. Let us now attempt a more systematic analysis of some dimensions of this notion of pollution as a basis for a status racism and its evolution during the Tokugawa period.

Pollution, the Elastic Idiom of Discrimination

Demographic evidence of contemporary burakumin communities, such as the Ministry of Welfare's survey of 1935, shows a strikingly uneven geographic distribution. Although *population* figures may be too low, by 100 to 150 percent, the data on the number and location of burakumin *communities,* harder to overlook, are considered to be fairly accurate.

It is immediately evident from table 21 that the western half of Japan's main island, Honshū (the Kinki and Chūgoku regions in the table), accounts for a disproportionately high percentage of buraku, with the highest concentration in the relatively small region around Kyoto. The eastern half, settled later, counts far fewer buraku, and in the northeast region there are virtually none. We shall return to this question of historical diffusion later. Also, in the Kinki area (another name for Kinai) buraku tend to be rather large, while in the east they are tiny and scattered.

This demographic variation, which goes back to the Tokugawa period, puts into question a theory that links discrimination against kawata directly to Shinto and Buddhist religious notions of pollution and indirectly to occupations involving the butchering and skinning of animals. This is not to deny that religious formulations and taboos played a part, representational or justificatory, in discriminatory practice against kawata. However, the almost total absence of kawata

Table 21. Distribution of Buraku Population, 1935

Region	Communities		Population	
		%	No. per thousand	%
Tōhoku (northeast)	9	0	1	0
Kantō (large Tokyo region)	835	15	104	10
Chūbu (central; around Nagoya)	751	15	75	8
Kinki† (Kyoto, Osaka, Kobe)	1,042	19	438	44
Chūgoku (southwest)	1,197	22	147	15
Shikoku	797	15	122	12
Kyūshū	736	14	112	11
Total	5,367	100	999	100

†Kinki is another name for Kinai.

SOURCE: De Vos and Wagatsuma, *Japan's Invisible Race*, 117; for a map, see ibid., inside back cover.

communities in northeastern Japan, a region not particularly less Shinto and Buddhist than the rest of the country, points to the inadequacy of such an explanation. Some people there must have disposed of dead animals and manufactured leather goods as well. Those who did may have been despised, as were many others, as senmin and subject to temporary pollutions, but as far as we know, they were not assigned a special social status on the basis of this pollution or subjected to discriminatory practices and laws.[48] In other words, the northeast may have been without eta, but it was not without kawata.[49]

It is important to note that during the Tokugawa period the linkage between certain occupations and kawata status was far from uniform

48. Watanabe, *Mikaihō buraku,* 128.

49. In several of his publications, the medievalist Amino Yoshihiko has argued for marked cultural differences between eastern and western Japan, one of them being the absence of a taboo against the consumption of horse meat and a weaker sense of pollution in eastern Japan (associated with the early prehistoric Jōmon period) than in western Japan (linked to the later prehistoric culture of Yayoi). See, e.g., his *Nihon no rekishi o yominaosu* (Chikuma shobō, 1991), 140–43.

or consistent. In some towns there were leather workers who were not categorized as kawata;[50] and other occupations that were considered polluted were not attached to kawata communities.[51] Certain provinces—Tosa, Iyo, Aki, Bingo, Awa, and Sanuki—had kawata fishermen.[52] Often the decision concerning which groups were to be legally stigmatized as kawata, that is, specifically categorized as "polluted," rested with the authorities and was reached in court.

That legal pronouncements played such a prominent role in identifying rather arbitrarily the grounds on which certain groups would be the object of hereditary discriminatory treatment may at first make this kind of discrimination seem quite different from that resulting from Western racism, based on skin color. But in the West also legal decrees often played a decisive role in deciding who belonged to one "race" or another, and membership sometimes could be purchased. Thus, in 1783 some blacks in Spanish America could become "white men" by fiat of the king of Spain; after 1795, legal white status was for sale, which only sharpened whites' sensitivity about race.[53]

Thus, the notion of pollution was not only used to separate certain occupations based on the belief that pollution was inherent in those occupations; it was also wielded as a weapon in intraoccupational disputes, where its strategic manipulation was harder to hide, since these disputes were settled by administrative fiat. In 1768, for example, the village group headmen from a district in Harima were given instructions about categories of polluted carpenters (*yogore daiku*), which included kawata carpenters working as cremators or as fabricators of instruments of torture and others such as basket makers or builders of houses of prostitution.[54] This taxonomic clarification appears to have

50. Watanabe, *Mikaihō buraku*, 100. Thus a decree of 1794, possibly as a response to an inquiry into a dispute, stipulated that although the making of bamboo hats and bamboo sandals was a kawata prerogative, *hamayumi* (exorcising bows used in ridge-pole-raising ceremonies; toy bows and arrows) could also be made by town artisans (Kobayashi, *Kinsei hōreishū*, 208).

51. Teraki, *Kinsei buraku*, 189.

52. Watanabe, *Mikaihō buraku*, 88.

53. Leslie B. Rout, Jr., *The African Experience in Spanish America, 1502 to the Present Day* (Cambridge: Cambridge University Press, 1976), 156; John Lynch, *The Spanish American Revolutions, 1808–1826* (New York: W. W. Norton, 1973), 20–21. I thank Igarashi Yoshikuni for calling these references to my attention.

54. Kobayashi, *Kinsei hōreishū*, 139.

been the result of an intratrade dispute in which certain groups of carpenters felt threatened by others and is, coincidentally, closely related to an advanced stage in the division of labor. Peasants in Hozu (discussed in chapter 4), frustrated over the course of a lawsuit by the kawata, obtained a ruling ordering the kawata to deliver their tribute rice on a different day from the day the peasants delivered theirs, allegedly to avoid creating occasions for trouble.

The notion of pollution was flexible to a certain extent. Activated and propelled by social, economic, or political forces, it was appropriated and applied in some situations but not others. From the existence of a general notion of pollution and its application at certain sites, one cannot deduce or predict where else it would also appear: its application could be customary (but custom is flexible), institutional (but institutions change), or situational (and therefore contestable). In the case of Mon, the kidnapped hinin woman, the introduction of the notion of pollution changed the tenor of the confrontation between the two villages. In the Bonboku Incident, the attempt to discredit a villager through association with the world of the kawata and other lowly occupations failed. Some Tokugawa Japanese raised the question why hunting, skinning, and eating wild boar was not considered polluting but the kawata were most concretely stigmatized for the skinning and slaughtering of cattle. Hunters (*matagi*), it seems, had succeeded by means of a lawsuit in 1694 to officially differentiate themselves from the polluted kawata.[55] As Pierre Bourdieu has pointedly remarked, "Practice has a logic that is not that of the logician."[56] One cannot essentialize pollution and grant it final explanatory value. Rather, one should historicize its functions and examine how and when it was used and not used.

Logic would lead one to expect that rice grown by kawata was considered polluted. And, indeed, there exists a decree to that effect, but it was enforced for only a short time. In 1720 the bakufu Office of Finance (Gokanjosho) issued an edict requiring kawata, who, like peasants, had paid part of their tribute in rice and part in cash, to now pay the total amount in cash and to store their bags of cash separately, marked *eta osame* ("eta tax"). The reason for this measure was revealed two years later, when the law was rescinded, for then it was ruled that

55. Mase Kumiko, "Ishiki no naka no mibunsei," MK: 274.
56. Bourdieu, *Logic of Practice,* 86.

"eta, hinin, and cremators could again, as before, contribute their polluted rice (*kegaretaru mono ni tsuki kome*) as tax."[57]

Here, then, the logic of pollution drained a precious and pure commodity of all exchange value. Analogously, a different commodity (one that was by nature polluted, one might say), namely, samurai excrement, took on a surplus valorization as a result of the high social status of its "producers": in the night soil market, samurai excrement fetched the highest prices.[58] One would expect the daimyo variety to have been even more valuable, but that does not seem to have been the case, perhaps because it was not for sale. These examples show that the logic of status valorization or devalorization is a contingent rather than an absolute one.

In 1558, Suwa shrine in Shinano recorded its taboos (*monoimi no ki*), which stipulated very circumscribed periods for bloodshed and contact with death: killing a person polluted the killer for one day, as did the removal of an animal carcass, and skinning an animal polluted a person for five days. This hierarchy of pollution, perfectly adapted to a country torn by warfare, suggests that there may not yet have been kawata in the region and that others may have handled dead animals at that time.[59] Nor was pollution a permanent, existential condition for certain classes of people: it was a temporary and removable stain.

Reference to Shinto's concern with pollution as an explanation for the kawata/burakumin's imputed state of inherent pollution misses the point that much of Shinto ritual focuses on the purification of individuals and their environment. No pollution was considered unremovable. Even Deguchi Nao (1837–1918), who founded the new religion Ōmotokyō in the late nineteenth century believing that humanity had lapsed into a fallen and therefore polluted condition, did not view this predicament as permanent or inalterable. Her millenarian vision predicted an imminent restoration of the world.[60] Thus, we need to address

57. Kobayashi, *Kinsei hōreishū*, 111, 115.

58. Walthall, "Village Networks," 295.

59. Banba Masatomo, " 'Buraku' no keisei ni kansuru kōsatsu: Shinshū ni okeru burakushi sobyō (1)," *Shinano* 12, no. 5 (1960): 18. In Amino's new interpretation (see above, n. 49), the Suwa taboos would constitute an argument for his thesis that pollution associated with killing was less developed in eastern Japan than in western Japan.

60. Emily Groszos Ooms, *Women and Millenarian Protest in Meiji Japan: Deguchi Nao and Ōmotokyō*, Cornell East Asia Series (Ithaca, N.Y.: Cornell University, East Asia Program, 1993).

not only the question why kawata/burakumin were associated with pollution but also what the permanent character of that association was.

As mentioned above, kawata joined peasants in some uprisings. They also cosigned with peasants oaths attached to lawsuits (Kashii village, Izumi, 1708).[61] Yet peasants were also particularly insulted when kawata were mobilized against them. In a confrontation between peasant and kawata youth in 1772 the peasants apparently shouted: "We can kill five or six eta without being struck by a curse (*tatari*) from anywhere!"[62] Later in the Tokugawa period, a similar devaluation of kawata lives was expressed by an official. In a well-known incident in 1859, a kawata visiting a Shinto shrine in Edo was killed by a gang of young men because he was "polluted." When Danzaemon requested the death penalty, the magistrate apparently responded that a townsman's life was worth that of seven kawata and that therefore the quota to justify the execution of a townsman had not been reached.[63] This ratio, it should be noted, was also applied to samurai and peasants, at least in rhetoric.[64]

In the seventeenth century, kawata not only served in villages as guards and *champêtres* but also worked in peasant households or as day laborers, perhaps replacing the bond servants who had been set free.[65] Yet, in the first decades of the eighteenth century, we find numerous prohibitions against kawatas' entering commoners' homes. That the segregationist laws were not an empty letter is shown by the ways they were circumvented and the punishments that followed discovery. Mixed marriages between majority Japanese and kawata occasionally functioned as channels for smuggling a number of kawata into peasant and merchant houses, sometimes over distances as far as seventy kilometers, to perform labor as servants. If discovered, the go-betweens, especially when they profited from the scheme, were punished more severely than the "illegal aliens" themselves were.[66] The

61. Teraki, *Kinsei buraku*, 152.

62. Ibid., 61.

63. Inoue Kiyoshi, *(Kaihan) Buraku mondai no kenkyū: sono rekishi to kaihō riron* (Kyoto: Buraku mondai kenkyūjo, 1959), 32–33; Saitō Yōichi, *Gorobe-shinden*, 243; Ninomiya, "Inquiry," 98.

64. Bix, *Peasant Protest*, 94.

65. Watanabe, *Mikaihō buraku*, 96, 107, 122, 132–33 (service); 125 (day laborers).

66. Hatanaka, "'Kawata' mibun," 333; Igeta Ryōji, "Kon'in sabetsu no rekishiteki shosō: Edo bakufu no hanketsu o tsūjite," in *Kindai tennōsei kokka*

mixed marriages, Ozaki Yukiya notes, were not unknown in Kita-Saku before the 1690s, and as a rule they were unproblematic for the authorities.[67] Gradually, however, increased administrative pressure for segregation, starting in earnest in the 1770s, led to severe sanctions against mixed marriages, now categorized with adultery; for commoners the punishment was status demotion to hinin underling (*tega*).[68]

Occupations—Degraded and Polluted

The term *senmin* ("despised people") was associated with certain occupations and has existed since the beginning of recorded history in Japan. Generally speaking, in all societies, past and present, certain occupations seem to be perceived socially as low and undesirable. Medieval Japan counted dozens of them. Danzaemon, the "national" head of the kawata/hinin since the 1720s, had fabricated his genealogy (at least in one version) through Heian warrior houses all the way back to China and listed no fewer than twenty-eight lowly occupations among his ancestors as an argument for his rightful dominant position among senmin.[69] Many of these occupations were still viable throughout the Tokugawa period, although this does not necessarily imply that they were hereditary. As mentioned above, Tokugawa Japan counted many more lowly and polluted occupations than those specifically held by kawata. Conversely, only some of the occupations, communities, and lineages of the kawata can be traced to late medieval times.

The term *eta,* first mentioned in texts of the thirteenth century, was written with the characters for "plentiful pollution" only some two centuries later, referring then to a subgroup of the *kawaramono,* or "riverbed people." The kawaramono lived on the riverbanks in Kyoto. They were ranked among the lowest of the many senmin categories.

---

no shakai tōgō, ed. Mahara Tetsuo and Kakeya Saihei (Kyoto: Bunrikaku, 1991), 12–18 passim.

67. Ozaki, *Shinshū hisabetsu buraku,* 177.

68. Igeta, "Kon'in sabetsu," 15. Satsuma domain, for one, in 1784 forbade intermarriage between peasants and "eta, kengo [?], etc."; made "eta and the like" live separately from peasants; and shifted its idiom for discriminated people from death to pollution when it changed the term from *shiku* (literally, "death pangs") to *eta* (Teraki, *Kinsei buraku,* 46).

69. These genealogies can be found in Kobayashi, *Kinsei hōreishū,* 27–49; and NSSS 14:427–38.

Riverbanks were not taxed, and their occupants—cleaners, plasterers, dyers, well diggers, gardeners, transporters of goods, and so on, and many highly skilled laborers—worked for the noble and warrior establishment or were attached to temples as jobbers. Kawaramono who earned their living cleaning estates, slaughtering animals, or working leather were specified as eta.[70]

During the wars that engulfed Japan throughout the sixteenth century, leather was in great demand for the manufacture of saddles, arms, and protective gear to equip the armies. Thus, some of the warlords (like the Imagawa in 1526 and the Hōjō in 1538) concentrated leather workers around their castles, subjected them to their immediate authority by cutting their ties with whoever might have claimed them as dependents, organized them under one head, exacted levies in leather from them, and forbade the export of leather goods to other domains. Later in the century other warlord houses, like the Maeda, the Ueda, and the Takeda, followed the same practice.[71]

These changes in the social organization of leather production were part of the gradually developing efforts by daimyo to mobilize all the sectors of society. Other artisans were similarly concentrated, organized, and forced, as the peasants were, to provide yaku (service that included materiel as well as corvée) to the new lords. Among those in the "low" occupations, the leather workers were most in demand. A number of them were moved from the countryside to castle towns, and when none were in the area, they were imported from the provinces around Kyoto. In Kaga, Noto, and Etchū leather workers were brought in from Ōmi and Tanba. The castle towns in Shinano were probably provided with kawata communities by Takeda Shingen (1521–73). As Banba Masatomo points out, leather workers in these towns may have suffered not only the prejudice associated with their "polluted occupation" but also that directed against outsiders and newcomers.[72]

Documents drawn up on the occasion of transfers of lords in Shinano in the 1580s and 1590s refer to already existing service relations between *kawaya sōgashira* or *kawata tōryō* (heads or leaders of leather workers) and lords whom they provided with leather goods and for whom they also performed policing duties such as guarding prisons,

70. Teraki, *Kinsei buraku*, 25–26.
71. Banba, "'Buraku' no keisei," 9–11.
72. Ibid., 21–23.

performing executions, cleaning castle grounds, checking the entering and exiting travelers at way stations, and so on.[73] These leaders were probably chosen from among the more prominent leather workers in the area. In order to perform the function of their occupation, these leaders had been moved to the castle towns and been put in charge of other kawaya or kawata. They were granted the privilege of wearing swords, received tax-free land (sometimes even called *chigyō* "fiefs"), and at times received stipends or collected "one sheaf" (*monnami hito-masu, momiko, hitowa ine*) per household from the villages they served. Their names became hereditary occupational names, like Danzaemon in Edo; Magoroku in Matsushiro, controlling four districts for a stipend of sixty bales; Hikodayū in Matsumoto, in charge of two districts; Kojūrō in Ueda. They formed the elite corps of the kawata, married into one another's lineages (Hikodayū was related through marriage to Danzaemon), lived in larger houses than their subjects, and enjoyed respect as officials. For instance, when Magoroku traveled on business to Edo he stayed in the daimyo's *nagaya*, the long house where samurai were lodged.[74]

Within kawata communities status divisions and concomitant tensions and power struggles developed along the same lines as in peasant villages. By the nineteenth century leadership positions had become hereditary, the number of main families had been frozen, and lawsuits initiated by kawata underlings (tega) concerning succession to office

73. The information that follows comes from ibid., 5–15. As a general rule, the execution of criminals was not associated with kawata executioners and guards in medieval times. There is mention of an execution performed by a *kawaramono* in 1488 (Watanabe, *Mikaihō buraku,* 139).

74. Banba Masatomo, "'Buraku' no sui-i to mibun kisei no kyōka: Shinshū ni okeru burakushi sobyō (3)," pt. 1, *Shinano* 13, no. 8 (1961): 33–34; idem, "Mibunsei no teppai e," 35. On the size of the homesteads (yashiki) in the Kamasu buraku, Komoro domain, in Kita-Saku, see Ozaki, *Shinshū hisabetsu buraku,* 61–63. Danzaemon's yashiki in Edo was about 1,000 *tsubo* (3,300 square meters), and he is said to have drawn income from 3,000 koku; other eta/hinin heads are said to have held 300,000 to 400,000 ryō, and a drum maker from Watanabe hamlet near Osaka is said to have held over 700,000 ryō (Kobayashi Shigeru, "Kinsei ni okeru Buraku kaihō tōsō," *Rekishi kōron* 3, no. 6 [1977]: 90–91; Ninomiya, "Inquiry," 103). Danzaemon in Edo was allowed to posture as a small daimyo on certain official occasions. For instance, when he paid New Year's visits to senior and junior counselors and to the three commissioners, he was carried in a sedan chair and accompanied by spear bearers (Mase, "Ishiki no naka no mibunsei," 270).

and abuses of authority were widespread.[75] It will be recalled that the domainwide struggle of 1856 in Okayama was forced upon the kawata leadership by their subordinates. In some of these disputes, shares in the privilege of patrolling villages (dannaba kabu) were at issue. These shares were controlled by the main houses, which were the equivalent of titled peasants in kawata communities. In Kamasu, for instance, only 30 percent of the households enjoyed such shares, which, as in peasant villages, could be transmitted or sold.[76]

After leather workers were forced to relocate to the castle towns, they were often moved to the outskirts as the towns' population expanded (this occurred, for example, in Kaizu, Sunpu, Odawara, and Kanazawa). The reasons were in part functional, for their work as prison guards or executioners or post attendants for checking travelers made it necessary for them to resettle outside the town; in part economic, the outskirts being inferior locations; and part cultural, having to do with notions of pollution.[77] In late medieval times similar separate communities had formed around market and temple towns, where a floating but semistable population of entertainers, tatami makers, and others had settled.

In the population rosters and land cadasters of the late sixteenth century many people were registered as "kawata," a reference to the leather workers or their fields.[78] Sometimes whole communities were registered as such, separate but not independent from peasant villages. Asao Naohiro stresses that on Hideyoshi's land survey, no kawata villages were registered as autonomous units; they were always appended

75. For details of internal governance of kawata communities, see Banba, " 'Buraku' no sui-i," pt. 1, 34–36; and Ozaki's study of Kamasu buraku in his *Shinshū hisabetsu buraku,* 75–76. For intrahamlet struggles in Shinano communities, see ibid., 20, 100–150, 296–99; Banba, "Mibunsei no teppai e," 36–39; and idem, "Ueda-ryō nai ni okeru 'eta' soshō jiken," *Shinano* 17, no. 11 (1965): 1–12, and 18, no. 3 (1966): 30–48.

76. Ozaki, *Shinshū hisabetsu buraku,* 85. Igeta notes that over the years some households succeeded in accumulating quite a large number of such shares, which did not automatically translate into leadership positions (Igeta, "Kuchi-Tanba," 107).

77. In Hozu village, for instance (see chapter 4), forty-two kawata households (including 250 people and 12 cattle) were relocated, not without some monetary remuneration, from the center of the village to a lowland closer to the Hozu River, which was exposed to frequent flooding (Igeta, "Mikaihō buraku," 112).

78. For this paragraph, see Teraki, *Kinsei buraku,* 35, 36, 86.

to peasant villages.[79] Sometimes the entries were hierarchized, as when kawata were listed after peasants but before *aruki* (messengers and jobbers on the payrolls of villages and towns). However, many were listed with their own kokudaka, some as owners of as much as twenty koku, although such entries are only found in rosters and cadasters west of Shinano. It is not quite clear whether these entries identified an occupation or what came to be their fixed hereditary legal status. One thing is certain: these entries were not discriminatory as such; the households thus identified were not subject to special discriminatory laws, and the kawata had not yet been organized "nationally," for this happened in the 1720s.

Only very rarely were leather workers entered on early Tokugawa records as "eta" (in Kumamoto in 1604, Awa in 1623). In the 1660s and 1670s, however, around the time when a new class of economically independent peasants was vying for political power in the villages, a great number of domains began to record kawata as eta. It is not clear to what extent the link between an increased competition among commoners and a stepped-up discrimination against kawata can actually be documented. At the same time, in some provinces around Kyoto, communities of kawata were relocated to less desirable locations that often were plagued by flooding or other natural disasters.[80]

Throughout the seventeenth century the bakufu and the various domains were engaged in haphazard efforts to regulate and order the marginal populations engaged in numerous "lowly occupations." Thus, for instance, the dyers of Kyoto, initially labeled eta, succeeded in being recategorized separately; in Omi province, however, dyers were organized into a kawata community.[81] Hunters also succeeded in separating themselves from the kawata. The expanding area of Danzaemon's control over the kawata, all of eastern Japan by the 1720s, and the extension of his jurisdiction over hinin and entertainers culminated in the recording of kawata (and Danzaemon's) genealogies in the early eighteenth century, which testifies to this ongoing effort at regulating the nonpeasant lower population strata. Yet judging from the frequent queries by various local authorities in other parts of Japan concerning

79. Asao, "Kinsei no mibun," 36.
80. Teraki, *Kinsei buraku*, 45.
81. Ibid., 189; NSSS 14:267n.

the locus of authority over kawata or hinin, it is evident that the situation was far from clear.[82]

Starting in 1678, the one kawata household of Kodaira village (Kita-Saku) was entered as eta in the population register. Around the same time, however, kawata in that area were also referred to as *chōri* ("officials"), often written with the homophonic characters meaning "removed, separate from the town." Sometimes they were entered as *yakunin* ("officials") on the temple rosters for memorial services (*kakochō*).

The practice of registering individuals in official records as members of a separate, defiled category of human beings came also to prevail in Buddhist temples around the end of the seventeenth century, whereby discrimination was extended into the afterlife. At Fukuōji in Kodaira, for example, the pre-eighteenth-century term *yakunin* had been replaced by 1725 by *eta*. Three decades later discrimination continued to grow: the names of deceased temple members who were kawata were now put on a list kept separate from the list of deceased peasant members. Moreover, posthumous names (*kaimyo*) with the additional character *kaku* ("tanned leather," also read as *kawa*, "hide," "pelt") were bestowed on kawata.[83]

Customarily, posthumous names were honorific titles that ennobled the deceased to varying degrees, depending on the sum of money paid by the family to their Buddhist temple. In the early nineteenth century the bakufu was sufficiently disturbed about the inappropriately high ranks commoners were being granted in the afterlife to pass legislation

82. See the numerous requests for clarifying questions regarding penal jurisdiction over kawata and hinin in Kobayashi, *Kinsei hōreishū*. Igeta discusses some of these requests regarding mixed marriages and incognito kawata servants in his "Kon'in sabetsu." See also Tsukada Takashi's interesting article on various suits by conflicting lower occupational groups that resulted in officializing the hierarchical relationships between them ("Kasōmin no sekai," 225–68).

83. On the numerous ways posthumous names on tombstones identified the dead as separate beings, sometimes as "humanoids," using the character meaning "to look like [humans]," sometimes even as beasts, *chiku*, see Kobayashi Daiji, *Sabetsu kaimyō*. Much of this study is concentrated on Ueda city and Chiisagata district, adjoining Kita-Saku district in Nagano prefecture. A temple in Nagano is said to have charged 3 million yen for converting a discriminatory posthumous name into a regular one (15). The oldest discriminatory posthumous name Kobayashi mentions dates from 1622 (180).

on the proper posthumous status for kaimyo.[84] The bakufu, however, did not have to worry about the kawata: the Buddhist clergy made sure they maintained their assigned status even in the afterlife. Discriminatory posthumous names were chiseled on tombstones, allowing for the immediate identification of kawata graves, a practice that continued well into the mid twentieth century, mainly in eastern Japan, where the tiny kawata communities often share graveyards with majority Japanese. Kobayashi Daiji reports a case of discriminatory posthumous names as recently as 1980.[85] The Sōtō branch of Zen Buddhism in Nagano also had the term *sendara* in its posthumous discriminatory repertory for kawata, *sendara* being the Japanese transcription in characters of the Sanskrit *candāla*, the name of an outcaste group in India.[86] In medieval texts *sendara* had been associated with butchers, labeled evil people (*akunin*).[87] Thus did mid-Tokugawa Buddhist monks recognize and sanction discriminatory practices against the Japanese kawata as similar to the casting out of India's "untouchables," long before modern scholars recognized the similarity.

The logic of discrimination penetrated the religious domain in other ways as well. Since families usually did not change temples, modern data on burakumin temple affiliations reflect quite accurately the Tokugawa situation. In regions scattered with tiny settlements, kawata shared temples with other commoners. Even then, they often went to special temples that served only kawata (*etadera*). A nationwide survey conducted in 1968 of all 1,470 etadera revealed that 91 percent were New Pure Land (Jōdoshinshū) temples. These "polluted" temples were orga-

84. For a law dating from 1831, see Narusawa Eijū, "Rekishiteki ni mita mikaihō buraku no kaimyō," in *Shūkyō to buraku mondai*, ed. Buraku mondai kenkyūjo (Kyoto: Buraku mondai kenkyūjo, 1982), 170–71.

85. Kobayashi Daiji, *Sabetsu kaimyō*, 15.

86. Ozaki, *Shinshū hisabetsu buraku*, 26–33; see also 329–35. For information on *sendara* and *candāla*, see Teraki, *Kinsei buraku*, 56. For the twentieth century, see Narusawa, "Mikaihō buraku no kaimyo," 158–87; and Wakamiya Yoshinobu, "Hisabetsu buraku ni totte no kami to hotoke: Komoro-shi Arabori de no minzoku chōsa o chūshin ni," *Nihon shūkyō to buraku sabetsu*, special issue of *Dentō to gendai*, no. 73 (1981): 79–112. I discuss the question briefly in the context of ancestor worship in my *Sosensūhai no shimborizumu* (Kōbundō, 1987), 171–72, 179–80.

87. For example, in the *Chiribukuro*, a mid-thirteenth-century dictionary; however, in an expanded version of the mid fifteenth century, the *Ainōshō*, the kawata are associated with pollution (Kuroda Toshio, *Nihon chūsei no kokka to shūkyō* [Iwanami shoten, 1975], 380).

nized separately into a specialized institutional hierarchy in direct connection, not with the sect's head temple in Kyoto (Honganji), but with midlevel head temples (*chūhonzan*) specifically for the kawata.[88]

There is a striking regional pattern to these temple affiliations. Almost all burakumin temples west of the central region are New Pure Land temples; only in Okayama and Takayama does one find temples affiliated with other Buddhist sects: Nichiren and Pure Land. East of Shinano (in the Tōkai, Kanto, and northeast regions) one finds a variety of Buddhist sects serving burakumin, including the Nichiren, Rinsai, Sōtō, Tendai, and Shingon sects. Moreover, fully 80 percent of the New Pure Land temples belonged to the Nishi Honganji branch, which claimed descent from the original line of the founder Shinran (1173–1262) after Tokugawa Ieyasu split up the sect in 1602. Ninety percent of these temples affiliated with Nishi Honganji are located in the Kinai area around Kyoto; there is not a single one in the central region or to the east of it.

Shinran's populist, egalitarian message appealed to the kawata.[89] Because kawata had been concentrated in the Kinai, where the most radical followers of Shinran, the Ikkō sect, had organized armed resistance (ikki) against warlords in the sixteenth century, before the Tokugawa period, Teraki Nobuaki tentatively linked kawata to the Ikkō ikki even though there is scant evidence for kawata participation in these ikki.[90] The close association between Nishi Honganji temples and kawata in the Kinai seems significant within the context of Teraki's argument, since a great number of these temples were established during the heyday of the Ikkō movement.

88. This and the following information on religious affiliation can be found in Teraki, *Kinsei buraku*, 55, 192–221.

89. Shinran (1173–1262) identified his followers, all believers in the sole power of *nenbutsu* (reciting the name of Amida Buddha), as human beings with the lowest karma: *toko* ("killers of dogs and sheep and sellers of sake"); and Nichiren (1222–82) wrote that he was the son of a sendara (Kuroda, *Nihon chūsei no kokka*, 388).

90. In eastern Japan, the Hakusan Shinto shrine in Kaga province is especially venerated by the burakumin. Hakusan seems to have been the protective god of socially marginal members of society, since he is also seen as especially protective of children (Shibata Michiko, *Hisabetsu buraku no denshō to seikatsu* [San'ichi shobō, 1972], 17–24). Teraki mentions a close link between the kawata communities and Hakusan belief in Shinano, and he writes of three thousand horsemen having been dispatched by two large Hakusan shrines in Kaga to join the Kaga ikki in the sixteenth century (*Kinsei buraku*, 193).

Toward a Legislated Racism

Just as Karl Marx argued that "the economic" constitutes the hidden or suppressed truth of past societies, now revealed to us by the workings of capitalist society,[91] one can make a case that racism reveals the quintessential operations of the ascription of any inherent inequalities, such as those that prevailed in a "society of orders" like Tokugawa Japan. Viewed from this perspective, which is not that of the logician, racism is not a particular variety of discrimination; rather, all forms of discrimination produce effects like those of racism. The Tokugawa history of today's burakumin points to practices and ideologies that betray racist sentiment developed from what was originally a status distinction.

We have seen how asymmetrical punishments meted out for kawata and peasants were following the 1843 Clog Thongs Riot. By the standards of late Tokugawa juridical practice, this was not unusual. In 1796 the bakufu's superintendent of finances, who had a seat at the Tribunal (Hyōjōsho), answered a query whether or not commissioners should conduct direct investigations of eta/hinin after preliminary interrogations by lower officials. The superintendent's answer was that there should be no distinctions in this regard between ordinary commoners (*heijin*) and eta-hinin. But, he added, their sentences should be different.[92] In 1839 it was decided that when peasants and kawata filed joint suits in court, they should be treated differently (*sabetsu*, discrimination): peasants should squat on straw mats, kawata on the gravel, or three shaku (almost one meter) lower.[93] Clearly this could be construed as an official strategy to drive a status wedge into possible solidarities among commoner groups.

Differential punishments for samurai and commoners were routine throughout the Tokugawa period, but the singling out of kawata around the turn of the nineteenth century was something altogether new. The first Tokugawa segregation law for "*eta, hinin, chasen,* and

91. Karl Marx, *Grundrisse* (New York: Vintage Books, 1973), 460. This thesis has been reformulated by Bourdieu, who argues for the pervasiveness of "interests" even in the symbolic realm; Foucault has substituted power for Marx's economic interests.

92. Kobayashi, *Kinsei hōreishū,* 217.

93. Ibid., 337.

the like" dates from 1778.[94] It expresses concern with the lawless behavior of eta, hinin, and chasen and with their "mingling incognito
with peasants or townspeople at inns, eateries, drinking establishments,
etc." This law was followed in 1804 by the first listing of special penalties for kawata and hinin.[95] The latter document refers to precedents
going back to 1771, but not earlier.

Bakufu regulations before the end of the eighteenth century mentioned kawata but did not legislate discrimination and segregation in a
comprehensive manner. In this the bakufu followed pre-Tokugawa
practice. For example, a kawaramono who in 1518 assaulted a silk merchant did not receive particularly harsh punishment from the Muromachi bakufu court.[96] Where official prejudice existed, however, it
was manifested in various ways. Teraki Nobuaki mentions a common
practice dating from the early Tokugawa period, the cartographic custom of leaving out figures for road sections passing through kawata
hamlets when computing distances between two points.[97] If maps are
representations of the land and its occupants, this practice may have
implied that the kawata did not belong in Japan. Similarly, a decree of
1763 required that hinin be removed from the road to Tokugawa
Ieyasu's shrine in Nikkō when the Korean embassy passed through.[98]
The image of Japan that was visible on maps (as seen through the eyes
of officials) and from sedan chairs (through the eyes of foreign digni-
taries) did not include kawata or hinin.

In reality, of course, kawata were far from being ignored by the
authorities. The first reference to kawata in Tokugawa edicts dates from
1657. They were mentioned only in passing, though, in an addendum
to the fourth article of a nine-point directive regarding the catching of
thieves. Kawata figured in a list of socially undesirable elements "one
should look out for," the list subsequently adopted in goningumi village

94. Ibid., 151–52; TKKz 5:474–75 (no. 3434). In some domains, *chasen*
(one of the many low occupational groups) were distinguished from kawata;
they performed similar functions as guards or at funerals under the direction of
kawata leaders (Teraki, *Kinsei buraku,* 48; KDJ 9:456).

95. Watanabe, *Mikaihō buraku,* 6, 155.

96. KDJ 3:758, s.v. "kawaramono."

97. Teraki, *Kinsei buraku,* 44. This cartographic practice was abolished by
law on April 2, 1869 (Ninomiya, "Inquiry," 107).

98. Kobayashi, *Kinsei hōreishū,* 136.

laws: "Buddhist monks, yamabushi (mountain ascetics), wandering ascetics, mendicant monks with flutes and bells, eta, hinin, etc."[99] Large cities conducted investigations and introduced reforms (*aratame*) and passed administrative measures for hinin (Osaka, 1644; Kyoto, 1654; Edo, 1674) and kawata (Kyoto, 1715; Edo, 1719).[100] These were efforts to tighten control over the floating population of senmin, who were neither samurai nor peasants, craftsmen nor merchants.

By the end of the seventeenth century the prevailing practice was to list kawata separately from peasants, sometimes in completely different population rosters. In Matsumoto domain (Shinano) beginning in 1722 kawata and hinin were even listed under the separate heading *jingai* ("outside humans"), written with the same characters, in reverse order, as today's pejorative term *gaijin* (foreigners).[101] Starting with Danzaemon in 1719 and continuing into the 1730s, the genealogies of kawata were being checked in Kyoto, Edo, and a number of domains,[102] apparently to build a data base around the membership of these classes. In later years these data were used in so-called eta hunts (*etagari*) in Edo, Osaka (1798, 1827, 1833), and Kyoto.[103] One such etagari conducted in Kyoto in 1831 yielded fifty-three kawata who were trying to "pass." In 1722 Danzaemon was established as a well-pedigreed "national" chief for the hinin and kawata in the eastern provinces (the eight Kanto provinces; Izu, Suruga, and Kai to the west of them; and the northeastern provinces).[104] In order to establish a clear hierarchy between hinin and kawata, the former were required to cut off their topknots and were forbidden to wear headgear.

The 1720s and 1730s constitute a watershed for segregation legislation aimed at kawata in many domains, perhaps prompted by the bakufu's retrenchment reforms collectively known as the Kyōhō Reforms.[105]

---

99. Ibid., 102. See article 1 of the goningumi rules (1662) of Shimo-Sakurai, Kita-Saku district, in appendix 3; cf. articles 2 and 3 of the goningumi rules (1640) of the same village in appendix 2.

100. Teraki, *Kinsei buraku*, 44, 46.

101. Banba, "'Buraku' no seiritsu," 56.

102. Watanabe, *Mikaihō buraku*, 108, 138.

103. Kobayashi Shigeru, "Buraku kaihō tōsō," 91.

104. For details of the national governance of the kawata/hinin, see Cornell, "Caste Patron," 56–70; and Ninomiya, "Inquiry," 99–100.

105. For an excellent, detailed discussion of these reforms, and the only one available in English, see Kate Nakai, "Kyōhō Reforms," in the *Kodansha Encyclopedia of Japan* 4:330–31.

This institutionalization of discriminatory practices against kawata and hinin gathered momentum with each subsequent reform (Kansei, 1780–1790s; Tenpo, 1830s), eventually culminating in the intra-race racism of the nineteenth century. Earlier some domains had issued status legislation for the kawata: Awa domain had decreed in 1699 that kawata should dress more coarsely than peasants, and Chōshū domain in 1713 had decreed that "eta, chasen, and the like" should not be extravagant in their clothing or home design and should not engage in occupations other than those authorized by the domain.[106] During the period of the Kyōhō Reforms a number of domains made a concerted effort to restrict social intercourse between kawata and other commoners. The domains of Matsumoto, Komoro, Iwamurata, and Okudono (Shinano, the latter three in Kita-Saku) all issued legislation for kawata in the year 1738.[107] In 1704 the Okudono domain (the location of the Bonboku Incident of 1771) acquired additional villages in Kita-Saku (around Tanoguchi) as a *tobichi,* or detached parcel. On that occasion the domain issued a comprehensive law comprising eighty articles, but none of them directly concerned the kawata. In 1738, however, the domain issued a seven-point directive aimed specifically at the kawata population. Reissued again in 1779 and 1809, this law constituted the domain's policy toward the kawata.

It is worth noting that in 1704 there were only eleven kawata households in the domain, spread over five (seven in 1738) of the twenty-five villages. By 1838 the kawata population, in ten villages, still numbered only 107 members. In 1765 in Komoro domain (15,000 koku), with a population of approximately the same size, the kawata population was 438 in ten villages, half of it concentrated in Kamasu, the largest kawata community in both Komoro domain and Shinano province.[108] How could such a minuscule "minority" population possibly represent a threat? What motivated domain officials to implement discriminatory and segregationist directives against the kawata in 1738? Judging from the regulations of that year and later, when they were reissued, the concerns seem to have been the following.[109]

106. Teraki, *Kinsei buraku,* 45; another example is Toyoura domain in 1683 (Kobayashi, *Kinsei hōreishū,* 103–4).

107. Ozaki, *Shinshū hisabetsu buraku,* 17, 72–74, 243–44.

108. Ibid., 52.

109. These rules, all from the Kita-Saku area, can be found in the following publications: for Okudono and Komoro in 1738, ibid., 73–74, 244–45; for

Standards of segregation, which were perceived as breaking down, were the main concern: the kawata were behaving too much like ordinary peasants. Concretely this involved reinstituting status-marking practices and creating new ones. Practices signifying status were fairly consistent throughout the area and the country, with only a few local variations. Laws consistently stated and restated that kawata could wear only straw sandals; wooden clogs were forbidden, as was the use of umbrellas or parasols; and clothing with family crests and haori jackets were proscribed. Kawata could not build new-style houses and were forbidden to hang streamers (*nobori*) from poles or roofs during village festivals.

These laws set kawata clearly apart from other peasants, although, as already mentioned, in certain places, such as Hozu village, titled peasants directed very similar taboos against other peasants. Social interaction was regulated and reduced to a minimum, usually only when official business was involved. As a rule, kawata were instructed always to be courteous and deferential toward peasants. Kawata could wear their short swords only when they were on official business, such as guard duty, and certainly could not parade about with them in other villages, posturing as officials. Even for one-day trips they needed permission from the village headman. At plays or entertainments they were to appear only in the line of duty, in accordance with instructions from the local headman, but not among the audience or as participants. Nor could they be seen at teahouses or drinking establishments. When going to the fields or mountains, they had to take back roads. They were forbidden to enter peasants' homes or even commoners' shops except on official business. Finally, they were not permitted to mingle with ordinary people (heijin), a regulation that led, as noted earlier, to a practical prohibition of mixed marriages. (For a translation of these and other regulations, see appendix 5.)

It was essential that these Japanese be identifiable as "other" at all times. While ultimately ancestry became the criterion for determining who were kawata, more visible signs were needed to differentiate them. In Tosa, persons of kawata status could not be in the streets after 4:00

Chiisagata district in 1819 and 1838, ibid., 323–26; and for Iwamurata in 1783, Banba, "'Buraku' no sui-i," pt. 2, *Shinano* 16, no. 9 (1964): 29.

P.M. (1780).[110] In Matsushiro domain, which had the largest kawata population in Shinano (380 households with a total population of 2,450 in 1869),[111] all kawata were required to carry a lantern so that they could be identified at night (1841).[112] As we saw in the Okayama uprising in 1856, they had to wear special clothing; elsewhere they had to wear pelts or pieces of animal fur.

Since kawata hamlets were set apart from society, fugitives sought refuge there. Others were lured to kawata hamlets by the opportunities of the sometimes lucrative leather trade.[113] That kawata hamlets were "hotbeds of criminals," as one Confucian scholar put it, is sheer derision. On the other hand, certain legal decisions criminalized the hinin and kawata population as a whole. In Osaka hinin status had become criminalized in 1680 by virtue of a decree stating that anyone buying clothes from hinin would be treated as a thief, the assumption being that hinin, already presumed to be criminals, peddled only stolen goods.[114] A new twist in the law regarding disinheritance (kandō, kyūri) had a similar effect with regard to the kawata. Disinheritance of an individual, it will be recalled, precluded the threat of punishment by vicarious guilt that made social groups (family, neighborhood, village) legally responsible and punishable for crimes committed by persons who had absconded. When a member fled the village, only after several active searches had failed to produce the fugitive could disinheritance be implemented. In the late eighteenth century numerous laws denied kawata communities any such protective clauses. If kawata absconded, a *nagatazune* ("long search") was ordered that did not end after a certain period, in other words, a search in perpetuity. Thus kawata communities were always responsible for crimes committed by their wayward members and held punishable for them.[115]

Popular views of pollution and its association with certain occupa-

110. Teraki, *Kinsei buraku,* 45.

111. Banba, "Mibunsei no teppai e," 41.

112. Banba, "'Buraku' no sui-i," pt. 2, 31.

113. Hatanaka documents the concentration of wealth in some kawata communities and in-migration there by non-kawata ("'Kawata' mibun," 308–9, 328–33).

114. Kobayashi, *Kinsei hōreishū,* 103.

115. For such bakufu laws issued in 1781, 1792, and 1802, see ibid., 162, 189–90, 252–54; for the difference between kandō and kyūri, see ibid., 312.

tions were officially sanctioned through legislation marking kawata as a visually identifiable class of people to be avoided. This led not only to perceptions of kawata as lawbreakers and their communities as "hotbeds of criminals" but also to racist views that naturalized the kawata as literally nonhuman. In Ōshū domain in Iyo (Shikoku) all male and female kawata over the age of seven were obliged to wear a piece of animal fur measuring fifteen square centimeters at all times; each kawata family also had to hang an animal pelt at the entrance to their home.[116] In Kaga in 1776, Matsumoto's term *jingai* was used in a notification stating that "since kawata are originally different from humans, they should not be in places where humans congregate."[117] As we shall see, a theory was developing that the kawata were indeed racially different from the Japanese. This view of the kawata as belonging to the realm of beasts was also adopted by intellectuals such as Kaiho Seiryō (1755–1817), rationalist and mercantilist, who wrote that they "are like animals (*kinjū dōzen*) . . . there is no morality in their heart (*kokoro ni zen'aku no naki*)."[118] But before turning to the question of racist ideology, we shall take a look at the economic dimension of segregation.

Economic Suppression

Discriminatory regulations were not only segregationist. Some were explicitly intended to control the kawata's economic status by either reducing them to poverty or keeping them there. Like peasants restricted to agriculture and required to deliver tribute (in principle, in rice), the kawata were required to engage in leather works. Represented by the authorities as a "privilege," this occupational restriction seems to have been fairly well established by the end of the seventeenth century.[119] Chōshū domain reissued such restrictive laws in 1743, 1771, and 1836. There were laws strictly forbidding the kawata to buy cows or horses and then slaughter them or to engage in other trades that ordinary commoners engaged in.[120] A bakufu edict of 1612 had already for-

---

116. Teraki, *Kinsei buraku*, 59.
117. Ibid., 45.
118. Ibid., 60.
119. Watanabe, *Mikaihō buraku*, 104.
120. Kobayashi, *Kinsei hōreishū*, 127, 142, 334.

bidden the killing of cattle, and in 1614 a kawata was crucified in Matsumoto because he had broken a similar law.[121] This prohibition was not new, however, since laws forbidding the slaughtering of horses and cattle had been issued some nine hundred years earlier, in 676, and again several times in the first half of the eighth century.[122] In Toyota village, reportedly, if common peasants removed dead horses, they would be considered kawata; elsewhere it was specified that the removal had to occur only at night.[123] In principle, the owner of a cow or horse lost ownership over it when it died; the carcass, taken to a designated place in the village, was taken possession of by kawata.[124] Nevertheless, a trade in live cattle for slaughter and consumption most likely existed anyway, since investigations were conducted, sometimes across whole provinces, into the slaughtering of cows and horses (e.g., in Bizen, Bitchū, and Ōmi in 1734).[125]

Status systems function to minimize competition by automatically excluding all holders of other ranks from the benefits or entitlements associated with a particular rank. This would apply also to the situation of the kawata: they held a monopoly, guaranteed by overlord authority, in leather working but were excluded from other trades. To explain the absence of kawata in northeastern Japan, Harada Tomohiko hypothesizes a link between increased discrimination against the kawata and increased competition among commoners generated by an expanding commercial economy. The commercial economy was weak in the northeast, and discrimination against kawata was absent there, as were the kawata, but discrimination against kawata was strong in the more commercialized regions where the kawata were concentrated.[126] Ian Neary suggests that the Emancipation Decree of 1871, which certainly did not result in equality, had the devastating effect for the kawata (perhaps intended) of bringing commoners in direct competition with kawata for

121. Ibid., 99; Banba, "'Buraku' no seiritsu," 55 n. 3.
122. Ninomiya, "Inquiry," 55, 78.
123. Kobayashi, *Kinsei hōreishū*, 498.
124. Teraki, *Kinsei buraku*, 49.
125. Kobayashi, *Kinsei hōreishū*, 124–25. Recent archeological excavations indicate the widespread consumption of animal meat, although not beef, in Edo (see Uchiyama Junzō, "San'ei-chō and Meat-eating in Buddhist Edo," *Japanese Journal of Religious Studies* 19, nos. 2–3 [1992]: 302).
126. Harada Tomohiko, *Buraku sabetsushi kenkyū* (Kyoto: Shibunkaku, 1985), 230–31. For a cultural explanation, see above, n. 49.

Table 22. Kamasu Buraku/Village: Population and Kokudaka Compared, 1723 and 1868

		1723	1868	% Change	B/V % Difference
Kokudaka (koku)	B	45	29	(−38)	
	V	108	108	(−0)	38
Population	B	120	237	(+100)	
	V	155	207	(+33)	67
Households (ie)	B	42	49	(+16)	
	V	32	46	(+43)	27
Taka holders	B	27	30	(−3)	
	V	23	36	(+6)	9
Average holder (koku)	B	1.7	1.0	(−42)	
	V	4.7	4.0	(−15)	27
Average per ie (koku)	B	1.1	0.6	(−46)	
	V	3.4	2.4	(−23)	23

SOURCE: Ozaki, *Shinshū hisabetsu buraku*, tables 5, 7, and 8 (pp. 66, 89, and 91).

modern businesses such as butcher shops or shoe manufacturing, which logically would have been the kawata's prerogatives.[127]

Competition for scarce economic goods was reflected by other restrictions. Iwamurata domain prohibited kawata from increasing their land holdings, and peasants were forbidden to sell them land. Fields owned by kawata were often of low quality and small, and access to water was often difficult to obtain. Thus, fields were mostly used only as a limited source of food and supplementary income, especially later in the Tokugawa period. The data for Kamasu, the largest kawata community in Shinano (located outside Komoro, Kita-Saku), illustrate this well (see table 22).[128]

Kamasu's kawata population doubled from 120 to 237 persons (42 to 49 households) between 1723 and 1868, but the holdings decreased from a total of 45 koku to 29. The average holding of taka holders (64 percent of all households in 1723, 61 percent in 1868) dropped from

127. Neary, *Political Protest*, 32.
128. Ozaki, *Shinshū hisabetsu buraku*, 66, 89, 91.

1.7 to 1 koku, which, averaged out over all households in the buraku (taka holders and nonholders), amounted to a drop from 1.1 to 0.6 koku per household.

In contrast, the figures for the Kamasu village peasant population are higher than the kawata figures at the beginning (155) and lower at the end (207), marking an increase of only 33 percent. (The kokudaka remained the same, 108 koku; the number of households increased from 32 to 46.) The average holding of taka holders (72 percent and 78 percent of all households) dropped from 4.7 to 4 koku, which, averaged out over all households in the village, amounted to a drop from 3.4 to 2.4 koku per household. It should also be noted that in the early nineteenth century the Kamasu kawata were strictly forbidden to purchase land or even mortgage their own.[129]

Kamasu's population growth was not exceptional. The dramatic universal increase in the number of kawata in comparison with the rest of the population, which stabilized after the 1720s, has long been noted by historians. The population of the Watanabe kawata community near Osaka increased fivefold between 1692 and 1856 (from 840 to 4,257), while the population of Osaka declined by 7 percent (to 320,780) during the same period.[130] In Ueda domain (Shinano) the kawata population increased from a total of 392 (70 households) in 1726 to 893 (110 households) in 1868.[131]

Historians have offered several explanations for this phenomenon, ascribing to it a combination of outside factors (the influx of drifters) and natural growth (facilitated by strong religious beliefs against infanticide), diet (kawata ate meat), and the growth of a market economy from which the kawata would have benefited (the price of leather went up, keeping pace with other rising prices).[132]

129. Ibid., 94.
130. Teraki, *Kinsei buraku*, 54.
131. Banba, "'Buraku' no sui-i," pt. 2, 16–17. The kawata population continued to increase well into the twentieth century. During the first sixty years after the Meiji Restoration (1868) the burakumin population increased by 400 percent, while the general population increased by only 80 percent (Ninomiya, "Inquiry," 114 n. 15). For a population diagram of three villages and their attached buraku between 1725 and 1875, see Hatanaka, "'Kawata' mibun," 313.
132. Steer hides fetched twice as high a price as horse hides, with cow hides in between. The price of steer hides increased from 0.700 to 1 *kanmon* (both dates unknown), then to 1.600 in 1781, 1.800 in 1812, and 1.900 in 1821

As the figures for Kamasu and Ueda indicate, while the population increased dramatically, the number of households did not. This was probably because of an attempt by the authorities to stem population increase by limiting the number of households. In the first bakufu legislation that dealt comprehensively with the kawata (1778), their "illegal (*hōgai*) population increase" was noted.[133] A decree of 1834 stated that "the number of kawata is increasing disproportionately in relation to that of the peasants. Someday this will become a source of problems. Henceforward only one male per household can take a bride. The other children must marry out. We will try to decrease the population one by one. Permission to marry must be secured from the appropriate officials."[134]

How widespread such population control measures were is not known. We do know, however, that one way of dealing with the undesirable growth of the local kawata population was to relocate them to other villages.[135] As we saw earlier, Umaji village, near Hozu, imported a whole kawata community in 1808 to work fields tenant peasants were trying to boycott. Some daimyo even had grandiose plans to utilize the kawata on a national scale to colonize Ezo (Hokkaido). Already by 1720 Arai Hakuseki, a retired shogunal adviser, had sorted out the available data on the island in his *Ezoshi*. Thus, interest in Ezo's economic potential antedates by several decades Tanuma Okitsugu's famous plan in the 1780s, based on a recent exploratory survey, to colonize the island with kawata.[136]

(Banba, "'Buraku' no seiritsu," 54–55 n. 2). Using tables to convert copper coins into silver value (*Nihonshi jiten [kaitei zōho]*, ed. Kyoto Daigaku bungakubu kokushi kenkyūshitsu [Sōgensha, 1960], 845) at exchange rates prevalent in Edo and price lists for Higo rice to be found on p. x of the appendix to any of the thirty-five volumes of *Nihon nōsho zenshū* (Nōsangyoson bunka kyokai, 1977–81), one finds that the value of steer hides remained fairly constant, being the equivalent of 0.25 koku of rice. Teraki (*Kinsei buraku*, 50) puts the value at 1 koku for the mid Tokugawa period.

133. Kobayashi, *Kinsei hōreishū*, 151.

134. Banba, "'Buraku' no sui-i," pt. 1, 36.

135. Ibid., pt. 2, 26.

136. Other books, less trustworthy in detail than Hakuseki's, appeared around the same time: Matsumiya Kanzan's *Ezodan hikki* and Itakura Genjirō's *Hokkai zuihitsu* (KDJ 2:271, s.v. "Ezoshi"). For Tanuma, see John Whitney Hall, *Tanuma Okitsugu, 1719–1788: Forerunner of Modern Japan* (Cambridge: Harvard University Press, 1955), 67, 100–105.

The kawata had become incorporated in an emerging "colonial" discourse in two ways. Through a fabricated etymological relationship between *Ezo* and *eta* the kawata were turned into aliens, literally alienated. As alleged descendants of captives from past wars with the aborigines of Ezo, the kawata were being signified by Tani Shinzan in 1717, among others, as genealogically non-Japanese linked to a non-Japan, Ezo.[137] Moreover, when the possibility of colonizing Ezo was actually being entertained, the proposal was made to utilize the kawata for this purpose on a grand scale. Thus in 1786/2 Matsumoto Hidemochi, the superintendent of finances, presented a scheme to Tanuma Okitsugu, the bakufu's chief political leader, for turning Hokkaido into one enormous shinden (new rice paddy):

> Because the native Ebisu would not be enough for this development project, we have conceived a plan to gather eta from various provinces and move them to Ezo. When we asked Danzaemon, without revealing the location of the project, whether he had ever thought of utilizing some of his subjects (tega) to develop new fields, he said that of the 33,000 eta in his jurisdiction, 7,000 eta/hinin could be made available for such purposes. This is not enough, but Danzaemon's authority, of course, does not extend to all the provinces. However, because he has on occasion issued rules to the various regional eta leaders, we could put him in charge of all the eta/hinin of the whole country, a population of some 230,000. This would enable us to move 63 to 70 thousand eta to Ezo, including Danzaemon.[138]

Hoashi Banri (1778–1852), a Confucian eclectic, scholar, teacher, and, at one point, elder in the domain of Hiji in Bungo province (Ōita, Kyūshū), combined the idea of colonizing Ezo with kawata (who he considered to be descendants from past captives from Ezo anyway) with that of liberating them first at a giant purification ceremony: "The ancestors of the eta are captives from Ezo. And, although they are assigned the task of apprehending thieves, [their communities] are hotbeds of crimes. So we should gather them all at the Great Shrine of Ise, purify them, make them heijin [commoners], send them to the land of

---

137. Morita Yoshinori, "Edo-ki ni okeru buraku e no shiteki kanshin," in *Kinsei buraku no shiteki kenkyū (1),* ed. Buraku kaihō kenkyūjo (Osaka: Kaihō shuppansha, 1979), 1:317.

138. Tsuji Zennosuke quotes a section of this proposal in his *Tanuma jidai* (Iwanami shoten, 1980), 300–302; for the whole text, see Kobayashi, *Kinsei hōreishū,* 175–77.

Ezo, and set them to work at agriculture or cattle breeding."[139] The "liberal" view of this Confucian betrays the depth of prejudice against the kawata. They are viewed as less moral than ordinary people and as property of the state who, like condemned criminals (with whom they were associated anyway), could be put to work to enrich the state. Interestingly, Hokkaido was eventually colonized and developed in the Meiji period by inmates condemned to forced labor.

The Contaminated Intelligentsia

Tokugawa discourse on society, while moving in a number of directions and shifting idiom, developed over time on a template provided by Confucianism. Whether traditional Confucian, neo-Confucian, anti-Confucian, eclectic, or Shinto, this discourse was always in dialogue with Chinese learning. Prominent in this "Chinese" tradition as it was "translated" in Japan was the view of society as divided into four classes: samurai, peasants, artisans, and merchants. It should be noted, however, that this "translation" took some time. Banba Masatomo writes that the shift in categories from the Chinese "ministers, high officials, gentlemen, commoners (*ch'ing, tafu, shih, shujen*)" to "samurai, peasants, artisans, merchants" took hold in Japan only around the 1720s.[140] Moreover, the expression does not occur in the *Tokugawa jikki*, which uses *senmin* ("lowly people," referring to the nonsamurai) or "peasants and merchants."[141]

Tokugawa scholars did not seriously confront the status and class system beyond these categories. Their "four-class" system, more a gen-

---

139. Quoted from Hoashi's *Tōsenfuron* by Teraki, *Kinsei buraku*, 62.

140. Banba Masatomo, *Nihon jukyōron* (Mikasa shobō, 1939), 172–77, esp. 176. Watanabe mentions Banba's interpretation (*Mikaihō buraku*, 137–38). For a more detailed analysis, see Asao, "Kinsei no mibun," 14–24. It is interesting that Banba, who after the war would pioneer new research into the Tokugawa past of burakumin, to my knowledge mentions eta only once in his book (131). Apparently following censorship guidelines, the word *eta* is not spelled out fully. Instead, it is printed as *xta*, an *x* replacing the *e* (meaning "dirt," "pollution"): even the character for "pollution" seems to have been taboo in those years. A similar practice governed the publication of Tokugawa village laws. In Hozumi Shigetō's *Goningumi hōkishū zokuhen*, the word *eta* is replaced by two blank squares (see, e.g., 1:97): the eta are erased just as their communities were expurgated from Tokugawa maps. Perhaps inspired by concern for burakumin sensibilities, the practice nevertheless maintained these communities as "the unnameables," the ones whose identity could not be spoken.

141. Watanabe, *Mikaihō buraku*, 137.

eral metaphor for hierarchy than a sociological concept, did not encourage discussion of status differentials within these classes, let alone
of subjects like the kawata, who fell outside the system.

Occasional references to kawata were limited to incidental remarks.
Texts on government policy and Confucian discussions of *jinsei* (benevolent government) do not contain compassionate references to
kawata. Kobayashi Shigeru, who compiled bakufu directives related to
kawata and hinin, found only one such reference, in the apocryphal
Tokugawa seiken hyakkajō (Tokugawa Constitution in One Hundred
Articles), most likely composed in the late eighteenth century, possibly
by a Buddhist priest.[142] The article reads: "Eta, beggars (*hoitō*), blind
men and women, and indigents who have no one to rely on (*tsuguru
naki*), who are outside the four classes, have since the ancient past been
treated with compassion so that they can make a living. One should
know that this is the beginning of benevolent government."

Other remarks expressive of a reasoned attitude include the following from early Tokugawa rulers and thinkers. Ikeda Mitsumasa (1609–
82), the famous lord of Okayama domain, was quoted as saying to a
vassal whom he took to task for prejudicial views: "Should we really
consider the eta different? They are also peasants. Skinning of wild
boars and badgers and eating their meat—don't a lot of people do
that (*dare tote mo sumajiki ni mo arazu*)? Why, then, do we look
with repulsion only at them?"[143] Whether or not he actually said this,
it is perhaps significant that these words were ascribed to a *meikun*
("model lord"). Kumazawa Banzan (1619–91), the Confucian scholar
in Mitsumasa's service and equally famous, expressed a similar logic,
undoubtedly shared by the kawata. In a passage critical of the Buddhist

142. Kobayashi, *Kinsei hōreishū*, 127. Inexplicably, Kobayashi gives Kanpo
2 (1742) as the date for this one article, although it is article 85 of the version of
the *Tokugawa seiken hyakkajō* (literally, the Tokugawa treasured legacy in one
hundred articles) reprinted in TKKz 1:59 and in *Kinsei buke shisō*, Nihon shisō
taikei, 27 (Iwanami shoten, 1974), 474 (hereafter NST 27). For a full German
translation of the three versions, see Rudorff, "Tokugawa-Gesetz-Sammlung,"
4–21. Hiramatsu Yoshirō writes that the articles "appear to have originated in
about the Kansei period (1789–1801), and it is strongly suspected that a Buddhist priest had a hand in it. There is also doubt whether they even reflect the
general Tokugawa legal consciousness" ("Tokugawa Law," trans. D. F. Henderson, *Law in Japan* 14 [1981]: 5, originally published as "Kinseihō," *Kinsei*
3, Iwanami kōza Nihon rekishi, 11 [Iwanami, 1976], 332–78).

143. Watanabe, *Mikaihō buraku*, 156–57.

clergy, he argued, "The eta are said to be polluted, but the Buddhist monks are even more so ... people are called 'eta' merely for handling dead cows and horses. But aren't those who handle dead people (*shijin*), consume meat, use clothes made from animal skins (*shihi,* "dead skin"), and live next to hundreds of graves big eta (*daieta*)?"[144] This view was rarely expressed in Tokugawa writings. Only in texts from near the very end of the period does one come across expressions of this view again. As discriminatory practices against kawata were institutionalized by official records and legislation, correlative theories developed to explain and validate this discrimination.

To justify segregation, Ogyū Sorai (1666–1727) does not appeal to the sages, as he did to rationalize the four-class system, but to the "customs of the Divine Country," Japan: "Not sharing fire with kawata is a custom of the Divine Country and unavoidable (*shinkoku no fūzoku, zehi nashi*)."[145] The expression "not to share fire," referring to an avoidance of kawata in order not to share their pollution, also appears in a letter circulated in 1748 by a bakufu intendant prohibiting the apparently *widespread* custom of "sharing fire, etc.," with kawata.[146] As we have seen, such prohibitions against "mingling" with the kawata became increasingly common in the second half of the eighteenth century: the "custom of the Divine Country" Sorai referred to was being upheld by law; that is, the state became the carrier of "customs," while the people seemed to be more accommodating. Ultimately, the authorities seem to have dreaded the reality of the kawata itself far less than the prospect of there being none.

On his official journey to the province of Kai in 1706 Sorai passed through a kawata community. In his official travelogue (the *Kyōchū-kikō*), he notes: "We pass through the village of Utsunoya. All are butchers. I wanted to smoke but could not ask for a light." This is a reworked version of his private travelogue, *Fūryūshishaki,* where the entry reads: "When we pass through the village of Utsunoya, we see women huddled together in a boisterous clamor. Bamboo peels

144. Teraki quotes this passage from Banzan's *Miwa monogatari* in *Kinsei buraku,* 60.

145. Ogyū Sorai, quoted from his *Seidan* by Teraki (ibid.). The quotation can be found in *Ogyū Sorai,* Nihon shisō taikei, 36 (Iwanami shoten), 286 (hereafter NST 36). For Sorai's justification of the four classes by appealing to the sages, see Maruyama, *Studies,* 214, 217.

146. Banba, "'Buraku' no sui-i," pt. 2, 16–34.

are soaking in the ditches under the protruding eaves of the houses [to be used for making leather-soled sandals, *setta*]. They are houses of butchers. I feel a great urge to smoke, but refined emissaries should not break customs. I could not ask for a light. I have a poem...." In this poem Sorai refers to age-old customs and to the ten categories for noble and base people that prevailed in China. In his *Seidan*, Sorai alludes to the theory that the kawaramono are of a different stock: "Prostitutes and kawaramono are considered lowly people; this is the same in China and Japan, both now and in the past. Because they are of a different stock (*genrai sono sujō kakubetsu naru*), they are considered lowly and entrusted to Danzaemon's rule. Nowadays, however, the old law is lost and ordinary commoners sell their daughters in prostitution and kawaramono become merchants, which is the greatest of evils."[147]

The unproblematic acceptance of the existence of an outcaste group by many Tokugawa scholars, regardless of philosophical or political bent, represents the rejection of a core tenet of Confucian thought, namely, the idea of a universal human nature.[148] This rejection derives perhaps from a perception of the rigid status divisions of the time as a "natural" state of affairs, and one closely linked to sacred customs dating back to Japan's divine creation. Embedded in this social or experiential "reality," Tokugawa scholars may have tended to downplay or ignore the notion of the universality of human nature so central to Confucianism. While they read social reality through Chinese texts simplifying society to four classes, they also read Chinese metaphysics through the practice of a rigidly differentiated status system that posited in a most radical way different degrees of "intrinsic worth" for members of different status orders ("six or seven kawata lives for one commoner").

147. For the quotations from the travelogues, see Watanabe, *Mikaihō buraku,* 153; for the quotation from the *Seidan,* see ibid., 152, and NST 36:283.

148. Nakae Tōju and Kumazawa Banzan seem to have been rare exceptions. For Banzan, see above, n. 144; for Tōju, see Kurozumi Makoto, "The Nature of Early Tokugawa Confucianism," trans. Herman Ooms, *Journal of Japanese Studies* 20, no. 2 (1994): 359–60, originally published as "Tokugawa zenki jukyō no seikaku," *Shisō,* no. 792 (1990): 117–18. Kurozumi discusses the difficulty Tokugawa thinkers had with the concept of a universal human nature (without linking it to social practice as I do here) on pp. 363–65 and 368–72 of the English text and 120–21 and 124–25 of the Japanese text. I am currently pursuing this issue and others in a full-length study of the kawata and *senmin* during the Tokugawa period.

Sung Confucianism, it has often been argued, constituted an advance in "rationalism" over traditional Confucianism and Buddhism. One may therefore conclude that the coexistence of Sung Confucianism and the "irrational" practices of segregation and indeed racism in Tokugawa Japan can only be explained by the faulty nature of this rationalism. The argument has been made, however, with regard to the development of Western racism that it is a strictly modern phenomenon and directly related to the concomitant emergence of rationalism.[149] It would be intriguing to explore this thesis for Tokugawa Japan, less to establish a causal relationship than to establish an affinity that goes beyond the observation that a Confucian-style rationalism had no difficulty making room for racist segregation.

That Tokugawa Japan's intra-race racism was expressed and fed by the "irrationalism" of cultural nationalism as it developed in nativist (*kokugaku*) discourse is more immediately plausible.[150] Given its emphasis on purity and pollution and the explicit hatred of foreign "others" (which was China and the West, according to Motoori Norinaga and Hirata Atsutane), it seems quite logical that kokugaku thought would validate and reinforce the creation of an "internal" group of despised others.

About the Dutch and the Russians, Atsutane writes: "The slenderness of their legs also makes them resemble animals. When they urinate they lift one leg, the way dogs do. Moreover, apparently because the backs of their feet do not reach to the ground, they fasten wooden heels

---

149. Christian Delacampagne, "Racism and the West: From Praxis to Logos," in Goldberg, *Anatomy of Racism,* 83–89.

150. While pointing out the connection between nativist ideology and the crisis of village leadership, Harry Harootunian leans far toward an uncritical acceptance of that ideology, which, he writes, "substituted friendship, affection, and reciprocity for the fragmentation and conflict reflecting the impersonal relationships of the authority system." His focus on the relationship between the village and the overlord causes him to overlook the discrimination that was increasing at the village level precisely when (and where) nativist thought became ruralized (see his *Things Seen and Unseen: Discourse and Ideology in Tokugawa Nativism* [Chicago: University of Chicago Press, 1988], 230–32, esp. 232). The province of Shinano, where traditional dogō families were very powerful in village affairs, counted the highest number of Hirata Atsutane's students (see Katsurajima Nobuhiro, "Hirata Kokugaku to gōnōsō," in Shūkan Asahi hyakka, *Nihon no rekishi* 91 [1988]: 9/74; see also Fukaya Katsumi, "Bakuhansei shihai to mura yakuninsō no kokugaku juyō," *Shikan* 91 [1975]: 13–23).

to their shoes, which makes them look all the more like dogs. This may also explain why a Dutchman's penis appears to be cut short at the end, just like a dog's. Though this may sound like a joke, it is quite true, not only of Dutchmen but of Russians."[151] It is interesting to note that Atsutane had to insist on his learned authority in this matter, anticipating that his readers might dismiss this information as a joke. It is also interesting to compare Atsutane's characterization of foreigners with an early-twentieth-century "popular notion" that burakumin had "one rib-bone lacking; they have one dog's bone in them; they have distorted sexual organs; they have defective excretory systems; if they walk in moonlight their neck will not cast shadows; and, they being animals, dirt does not stick to their feet when they walk barefooted."[152]

As Etienne Balibar notes, "the racial-cultural identity of the 'true nationals' remains invisible, but it is inferred from (and assured by) its opposite, the alleged, quasi-hallucinatory visibility of the 'false nationals.'"[153] And as deconstructionists are wont to say, (national) identities can only be established impurely, by incorporating through negation their others, which in due course they produce. Hence, it is perhaps no coincidence that in Motoori and Atsutane's discourse exclusion served as a central structuring device and that the discourse developed at a time when efforts were being made to reinstitute and reinforce kawata segregation through discriminatory laws and regulations.

As mentioned earlier, pre-Tokugawa explanations of the term *eta,* which are still used widely today, were occupational and linked to some low occupations or religious taboos because they were associated with bloodshed or the consumption of meat. The term *eta* (initially not written with the characters for "plentiful pollution") was first mentioned in a mid-thirteenth-century dictionary, the *Chiribukuro,* which explained it in association with *kiyome,* or purifiers, who removed polluted items from sacred places, and linked it etymologically to *etori,* feeders of hawks, and associated the Indian outcast candāla with butchers. These explanations were repeated in later versions and sup-

151. Donald Keene, *The Japanese Discovery of Europe, 1720–1830* (Stanford: Stanford University Press, 1952), 170. For a long, virulent analysis and indictment of antiforeignism in Tokugawa thought, see Sajja A. Prasad's three-volume *The Patriotism Thesis and Argument in Tokugawa Japan* (Samudraiah Prakashan, 1975–84).

152. Quoted in Ninomiya, "Inquiry," 56 n. 18.

153. Balibar, "Paradoxes of Universality," 285.

plements of the *Chiribukuro* with a Buddhist slant (the *Ainōshō* of 1446, using for the first time the characters meaning "plentiful pollution" for *eta*, associating the kawata with pollution, and the *Jinten ainōshō* of 1532) and throughout the Tokugawa period in various writings.[154]

Not until the beginning of the eighteenth century was there mention of a different origin for the kawata. In 1712 Terajima Ryōan, a medical doctor at Osaka castle, mentioned that kawata were butchers, gave them the (Sinified Indian) caste name *sendara*, and noted that one should not share fire with them, that they were of a different stock (*seishi o koto ni su*).[155] In 1725 Sorai alluded, as mentioned above, to a theory that kawaramono had a different parentage or lineage or nature from that of other Japanese (*genrai sono sujō kakubetsu naru*). *Sujō*, the term rendered as "parentage," "lineage," "nature" (literally, "seed-nature"), indicates, according to Kuroda Toshio, that in medieval times differential human qualities were attached to status by birth, the nobility being the *kishu* ("noble seed"). On the other hand, the nobility were sometimes spoken of as "not of human seed but partaking of the imperial nature." At the other end of the social scale, the kawaramono were described in one fifteenth-century text as "humans, but like beasts." According to Kuroda, the medieval social imaginary was genealogical throughout and originated in, and was maintained by, the Buddhist karmic world-view. Kuroda sees *sujō* as none other than a translation of the Indian term for "caste."[156] In this context, it is worth noting that other derogatory terms for classes of low people also originate in Buddhism; Kuroda mentions *bonge* (commoner) and *hinin*.[157] Yet, we should keep in mind that there was considerable mobility among the various lower strata, occupations, and statuses of medieval society.

This genealogical imaginary, as we shall see in a moment, continued to be applied to status groups in Tokugawa times. However, while most of the karmic connotations such constructs may have had in medieval times were eventually lost, to ancestry was added a racial dimension. As already mentioned, some writings suggested that the origins of the kawata were in Ezo, in a racially distinct group. In the 1720s and 1730s,

154. Teraki, *Kinsei buraku*, 25–26; Morita, "Buraku e no shiteki kanshin," 308, 318; Kuroda, *Nihon chūsei no kokka*, 380.
155. Morita "Buraku e no shiteki kanshin," 311.
156. Kuroda, *Nihon chūsei no kokka*, 361, 372, 375, 381, 388, 391.
157. Ibid., 376, 388.

when Danzaemon fabricated, in one of his genealogies, a Chinese ancestry for himself, stories about the foreign origin of the kawata started to circulate. Thus *Kyōhō sewa,* a record of daily life of that period, explains that the kawata were descendants from Chinese refugees who had lived in the wild and eaten animal and bird meat and were considered polluted. For that reason they were avoided by good people and forced to live apart.[158] Nativists did not have to specify where the kawata came from. For them it was sufficient to know that they were not Japanese. Writing in 1795, Tamada Naganori wrote that "butchers, although living in the divine country, are not of divine descent (*shinson*); they therefore do not venerate the gods, do not wash their hands after relieving themselves, do not use mourning garments for relatives, and do not spit when they see impurities."[159] Not to discriminate against butchers would be against the Way, wrote Ban Nobutomo in 1847. He maintained this orthodoxy, although he clearly understood that such discrimination may have had historical explanations and that people may have had mixed feeling about such practice in his own day:

> Butchers of wild animals came to be treated as if they were not human beings. If one inquires about their ancestors, many are found to hail from respectable families, and it is regrettable that it is impossible for them to become good people (*ryōmin*). If, however, today we would not despise them as defiled, this would be against the Way, because this would be the same as not being repulsed by the pollution of the meat of wild animals.[160]

The transition from a medieval genealogical to a racialized social logic was apparently completed in the early eighteenth century— around the same time that the nobility in France argued its racial superiority over the common Gaulois because of their Germanic-Frankish descent![161] It should be noted that by then a quasi-genealogical or

158. Morita, "Buraku e no shiteki kanshin," 312; see also 317.
159. Ibid., 318.
160. Ibid., 330.
161. André Devyver has traced a similar genesis of racial philosophy of "pure blood" among the French lesser nobility between 1560 and 1720, culminating in the racist writings of Henry de Boulainvilliers (see his *Le sang épuré: Les préjugés de race chez les gentilshommes français de l'Ancien Régime [1560–1720]* [Brussels: Éditions de l'Université de Bruxelles, 1973]). According to Noël du Fail, an earlier contributor to this discourse, one of the worst marriages a country noble could contract was with the wife of a butcher, which

racial concept of Christians had also been codified in Tokugawa law. In 1687 and 1695 laws were issued against former Christians who had publicly abandoned their faith but were suspected of having done so only for the sake of appearances.[162] Therefore all agnatic and affinal relatives to the fourth degree and direct male descendants to the sixth generation were put under the close supervision of local officials, who had to report twice a year on their occupations, marriages, deaths, divorces, travels, and so on. The taint of Christianity, like the stigma of pollution, could not be removed and was passed from generation to generation. Similarly, in sixteenth-century Spain the Inquisition paid special attention to *conversos*, who were always suspected of not having become genuine converts.[163] The French nobility (especially the lower rural nobility), Spanish converted Jews, Japanese ex-Christians, and the kawata—all more or less contemporaries—were all minorities, either threatened (the French nobles by the ennoblement of many bourgeois) or threatening (economically competitive Jews and kawata), racialized in order to set them further apart from an otherwise undistinguishable majority.

The kawata did not accept being called eta, and they did not subscribe to the genealogical and racial portrayals of themselves by majority Japanese. Using the same discourse but inverting its values, they pictured themselves as genealogically noble and racially Japanese. The major difference was that their counterdiscourse was private. We find mythological genealogies kept in the important houses of the kawata, but only very recently have they been studied seriously as avenues to the consciousness and self-representation of this oppressed minority.[164] In the early seventeenth century the kawata from the Kinai region traced their ancestry back to Indian nobility, a certain prince Entara—phonetically close to *eta* and *sendara*—whose line was punished because he

---

would make his offspring bloodthirsty (181). Unlike in Japan, the French "noble race" was not said to be indigenous, since its origins were allegedly Frankish: they were the fifth-century conquerors of the aboriginal Gallic Celts, the ancestors of the common Frenchmen. Historically, the nobility traced itself back to Germany, mythologically sometimes to Abel (10, 11, 27).

162. Yokota, "Kinseiteki mibun seido," 72, 76; see also KDJ 4:441, s.v. "Kirishitan ruizoku shirabe."

163. Devyver, *Le sang épuré*, 50–55.

164. See Mase, "Ishiki no naka no mibunsei," 270–72; Wakita, *Kawaramakimono*.

had committed cannibalism, or to the Japanese mythical figure Somin-shōrai, a poor man who had become wealthy because he had lent his humble abode to a god. In the eighteenth century imperial ancestors (the emperor Ōjin or Suzaku) and divine origins (Hakusan or Ebisu) were invoked. In the nineteenth century, far removed from the original sin of cannibalism that constituted a complicitous theo- or sociodicy of their low status, the kawata imagined themselves descendants from the Minamoto shogun (ancestors of the Tokugawa) or considered themselves simply to be codescendants of the gods with all Japanese.[165]

People locked into a status system usually seek to improve their position within it, yet their struggles often strengthen the system that oppresses them. A status system will keep on reproducing itself unless some independent institutions develop and a counterhegemonic practice and philosophy or ideology is produced. Cataclysmic social or political events force fundamental questions about the system's utility and rationale. Tokugawa Japan had neither institutions such as churches nor independent courts to challenge the principles of the prevailing political practice. In principle and practice, reason could not prevail over law, nor law over authority. The collapse of the regime in 1868 was perhaps the cataclysmic event that offered the most opportunity for change. But the change that occurred fell far short of what the kawata might have hoped for. On the surface (tatemae), the 1871 decree declared that that official class status was abolished and that in terms of occupation and social standing the kawata would be like other commoners. But in reality the discrimination against them continued: they were entered in the early Meiji population registers, not as citizens like everyone else, but as "new commoners (*shinheimin*)." A public record of difference was thus established that provided an official ground, and the only one, upon which to base future discrimination. An important step toward the elimination of such a basis for genealogical racism would be to do away with the Meiji records that document it.

Until recently, access to these records was open to anyone. In 1976, through the amendment of Section 10 of the Family Registration Law, "the government restricted access to family registries to family members, their legal representatives, and officials whose job required it." This, however, is another instance of a tatemae aspect of law, for en-

165. Mase, "Ishiki no naka no mibunsei," 271–72.

Investigation Services

Survey Japan Helps You
With All Types of Investigation and Information Gathering And in the Best Interest of Your Clients

For more than 10 years, Survey Japan has built up its reputation as a unique intelligence unit serving foreign corporations, law firms and individuals. Our motto is:

Accuracy, Speed, Sincerity and Confidentiality

Our services include:

- Corporate information gathering, reputation check, credit research, asset search, property check, litigation check, confirmation of nationality and family registration, including matrimonial history, collection of evidence, survey on the infringement of patents and trademarks, market research, locating of missing persons, identification of unknown persons and any other type of investigation required for litigation or negotiations with opposing parties.
- Risk control for criminal prevention with various measures
- Representation and Negotiations

We can serve you in Japan as well as abroad with our established international networking. Rates are available upon request. Please feel free to call

Survey Japan Tel: (03)3262-7476, Fax: (03)3262-7453

Plate 7. Advertisement for Genealogical Tracing. The investigative services advertised here include "confirmation of nationality and family registration, including matrimonial history," which practically targets Koreans and burakumin. *Japan Law Journal* 6, no. 2 (1993): 2.

forcement is very lax; "local registrars do not consistently enforce the prohibition on securing copies of unrelated individuals' family registries."[166] Plate 7 shows an advertisement in English for genealogical tracing services.

One late Tokugawa voice on behalf of the kawata was Senshū Fujiatsu's (1815–64), a loyalist rebel who was ordered to commit seppuku because of his anti-bakufu activities. In a very short tract, *Eta o osamuru gi* (How to govern the eta), Fujiatsu articulated a vision of a new Japanese social order that included the emancipation of the kawata.[167] Like the agricultural utopia that figured in the writings of Andō Shōeki (1703–62), Fujiatsu's imagined new social order made no

166. Taimie Bryant, "For the Sake of the Country, for the Sake of the Family: The Oppressive Impact of Family Registration on Women and Minorities in Japan," *UCLA Law Review* 39 (1991): 120, 121. I thank my colleague Bryant for referring me to the advertisement shown in plate 7.

167. Fujiatsu, a retainer of the Kaga domain, was an instructor at the Hayashi College in Edo and then in his domain school, and finally he served as tutor to the successor of the daimyo in his domain. He was one of the leaders of the small band of Kaga loyalists. A short biographical sketch serves as the preface to his tract on the kawata, which is published in NSSS 14:565.

immediate political or social impact; his tract was not discovered until after the Tokugawa period, and it did not appear in print until 1924. Like Shōeki, Fujiatsu provided evidence of views opposed to the Tokugawa status system, and to the position of the kawata within it.

Unlike Shōeki, who constructed a counterideology that was complex and decidedly utopian, the work of an intellectual, Fujiatsu, in his indictment of discrimination against kawata, offered a critical analysis of its sources and a realistic program for its abolition, the work of an official. He listed theories and rationalizations (historical, genetic, and cultural) used to justify discriminatory practices and rejected them all. For example, he dismissed as a myth the idea that the kawata originated in Ezo (Hokkaido); and he countered the idea that the kawata were not human but animal in nature by asking, "Would Heaven and Earth produce such a thing? If they are not humans, then they would be beasts or birds, grass, trees, dirt, or stones, but how could they have an animal nature if they have a human body?" Fujiatsu argued against the popular notion that those who engaged in "low" occupations were by association polluted or base: "In our country there are prison officials, but that does not make them necessarily base; burials are taken care of by monks, but that does not make them necessarily base; people in the mountains kill wild boars as an occupation, but that does not make them necessarily base ..." He believed that nothing comparable to the situation of the kawata existed in the West and concluded that the kawata must be the result of the government's status system. He then recommended that the status system be abolished and that the kawata be registered as "good people"—advice that was not followed by the Meiji government—and he urged public assistance for the economic emancipation of the kawata through agricultural start-up programs.

CONCLUSION

One could say that the Tokugawa status system, like status systems everywhere, served to retain "privilege among the powerful and power among the privileged."[168] Inherently discriminatory, it was developed and expanded for specific economic and political purposes by and for those who had the power and privilege to determine those who should have less or none. Status stratification sets limits on what people can

168. Berreman, *Caste,* 198.

realize; consequently they are induced to look upon those immediately above them with deference and envy and upon those immediately below them with contempt and fear.

Such dispositions are the result of man-made laws and rules of social practice, which are effective only in that they are misrecognized as something other than sheer coercion. Prescriptions in the guise of descriptions transform originally political, economic, and legal objectives into the "natural" order of things. The *ought* of the law slides under the *is* of an imaginary order structured according to symbolic categories such as nature, descent, purity, and pollution, which are presented as direct readings of reality but are in fact nothing but political values or social norms. Etienne Balibar notes in a discussion of racism that "the criteria of differentiation cannot be 'neutral' in practice; they incorporate sociopolitical values that are often challenged and that have to be imposed via the detour of ethnicity or culture.... Classification and hierarchy are above all else operations of naturalization, or more accurately, the projection of historical and social differences onto an imaginary nature.... The nature of racism is not one of proportional causes and effects, immanent regulations: it is a nature that is 'inherent,' 'immemorial,' 'always already valorized.'"[169] Like the title "titled peasants," such symbolic constructs have the potential to develop a power within their own logic and to withstand alternative, critical readings of reality.

The escalating discrimination against the kawata in Tokugawa Japan provides an excellent illustration of this logic of practice and representation. Based on popular prejudice, accentuated by economic rivalry, articulated further and given a new layer of reality by legislation, rationalized by racial explanations and racist theories, discrimination and segregation produced, and kept on producing, a great amount of particularly painful social suffering that from today's perspective it is hard not to see as akin to racism. That the predominant idiom in Japan was and is pollution rather than the pseudoscientific notion of race, although that aspect was not absent, makes no difference to those who suffered and continue to suffer from its effects. Ritual pollution, the central concern of Shinto, may be contingent and circumscribed, but pollution ascribed to bestial origins is an existential, inalterable predicament.

169. Balibar, "Paradoxes of Universality," 290.

Pollution is not an adequate social marker of difference, for it is still an imaginary, spiritual state. The construction of racial and racist theories was an attempt to make sense of the world as fashioned by bakufu laws. The Tokugawa authorities legislated visible but nonexistential, sartorial, "attachable" (and therefore also detachable) marks of social status; that is why "passing" was a major concern. Ultimately, only official records of ancestry and birthplace could identify sites of pollution; status racism became a state racism because bakufu law constructed the legal ground for an intra-race racism.

Only with the formal collapse of the Tokugawa system did emancipation become a possibility. By then, however, the intensification of discriminatory and segregationist legislation had succeeded in giving new authority to values and practices that are now viewed as part of Japanese culture. Somewhere near Shimoda, at the site of the first foreigners' residence after Japan was opened in 1853, a memorial plaque enshrines in Japanese and English a lie that establishes an official truth, suggesting also perhaps that gaijin belong to the realm of jingai:

> This monument, erected in 1931 by the butchers of Tokyo, marks the spot where the first cow in Japan was slaughtered for human consumption (eaten by Harris and Heusken).[170]

170. Townsend Harris (1804–78) was the first consul general to represent the United States in Japan. He arrived in Japan in August 1856 and established his post in a temple in Shimoda. Henry Heusken (1832–61) was Harris's secretary and served as his Dutch-English translator.

6

The Tokugawa Juridical Field and the Power of Law

"Unreason < Reason < Law < Authority < Heaven"
                                        Tokugawa dictum

"I'll go to Edo"
            Ken; Kami-Kaize village officials in
            the hinin kidnapping case; Chūemon's
            relatives in the Bonboku Incident; Others

In this study, the intravillage/extravillage dichotomy, especially the ways in which the intramural and extramural were mutually imbricated, is a major theme. Villages had two sets of regulations, laws with an extramural origin and internal codes, and the relationship between them changed over time. With regard to village justice, penal practices in principle existed by sufferance from the overlords and often functioned in "illegal" ways. Certain informal practices suggest that the overlords silently acknowledged some of these irregularities. Probably more often than not, village and overlord authorities were in mutual agreement about administrative matters, whether openly or silently.

ORDER, JUSTICE, INSTRUMENTALISM, AND FORMALISM

The principal concern shared by overlord and village authorities was the maintenance of *order,* which did not necessarily always mean the same thing to both. This parallel interest also governed and informed legislation and judiciary practice. As the first epigraph above indicates, authority does not yield to law. At the same time, however, commoners who were dissatisfied with that order as it affected them personally often threatened to go or indeed did "go to Edo" in the hope of finding *justice* there.[1]

---

1. While this perspective of justice informs some of the cases analyzed in this study, I came to see its importance clearly through discussions with Maeda Ichirō and other participants in the seminar at Otani University in Kyoto in the

Order and justice—these two Tokugawa perspectives on the role of judiciary practice also implicate the village in the wider field of power, but more important, they represent two opposing views of the relationship between the juridical domain, including legislative and judiciary practice, and the field of power. For the rulers (and scholars who, with them, view Tokugawa society from the top down), an *instrumentalist* view is almost inescapable: the juridical domain is foremost a means to maintain the power distribution over which the rulers preside. Obvious on a macro-, social scale, this is also valid at a micro-, local level. The internally generated "village" rules regarding status in Hozu village and the whole Mino region (for genin and small peasants) or Tanoguchi village (for newly established titled peasants) are clear examples. The system of "titled" peasants, "shares," and status differentials among peasants served the same purpose.

On the other hand, commoners turned to petitions, suits, and the courts to seek redress, right wrongs, and, ultimately, find justice, perhaps hoping that something else—reason, good sense, empathy?—might prevail besides or against the authorities' vested interest in order. The imagined locus for finding this *formal,* meta-institutional justice was most stereotypically Edo, but no petition or suit was devoid of that expectation. Thus, the assumption underlying the practice of many commoners was that the juridical field was (should be) somehow independent of worldly powers and institutions; otherwise, why bother petitioning or suing at all? In the course of this study, we have encountered a number of such instances. Ken threatened to go to Edo, as did Kami-Kaize's village officials in the kidnapping case of Mon, the hinin woman. When a certain Seigorō was voted into jail without evidence that he was the Higashi-Kami-Isobe village arsonist, his relatives marshaled all possible resources to set him free. The kawata also resorted to petitions and suits: Nagase hamlet (the Clog Thongs Riot) brought a suit against Ogoseimaichi village; before staging their protest, the kawata of Okayama domain resorted to petitions; Hozu's kawata sued the small peasants with good effect; and kawata sued one another.

At a more general level, an institution like the kokudaka system, a means used by overlords to systematically extract their subjects' sur-

---

summer of 1994 and with Christine Schoppe at UCLA, whose contributions I gratefully acknowledge here.

plus, was used as leverage by the peasants to obtain greater fairness in the allocation of burdens at the village level. The plaintiffs' sense of justice only rarely caused them to target status institutions as such, as it did in the instance of Hozu's peasants' demand that they cease to be treated as hereditary vassals by the gomyō, who considered themselves rural samurai; or when a group of clients (kakae) in Kodaira village demanded that the system of main and branch houses (kakae and kakaeoya) be abolished; or when kawata questioned the official discriminatory policies, arguing that they were, after all, tribute-paying peasants.

At first sight one might be inclined to generalize the contrast between the institutional status order and the personal sense of justice as one between particular and universal values if it were not for the fact that any explicit justification one might identify as universal or natural is to be found on the side of the status order This sense of justice, rarely expressed discursively, is limited almost exclusively to the level of practice. I have attributed this practical sense to assumptions about the possibility of finding formal justice in the juridical sphere apart from the administrative dictates of social order.

Structurally, of course, the juridical domain in Tokugawa Japan was not independent from the administrative apparatus but an integral part of it: administrators also functioned as judges. In terms of the categories Bourdieu uses to characterize a longstanding dichotomy in the interpretation of the status of the jurisprudential field—instrumentalism and formalism—historians of Tokugawa Japan would readily side with the instrumentalists. The instrumentalists conceive the world of law as a direct reflection of the world of power and therefore as an instrument of domination pure and simple.[2] This view holds that the juridical field, a mere superstructure without autonomy, permeated throughout by heteronomous social power, generates no specific force of its own. In contrast, formalists posit (modern) law as a domain closed off from the social world and hence as functioning solely according to its own specific dynamic, logic, or rules.

The value to a discussion of Tokugawa Japan of the polemical scheme that has structured a debate about the relationship between modern society and law may seem limited. Here, all will agree, the issue is clearly settled structurally and institutionally in favor of the instrumentalist interpretation. Yet, further questions need to be addressed.

2. Bourdieu, "Force of Law," 814–17.

First, it remains to be seen not whether but how an explicitly instrumentalist juridical institution contributes in its own specific, symbolic but real way (as transformed, surplus social power) to the social forces that created it. In this respect, Bourdieu speaks of oblique and misrecognized ways in which outside (heteronomous) forces affect juridical activity that in turn deploys functions that are not identical but homologous to the operation of these forces. Second, at times the instrumental function clashed with the commoners' practice springing from a desire for a kind of justice (which I call formal or meta-institutional) that was not simply a conduit for domination. Attention to such areas of practice will modify our natural inclination to view the juridical as an instrument of power in premodern, "feudal" societies. Third, since juridical practice, even when it is instrumentally overdetermined, as in Tokugawa Japan, generates its own specific symbolic power, one has to examine (1) where such development starts to function through the formalization and routinization of its own practice, as a brake on the arbitrary use of heteronomous power, and (2) how this symbolic power was put to use by plaintiffs for their own struggles, which had nothing to do with the rulers' instrumentalist intentions.

Formalist legal history pays scant attention, if any, to law's embeddedness in society. Its narratives typically do little more than trace the genesis of modern juridical concepts, seemingly for the exclusive entertainment of practitioners of law. Strange as this may seem today, all prewar and most postwar Japanese *legal* historians, following German models, organized their analyses in this fashion.[3] Postwar *social* historians, however, bringing the study of law within the ambit of social history and fully aware, from a modern perspective, of the underdevelopment of an autonomous judiciary in premodern (and prewar) Japan, have aligned themselves until recently with the instrumentalist (Marxist) position.[4] Since the 1980s, Mizumoto Kunihiko and other historians have explored another dimension. One can loosely theorize their

3. See, e.g., Nakada Kaoru, "Tokugawa jidai ni okeru mura no jinkaku," *Kokka gakkai zasshi* 34 (1920): 8, reprinted in *Hōseishi ronshū*, vol. 2 (Iwanami shoten, 1938), 963–90. See also the introductory remarks to chapter 4, above.

4. Kodama Kōta, in his review of Maeda Masaharu's classical study of village laws, *Nihon kinsei sonpō no kenkyū*, seriously questions the latter's thesis of even limited autonomy mainly in terms of the origins of village laws, which, as Maeda readily admits, were skillfully used by the authorities and gradually absorbed by them (see Kodama's "Hihyō to shōkai: Maeda Masaharu, *Nihon*

position as closer than the positions of the instrumentalists and formalists to Bourdieu's notion of field and field-specific power used from below for specific local interests not immediately related to the forces that shaped the field in the first place.[5]

Although Bourdieu emphasizes the relative autonomy of the juridical field and its specific "world-making" power, he nevertheless sees this field's output almost exclusively as feedback to society sanctioning the power structure of that society. He would probably argue that any subversive power that law might possess is itself ultimately subverted by the social and class embeddedness of the juridical field—an argument that would hold *a fortiori* for more neutral uses of the law from below. Because legal action has to follow the rules of the juridical field in order to be *legal* action, and insofar as these rules themselves serve heteronomous power (which for Bourdieu is very far, if not all the way), there would be "in the last instance" no "neutral" use of the law.

In this final chapter, then, I shall try to specify how the juridical field, on both the legislative and the judiciary side, exercises its instrumental function and where and how that instrumentalism meets internal and external limits.

CONTEXTUALIZING TOKUGAWA LEGISLATION

Let us start with some very broad strokes at the risk of stating the obvious. Legislation of the Tokugawa period was *Tokugawa* legislation, which means that it was created over the course of two and a half centuries. This suggests two things: qualitatively, that it was by and large new, and quantitatively, that there was much more of it at the end, in the 1860s, than in the early 1600s.

Tokugawa legislation was new because it replaced earlier codes. The eighth-century Ritsuryō codes, supplemented by the Kamakura and Ashikaga shogunal formularies of the thirteenth and fourteenth cen-

---

kinsei sonpō no kenkyū; furoku sonpōshū," *Shigaku zasshi* 60, no. 9 [1951]: 66–70). Any grand-scale analysis of the function of the Tokugawa legal system winds up as instrumentalist almost by necessity; see, e.g., Mizubayashi Takeshi, *Hōkensei;* and idem, "Kinsei no hō to kokusei kenkyū josetsu," *Kokka gakkai zasshi* 90, nos. 1–2, 5–6 (1977), 91, nos. 5–6 (1978), 92, nos. 11–12 (1979), 94, nos. 9–10 (1981), 95, nos. 1–2 (1982).

5. Asao Naohiro reports on this new trend in Japanese scholarship in his "Kinsei no mibun," 24, 35, 38.

turies, were partially superseded by the military provincial laws of the sixteenth-century daimyo, all of which, in turn, were replaced by Tokugawa legislation.

It is no exaggeration to say that virtually all of the warrior codes from the sixteenth century were abandoned and replaced with new legislation, which no doubt retained certain of their stipulations; conspicuous are cruel punishments. Harafuji Hiroshi cites just one example as an exception, a house law enacted in 1555 that was applied in the late Tokugawa period.[6] It should also be mentioned that the Ritsuryō model had some formal influence on Yoshimune's *Kujikata osadamegaki* of 1742, according to Dan Fenno Henderson "the high point of written native law in Japan," and on the Tokugawa reformatting of the imperial institution.[7]

Tokugawa legislation surpassed that of the past also in volume. Various factors account for this increased legislative activity, which was aimed at regulating ever more areas of daily practice. Legislation became calibrated to a much more finely tuned status society. This set severe limits on its potential to universalize, because what could otherwise have been general norms required multiple refractions, a striking example being the discriminatory legislation introduced during the eighteenth century against the kawata. Moreover, legislative growth was stimulated, mainly in the second half of the period, by the requirements of an unprecedented expansion of commerce, which could not be accommodated by status legislation. In addition, laws and regulations were issued not only from the higher authorities, shogun, daimyo, and their representatives, bannermen, or intendants (lordly law), but also from various constituent social units, such as villages or status orders

6. On these points, see his "*Han* Laws in the Edo Period with Particular Emphasis on Those of Kanazawa *Han*," *Acta Asiatica* 35 (1978): 51–53.

7. Dan Fenno Henderson, "The Evolution of Tokugawa Law," in Hall and Jansen, *Studies*, 204. See also idem, "Introduction to the Kujikata Osadamegaki (1742)," 539–40. For Mizubayashi Takeshi's recent theories on the importance of the Ritsuryō system for a proper understanding of the imperial institution in Japanese history, including its particular institutionalization under the Tokugawa, see his "Bakuhan taisei ni okeru kōgi to chōtei," NNS 3:120–58; "Kinsei tennōsei kenkyū ni tsuite no ichi kōsatsu: kinsei tennōsei no sonzai hitsuzensei ni tsuite no shogakusetsu no hihanteki kentō," *Rekishigaku kenkyū*, nos. 596 (1989): 18–27, 597 (1989): 19–33, and 598 (1989): 57; and "Ritsuryō tennōsei ni tsuite no ichi kōsatsu (1)," *Tokyo-toritsu Daigaku hō gakkai zasshi* 30 (1989): 1.

("corporate law"), where, moreover, practice was also regulated by local tradition (customary law).

The Tokugawa period no doubt witnessed not simply a multiplication of laws but the constitution of an increasingly complex juridical field that was structured quite differently from either its modern or its medieval counterparts if only because of the different relationship it had with sociopolitical power. As stated above, in Tokugawa Japan, rulers were also both legislators and judges. This fact alone, one may presume, reduces the autonomy of the juridical field to virtually a zero-degree level, and the very notion of such a field to little more than an artificially (anachronistically) constructed category of dubious heuristic value. The assumption, however, is that the application of sufficient analytical pressure via the notion of "juridical field" will yield more insights about the absence in the Tokugawa legal system of a separation of powers or a formal rationalism.

Max Weber's elementary typology of law distinguishes between an "interpretation of law on the basis of strictly formal concepts" ("formal rationalism") and "adjudication that is primarily bound to hallowed traditions" (substantive rationalism). He argued that for settling ambiguous cases the latter is supplemented by (a) charismatic justice, by oracle or ordeal; (b) kadi justice, "informal judgments rendered in terms of concrete ethical or other practical valuations"; and (c) empirical justice, based on analogical reasoning and reliance on precedents.[8] Weber warns against a simple identification of modern legal systems or democratic systems of justice with formal rational adjudication: kadi justice is still very prevalent in England, as empirical justice is in America. But he suggests that formal rationalism in the juridical field does not develop without a bureaucratization of the polity.[9] These precautions

8. Weber, *Economy and Society,* 2:976. Weber does not type traditional justice as a form of "substantive rationalism." In view of the way he defines formal and substantive rationality in terms of economic action (ibid., 1:85–86), however, the term *substantive rationality* is appropriate for describing traditional justice since it refers to the application of "certain criteria of ultimate ends, whether they be ethical, political, utilitarian, hedonistic, feudal (*ständish*), egalitarian or whatever, and measure the results of economic action, however formally 'rational' in the sense of correct calculation they may be, against these scales of 'value rationality' or '*substantive* goal rationality.'" A few lines further on he adds "social justice" as a possible value (see Bourdieu, "Force of Law," 825 n. 33, 842 n. 59).

9. Weber, *Economy and Society,* 2:976–78.

by Weber notwithstanding, Bourdieu suggests that Weber idealistically assumed the possibility of "rational law," but Bourdieu argues that predictability and calculability should be measured in terms of the consistency and homogeneity of a historically specific habitus rather than against an abstract "rationality."[10] For Bourdieu, therefore, there exists only one kind of rationalism, substantive rationalism.

The juridical field of Tokugawa Japan was marked by substantive rationalism. Lordly law was a mixture of kadi justice and empirical justice. In village law and practice, as we have seen, a form of charismatic justice was often added to this mixture by the custom of "ordeal by voting" in the absence of any concrete evidence on the identity of thieves or arsonists. Formal development, however, was not totally absent. It was made possible, but not necessary, by the development of a bureaucracy during the Tokugawa period.

The newness of the Tokugawa juridical field can be explained in a straightforward functionalist manner by pointing to the new configuration of forces that forged a sociopolitical field that differed from the one that preceded it. In the sixteenth century institutional arrangements and power relations that had prevailed since the early Middle Ages, considerably weakened since the fourteenth century, were completely scrambled and reconstituted on a new basis, first by daimyo and then, toward the end of the century, by superdaimyo such as Oda Nobunaga and Toyotomi Hideyoshi. The sociopolitical field, traditionally structured as a tripartite power block of nobles, clergy, and warriors, who were buttressed economically by the shōen, or estate, system and legally bound to the Ritsuryō system and shogunal law, was replaced by the daimyo's monopolistic hold on power and territory, secured through sheer military force.[11] The Tokugawa system guaranteed the preservation of this monopoly and gave it a hierarchical structure under the hegemony of a shogun who was more powerful than any daimyo at the time or any shogun (or emperor) of the past.

The Tokugawa system is thus perhaps better rendered as a regime of conquest than as a feudal order. The shogun, daimyo, and warriors by

10. Bourdieu, "Force of Law," 833.
11. Neil McMullin reports that during the Muromachi period more than 25 percent of the land in Japan belonged to temples and shrines, while during the Tokugawa period the number of temples increased but land shares dropped to a mere 2.5 percent (*Buddhism and the State in Sixteenth Century Japan* [Princeton: Princeton University Press, 1984], 23, 251).

and large constituted a new class that achieved domination of the whole national territory and population through the application of unprecedented military force. And they sought to secure their gains through a peace settlement whereby coercive violence was reduced to a threat and a remedy of the last resort, supplemented by the authority of law—a form of symbolic violence that was also of unprecedented magnitude.

The context of conquest, needed to properly understand some of the dominant features of Tokugawa society and law, such as an obsession with the maintenance of hierarchy, population control, social order buttressed by an overall lack of juridical autonomy that lasted throughout the whole period, is in fact a context of two conquests. First was the complete domestic victory of warriors over all other warring and nonwarring groups (other warriors, religious institutions, organized peasants, autonomous towns), a victory accompanied in the last three decades of the sixteenth century by specific institutional arrangements and measures of social control, which were spelled out in *local* legislation. Second, in the late 1580s and 1590s, with the formation of Hideyoshi's paramount military power and the extraordinary emergency requirements for foreign conquest (aimed at China but successful only briefly in Korea), regulatory creativity, both institutional and legislative, expanded and took on a *national* character (within limits set by the division of power between Hideyoshi and the daimyo).

Many commoners, although often victims of the first conquest and shouldering the inevitable sacrifices of the second, probably felt relief at the stabilization that followed a century or more of civil war. There is little doubt that control deepened as a result of the national effort of foreign war and the extraordinary need to secure the domestic peace for the production and procurement of military supplies and manpower. And these emergency measures did not end when the troops returned home, but remained in place throughout the Tokugawa period, when they were articulated further.[12]

12. Fujiki Hisashi's contextualization of Hideyoshi's "Peace Laws," which laid the basis for the Tokugawa system (*Toyotomi heiwarei to sengoku shakai* [Tokyo Daigaku shuppankai, 1985]), has drawn new attention to the military character of Tokugawa governance. Chapter 2, above, presents Takagi Shōsaku's elaboration on the theme of Tokugawa Japan as a "garrison state." Many Tokugawa thinkers shared the view that Tokugawa governance (institutions, tax burdens, and so on) had come into being in the context of the warfare of the sixteenth century and were inappropriate for peacetime. For Arai Hakuseki, see

Consider for a moment some elements of the ruling apparatus assembled during those years: data on the size of the population and the productive potential of the land, legislation binding peasants to agricultural production, monopoly on juridical power, and the exercise of violence by the highest authorities, rights that earlier had rested with local communities and guaranteed them varying degrees of self-determination. This whole ensemble of regulations, arrangements, and measures was implemented on a national scale to launch the Korean expedition. It was with that aim (or under that pretext?) that Hideyoshi could inform himself of the economic potential of the whole country, get accurate estimates of available supplies for his armies, make sure that there were producers to produce them, and secure domestic peace so that his military adventure abroad would not be hampered by interruptions or trouble at home. Thus, institutions developed in the extraordinary context of conquest and accordingly provided with high degrees of control (surveillance, harshness, and alarmism turning mundane tasks and activities into duties for the public authority, the country, in short, "patriotic" duties) became permanent features of Tokugawa normalcy. Two hundred and fifty years of virtually unchallenged military hegemony and pressures of commercial development attenuated somewhat the tenor of institutional and legal arrangements launched under such extraordinary circumstances. Still, the Tokugawa system continued to bear its birthmarks until its demise.[13]

The general allocation of power under this regime, its dispersion and limits within the social field, especially in the early period, is directly relevant for an understanding of the juridical field and its own specific

---

Kate Wildman Nakai, *Shogunal Politics: Arai Hakuseki and the Premises of Tokugawa Rule* (Cambridge: Harvard University Press, 1988), 293–94; for Sorai, see J. R. McEwan, *The Political Writings of Ogyū Sorai* (Cambridge: Cambridge University Press, 1969), 33, 96; for Motoori Norinaga, see his *Hihon tamakushige*, in *Motoori Norinaga zenshū*, vol. 8 (Chikuma shobō, 1972), 336 ff.

13. Takagi Shōsaku argues that samurai status rankings were rooted in the military functions of very early Tokugawa times (NRT 3:203–23). And Kurushima Hiroshi demonstrates, as mentioned in chapter 2, that perceptions by commoners of their duties of military support and assistance, duties originally defined in the 1630s but nominal for much of the next two centuries, were still very strong and functional in the civil war that brought about the fall of the Tokugawa (Kurushima, "Kinsei gun'yaku").

structure and power.[14] Once the wars were over, the matter of ruling the realm, that is, of ensuring the continuity of the new order fashioned after the victors' interests, could not be dispensed with (as the Mongol or Manchu conquerors did in China) by relying on already established institutions or legislation. There were no national government organs that could do the conquerors' bidding. They had to invent the state—anew, one might add, after its first institution in the seventh century.[15]

Like a colonial conquering power, these would-be rulers had to operate within the limits imposed by the existing social infrastructure, which even the most totalitarian modern regimes are incapable of refashioning completely at will. The only social groups that were eliminated, or forced into underground existence, were religious organizations such as the Catholic Church and the Buddhist Fujufuse sect. This limitation on power's downward reach was further aggravated by the decision, made in order to better block at the source possible challenges from within its own ranks, to hold the ruling class hostage to itself (alternate attendance), which was misrepresented as host to itself, in urban centers.

These circumstances greatly determined the shape of the field of power, which was allowed—indeed, forced—to follow the general contours and inner divisions of the social field. Lordly power first of all added legal sanctions to already existing social divisions and thereby claimed the authority to control them. In this way, overall social stability was built by strengthening inwardly the separate spaces of all the constituent units—the villages, domains, towns, status groups—and by controlling these spaces indirectly from the outside by ensuring that

14. Relational concepts of power fields allow one to bypass the academic debate concerning whether, or to what extent, Tokugawa Japan was feudal or absolutist. For the latest additions to this debate, see Mary Elizabeth Berry, "Public Peace and Private Attachment: The Goals and Conduct of Power in Early Modern Japan," *Journal of Japanese Studies* 12, no. 2 (1986): 237–71; and James White's response, pointed and to the point, "State Growth."

15. In a series of recent articles, Mizubayashi Takeshi has drawn attention to the importance of the imperial institution for the organization of the Tokugawa polity. He argues that the institution was saved and resurrected (in its religio-ritual aspects only at the very end of the seventeenth century) by the bakufu to meet specifically structural needs (see his works cited in n. 7, above). This supplements my treatment of this subject in my *Tokugawa Ideology*, esp. 28–35 passim, 51–55, 162–73.

coopted prominent insiders were held responsible for intragroup law and order, shouldering the costs thereof.

The superordinate powers of the shogun and daimyo subcontracted members of commoner groups for "administrative" purposes, foremost for supervising the production and delivery of tribute, which supported the rulers; at the same time, they handed over to prominent local families the burdens and privileges of maintaining local law and order. More than "subcontracting" was involved, however. Legally sanctioned because they were connected to ruling power by official duties, these groups were transformed into something more than they had been, one of the practical effects of "world-making" typical of state power.[16] The state, or more accurately, the lords, did not merely subsume groups but subjected them to a social and economic logic, telling them what they were to be and what they were to do. Lineages were still effective, but now their contours acquired new significance by way of new institutions and leadership positions (goningumi, kumi heads, titled peasants). The outside appointment of village heads set in motion internal power struggles.

These structural constraints distanced the dominant class, the warriors, from the sites of production, the villages, while they made direct infrastructural reach unnecessary. At the same time, the rulers pushed as far as was necessary and feasible the principle of a single sociopolitical hierarchy; it was in their interest that there be only one such hierarchy and that they control it. The position of the emperor made such an effort problematic at the top. While the emperor was politically neutralized and controlled by shogunal regulations, his very existence raised the question of the hierarchical apex: should it culminate in the shogun or in the emperor? As John Haley has remarked, "Neo-Confucianist views of suzerainty were more than inadequate in rationalizing the respective roles of emperor and shogun ... law sourced in the will of the shogun ... law and lawmaking [were transformed] from simply an expression of legislated regulation, custom, and precedent into a manifestation if not source of legitimacy as well."[17]

16. On the dialectic involved in legal "world-making," of creating or instituting a social reality that already exists, see Bourdieu, "Force of Law," 838–39, and his *Ce que parler veut dire: L'économie des échanges linguistiques* (Paris: Fayard, 1982), 125 ff.

17. Haley, *Authority without Power*, 54, 55.

Two solutions were proposed to end this ambiguity—clearly testifying to the desirability of a single hierarchy. In the early eighteenth century Arai Hakuseki's effort to raise the shogun's legal status to that of a king and Ogyū Sorai's proposal that the bakufu devise its own rank system independent from the court were obvious attempts at clarifying the position of the shogun vis-à-vis the emperor by making the former unambiguously the pinnacle of a single hierarchy.[18]

Through hierarchization, the shogun and daimyo fixed directly the positions of all constituent groups, including the nobility and the clergy (no longer partners in government with the warriors as they had been in medieval times), and through them indirectly made (new) subjects of everyone. This strategy entailed two consequences: (1) the unavoidable and essential reliance on regulations, laws, and practices to determine and express hierarchical status while representing it as natural; and (2) the dual origin for laws and practices, namely, the bakufu and lords, and the corporate (territorial and status) units.

The lords' primary concern lay with *any intergroup* jurisdictional problems—among domains or villages, between court and warriors, among kawata or temples, and, for commoners, among occupations—because such discord tested the ability to maintain the principles of hierarchy, and with the *serious* and potentially explosive problems of maintaining *intragroup* order, because they could affect the position of the constituent units within the one hierarchy. The corporate groups also produced internal laws and regulations to the extent that they were entrusted with juridical matters.

It should be noted, however, that the infrastructural reach of superordinate (public, "state") power, although subject to the above flections, extended deeper during the Tokugawa period than previously. In medieval times, self-redress, the armed variety in the form of vendettas, was a socially accepted and legally sanctioned remedy, whether among individuals, clans, villages, village leagues, towns, temple communities, city wards, or warrior bands. Warrior courts and public investigations were available, but only upon the request of the parties involved: "even

18. On Hakuseki, see Nakai, *Shogunal Politics,* chap. 8; on Sorai, see McEwan, *The Political Writings of Ogyū Sorai,* 90–94. On the neutralization of the emperor during the first Tokugawa century, see my *Tokugawa Ideology,* chap. 5.

a murder in front of the jail [i.e., under the eyes of the authorities] should not be investigated unless someone initiates a lawsuit."[19]

The Tokugawa as "state," however, monopolized in principle the use of coercive force: armed self-redress was outlawed, and all serious crime had to be reported to the lordly authorities. In the case of violent quarrels, the authorities, while insisting on their monopoly over law and violence, never played the role of administrators of social justice; they refused to examine the relative merits of parties involved (as was done in pre-Tokugawa courts) and instead punished both parties according to status and regardless of respective innocence or guilt (kenka ryōseibai). One could say that it was a case of martial law applied in peacetime.

For personal vendettas, official permission was needed, and private settlements functioned through a mechanism whereby a subject was temporarily entrusted with the penal authority that in principle rested only with the higher authorities. One of the legal flaws of the celebrated action by the forty-seven rōnin from Akō was not that the murder of a bakufu official was a vendetta but that it was an illegal execution, permission having been neither sought nor granted. In addition, there was the question of legal definition: was it a violent quarrel (in consequence of which both parties, including Lord Kira, should have been punished rather than only Lord Asano's being ordered to commit seppuku), or was it an attack by one party only (Lord Asano, since Lord Kira had not struck back when wounded, in which case the rule of kenka ryōseibai would not apply and it would have been proper that only Lord Asano be punished).[20]

We can summarize the structural characteristics of the juridical field of Tokugawa Japan as follows. First, its location within the social field as an integral part of the ruling (military) apparatus made for its thorough penetration by heteronomous power, making the possibility

19. Mizubayashi Takeshi, "Kinseiteki chitsujo to kihan ishiki," in *Chitsujo*, Kōza Nihon shisō, 3 (Tokyo Daigaku shuppan, 1983), 114. See also Haley, *Authority without Power*, 40: "Law enforcement by the Kamakura authorities could only be activated by outside complaint or accusation generally, and the process remained subject to the initiative and direction of the litigants."

20. This argument is central to Tahara Tsuguo's discussion of the incident in his *Akō shijūrokushi-ron: Bakuhansei no seishin kōzō* (Yoshikawa kōbunkan, 1978).

of developing an autonomous juridical field virtually impossible, this in contrast to the medieval conjuncture, and in even greater contrast to that of modern times. Second, the reach of the law was greater than that of its medieval counterpart and, arguably, even its modern counterpart. This was because (*a*) the greater imbalance of power between the centers (shogun and daimyo) and their areas of control (villages and towns) reduced local autonomy, this only in comparison to medieval Japan; and (*b*) the law treated as public, and hence subject to status control, many matters that were considered legally neutral and private in both pre- and post-Tokugawa times. Third, since the expansion of legislation, although the result of a heavier concentration of sociopolitical power by a military force than in medieval times, did not emanate solely from one source, the Tokugawa juridical domain was imperfectly unified, constituted as a complex network of mutually reinforcing and partially overlapping subfields.

Since this study focuses mainly on legal and juridical matters with regard to village practice, the structural and historical analysis of courts, jurisdictions, and legislative centers as they pertain to specific social formations such as cities, temples and shrines, and specific status groups need not preoccupy us here.[21]

THE TOKUGAWA JURIDICAL FIELD WITHIN THE FIELD OF POLITICAL POWER

The undeniably strong presence of heteronomous (political) power in juridical matters predetermines the relative possibilities, findings, and strengths of formalistic and instrumentalist interpretations. The latter are particularly forceful since lordly law was foremost a continuation of war by policy, a substitution of coercive (symbolic) violence for real violence aimed at maintaining the structure of domination established by military conquest. Hence differential punishments for the same crime depending on whether the parties were rulers or ruled, and more gen-

21. Good descriptions and analyses of these matters can be found in Henderson, "The Evolution of Tokugawa Law"; idem, *Conciliation*, vol. 1, chap. 4; Hiramatsu, "Tokugawa Law"; Haley, *Authority without Power*, chap. 3; Steenstrup, *A History of Law in Japan*, chap. 4; and, for the kawata, Cornell, "Caste Patron," 56–70, and Ninomiya, "Inquiry," 99–100. For a general description of the route petitions and suits took, see the introduction.

erally on whether they were of superior or inferior status in relation to one another.[22]

Thus, even a formalistic study of the dynamics of Tokugawa law could not but expose the levels and lines of impact of the forces of domination. Such an analysis of Yoshimune's great legislative codification of the 1740s, the *Kujikata osadamegaki,* would reveal that many of the articles are no more than casuistic status cases, a multiple unfolding into every nook and cranny of a penal code according to the fundamental hierarchizing "imaginary" that informed the Tokugawa system.[23]

Very concretely, a comparison with legislation a few decades earlier exposes the operation of this logic, since it shows that the range of serious crimes against status hierarchy was increased by moving up certain categories to make them subject to more severe punishment. The *Kujikata osadamegaki* increased the level of seriousness of certain crimes against superiors and decreased that of certain crimes against inferiors: the penalty for the murder of a former lord moved up two notches, from simple crucifixion to crucifixion preceded by exposure in a public place (a bridge in Edo); of a parent or teacher, up two notches, from gibbeting to crucifixion; of a relative of one's lord or master, one's father-in-law, uncle, aunt, elder brother, or elder sister, up four notches, from beheading to gibbeting after ambulatory exposure. But the penalty for the unintentional killing of a child, younger brother, younger sister, nephew, or niece moved down one notch, from beheading to banishment to a remote island and confiscation of the criminal's land, house, and personal effects.[24]

As mentioned in chapter 4, a formal diachronic analysis of village codes indicates that although punishments were lessened as time went on, for example, by substituting fines for physical punishments such as

22. See article 71 of the *Kujikata osadamegaki* (on punishments for killing and wounding) in Hall, "Japanese Feudal Laws III," 766–71. There was also a Tokugawa saying, already mentioned, that the life of one samurai was worth that of seven commoners, and another one that the life of one commoner was worth that of seven kawata.

23. Cornelius Castoriadis, *The Imaginary Institution of Society* (Cambridge: MIT Press, 1987). Castoriadis uses the term *imaginary* to refer to a (socially) unquestioned social metaphor that functions as a template for common sense, or, to use computer language, a default category through which a society at a particular time organizes, perceives, and partly misrepresents itself.

24. Mizubayashi, "Kinsei no hō to saiban," 163–65.

mutilation or banishment, the codes converged increasingly with lordly authority in the second half of the period, precisely when, it is generally assumed, the lords were losing their grip on local communities.[25]

Imperfect Instrumentalism

As this late convergence suggests, village codes in the first century of Tokugawa rule were perhaps less immediately responsive to, or less in tune with, lordly laws than in the second half of the period. Thus, an unqualified instrumentalist understanding of Tokugawa law as always serving directly the interests of the superordinate powers may suffer from overinterpretation. We can identify at least four areas in which that may be the case: village codes, the interplay between village codes and lordly law, commercial law, and the emergence of legal specialists.

The village codes. We do not have in the archives today sixty thousand village codes, one for each Tokugawa village; many have been lost, many seem never to have been written down, and many were rewritten several times. Those that remain are rather short, consisting often of fewer than ten articles—much shorter than the written village laws that the lords drafted and that to a degree influenced the codification of village codes in the eighteenth century. Yet all villages were governed by norms, whether written or oral, the latter undoubtedly covering a much wider area of practice than the former but not necessarily an older stratum of practice; codification often signals not the formulation of new rules, but the recording of existing ones. It is thus very likely that most of the extant village codes, at least those recorded in the seventeenth century, pertain to pre-Tokugawa practices and thus were not consciously geared toward heteronomous lordly interests.

Peasants, however, were far from insensitive to the possibilities for manipulating intra-village power distributions by contesting village codes or using them to advantage, a fact overlooked by those who stress the autonomous character of village laws in relation to heteronomous lordly power. In Hozu village and in the whole Mino region, for instance, village codes configured relationships between (ex-samurai) titled peasants and the other peasants on a samurai model of vassalage.

The relation between lordly law and village codes. The traditional instrumentalist position has held that village codes were simply an extension

25. Ōide Yukiko, "Kinsei sonpō," 98–110.

of lordly law, and a tool of lordly domination. This view has been challenged by a semiformalist interpretation, but by failing to problematize power relations within the village, this interpretation has come to understand village codes as unmediated expressions of the survival needs of the village as an organized social community (kyōdōtai) that was indifferent or even opposed to lordly power. Recent scholarship, such as Mizumoto's, however, has broken with (antagonistic) essentialist views of law by positing a space amenable to strategic manipulation rather than the presence or absence of a fixed barrier between the "autonomous" juridical subfield of village codes and the far larger "heteronomous" juridical subfield of lordly law.[26]

While in general village codes did not contradict lordly law, the latter was not necessarily applied; in practice, village officials could exercise discretion in the implementation of lordly laws, especially if noncompliance could be legally camouflaged. Village officials could activate lordly power without actually implementing lordly laws by the mere threat of using them, thus obliging obedience. Thus, paradoxically, lordly law was implemented at the same time that its formal power was being manipulated by being redirected, "borrowed" as the mere threat of implementation.

Commercial law. From the beginning of the eighteenth century shogunal courts were forced to (very reluctantly) address civil suits, whose volume had increased enormously with the expansion of commerce. Civil cases (property or money suits) can be considered somewhat neutral to the ruling class's political or economic interests because they were irrelevant to the maintenance of hierarchy; their adjudication constituted, therefore, an unwelcome burden and expense. Yet in this area the rulers were forced to add to their role as rulers the role of administrators. Hence commercial law constituted a juridical subfield for which a simple instrumentalist interpretation falls short. Indeed, as Dan Fenno Henderson has argued, it is the level at which one can identify a formal development of a juridical field,[27] propelled by its own dynamic, and where the interference of heteronomous social power was weakest.

The adjudication of violent quarrels followed the kenka ryōseibai

26. Mizumoto, *Mura shakai,* chap. 6; idem, "Kōgi no saiban."
27. Henderson, *Conciliation,* 1:11; idem, "Introduction to the Kujikata Osadamegaki," 525.

principle; no evidence of either party was relevant, and both sides were punished, an unmitigated application of coercive force. In criminal cases the only decisive evidence was the suspect's confession; hence the use of torture, an extreme form of coercive force. In civil cases, however, attention to the relative merits of the litigants through an examination of documented evidence became important. Max Weber noted that in England "the royal power introduced the rational procedure of evidence primarily for the sake of the merchants," a development that was, therefore, "strongly influenced by structural changes in the economy."[28]

In this regard one can draw attention to two points. First, every effort was made, even during preliminary hearings (i.e., after the judicial process had been initiated), to reach a settlement before arriving at a final verdict.[29] This emphatic preference for conciliation on the part of the authorities testifies to their reluctance to function as judges in cases that did not affect the power of the dominant class directly. In other words, overlords used their authority to order a binding private settlement, the terms of which were to be determined by the litigants with or without a mediator. As we saw in the ostracism case that came before the attendant (chapter 4), such practice also prevailed in noncommercial disputes. Second, the form this conciliation took, often under threat of dire punishment if the law were applied to the letter— revealing the force of law as such—was as an application of the kenka ryōseibai principle, dividing the blame, although not necessarily evenly, between plaintiff and defendant to the detriment of the nonguilty. In the end both sides were guilty. Yet the application of this principle here was not directly the result of an open application of coercive force, because conciliation was achieved by the parties involved—tatemae—under the paternalistic prodding of the judge, abdicating momentarily his official position as judge to adopt the posture of a private go-between. But this was momentarily only, because the next moment he could threaten to let the case come to a much more dreaded final verdict: honne.[30]

Ishii Ryōsuke has drawn attention to one particular aspect of con-

28. Weber, *Economy and Society*, 2:977.

29. Henderson, *Conciliation*, 1:7, 127, 147, 150.

30. See ibid., 128, 150, 154, and esp. 156, for attempts at reconciliation in a court case analyzed by Henderson; 149, 153–55, for instances of the use of threat in the same case. The similarities between the present-day practice of conciliation and the Tokugawa variety have been explored by Henderson in vol. 2 of *Conciliation*.

ciliation, namely, that the fact that it is often ordered under threat is revealing of its coercive nature. The "interrogations in both the inquisitorial procedure and in the Adversary Procedure (*deiri-suji*) were handled by the same officials. Thus the thinking behind the inquisitorial procedure [where torture was an option] ... influenced the conciliatory procedure of adversary proceedings; and it was held that in any event, a private settlement cannot be established without basing it on the free will of the parties. Consequently, 'provisional imprisonment' was used to coerce it."[31]

The emergence of legal specialists. The existence of a corps of legal specialists is necessary for an autonomous juridical field. Several developments during the Tokugawa period led in that direction. Starting as early as the last decades of the seventeenth century, the recruitment of investigative and recording officers for the shogunal court was narrowed to the personnel from one office within the shogunal bureaucracy; these positions ultimately became hereditary, shared among a few families.[32] Their accumulated knowledge of precedent furthered consistency in verdicts, for practice turned these officers into experts, and their opinions became authoritative not only regarding the results of the investigations they conducted but also regarding the penalties; they functioned increasingly as judges. Yoshimune tapped into this experience when he started to codify standards for judgment in shogunal courts, which had a formalizing impact in the daimyo courts as well.[33]

Since Yoshimune's *Kujikata osadamegaki* was intended only for internal use in bakufu courts and hence was not publicized, knowledge of its codes filtered out to commoners indirectly through court decisions, slowing the regulatory effect the predictability of justicial outcomes might have on social behavior. Yet regularity was enhanced by two practices that limited arbitrariness: internal queries by intendants or commissioners were sent to higher authorities, and commoners began to make use of legal consultants (suit inns).

When bakufu intendants or commissioners had to pass judgment on difficult cases, or when the proposed penalty exceeded their penal

31. Ishii, review of *Conciliation,* 223.

32. Henderson, *Conciliation,* 1:66–67, 69, 139; Hiramatsu, "Tokugawa Law," 10–11.

33. Henderson, "Introduction to the Kujikata Osadamegaki," 506; Hiramatsu, "Tokugawa Law," 20–21.

powers, they queried higher-ups, which ultimately meant the members of the Senior Council. The senior councilors, in consequence, gathered together all the serious cases from the bakufu courts, examined the proposed sentences to determine whether precedents were applied consistently, and sometimes consulted further with the Tribunal (Hyō-jōsho), which functioned to some extent to standardize the verdicts of all courts throughout the country.[34] Such formalization put constraints, however limited, on arbitrary judgments.

Igeta Ryōji analyzes a number of queries regarding penalties for kawata who had married commoners and, in addition, often helped channel other kawata as illegal labor into commoner households. In the latter case, the Tribunal almost always lowered the proposed sentences.[35] However, according to Igeta, the verdicts alone give a slanted picture of juridical practice for two reasons. First, in the case of the kawata in the Kinai region, which was beyond Danzaemon's jurisdiction, decisions on penalties and their execution were entrusted to the elders of the kawata community from where the offender came; since they produced no documentary evidence, we do not know whether these sentences were harsher than those suggested by the bakufu Tribunal. Second, the juridical process included provisional incarceration of suspects until a verdict was reached. A sizable percentage of the suspects died in prison, an understandable deterrent that added considerable coercive power to the "power of the law" as such. Among those who died during pre-sentencing detainment were 16 of 102 kawata in the Clog Thongs Riot over a span of two years; 6 of 12 in the Okayama Riot over three years; and 8 of 55 in a mere two months after the "eta hunts" in Kyoto in 1831.[36]

In the final seventy years or so of the Tokugawa period commoner specialists in legal matters who were sufficiently knowledgeable in complicated Tokugawa legal procedures and in substantive law introduced their skill and knowledge to the market. Litigants came to avail themselves of the business of these consultants at their kujiyado (suit inns) near the shogunal courts in Edo. The litigant in the ostracism case analyzed in chapter 4 seems to have successfully relied on these spe-

---

34. Hiramatsu, *Edo no tsumi to batsu*, 46.
35. Igeta, "Kon'in sabetsu," 9.
36. For the general statement and the figures for 1831, see ibid., 19; for the other figures, see chapter 5, above.

cialists for drafting his suit. The existence of these private legal assistants testifies to the advanced degree of formalization reached in at least one sector of the juridical field, although their function was limited to cases coming before the shogunal court. The authorities, although concerned about abuses,[37] understood the benefits commoner assistants offered for the smooth functioning of the courts and enrolled their services by sanctioning their activity with a license.[38]

Levels of Formalism

The degree of legal formalization and codification is one indicator of the juridical field's degree of autonomy. When discussing legal formalization, it is useful to distinguish between levels of formalism. An initial formalism, to which great attention was paid in Tokugawa Japan (as in China), relates to the recognition that cases should be grouped and filed under specific categories (water and border disputes, money suits, etc.).[39] This first procedural decision was to determine the nature of a case in order to channel it to the appropriate judicial authorities and to apply to it the appropriate law. As Henderson remarks, this could not but also reflect "the relative substantive value attached to ... [the] underlying claims [of each type of case]."[40]

More fundamentally, one could say that this is the point where a dispute or incident gets converted into legal matter, the creative power of legal naming reveals itself, and law has its field-specific effect on social reality. The decision to allow some events to become legal matter and to deny this to others creates a quasi-ontological divide in social reality;[41] and the effect is not always to enhance the importance of the former over the latter. Thus, the stipulation that murders and border disputes had to be brought to court certainly turned such incidents into public events and introduced a new element of power into them. An-

37. Henderson, *Conciliation*, 1:145 n. 59.
38. Ibid., 167–68. The status of the suit inns contrasts sharply with the illegal status of pettifoggers in China (see Melissa Macauley, "Civil and Uncivil Disputes in Southeast Coastal China, 1723–1820," in *Civil Law in Ch'ing and Republican China,* ed. Kathryn Bernhardt and Philip C. C. Huang [Stanford: Stanford University Press, 1994], 85–121).
39. See Henderson, *Conciliation*, vol. 1, chap. 5, for the main categories of "civil suits."
40. Ibid., 102.
41. Bourdieu, "Force of Law," 837–40, 846.

other example is the prosecution, started in 1773, of mixed marriages between kawata and commoners as "adultery," resulting in status demotion from commoner to hinin, whereas such marriages had been legally neutral prior to that date.[42] That courts refused to consider cases initiated by inferiors against their superiors (lower samurai against higher samurai, sons and daughters against their fathers—*Osadamegaki*, art. 65), however, did not mean that such "authority-related" cases were deemed less weighty than, say, border disputes; rather it signaled that a certain reality, namely, authority, was above the law. After all, "unreason does not prevail over reason; reason not over law; law not over authority; authority not over Heaven."[43]

A second type of formalism concerns the bureaucratic procedures whereby an incident, once transformed into a case, must be submitted in proper form to appear in court. This is the all-important area of legal language and format, which became quite intricate in Tokugawa Japan, although, and in part because, it was by no means made uniform. The procedures themselves could be lengthy and complex. Dan Henderson's detailed analysis of a money suit by a villager reveals that a settlement (not a verdict) was reached after four months, after attempts to settle the suit at the village level.[44] First the village headman's endorsement was secured, then the local overlord's;[45] subsequently misphrasings underwent correction, the petition had to be endorsed by the court, and the suit initiated, and after twelve postponements, five stalemates, one hearing before the commissioner, and six hearings before the recording officer, only a settlement was reached. In another case, involving eight commissioners, over the establishment of a new market, Henderson

---

42. Igeta, "Kon'in sabetsu," 10.

43. Mizubayashi, "Kinsei no hō to kokusei kenkyū josetsu," *Kokka gakkai zasshi* 90, nos. 1–2 (1977): 6 ff.; for a different interpretation of this dictum, critical of Mizubayashi's, see Nanba, "Hyakushō ikki no hō-ishiki," 47–62. The "reason does not prevail over law" part of the dictum was incorporated in the third article of the Warrior Code (*Bukke shohatto*) of 1615 (NST 27:454; for the English translation, see Lu, *Sources*, 1:201–3).

44. Henderson, *Conciliation*, vol. 1, chap. 6.

45. Ishii Ryōsuke (review of *Conciliation*, 216) questions Henderson's assertion that the headman's *approval* was needed, which Henderson also argues on p. 129 of his book. The headman, however, had to endorse with an accompanying letter any suit by a villager. As we saw in the Kasuga village case (chapter 3), it was considered an abuse of authority by the headman to forward such a case without his endorsement, which meant that the case would be immediately rejected by the intendant.

estimates that plaintiffs from three villages located the distance of a five-day trip from Edo must have traveled some thirteen hundred miles before obtaining a (negative) final verdict.

Similar documents differed from one another depending on whether they recorded the testimony of a commoner (*kuchigaki*) or a warrior or priest (*kōjōsho*) or an offense by the former (called *kyokuji*) or the latter (*otsudo*), or depending on the commission involved (the Temple and Shrine Commission called complaints not *meyasu* but *sojō*).[46]

The complexity of the above two types of formalism created a special world having a very specific effect on any commoner who entered it. A veritable arsenal of symbolic devices was marshaled to turn him or her into more of a subject than he or she was in daily life. First of all, one could not enter this world simply on one's own volition. Endorsements from the authorities (headman and overlord) were needed, and the language of that specialized world was formulaic and determined in an authoritative way, severely restricting spontaneous, quotidian expressions. Its tenor was one of supplication and submission, *osorenagara,* or "[submitted] with fear and trembling," being the ubiquitous formula.[47] The effect of distance from an accustomed world increased the subject's isolation and vulnerability, pure subject confronting pure authority. The distance was reinforced by the layout of the court (called *shirazu,* "white gravel"), where commoners literally had to grovel in the gravel one level below the officials, who were seated on a raised wooden or tatami floor.[48] In the late Tokugawa period, when peasants and kawata appeared in court together, the gravel (or a place located three shaku below the peasants) was reserved for kawata, while peasants squatted on straw sacks.

A third type of formalism concerns the predictability of the judicial reasoning that leads to legal conclusion. The higher the degree of formalism and the clearer and more publicly spelled out the principles applied or weight given to precedent, the more circumscribed the realm of arbitrariness or discretion of the judgments will be and the greater the likelihood that political power will be bound by law.

Yoshimune's *Kujikata osadamegaki* (1740s) constituted the apex of

46. For the two cases, see Henderson, *Conciliation,* 1:137, 161–62, 166; for the terminology, 166 n. 98, 140 n. 42; 165 n. 95.
47. Ibid., 151–52.
48. Ibid., 145–46.

白洲
之
圖

Plate 8. Court at an Intendant's Residence. Hanging from the wall at the left are instruments of torture used to obtain confessions of guilt in criminal cases. From Andō Hiroshi, ed., *Tokugawa bakufu kenchi yōryaku* (1965). Reprinted with permission from Seiabō Publishing Company.

legal systematization during the Tokugawa period. Yet the degree of formalization in the third sense was very limited because it was not a publicized "code" but a manual to which access was restricted to shogunal officers of justice, especially with regard to determining penalties. This meant that (1) its principles were intended only for shogunal courts, and not for application in village or domainal justice; (2) it was "secret" knowledge, not to be divulged in the commoner world; and (3) its stipulations were no more than suggestive guidelines for judges that were partly based on precedent but did not limit their penal powers.

The net effect (likely purpose) of the restricted nature of this formalization was the preservation of a discretionary leeway for judicial officers, which meant, of course, the preservation of the power of the warrior class. Nevertheless, insofar as investigative and recording officers developed a "legal" habitus, however weak, simply by acquaintance with precedent—knowledge that found its way into the weighty responses of the Senior Council or the Tribunal to queries from below—formalization was a legal, if limited reality.

Practitioners of deconstruction, with their predilection for discursive moments of undecidability, have argued that the one-time arbitrariness at the origins of laws, meant to eliminate future arbitrary coercive violence by substituting the rules of law, is in fact reactivated when decisions are made concerning the (degree of) applicability of the laws in each case that comes before a judge. Typically, however, they have nothing to say about interests orienting the judge through this moment of undecidability toward closure. Bourdieu's solution to this problem is to be found in his notion of the social construction of the legal habitus.[49]

Thus, courts were foremost an instrument of the rulers to preserve order, ensuring a slanted distribution of sociopolitical power. Hence the emphasis on "settling" disputes by restoring peace rather than righting wrongs. Since there was no break between heteronomous power and the juridical field, "truth" and "justice" accordingly were quite openly secondary considerations.

EXPANSION OF THE JURIDICAL DOMAIN

The extension of the legislative and juridical reach into ever more areas of daily life through prohibitions of all sorts pertaining to both production and consumption, affected all commoners. People thereby somehow became "officials," as Suzuki Shōsan (1579–1655) and Ogyū Sorai (1666–1724) put it;[50] they were forced to alter their comportment and lifestyle to fit their assigned status, which was related to their ability to contribute to production (tribute) in support of "the realm" (the rulers). This affected virtually all items of material and symbolic culture. The logic propelling this legislation of the shogun and daimyo was one of gradual and reactive comprehensiveness, covering more and more items, in an effort to keep up with cultural developments that came to be perceived as potentially challenging to the formal status order.

---

49. See Jacques Derrida, "Force of Law: The 'Mystical Foundation of Authority,'" in *Deconstruction and the Possibility of Justice,* ed. David Gray Carlson, Drucilla Cornell, and Michel Rosenfeld (New York: Routledge, Chapman and Hall, 1992), 13–14, 23–24. Note the similarity between Derrida's title and Bourdieu's "The Force of Law."

50. Ooms, *Tokugawa Ideology,* 131.

Regulations concerning social practice included prohibitions against the production of luxury items such as tobacco and certain publications, restrictions on consumption of certain items, such as rice, or the use of palanquins and horses; dress codes specifying the allowed number of layers of cloth, the cut, and the quality of material (cotton or silk) in a garment; architectural specifications for peasants regarding the size and/or number of their dwellings, whether or not they could have gates and what kind, whether or not they could have ceilings, and so on; formalized language necessary for forms of address and forms of documents (such as petitions); restrictions and prohibitions on forms of entertainment (kabuki, gambling, Western playing cards); the outlawing of certain religious sects and prohibitions against "new teachings" or the improper granting of posthumous names; and control of the movement of people traveling, making pilgrimages, or changing domicile.[51]

Hierarchy seems to be present in all societies at all levels as the result of an informing ideological principle, the effect of the exercise of power, or the combined effect of both; undeniably, Tokugawa Japan presents us with an extreme example. In this society hierarchy was, to borrow Castoriadis's term, the "central social imaginary," based consciously or not on the paradigm of the army. The military model, one could say, provided a far more refined hierarchizing operator than the five relationships of Confucian teachings could ever have devised.[52] Obviously, this does not mean that practice followed the law or that laws never went too far in hierarchizing penalties. Laws were often broken, sometimes not enforced, occasionally rescinded. This did not detract from the pervasive formative force of hierarchizing operators, which were

51. It would be nearly impossible to give even elementary bibliographical references for this vast area. Suffice it to refer to two unusual items on this list. For the prohibition against Western playing cards during the Genroku period, which was later rescinded, see NRT 3:151; for the 1831 prohibition against using improper posthumous names for the deceased, showing disregard for their official status, see Narusawa, "Mikaihō buraku no kaimyō," 170–71.

52. In this context, it is perhaps worth noting that the comparative sociologist Stanislav Andreski, in his search for a qualifier for a typically feudal society, a "type of society where a stratum of warriors dominates unarmed masses," decided to call it "bookayan, and the dominating warrior stratum a bookay," deriving these terms "from buke—the Japanese word for military nobility" (see his *Military Organization and Society* [Berkeley: University of California Press, 1971], 144).

sufficiently powerful to permanently mark a great number of salient features of Tokugawa society and culture.

The various grades of banishment from Edo, introduced in the *Kuji-kata osadamegaki* in 1742, differentiated between major, medium, and minor banishment from Edo and gradations of three, five, seven, ten, or twenty miles (ri), although they were virtually nonexistent prior to 1742. An examination of 974 verdicts handed down between 1657 and 1699 reveals that the most common distance of banishment from Edo was ten miles. Thus in 1745, only three years after the introduction of these multiple gradations, previous practice was reinstated by decree, declaring that henceforth the distance of banishment from Edo for commoners would always be ten miles.[53]

The net overall social effect of such an imaginary was the conversion of an extensive field of (private) cultural practice into an explicit (public) politically informed practice. Legislation and the accompanying jurid-ical pronouncements have a transformative power, an "illocutionary" force that by naming reality in legislative utterance or juridical verdict thereby creates, reinforces, or transforms it.[54] In this way, discursively unarticulated (dispersed) "elements" of private cultural practice whose meaning was previously heterogeneous, open-ended, and unstable are by edict transfigured into articulated "moments" of a public space, their meaning now homogeneous, closed, and predictable.[55] This, at least, one may perceive as having been the intention behind many of the cul-tural regulations that multiplied during the Tokugawa period, although no power could ever achieve signifying closure that would prevent the generation of new signifieds, a point to which we shall return.

The modality of legal expansion in the Tokugawa period is homol-ogous to that of the expansion of knowledge in the Sung Confucian tradition. Both reveal an unlimited capacity to recreate (through legis-lation) or rediscover (through knowledge) again and again in ever new sites, social hierarchy in the former case, natural hierarchy in the latter.[56] It can be argued, however, that legislative or juridical practice

53. Tsukada Takashi, "Kinsei no keibatsu," 96–97.
54. See n. 16, above.
55. For the distinction between politically free-floating "elements" and politically mobilized and structured "moments," see Ernesto Laclau and Chan-tal Mouffe, *Hegemony and Socialist Strategy* (London: Verso Press, 1985), chap. 3, esp. 105–6, 127–28.
56. Ooms, *Tokugawa Ideology*, 95, 240–41.

was more powerful than teachable doctrine because law restructures the context and thereby reconstitutes the nature of social practice, including the production of representations specific to that practice, that is to say, social knowledge.

It goes without saying that any power to fashion sociocultural practices and representations, a power to create society through "vision and division,"[57] must be backed by the necessary weight of coercive force if it is to secure a sufficient degree of implementation. On the one hand, the power of law, in its thematizing and unifying effect of social vision and division, extends well beyond the range of social practice as merely regulated by law enforcement. The comprehensiveness and the thematic consistency of Tokugawa law more than made up for an alleged "shallowness" (Henderson)[58] because it gave public meaning to so much of daily practice. The purpose of this strategy was not to provide a supplement to private meaning but to erase it and produce a formal substitute. Dress codes were not an addition to fashion, but were supposed to replace sartorial expressions of individual idiosyncrasy, taste, or wealth, of privately imagined selves, with the markings of a hierarchical position in the body politic, expressions of publicly assigned selves. Yet semiotic reality is such that signifiers such as clothing always produce potentially ambivalent or polysemic signifieds: what the authorities produced, intentions notwithstanding, were not substitutes but supplements of meaning.

This ruling strategy, in imposing a single signified (hierarchy) on a large number of heterogeneous signifiers, established an authoritative orientation for the production of cultural meaning. In other words, the hierarchizing principle expanded beyond juridical matters through the initiative of nonrulers, which converted more and more heterogeneous signifieds and made them converge into the one signified of the central imaginary. For example, as mentioned earlier, there was no law fixing the price of samurai human waste in the market of fertilizers higher than that of commoners, yet it was the case that the exchange value of human excrement was not determined "rationally" by the market or by

57. Bourdieu, "Force of Law," 838.
58. Henderson, speaking specifically about shogunal law rather than Tokugawa law in general, says, "The coverage of Shogunate law was quite shallow, both in terms of territory controlled directly and persons affected directly" (*Conciliation* 1:62; see also 100).

its use value but was measured according to the status hierarchy of its producers: samurai night soil fetched a higher price than that of commoners.[59] Similarly, the production of etiquette booklets as guidelines for proper hierarchical human interaction indicates the necessity and aspiration to conform to one social model, that of the samurai.[60]

The complicity between subjects and authorities is also illustrated by the readiness of some parents to redefine unfilial behavior as the authorities had done, from ethically reprobate behavior to a legally punishable crime. In the second half of the seventeenth century a number of parents requested that their unfilial sons be temporarily jailed, and in the eighteenth century parents often asked that they be temporarily committed to a penal colony or stockade.[61] In Kodaira village, for example, as we saw, commoners stretched the limits of hierarchizing status further than the authorities intended; statuses could be split almost endlessly to simultaneously accommodate efforts aimed at social mobility while safeguarding the power elite against such ambitions. Competing proximate occupational groups often went to court hoping to have the authorities settle conflicts over territory or hierarchy to their advantage. Status thus became a weapon and a prize, for example, for the carpenters from a district in Harima who requested clarification on which of their subcategories were polluted; in disputes in Azumi district between Ebisu, lion dancers, and kawata; in suits whereby hunters and Kyoto's dyers succeeded in dissociating themselves from the kawata—all examples of commoners seeking advantage within the rules of the rulers' game of social ordering, which by publicly, legally sanctioning groups thereby created status positions for them.[62]

To a large extent, the net social effect of the incorporation of legal constraint into practice was the naturalization of social practice thus constructed. In the hierarchical structure that was sanctioned, recreated, and expanded in this way, each status position, because locally specific

59. Walthall, "Village Networks," 295.

60. Eiko Ikegami, "Disciplining the Japanese: The Reconstruction of Social Control in Tokugawa Japan" (Ph.D. diss., Harvard University, 1989).

61. For the jailing, see Tsukada Takashi, "Kinsei no keibatsu," 100–101; for the penal colony (the stockade, or *yoseba*) of Ishikawajima, an island in the lower Sumida River in Edo, see Hiramatsu Yoshirō, "History of Penal Institutions: Japan," *Law in Japan* 6 (1973): 11, 15.

62. For further examples, see Asao, "Kinsei no mibun," 35, 37–38; and Tsukada Takashi, "Kasōmin no sekai."

and immediately differential only with regard to the positions immediately above and below it, narrowly limited what was possible or
impossible, forming a localized, circumscribed habitus. Limited aspirations precluded ambitions challenging superordinate powers more
effectively. The farther removed the status in question was from superordinate powers, the more effectively limited aspirations precluded ambitions challenging those powers. We have seen a number of "emancipation suits" that illustrate this kind of mechanism.

Structurally, one can say that a tenant peasant (tribute *producer*)
might aspire to succeed to becoming a tribute-*paying* peasant with land,
but not a village headman, at least not immediately. And he feared
becoming a hinin or registered beggar. A landowning peasant might
covet the post of headman or membership in the shrine association
(miyaza) or "nominal" samurai privileges (wearing one sword and using
a surname) but not full membership (not even in the lowest strata) in
the ruling class. The peasant's greatest fear, of course, would be to end
up landless. A commoner's daughter might hope to serve in a samurai
household or to marry into a lower-class samurai family, but she also
dreaded being handed over to such a family as a virtual slave as part of
the punishment for a crime committed by her father or husband.[63]

Moreover, in regard to a regime where authorities at all levels—
shogun, daimyo, as well as village elite—invested much symbolic power
in explicitly shaping cultural and social practices, and where that effort
was met halfway by the colluding practices of the dominated (their
aspirations revealed by suits and petitions), the question whether legitimacy was an internal matter of acceptance or consent or an external
matter of coercive power and resistance becomes difficult to answer.
Indeed, it may be irrelevant if one considers the objective relations in
this conjuncture of legal imposition from above and practical complicity from below.[64]

This publicly created (political) equivalence of all signs—through
their restricted single signified, the division between rulers and ruled, and

63. On legal stipulations concerning, and real cases of, wives, daughters,
and sometimes sons of criminal commoners given as "slaves (*dohi*)" to samurai
families, see Tsukada Takashi, "Kinsei no keibatsu," 101–2.

64. Concerning this line of argument, see Bourdieu, "Force of Law," 841,
844. On the effects of universalizing values promoted by juridical formulations,
discussed in the following paragraph, see ibid., 838, 845; and idem, *Ce que
parler*, 72–73.

its numerous refractions and reflections in "civil society" as the separation into superior and inferior—expanded the spheres of domination. At the same time, however, it also increased the system's vulnerability, because it multiplied pointillistically the sites where behavior could be interpreted as illegal or rebellious behavior. If etiquette "manages to extort what is essential while seeming to demand the insignificant [and] concessions of politeness always contain political concessions,"[65] by the same token, the essential can be denied while refusing the insignificant. Thus, within this setting, cultural practices could as easily be redefined as deviant illegal behavior because of the implied rejection of the universally signified. It suffices to recall the geta incident in Hozu village (chapter 4), in which both sides held precisely opposing views regarding what was essential and what was insignificant in the peasants' disregard for the prohibition against wearing wooden clogs. Hence almost anything could become subversive through the creation of a new signified or the restoring of a suppressed one for any publicly marked cultural signifier.

To suppress the social tumult caused by the sexual and erotic commotion surrounding the early kabuki theater, the bakufu tried to eliminate a signified (provocative sexuality) by doing away with its signifier (female actors), assuming that there was only one possible signifier (females) for that signified, when it banned women actors from the stage in 1612. Yet, since gendered sexuality is not necessarily linked to sex, female impersonators (*onnagata*) circumvented the effect of the ban with clamorous success. The bakufu then thought that it was striking at the heart of erotic signification when it required, in 1652, that all actors shave their forelocks, which at first made them look, in the eyes of one contemporary, like "cats with their ears cut off."[66] The actors, however, re-created erotic allure by wearing scarfs, caps or even wigs. By legislating political values into cultural practice, the bakufu multiplied sites for flaunting the law and displaying contempt for authority, yet infringements of cultural prescription constituted no ultimate threat to the order of domination.

To the extent that it was accepted that behind Tokugawa norms lay a norm of norms, namely, the natural order portrayed by Confucian

65. Bourdieu, *Logic of Practice,* 69.
66. My interpretation is based on data found in Donald H. Shively, "*Bakufu* versus *Kabuki*," in Hall and Jansen, *Studies,* 236–39.

teachings or the divine order taught by Shinto,[67] the bakufu was safe from the critique implied in cultural practice's deviation from those norms. Of course, the crucial question is to what extent this "to the extent that" is applicable, especially since a "natural" or "divine" order is but a *description* elucidating a world-view. As Lyotard has pointed out, description and *prescription* (norm) are two intrinsically different "language games" that can be engaged only sequentially by shifting from one game to the other, without description's ever, strictly speaking, by itself yielding prescriptive force or providing its ground, because the two are incommensurable. Since prescription contains its raison d'être and authority within itself, its oblique reliance on description makes it, at least in principle, vulnerable to questioning. This postmodern viewpoint is not different from Derrida's deconstructionist denial of any foundation for authority; see his qualification of it, mentioned earlier, as "mystical." Such interpretations are generated in part by the linguistic theory of performatives. Bourdieu has incorporated this view, since he writes of "performative utterances" as "magical acts which succeed because they have the power to make themselves universally recognized." On the other hand, he speaks elsewhere of the power of a "norm of norms."[68]

Moreover, insofar as prevailing linguistic usage was an embodied expression of order in a practical, unreflective, and "natural" way, in contrast to the conceptual, reflective, and disputable Way of teachings, language constituted an additional rampart of defense against ideological challenge. As Anne Walthall's recent research indicates, women could step beyond the bonds of propriety and speak out politically on *their* concerns; protesters could use "vulgar" language to address the authorities in the heat of protest, attempting to force the addressees to *their* own level.[69] Yet, these attempts by commoners to submit the

67. Ooms, *Tokugawa Ideology*, 250–62, 281–86; idem, "Yamazaki Ansai no 'Kamiyo no maki' ni okeru kaishakugaku—tenkeiteki ideorogii-keitai to shite," *Shisō*, no. 766 (1988): 15–18.

68. Jean-François Lyotard, *Just Gaming* (Minneapolis: University of Minnesota Press, 1985), 45, 52–54, 59, 99; Bourdieu, "Force of Law," 838.

69. Anne Walthall, "Representations of Women in the History of Japanese Peasant Uprisings" (paper read at the Western Conference of the Association of Asian Studies, Long Beach, Calif., October 1989); idem, "Edo Riots" (paper read at the Southern California Japanese Seminar, UCLA, December 8, 1989).

authorities to their own rules of communication and signification by disrespectfully rejecting the order of respect and power were doomed to failure not only because such attempts were sporadic and limited or gambled against overwhelming odds but (perhaps mainly) because the very modalities of reversal or trespassing were dictated and controlled by the field of power as it was structured by the authorities. In other words, the same rules dictating the maintenance of the field of social forces also informed the shape of attempts to reorder it. Women were socially stigmatized by such behavior as "beyond the pale" or as behaving "like men," that is, behaving "unnaturally." Paradoxically, hierarchy was reaffirmed through acts of denial that were rejected as socially unacceptable.

Only critiques that took as their target the historically contingent unequal distributions of power or the malleability of the social imaginary of hierarchy (informing legal or natural representation) escaped the stigmatizing hold of hierarchy, because such critiques unmasked and exposed the misrecognized interested power behind ideology. The first attempt of Kodaira's kakae peasants to do away with the patron system and the demand by Hozu's small peasants that the titled peasants of the gomyō stop treating them as vassals partake of the nature of a practical critique. Senshū Fujiatsu provided a succinct but radical critique of the status system, which he singled out as the sole cause of the kawata's plight. At the level of discourse, a student of the famous Confucian scholar Satō Naokata (1650–1719) recorded his teacher's remark that Hideyoshi and Ieyasu were like two brigands who took what did not belong to them by killing others.[70] In the writings of Kamo Mabuchi (1697–1769), the renowned nativist scholar (*kokugakusha*) patronized by Yoshimune's son Tayasu Munetake, one can find a similar sentiment hidden in a text attacking the idea of religious retribution:

> In former times,... everyone was waging war with everyone else and killing people. Those who killed nobody then is today just a nobody [literally, "a commoner"]. But if one killed a few, one got to be called "bannerman"; and a few more, "daimyo"; and even more, "super daimyo of a whole province." However, he who killed an exorbitant number became the most highly regarded person [shogun] and flourishes gen-

70. Satō Naokata, "Satō Naokata sensei setsuwa kikigaki: 5-hen unzōroku, maki 2," Mukyūkai Collection, Tokyo, 30b.

eration after generation. Where is retribution in all this? We see that it comes to the same whether one kills men or insects.[71]

Andō Shōeki (1703?–62) is well known for his full-scale attack on the principle of hierarchy itself:

> From Fu Hsi to Confucius, there are eleven men called sages. They all violated the true way of nature. Their desire to rob the world and the state have plunged the world into war.... It is indeed lamentable that the sages, being ignorant of nature, established private laws ... beginning with Fu Hsi, ... the Yellow Emperor, ... the Duke of Chou ... and all the sages, saints, and Buddhas down the generations ... all the scholars ... including Hayashi Razan and Sorai, were nontillers and violated the way of heaven by robbing the common people who engage in direct cultivation. They have gluttonously devoured the people's surplus grain ... they distinguish between high and low, and proclaiming this to be the law, they claim to possess princely characters and place themselves above others ... teachings that are based on separating everything into two [correspond to the] world of law, [of gluttonous noncultivation]."[72]

Yet it is significant that none of these critiques were public statements. A later reader of Naokata's remark, jotted down by a disciple, wrote in the margin, "This ought to be erased." Mabuchi's critique was published only after his death, and Ando Shōeki's writings were made public only in the Meiji period, as was Fujiatsu's political essay. Tokugawa censorship, implicit or legislated, had the power to control public discourse that was critical of the social imaginary; here the force of law was effective.[73]

CONCLUSION

What are we to make of the development of the vast juridical domain in Tokugawa Japan? A structuralist perspective will almost inevitably lead to an instrumentalist conclusion of the function of law; a strictly modern perspective would question the significance of the Tokugawa field

---

71. Kamo Mabuchi, *Kokuikō*, in *Kinsei Shintōron; zenki kokugaku*, Nihon shisō takei, 39 (Iwanami shoten, 1972), 388–89.

72. Andō Shōeki, quoted in Maruyama, *Studies,* 254–55, 258, 260.

73. Jacques Joly would disagree with my attribution of critical importance to Andō Shōeki's writings. See his "L'Idée de shizen chez Andō Shōeki" (Diss., Université de Paris VII, Unité Asie Orientale, 1991), and idem, "Spontanéité et nature: Le cas d'Andō Shōeki. Comparatisme et récupération," *Revue Philosophique de Louvain* 92, no. 4 (1994): 546–69.

of law because of the lack of even a minimal relative autonomy; and positivists would be negativists, pointing out the great discrepancy between the number of laws on the books and the questionable level of enforcement. By focusing, following Bourdieu, on "world-making" and "social consecrating" effects of the symbolic power of law, however, we may appreciate in a new way the importance of the creation and growth of a Tokugawa juridical field.

In this regard, James White, in reopening the old question whether and in what sense the Tokugawa regime constituted an absolute state, has made a useful distinction between actual (state) development or growth and capacity. He posits that the "central assertion of a claim to such [legitimate] control [of coercive resources] ... which either is not widely questioned or is actively confirmed by significant political actors constitutes state growth, even if *de facto* realization [i.e., capacity] of the claim takes some time and even if the claim is effectively institutionalized for less than the lifetime of the regime in question. Such claims, even if unexploited, are the stuff of which modern nation-states are made."[74] He argues that "centralization and state development continued" in Tokugawa Japan, although "state capacities deteriorated over time."[75] White's assessment can be read as a positive evaluation of the symbolic importance of Tokugawa law.

The claim, tatemae, to legitimate control of coercive resources, whether violent or symbolic, by the superordinate powers was never widely or publicly questioned in Tokugawa Japan. This does not mean that the situation was one of an authoritarian regime in supreme control of its subjects. In practice, this claim did not translate into a direct monopoly on the exercise of authority by the warrior rulers. Many *commoners* were "subcontracted," that is licensed, delegated, or simply allowed to oversee the maintenance of law and order. Positions of authority below that of the intendants—those of their assistants, village group headmen, village headmen, village officials, in the early period even including a number of intendants themselves—were usually filled by coopted prominent local bosses, who were often economically better-off than their dependents but always buttressed by relatively ele-

74. White, "State Growth," 9.
75. Ibid., 11. Philip Brown makes extensive interpretive use of White's categories for state development and state capacities in his *Central Authority*, 12, 25–26, 231 ff.

vated status and concomitant privilege. Although the rulers were warriors, they delegated to others even the ultimate use of violence, the killing of life (when no valor or honor was involved): hunters were licensed for "killing life," and kawata were called upon to take part in armed confrontations with peasants and to execute criminals.[76]

Similarly, laws and regulations often incorporated existing commoner *practices*, such as ways of locally adjusting individual tribute contributions by households when villages were affected internally and unevenly by partial crop failures; crime voting and banishment (if reported at least after the fact) in the realm of penal justice; the proliferation of status distinctions among commoners. Thus the rulers had to compromise not only with local elites but with their practice as well. World-making by the rulers often followed the contours of the world commoners had already made, admittedly in the process consecrating that world.

Non-elite, common commoners had little choice but to play the social game by the rules set for them by their immediate and distant superiors. Both levels of authorities were not merely concerned with maintaining law and order; they were obsessed with it and extremely sensitive to any potential disruption of the peace. This obsession may explain the martial-law solution of punishing both parties in violent quarrels and its extenuated form as a propensity to spread guilt to both sides in conciliation settlements and the practice of nipping occasions for private vendettas in the bud by producing perpetrators of theft or arson through the ballot box. Nevertheless, commoners, undeterred by such practices, which restored order but failed to satisfy their demands for justice, forced the authorities to spend far more time and energy than they wished responding to petitions and lawsuits; because these practices were officially discouraged, those who initiated them were stigmatized as troublemakers.[77] The presumption by all subjects, including the kawata, that they had a "right" to petition or sue was perhaps a result (unintended by the authorities) of the fact that, unlike in pre-Tokugawa times, everyone was now recorded in the population registers and thus identified as a subject with public duties.

Local elites and common commoners, by making the system work to

76. The need of a license for hunting ("the killing of life") is mentioned in village laws; see art. 20 in appendix 3.

77. See arts. 16 and 54 in appendix 3.

their own advantage as best as they could (often in opposite directions), thus contributed to widening the scope of the warriors' role in society beyond what they originally intended. Law, in its individual use in petitions and suits, must thus be seen as something more than a pure instrument of domination, although structurally there is no denying that it was predominantly instrumentalist.

Settlement of a Dispute between *Kumi* Heads and Small Peasants, 1760 (Iribuse, Kita-Saku District, Shinano)

1. Since the ancient past, the offices of kumi heads and peasant representative in the village of Iribuse in Saku-gun have been filled from among the twenty-four titled peasant households. Now the small peasants are fighting to establish their own [representatives], and a dispute has erupted between the two sides. The shogunal office has conducted an investigation. Tachū, from the way station Hiraga, and Tokorozaemon, headman from Gorobe-shinden, submitted a petition for settling the dispute that this office, having heard both sides, endorses. The content of the agreement is as follows.

2. Goningumi. According to the law, the twenty-four titled peasants have been divided into groups of five to form five kumi. In each kumi these five titled peasants, together with the small peasants of each kumi, have elected their kumi head from among these five titled peasants. Of course, the small peasants cannot insist that one of theirs be elected. Now, it has been decided that when it becomes unavoidable that a titled peasant relinquish his office as kumi head, the transfer has to occur with the full consent of the titled peasant; it cannot be done without his consent.

3. When five kumi are made out of the twenty-four titled peasants, one of the kumi will have the headman; which of the five kumi this will be has to be decided by the titled peasants and the small peasants in a meeting, and the kumi from which the headman is selected will be the headman's kumi; the other four kumi decide on their heads as men-

---

The Japanese text can be found in NAK-KS2 (1): 963.

tioned above. Among these four kumi, one kumi head's seat will be empty and the three other kumi leaders will function instead, the vacant post shifting every year to another kumi [this vacancy related only to the village council, not to intra-kumi matters].

The stipend for the kumi heads is, as stipulated in the past, four bales per head, which makes twelve bales for three heads. The headman is especially important; hence the titled peasants and the small peasants, without discrimination, shall elect him from among the twenty-four titled peasants at a meeting of the whole village. From now on, the kumi head will be decided on by the kumi.

4. The peasant representative: to be selected by the small peasants from now on and to rotate among them. His stipend will remain at four bales, as it has been in recent years, and we shall not go back to the two bales of eight years ago; this by a decision of all the peasants. Until now the positions of headman, kumi heads, obviously, and the peasant representative have been limited to the twenty-four titled peasants, and the small peasants could not serve in these functions. This is not according to the law. From now on the peasant representative shall be selected from among the small peasants, and the office will rotate. In anything that does not relate to business with the shogunal office, he will function as an equal to the kumi leaders. Of course, in relation to the village budget, utmost care has to be taken to avoid unnecessary expenditures; an earnest effort has to be made that quarrels do not erupt again and again.

Goningumi Rules, 1640
(Shimo-Sakurai, Kita-Saku District, Shinano)

1. Goningumi should not be formed only with kith and kin; membership should be diverse.

2. *Re:* The yearly investigation of affiliation with Christianity. There is not a single Christian in this village. The peasants are investigated every month, and comings and goings are checked with the pertinent temple in each case to verify affiliation. Therefore, should there be a Christian in this village, not only his goningumi and the headman but the entire village will be punished.

3. If there is a thief in the village, it should be reported to the shogunal authorities. Presently there are none. If one is found, the person will be apprehended immediately and turned over to the shogunal authorities.

4. The term of indentured servants is limited to ten years, as ordered. Anyone exceeding this term by even one month will be punished by the shogunal authorities. A person whose term is completed should know that he cannot come and go or deal with his employer [as if he were still employed].

5. Prohibitions against traffic in human beings have been issued. Henceforward both parties in these transactions will be punished.

6. Wells should be dug and rivers cleaned in due time; cultivation engaged in without delay; yearly tribute paid in full.

The Japanese text can be found in virtually the same form in Ichikawa Yūichirō, *Saku chihō,* "Shiryōshū," 1–3; and Hozumi Shigetō, *Goningumi hōkishū zoku-hen,* 1:18–23. This is one of the oldest goningumi laws from a bakufu territory (Hozumi lists one other, comprising six articles, dated 1629).

7. Turns for guarding the storehouse should be faithfully kept to avoid arrears in tribute rice; in case of fire or theft, loss has to be made up by the entire village.

8. If someone commits the offense of not paying tribute in full or absconds without paying it because he or she cannot make ends meet, the entire village should share the unpaid portion and pay it promptly in full.

9. Nothing that has to be turned in to the shogunal authorities can be sold to others.

10. Wives of headmen and peasants cannot wear starched silk or silky fabrics; peasants can only wear clothes made of cotton or thick paper at any time.

11. Roads and bridges have to be fixed regularly to keep them in good repair.

12. Bamboo cannot be cut without official permit.

13. Gambling, lotteries, and games of any kind are prohibited.

14. Business trips have to be reported to the headman and gonin-gumi before departure, stating the purpose and the places where one will stay; if no such notification occurs and an investigation is made by the shogunal authorities during one's absence, this offense will be punished.

15. All orders from the shogunal office must be obeyed; circular letters from the intendant's assistant should be passed on without the slightest delay; negligence in delivery will be punished.

16. The width of silk and pongee should be of standard size.

17. Wounded individuals cannot be given lodging.

18. Peasants who fix up their hair in bamboo-whisk style, wear long swords, disobey their parents or master, or do not engage in cultivation but spend their days in idleness must be reported to the authorities and cannot be concealed even if they are one's children or servants.

19. People with complaints can lodge suits only on their own; they cannot encourage others to do this, invoking gods' names; as a matter of course, they cannot become involved in others' complaints elsewhere.

20. This document should be rewritten every month, and all villagers, gathered at the headman's, should affix their seals to it, and the certificates should be handed over to the intendant's assistant.

21. Oak, lacquer, and mulberry trees, obviously, but also any kind of tree and bamboo should be planted with due diligence.

The above articles should never be violated.

[Date.]
[Signatures.]

We have grouped all villagers, including semi-independent branch houses (kadoya), into goningumi. If we have missed anyone, we understand that we shall be punished according to the shogunal law.

Goningumi Rules, 1662
(Shimo-Sakurai, Kita-Saku District, Shinano)

1. *Re:* Christians. Following the investigations of the past, each and
every one, down to the last person, has been thoroughly examined: not
only house owners, [but also] men, women, children, servants and semi-
independent branch houses (kadoya), renters, fully established branch
houses (kakae), down to Buddhist monks, Shinto priests, yamabushi,
ascetics, mendicant monks with flutes or bells, outcastes, common beggars and hinin, and so on—to make sure that there is not a single Christian in the village. If villagers see or hear about Christians, regardless of
whether they are in the village or somewhere else, they must report

---

This text can be found in Ichikawa Yūichirō, *Saku chihō*, "Shiryōshū," 3–8.
Ichikawa lists six identical goningumi laws from Kita-Saku, dated between
1635 and 1760, for other villages from bakufu domains, bannermen fiefs, and
the Tokugawa Kōfu domain (among them one for Makibuse dated 1687); and
another four that have supplemented the former goningumi law with the same
number of articles (pp. 17, 29). The translation is based on Ichikawa's text.

Hozumi Shigetō, in his *Goningumi hōkishū zokuhen*, vol. 1, has the same
text, with some slight variations, for Shimo-Sakurai and two other villages, one
from Ōmi province; for Shimo-Sakurai he has seven texts, the last one from
1869, all of them consisting of virtually the same fifty-six articles. This means
that the same goningumi law governed village life in some locales for nearly two
hundred years.

The basic text can be found on pp. 96–103. There are only two remarkable
differences between Ichikawa's and Hozumi's versions. First, in the addition to
art. 38 Hozumi's text does not mention the headman as the source of exploitation because of interest rates he charged peasants at the end of the year on funds
he advanced for corvée expenditures. Second, kawata are not mentioned in
Hozumi's text; where they should appear, two character spaces are left blank. I
do not know whether this reflects the original texts or official Meiji/Taishō
"sensitivities" (probably the latter).

them to the authorities at once and receive the appropriate reward. If intentionally no report is made and then someone else reports it, not only the headman and the goningumi but the entire village will be punished.

Add: Those employing people that move in from the outside or bond servants (genin) should investigate their religious affiliation and secure a certificate from the Buddhist temple where they are registered.

2. Christians, obviously, but also murderers, thieves, or other rascals should be investigated, and all the villagers should arrest them; if it is beyond the community's capacity [to do so], the village should see to it that they do not escape, and this should be reported without delay.

3. Masterless samurai (rōnin) of unknown provenance should not be put up; the headman and goningumi should investigate them, and if they are certified and guaranteed by relatives or in-laws, they should arrange to seek permission from the shogunal authorities.

Add: This applies also to people moving in from the outside.

4. If there are people who have killed someone, no matter whom, or strangers who hang out about shrines or in mountain forests, the villagers, together with people from neighboring villages, should arrest them, tie them up, and hand them over to the authorities. If it is difficult to catch them on the spot, then you have to pursue them, however far, and catch them where they settle. But no matter what kind of people they are, you cannot kill them.

5. If evil parties come fleeing to the village from out of nowhere, you have to detain and report them quickly.

6. Gambling, lotteries, and all kinds of games are forbidden.

7. Traffic in humans is forbidden, and terms of indentured servants cannot exceed ten years.

8. The permanent sale of paddies and fields is forbidden; sales should be made for fixed terms, and contracts must have the seals of the headman and goningumi.

9. As a precaution against thieves, a lookout post should be built in every village in a good spot for night watches. If a thief is discovered, whether in the village or in a neighboring village, one should shout out loud, and everyone should gather and catch him without negligence following the usual arrangement of headmen and peasants.

Add: One should always investigate very well whether Buddhist monks, Shinto priests, yamabushi, ascetics, mendicant monks with flutes or bells, outcastes, common beggars, hinin, and so on, shelter thieves or are among their number.

10. *Re:* Peasant dress. Headmen can wear woven silk and cotton cloth, other peasants only the latter; silk cloth cannot be worn even in collars or sashes, and nothing can be dyed purple, crimson, or plum.

11. Palanquins cannot be used by headmen or peasants, male or female.

12. All luxury items are prohibited. Trespassing one's status is not allowed even in religious ceremonies, festivals, rituals, and so on.

13. Apply your mind to cultivation; the yearly tribute, as ordered, should be paid in full promptly before the fifteenth of the twelfth month.

Add: Pay the kuchimai tax as decided earlier.

14. If peasants seem set on absconding without paying their tribute, the goningumi should investigate, consult with the headman, and stop them; if they are negligent and do abscond, their arrears should be made up by the goningumi and a search organized.

Add: When it obviously concerns a peasant who cannot make ends meet and has not paid his taxes in full, then first the goningumi and next all the peasants will be ordered to pay the tribute for him. This has to be done in full by the due date.

15. *Re:* Shogunal business. No matter who transmits it, the business should be carried out without the slightest delay; circular letters have to be delivered promptly to their next destination.

16. People who are not engaged in cultivation, trade, or any other occupation, or withdraw from consultation with the village, or like quarrels and lawsuits, or do all kinds of bad things should not be hidden [but reported].

17. No peasants should engage in banding together to plot evil things.

18. In the case of quarrels and disputes, the locals have to gather, put a stop to them, and settle the matter; if no private compromise can be reached, both parties have to report their complaints. Of course, if injuries occur, the parties involved have to be restrained immediately.

Add: The dead whose provenance is not known need to be reported.

19. Bad spots not only on highways but also on roads and bridges have to be repaired without negligence.

20. No killing of life [hunting] is allowed except by those who have a permit.

21. Expanding fields by making ditches or roads narrower is forbidden.

22. Under no circumstance can absconded peasants and fugitives be sheltered, not even by relatives or in-laws.

Add: Buddhist monks, Shinto priests, yamabushi, ascetics, mendicant monks with flutes or bells, common outcastes, beggars, hinin, and so on, and strange persons cannot be rented rooms even for one night.

23. Aside from those who come for business, people who often come from elsewhere without having some business in the village cannot be put up.

24. When one has to stay overnight somewhere else, whether on business or on a pilgrimage, one has to report the details to the goningumi.

25. If a single peasant cannot work the fields because of illness, the whole village, starting with his goningumi, has to engage in mutual assistance, work the fields, and pay the tribute.

26. No peasant, no matter how poor, can arbitrarily be banished.

27. One cannot force a well-established peasant into bankruptcy and then add his fields to one's own; even in the case of death without a successor, one cannot add those fields to one's own without first seeking permission from the shogunal authorities.

28. That the fixed tribute has to be paid on the main paddies and fields goes without saying, but the same is true for waste fields and newly developed fields: all, down to the last bu [four square meters] have to be reported and taxed. No matter how low the quality of a piece of land, it should not be left waste.

Add: If there is grassland or old wasteland that should be turned into fields or paddies, permission for its development ought to be secured from the shogunal authorities.

29. Before one turns a paddy into a field because the plot is unfit for wet cultivation, shogunal permission has to be sought.

Add: Permission is also needed to convert fields and paddies into a homestead, or vice versa.

30. In the event of fire within the village, everyone has to rush to the storehouse to protect it. Of course, if the storehouse is safe, everyone should go to where the fire is, and everyone should always be very fire-conscious.

31. Trees and bamboo in the shogunal forest cannot be cut; this applies also to undergrowth, bushes, and grass.

Add: Peasants should not lay waste bamboo and other trees around their house.

32. Favoritism by intendants' assistants (tedai) and irregularities all the way down should be reported.

33. No presents whatever should be given to assistants.

Add: It goes without saying that under normal circumstances, and a priori, when intendants' assistants visit the village for official business, the peasants should not entertain them.

34. When one is to supply men and horses for any official business, one has to secure a note from the intendant's assistant before proceeding; also, any official document has to be signed by the assistant and bear the headman's seal.

35. At the time of the allocation of tribute, all the peasants, including those with fields in other villages, shall gather, reach decisions together, and affix their seals to the document to signify that they have seen it and deposit it in the headman's office.

Add: The peasants should also have a copy of the document.

36. When the tribute document, based on a visual inspection of the fields by the shogunal authorities, arrives [from the intendant's office], all the peasants have to gather, divide the amount due, and affix their seals to a proviso saying that they have seen and examined the allocation and return it to the intendant's assistant.

37. When the rice and cash tribute registers are closed, the headman and four or five small peasants have to affix their own seals and secure the seal of the intendant's assistant. Each time someone pays his tribute, he shall affix his seal to the register under his name and be given a receipt by the headman.

38. None of the items that comprise the corvée cash tax (busen) can be lumped together with the allocation of rice tribute.

Add: It happens that headmen do this, advancing money and then charging interest on the amount. This causes hardship to the peasants; therefore, corvée cash tax should be allocated at each occurrence and settled at that moment.

39. When tribute rice is stored, the storehouse has to be padlocked and sealed with the seals of the intendant's assistant, the headman, and the peasants. The assistant keeps the key, and when payments are made, he has to come and open the storehouse. Of course, if any rice is handed over to someone, a receipt with the amount has to be recorded.

40. In the case of a minor as head of a household, the relatives,

headman, and goningumi have to confer and through a deed entrust the paddies and fields to someone and have that person pay the tribute and perform corvée. When the head of household reaches adulthood, the entrusted goods will be handed back *in toto* to the person in question, who then will become [registered as] a peasant.

41. A name register has to be presented [to the authorities].

42. The peasants should have a copy of the name register, and the tribute allocation should be specified in detail.

43. Not only all accounts of the intendant's assistant, headman, and the peasants but also the smallest transactions have to be balanced with the bills.

44. *Re:* village headmen. Since all the peasants in consultation put up a man they verify to be reliable, if irregularities occur with the balance of the tribute or other matters, responsibility falls on all of them.

45. Suspicious expenditures related to corvée cash or any other matter and allocated by the headman should be investigated immediately in every case.

46. What goes for disputes with people from other places applies also to difficulties among fellow peasants: the headman and the titled peasants (osabyakushō) have to conduct a joint investigation and settle the matter. They have to report cases in which no reasonable private settlement can be reached; favoritism is not allowed, not even for relatives and in-laws.

47. No negligence is tolerated in one's rotation duty to guard the storehouse.

48. No owning of guns is allowed except by those licensed for official use.

49. The storehouse should not leak; obviously, attention should be paid to the walls and even to the matting.

Add: In stormy weather, the storehouse should be checked and any damage reported to the intendant's assistant and repaired.

50. When an intendant's assistant passes through the village on official business, one horse and one boatman will be made available to him. Without permission, men or horses cannot be put out for anyone else. Of course, if an assistant passes through on private business, then he has to be charged the fixed rate for a pack horse.

51. At times, in some places, there are horse thieves about. If there are suspicious-looking people passing through with roped horses or cattle, whether by day or by night, one should inquire about their des-

tination, and if incongruencies are noted, one has to correctly inform the village and subsequently the headman and goningumi of their destination.

Add: No cattle or horse trading should occur without a bona fide go-between.

52. If it is reported that people of the village or from another locale have seen or heard about a thief's stored goods, the headman and goningumi have to get together without delay and investigate the matter.

53. If in some way things have been taken by thieves, or things have been found, or suspicious things occur, they have to be reported.

54. All peasants should endeavor to take the shogunal rules to heart and always investigate to keep things on the right track so that lawsuits do not develop.

55. Replacement of seals affixed to this document is not allowed; the same seals must be used for all other deeds. If a seal gets lost, the owner presents the new one to the intendant's assistant in charge of certifying seals with a note indicating the date of replacement, and he affixes it to the goningumi roster.

56. A copy of this document is deposited with the headman; it should be read aloud whenever the peasants meet in council. The shogunal law should be kept in everything. The above articles are not to be deviated from in the slightest. Therefore, they have been examined in the presence of the headman and the peasants, and the goningumi present this document to the authorities. If anyone breaks these rules, then, starting with the goningumi, the headman and the titled peasants can expect any punishment. In witness whereof, we set our seals hereunto.

Addressee: the intendant.
[Date.]
[Signatures, seals.]

Regulations for the Villages of All Provinces— The Keian Edict, 1649 (and 1665)

INTRODUCTORY COMMENT

This is the famous Keian Edict of 1649 (Keian 2).[1] The translation is based on an expanded version (the expanded portions given here in italics) dated 1665, from the Mikage intendant's office in Kita-Saku, which Ichikawa Yūichirō found in the house of the descendant of the headman of (Maki)buse village.[2] The bracketed second sentence of article 5 (against buying firewood) is the only section from the 1649 document left out in the 1665 version; it is replaced by the long section enjoining peasants to manage things so that they can sell firewood.

Recently some scholars have questioned the authenticity of this important edict. Maruyama Yasunari argues the most radical thesis, that this "forgery" was produced in the second half of the eighteenth century.[3] According to him, at that time some intendant would have felt the need to shore up the status and authority of titled peasants and wrote an exhortative tract, the *Hyakushō mimochigaki*, which was compiled from early and mid Tokugawa edicts, goningumi laws, and educational booklets. This tract, which became quite well known, was expanded and eventually reworked as the famous Keian Edict. And it was as such that it found its way into the *Tokugawa jikki* and the *Tokugawa kinreikō*.

1. TKKz 5:159–64 (no. 2789).
2. Ichikawa Yūichirō, *Saku chihō*, "Shiryōshū," 21–26.
3. Maruyama Yasunari, "'Keian ofuregaki' ron no sui-i to sono sonpi o megutte," in *Kinsei-kindaishi ronshū*, ed. Kyūshū Daigaku kokushigaku kenkyūshitsu (Yoshikawa kōbunkan, 1990). Fukaya Katsumi refers to this text (see the following note).

Fukaya Katsumi, on whose refutation of this thesis I rely, presents the Maruyama argument as follows.[4] The Keian Edict does not figure in two famous collections of Tokugawa edicts. The edicts of 1642 and 1643 are reflected in goningumi laws, but there is virtually no trace of the Keian Edict in these laws. The Keian Edict does not touch upon the proscription of Christianity or the prohibition of the sale of land; it is not often quoted in manuals for local administrators (the few exceptions being the *Bokumin kinkan,* the *Jikata hanreiroku,* and the *Minkan seiyō*), and it is silent on sartorial distinctions between peasants and headmen, which figure in many goningumi laws of the time. The extant versions are both rare and late (nineteenth century).

Fukaya points out, however, that no revisionist has explained why a forgery should be given the date Keian 2.[5] In addition, the absence of any mention of the office of peasant representative (hyakushōdai) in an edict allegedly on village governance may indicate that it was composed before that office existed.[6] His main argument, however, rests on a close analysis of the content.

The Keian Edict is an agricultural treatise, not a manual for local administrators; most of its articles are addressed directly to the peasants.[7] Its emphasis, as the analysis in chapter 4, above, also indicates, is on individual responsibility and economic improvement. Unlike most Tokugawa edicts, it is not prohibitory (and hence does not figure in collections of such edicts).[8]

TEXT

1. One should obey the shogunal law, respect district officials and intendants, and consider headmen and goningumi heads as one's real parents.

2. Those functioning as headmen and goningumi heads should respect district officials and intendants, pay tribute in full, observe the shogunal law, and see to it that the small peasants behave properly. If

---

4. Fukaya Katsumi, "Keian ofuregaki no kōsei to ronri," in *(Ronshū) Chūkinsei no shiryō to hōhō,* ed. Takizawa Takeo (Tōkyōdō shuppan, 1991), 345–72; see 346 and 348.
5. Ibid., 349.
6. Ibid., 370.
7. Ibid., 350.
8. Ibid., 345.

headmen and goningumi heads fail to perform their duty or are in poor standing, they will not earn the respect of the small peasants, who will not obey even shogunal orders. Therefore, headmen and goningumi heads should always behave properly and try to be successful in life.

3. Headmen should not mistreat people, including those with whom they do not get along well; no favoritism should be shown to anyone, no matter how close a friend. Headmen should be close to the small peasants and allocate tribute and corvée to each of them equally and fairly. On the other hand, the small peasants should not disobey the orders of headmen and goningumi heads.

4. Apply your mind to cultivation; if you take as good care of paddies and fields as you would of trees, keep fields from becoming grass-covered by weeding them often, and plow the land often between cultivations, you can expect a promising crop and a rich harvest.

Add: Plant soy and adzuki beans and such along the edges of fields; you should cultivate even the smallest empty plot.

5. To go buy and drink sake or tea is prohibited; this applies also to wives and children. [Plant bamboo around the homesteads, collect fallen leaves, and see to it that you do not have to buy firewood.] *It makes sense to plant saplings in the village and grow a forest and bamboo grove. At first this may be troublesome for the peasants. However, the fallen leaves and wood can be used for various things, such as digging wells, cleaning rivers, building houses, and making bridges. Furthermore, in the end, when the forest is full-grown, one can sell firewood from it and make a profit. Moreover, economically pressured earners can have tools made for peasants to build houses. One who makes it in this business can be successful for generations, passing his wealth on to his offspring, because peasants, unlike officials, who change positions, continue living in the same place. If one plants mulberry, lacquer, and oak trees at the borders of paddies and fields, one can also plant tea. In twenty or thirty years this will result in many tea groves and full-grown mulberry, lacquer, oak, and other trees in the mountains. This will bring great [economic] ease to the village. Therefore, the headman and goningumi heads should consider planting trees as often as possible.*

6. All seeds should be selected carefully at the beginning of the fall season. Only good seeds should be sown; otherwise one cannot expect a rich harvest. *Also, it is important to plant rice seedlings suitable to the soil. After rice has grown and been harvested, the ears should be*

checked for the number of grains. Check the possibility of single- and double-crop farming, which depends on the quality of the soil: some fields are good for soy and adzuki beans, others for foxtail millet, barnyard grass (millet), greens, radishes, and potatoes. It is important to consult often with skilled farmers, raise the crops in season, and harvest them on time.

Add: Some crops need humidity, others don't; take this into consideration, and you will be able to harvest even from low-grade paddies and fields.

7. One should sharpen hoes and sickles every year before the eleventh day of the first month. If paddies or fields are cultivated with a dull hoe, little progress will be made. The same is true for dull sickles.

8. A peasant must take special care in preparing manure and ash; therefore, he should make a large night-soil reservoir in such a way that it keeps the rain out.

Add: If a couple lives all alone and cannot afford to make a toilet, they will have no night-soil reservoir (pot). In that case, they should dig a hole in the yard, three shaku [about one meter] wide and two ken [about four meters] deep and relieve themselves there; they can also add weeds from the roadside and lead water into it to make manure and use it for cultivation.

9. Peasants lack judgment and do not think ahead; hence they carelessly feed their wives and children rice and other grains when these are harvested in the fall, but they should always take as good care of food as they do in the first, second, and third [winter] months of the year.

Add: While cereals are the main products, wheat, foxtail millet, barnyard grass, greens, radishes, and any other grains should be planted so that rice is not depleted by eating it in great quantities. If you keep famines in mind, then the leaves of soybeans, adzuki beans, cowpeas, and even the fallen leaves of potatoes will not be wasted.

10. [Everybody], from the house owner down to his children and servants, and so on, should normally eat plain food. However, at times of demanding labor, like planting rice seedlings or harvesting, slightly better food should be made available in large amounts. If one shows such consideration regarding food, everyone will be content and work hard.

11. *Wealthy peasants, such as those who employ seventy or eighty male and female servants, often limit themselves to giving them orders*

about work but leave everything to their servants' judgment and do not check things for themselves. While they are well-off, their weak points do not reveal themselves, but when their ease and comfort have been taken advantage of and their wealth has declined, they are forced to reduce the number of servants, and finally they have to cultivate by themselves. The comfort they had in the past now kills them. Keeping this in mind, they should, as a rule, get up in the morning, wake up the servants, and send them to weed during the morning; after they return, take them to do field work and be with them to direct them. Then the servants will apply themselves to their work with diligence.

12. *For instance, when one goes out to the field and feels that it might rain the next day, one should be engaged in harvesting rice or wheat, sowing in the dry fields, or doing something first that normally cannot be done on a rainy day. This sort of planning should be done on a daily basis so that one can work without delay: on a rainy day one cultivates or mends paddies, and on a fine day one cultivates or weeds fields. In the evening one should plait rope or weave straw rice bags. Be* always diligent in whatever you do.

Add: When servants have to do back-breaking work, show concern for their hard work and give them some time off.

13. One should make efforts to have a good-quality bull or horse. The better the bulls and horses, the better the manure. Needless to say, the poorer peasants should take this to heart. *Furthermore, these animals need solicitous care* (fukaku awaremu). *Think about them once in a while. They cannot ask for water when thirsty or food when hungry. They cannot complain about the pain in their backs from a rough saddle even when it penetrates to the marrow. Sometimes they collapse near death under a heavy load on a mountainside. Since they cannot throw off their burden by themselves, their suffering must be unspeakable. There is a saying that even an ant's wish is granted by Heaven, but a horse or bull's wish must be far more profound than an ant's. It is said that sometimes people get seriously ill or even die from an unexpected disease because of a curse* (tatari) *from horses or bulls. Furthermore, when a poor peasant kills a horse, which costs three bu to one ryō, he cannot compensate for the loss even after five or seven years. In fact, nobody gains from shrugging this off with the saying that this is the horse's or bull's karma and my loss. Therefore, make saddles comfortable for horses and feed them well. If poor peasants cannot afford to feed them ample fodder and soybeans, they can simply take good*

care of them and understand their suffering. Sometimes young children and servants may not feed them as they should, although they may tell their parents and master that they have fed the animals. In that case, the poor animals have to be without food all day and all night. This may happen often if one does not consider feeding them rice bran and fodder oneself and personally checking the stable often. It is regrettable to neglect the animals, when they contribute to support the peasants with their endurance. Also, in early fall a peasant should prepare food to be given to the horses and bulls during the spring season.

14. Both husband and wife should work for a living: the husband in the fields, the wife at the loom and preparing the evening meal. If a wife neglects her husband, drinks a lot of tea, and likes pleasure trips, she should be divorced even if she is good-looking. The only special cases are when a couple has many children and when a husband has a prior debt to his wife. Furthermore, a husband should take good care of a wife who is not good-looking but is devoted to him.

15. The shogunal law must be observed in everything. Specifically, a criminal whose provenance is not known cannot be patronized (*kakaeoku*) in the village. If someone secretly shelters criminals such as burglars or lawbreakers and this is reported, he will be taken to the shogunal office and examined. The entire village will be put under severe strain if the investigation takes long. Also, one should behave honestly and faithfully so as not to be scorned by the headman, gonin-gumi heads, titled peasants, and the entire village.

16. Peasants can wear cotton cloth only; nothing else can be used even in sashes and collars.

17. One should try to raise one's living by becoming a little business-minded. That is to say, when one sells or buys grains to pay the tribute, one will be taken in if one does not have a business mind.

Add: There is an old saying that it is better to draw water to each field near you rather than attempt business far away. If water is drawn to each field, it will fertilize the soil, make the rice stumps rot, and eventually produce a rich harvest.

18. Apart from the rich, the poor who do not own large fields should think well about a means of living throughout the year; for instance, if there are many children in a family, some can be given away [for adoption?] and some can be sent out as servants.

19. *Peasants should learn early not to spoil their children with love. They should know that too much love makes them play and be*

worry-free. When children grow up, they may not know how to culti-vate fields, or they may associate with outlaws and cause trouble to their parents. Given the instability of this world, they may be separated from their parents when still young. Then they will be frightened like monkeys that are separated from the trees. They will try to perform their duties on the fields and budget the housekeeping, but because they lack training in such things, often they will lose everything and never attain old age. If one truly loves one's children, one must nurture their individual talents when they are young, and when they grow up they should be taught housekeeping. They have to be made to get up in the morning and check around the fields with the servants. Indeed, if they can experience rough times when they are young, they will not be worried when a parent suddenly dies. Then that will be the parents' great blessing to their offspring.

20. The yard should be kept clear and face south. This is because if the yard is not clean, when a peasant winnows rice and wheat, threshes soybeans, and handles cereals, soil and sand will be mixed in with these grains. In that case, he will only get a low price for them, and he has no other resources.

21. It depends on the location, but [as a rule] one should under-estimate the area of a prospective wheat field. Then, if one expands wheat fields one after another, they will bring a greater profit to the peasant in the end. Once a village succeeds in developing land as wheat fields, the neighborhood villages will follow this example.

22. One should always attend to one's health by getting a moxa treatment in spring and autumn. No matter how hard one is willing to work at cultivation, if one falls ill, one cannot be engaged in work that year and eventually becomes bankrupt. One should give this the greatest consideration. The same applies to wives and children.

23. Smoking is prohibited. Tobacco is no substitute for food; on the contrary, it causes illness. In addition, it takes time and money and constitutes a fire hazard. It is disadvantageous to everyone in every respect.

24. Regarding the allocation of tribute: the amount is allocated either per tan in the case of tan units or per koku in the case of taka units, and the tax roster is issued by the intendants. Accordingly, peas-ants should apply themselves earnestly at cultivation. If they reap a rich harvest, it becomes their profit. If they harvest poorly, it will be their loss.

25. Regarding full payment of tribute: when they have no other alternative to make up for the shortage of rice, peasants often borrow from other villagers in the amount of five or six shō to one *to* [between 10 and 18 liters]. At the time the tribute is due, everyone becomes short of rice and cannot loan to others. It does not make sense to sell a child, horse, or bull for a small amount of rice, such as five shō or even one shō. Although good tools and cutlery can be sold, it is loathsome to sell them for one bu or five or six shō of rice. Some without anything to sell have to borrow at a high interest rate, and then their loss becomes larger. At the time of the allocation of tribute by the intendant, peasants should estimate the amount of tribute and borrow the shortage in advance. Getting an advance results in a low interest rate, and then selling something for a loan payment is easier. It is better to pay the tribute promptly. If one waits to pay, it may result in a large loss due to rats, theft, fire, or any other damage. One should dry the unhulled rice completely and thresh it to grains; otherwise rice often gets cracked. Keep this in mind.

26. If one has to borrow rice, say, two bales, because one failed to act properly or in order to supplement one's yearly tribute payment, after five years the principal and interest of that loan will be fifteen bales because of the yearly compounded interest. *It will be over one hundred fifty-five bales within ten years,* and by that time one will be bankrupt. One will sell one's wife and children and even oneself, and future generations will suffer for it. One must consider this well and act properly. At first two bales of rice seems little, but the interest adds up yearly and becomes [an enormous amount], as seen above. On the other hand, if one manages two bales of rice by oneself, with the interest one will have one hundred and seventeen [*fifty-five*] bales of rice ten years later. Peasants should not be negligent in this.

27. Both people working in the mountains and those working at the seashore should apply their minds and work hard every day without negligence. It may happen that one is not able to work because of bad weather, rain or wind, or long illness; one therefore should not waste one's earnings.

28. Mountains and seashores are sparsely populated; therefore people can make a [good] living there. People in the mountains bring down firewood and timber and sell citrus fruit. People at the seashore produce salt and catch fish and always make a good living selling them. But they tend to spend their earnings then and there, thoughtlessly,

without regard for the future. It is said that in time of famine they suffer much worse than villagers and that more of them die of starvation. They should always keep in mind sufferings of times of famine.

29. When a peasant who is single cannot cultivate his fields because of the time he has taken off or because of illness, his goningumi should help with cultivation and maintain the condition of the fields. Furthermore, if a single peasant has plowed the paddies, picked up and prepared seedlings, and planned to bed them out the next day and is then appointed for corvée at the intendant's office or for some other official duty, he will have to take time off from his work for three or five days. The rice seedlings that he had already taken out of their beds for transplanting will turn bad. Other plants will also become knotty, and because he missed the right time for planting, his rice will not grow well that year. He will have a poor harvest and then become bankrupt. This is also true for crops in dry fields. If the opportune time for sowing or planting is missed, crops will not grow well. The headman and goningumi head should take this into account, and if a peasant who lives alone is assigned an official task, they should try to find a substitute for him from among a wealthier peasant's servants.

30. A husband and wife who live all by themselves and have a hard time making a living are the daily object of the villagers' scorn. If they then start to raise their living, obtaining much rice and money, they will begin to be treated nicely in word and deed. The headman, titled peasants, and then others will address them politely, upgrade their seating rank [at meetings], and entertain them. In contrast, once a rich peasant fails in his business and becomes poor, he is disdained and not spoken to by anyone, including his family, relatives, headman, and goningumi heads. Therefore, one should behave well and see to it that one makes a good living.

31. If there is one person in the village who works hard at cultivation, behaves well, and is wealthy, all will learn from him and apply themselves better. If there is one village like this in a county, the entire county will become wealthy. Consequently, a province becomes rich, and then the neighboring provinces will be influenced by this. Intendants shift office all the time, but peasants leave their fields to succeeding generations and make a good living. If peasants work hard and attain wealth, is that not their success and merit? On the other hand, if there is one lawbreaker in a village, the entire village is affected and peasants and servants will engage in endless quarrels. If one person breaks the

law and is taken to court, high and low will have to work harder, and the village will have heavy expenses to bear. Everyone should take care not to get involved in any violation or crime. Headmen should keep this in mind and inculcate the peasants. The peasants should entertain good relations with neighboring villages and not engage in suits with people from other domains.

32. *Even a stranger of unknown provenance can be kind to us; [therefore,] it is not filial piety if one is devoted to good parents. True filial piety is to show great devotion to parents who are unreasonable, immoral, and selfish* (murihidō nite wagamama). *Filial piety means to be well-behaved, have a good reputation, and as brothers have good relations.* The older brother takes care of his younger one, who is obedient to him. Moreover, one can make one's parents happy if one does not go buy and drink much sake, is not quarrelsome but obedient from the bottom of one's heart. If one observes this, gods and Buddhas will bestow their blessings, the Way will be observed, fields will be cultivated, harvests plentiful. On the other hand, no matter how devoted one may be toward one's parents, it is difficult to be filial when in misery. Therefore, one should try hard to be successful. Poverty may cause illness, warp one's mind, make one steal or break the law, and one will wind up tied up, arrested, put into a prisoner's sedan basket, receive the death penalty, and be crucified, and so on. How painful this must be for the parents! Moreover, one's wife, children, brothers, and lineage will feel shame and grief. One should ponder this day and night, behave well, and do nothing unbecoming.

33. If, no matter how hard one works or how much gold, silver, rice, and money one has or how good a homestead, one violates the shogunal law or does not observe the intendant's regulations, one will be arrested and sued. Also, one who drinks much, is violent-tempered, quarrelsome, and selfish will go bankrupt. Be sure to be merciful and honest and not violate the shogunal law. Headmen should stress this a great deal with the small peasants, and parents with their children.

34. Village bridges and roads must always be kept in good condition. If they are bad, travelers will be inconvenienced, people and horses from the village will be troubled, and this will result in mishaps. Headmen and goningumi heads should always be concerned with this and use slack times or holidays to fix them.

35. If we are right-minded, no one treats us badly. If someone treats us badly, that is because our heart is not in the right place. The

same is true for all relationships between intendants and peasants, masters and servants, parents and children, husbands and wives, fellow peasants, and headmen and the peasants. If the headman and the peasants respect the intendants, are well-behaved, do not violate the shogunal law, and apply themselves to everything, the intendants will not harbor any bad feelings. Keep this respectfully in mind every day and do not oppose others. In all these matters, take good care and apply yourself earnestly. When one's living improves and one comes to have rice, silver, and grains, one can afford to build a house and buy clothes and food as often as one wants. Even though one has lots of rice, gold, and grains, the intendants will not take it away. Since this is a time of great peace in the realm, no one will forcibly take it away. One can, therefore, live comfortably for generations, and even during famine will one be able to take care of wife, children, and servants. Nobody lives better in peace than a peasant who has paid his taxes. You should understand this well, teach it to your children and grandchildren, and make a good living.

Regulations for Outcastes in Various Jurisdictions in Shinano

1. KOMORO DOMAIN, KITA-SAKU DISTRICT (1738)

1. Obviously, kawata should be courteous and avoid any insolence toward servants in warrior households, but they also should not enter commoners' houses or shops; in matters of fires, quarrels, and disputes they should follow instructions.

2. They should not hassle for bargains in the towns or countryside, and they should not frequent teahouses or places that sell sake or be self-indulgent (wagamama).

3. They should not wear short swords all the time, but only, following directions, when they are on duty.

4. They cannot enter the castle to sell sandals or enter homes.

5. They cannot act selfishly (wagamama) when they venture into the countryside; when women sell needles in summer and fall, they should do so properly and not hassle people.

Add: It is strictly forbidden for them to go to the towns or countryside and pressure people into lending them money.

6. They should settle quarrels and disputes and apprehend pickpockets at festivals, exhibits, rituals, shows, and so on, but should not pass as ordinary commoners (heijin) and mingle with crowds of onlookers; we have heard that they behave in a self-indulgent and rude manner, and therefore they should not mingle with commoners except in their official capacities; women and children at shows should stand beside the eta and not hinder the heijin....

Ozaki, *Shinshū hisabetsu buraku*, 73, 244, 323–24, 43–44, 325–26.

II. OKUDONO DOMAIN, KITA-SAKU DISTRICT (1738)

1. It is forbidden from now on for eta to wear sandals (*zōri*) when going to the village; they need to wear straw sandals (*waraji*).
Add: They cannot enter the homes of peasants.
2. They should not be discourteous toward villagers in their dannaba or when going to villages beyond it.
3. As eta, they cannot wear short swords.
Add: They need permission from the village headman for trips, even day trips without overnight stays.
4. It is strictly forbidden for them to go to plays or entertainments.
5. They should not quarrel or fight at festivals, markets, or shopping districts.
6. When they are requested to patrol plays and entertainment in villages of a dannaba in a different domain, the requests and directives of local headmen should be followed.
7. They should not temporarily put up people who have been banished, have absconded, or are of unknown provenance; this obviously pertains to persons from other domains, but it also pertains to persons from the villages in the dannaba....

III. CHIISAGATA DISTRICT: THE VILLAGES OF TATSUNOKUCHI, KOSHIGOE, NAKAMARUKO, IINUMA, MITAKEDŌ (1819)[1]

1. House or storehouse rentals, smoke outlets, and billboards are forbidden.
2. Wearing of short swords on private occasions is forbidden.
3. Umbrellas, geta, and leather-soled sandals cannot be used.
4. Children's forelocks should be kept short.
5. Haori coats or parasols cannot be used.
6. No silk garments of any kind can be used.
7. When going to other villages, you [cannot] look like titled peasants.
8. When meeting murakata [probably "villagers" rather than "officials"], you cannot extend greetings.

1. The first two villages were part of a bakufu fief from 1704; the other three, part of Iwamurata domain from 1711. Today all five are part of the town of Maruko, south of Ueda.

9. When interacting with murakata, you cannot proceed further than the extended eave and enter their homes.

IV. CHIISAGATA DISTRICT, NETSU HATAMOTO FIEF: NETSU VILLAGE, (1838)[2]

1. As decreed in past years, you should always be polite, and never rude, toward titled peasants.

2. You should not be rude toward titled peasants on your way to work or to the mountain forests.

3. Never engage in extortion or be rude in your dannaba.

4. When going to festivals, obviously in your own locale but also in others, men, women, and children should dress according to their status without standing out.

5. Modesty is required in hairdos for women and children.

6. No entertainment or musical accomplishments are allowed.

7. New-style houses or multiple front entrances are forbidden.

8. No cutting of standing trees is allowed.

9. No building of new houses, not even one, is allowed.

10. Backroads are to be used for going to the plains and fields.

11. No taking of more than one sheaf is allowed; in other domains, however, you can do as you please.

12. When leaving the village, no umbrellas, geta, leather-soled sandals, lining, or tabi are allowed, only straw sandals.

13. No streamers or decorations are allowed at the Boys' Festival on the fifth of the fifth month.

14. When going to other places, you cannot look like titled peasants, but should set yourself apart from them; this applies to both men and women.

15. Clothes with family crests are absolutely forbidden.

16. *Momohiki* (drawers) and fine patterns are not allowed for titled peasants and certainly not for eta.

17. As ruled before, obviously in the dannaba but also elsewhere, neither old nor young, neither men, women, nor children, can proceed beyond the place under the protruding eaves into the homes....

2. These rules were issued in the context of a reform that stressed frugality, as explained in the preamble (not translated). As Ozaki remarks (327), this is really a transference, even in the language used, of warrior prescriptions for proper behavior of peasants toward them to the manner kawata should adopt toward peasants.

List of Characters

Note: The characters for names of authors appearing in the bibliography are not included.

Aida　會田
Ainōshō　壒嚢鈔
Aizu　会津
Akashina　明科
Aki　安芸
Akita　秋田
Akō　赤穂
akunin　悪人
Andō Shōeki　安藤昌益
Aoyama　青山
Arai Hakuseki　新井白石
arakamisama　荒神様
aruki　あるき
Asama　浅間
Asano　浅野
Asashina　浅科
ashida　足駄
Ashikaga　足利
Awa　阿波

bakufu　幕府
bakurō　馬喰
Ban Nobutomo　伴信友
betsudan ofuregaki　別段御触書
Bingo　備後

Bitchū　備中
biwahōshi　琵琶法師
Bizen　備前
bonboku　ぼんぼく
bonge　凡下
bu　分
bugyōjo　奉行所
bumai　武米
Bun'emon　文右衛門
Bungo　豊後
bunke　分家
Bunshirō　文四郎
buntsuke　分付
Bunzō　文蔵
buraku　部落
burakumin　部落民
busen　夫銭
bushi　武士
buyaku　夫役

chasen　茶筅
Chiba　千葉
chigyō　知行
Chihara　千原
Chiisagata　小県

377

chiku　畜
Chikuma　千曲
ch'ing　卿
Ch'ing　清
Chiribukuro　塵袋
chōgai　帳外
Chōjirō　長次郎
chōmen　帳面
chōnai　帳内
chōnin　町人
chōri　長吏，町離
chorippo　チョリッポ
Chōshū　長州
Chūbu　中部
Chūemon　忠右衛門
Chūgoku　中国
chūhonzan　中本山

daidai　代々
daieta　大穢多
daikan　代官
daimyo　大名
Daitokuin　大徳院
dannaba　旦那場
dannaba kabu　旦那場株
Danzaemon　弾左衛門
Deguchi Nao　出口なを
deiri-suji　出入筋
dogō　土豪
domen　土免
dono　殿
dōshin　道心

ebisu　夷
Ebisu　恵比寿
Echigo　越後
Edo　江戸
Edohyō　江戸表
egō　穢郷，江郷
enryo　遠慮
Entara　縁太羅
enza　縁座

eta　穢多
eta osame　穢多納
etadera　穢多寺
etagari　穢多狩
etagashira　穢多頭
Etchū　越中
Ezo　蝦夷
Ezodan hikki　蝦夷談筆記
Ezoshi　蝦夷志

fuben　不べん
fūbun　風聞
fuchōhō　不調法
fudai　普代
fujittai yue yowatari　不実体故
　世渡
Fujufuse　不受不施
Fukuda Tokuzō　福田徳三
Fukuōji　福王寺
Fukuyama　福山
furusato buumu　故里ブーム
Fuse　布施
Futamori　二森
fuwa　不和

gaijin　外人
gaikokujin　外国人
Gakushūin Daigaku　学習院大学
gejo　下女
Gendayū　源太夫
genin　下人
genrai sono shusei kakubetsu
　naru　元来其種姓各別ナル
Genzō　源蔵
geshunin　下手人
gesugerō no mibun　下司下﨟の
　身分
geta　下駄
gizetsu　義絶
gō　郷
Goemon　五右衛門
goikō　御威光

gokōgisama　御公儀様

gokōgisama godōgu　御公儀様
　御道具

gomyō　五苗

gonai-i　御内意

goningumi　五人組

goningumichō zensho　五人組帳
　前書

Gorobe-shinden　御郎兵衛新田

Gorōemon-shinden　五郎右衛門
　新田

gosahō　御作法

gosanke　御三家

gōshi　郷士

Goshioki saikyo chō　御仕置裁
　許帳

gōso　強訴

goyakushosama negai age　御役
　所様願上

Gunma　群馬

hakama　袴

hamayumi　破魔弓

hanao　鼻緒

Hanbei　半兵衛

hangashira　半頭

hangashiradai　半頭代

hanyakunin　半役人

haori　羽織

Hara　原

Harima　播磨

hatamoto　幡本

Hayashi Razan　林羅山

Heian　平安

Hei'emon　平右衛門

heijin　平人

Heijirō　平次郎

heimon　閉門

Heizaemon　平左衛門, 兵左衛門

Heizō　平蔵

heya-sumi　部屋住

Higashi-Kami-Isobe　東上磯辺

Higashi-Tenkawa　東天川

Higo　肥後

Hiji　日出

hikan　被官

hikiyoseru　引き寄せる

Hikodayū　彦太夫

Hikozaemon　彦左衛門

hinin　非人

Hino　日野

Hinoya Kiee　日野屋喜兵衛

Hirabara　平原

Hiraga　平賀

Hirata Atsutane　平田篤胤

Hiroshima　広島

hissoku　逼塞

hitogara　人柄

hitowa ine　一把稲

Hoashi Banri　帆足万里

hōgai　法外

hoitō　哺啜

Hōjō　北条

Hokkai zuihitsu　北海随筆

Hokkaido　北海道

honbyakushō　本百姓

honden　本田

Honganji　本願寺

honke　本家

honne　本音

Honshū　本州

honyakunin　本役人

Hosokawa Takakuni　細川高国

Hozu　保津

hyakushōdai　百姓代

hyō　俵

Hyōgo　兵庫

Hyōjōsho　評定所

Ichijōji　一乗寺

Ichikawa Gohei　市川五兵衛

ichiwa　壱把

ie　家

iegara　家柄

iekazuchō　家数帳
Iemon　伊右衛門
iewari　家割
Ikeda Mitsumasa　池田光政
ikki　一揆
Ikkō　一向
Imabori　今掘
Imagawa　今川
Ine　いね
inkyo bunke　隠居分家
Innai　印内
irefuda　入札
Iribuse　入布施
Iruma　入間
Ise　伊勢
Ishimoda Shō　石母田正
Itakura Genjirō　板倉源次郎
Iwamurata　岩村田
Iwaya　岩屋
iyashii　卑しい
Iyo　伊予
Izu　伊豆
Izumi　和泉

jigeuke　地下請
Jihei　次兵衛
jinarashi　地ならし, 地並
jinbetsu aratamechō　人別改帳
jindatesho　陣立書
Jin'emon　甚右衛門
jingai　人外
jinsei　仁政
Jinten ainōshō　塵添壒囊鈔
jinya　陣屋
Jirōemon　次郎右衛門
jizamurai　地侍
Jōdoshinshū　淨土真宗
Jōfukuji　常福寺
Jōmon　縄文
Jūzaemon　十左衛門

kabu　株

kabuki　歌舞伎
kabushiki kaisha　株式会社
kabuwake　株分
kadoya　門屋
Kaetsu　下越
Kaga　加賀
Kai　界
kaikaku　改革
kaimyo　戒名
Kaizu　海津
kaka　かゝ
kakae　抱
kakaeoya　抱親
kakaeya　抱屋
kakochō　過去帳
kaku　革
Kamakura　鎌倉
Kamasu　加増
Kameoka　亀岡
Kameyama　亀山
Kami-Hosoya　上細谷
Kami-Kaize　上海瀬
Kami-Kawarabayashi　上瓦林
kamishimo　裃
Kamo Mabuchi　賀茂真淵
Kanazawa　金沢
kandō　勘当
Kan'ei　寛永
Kanesuke　金助
Kanji　官治
kanjōbugyō　勘定奉行
kan(me)　貫（目）
kanmon　貫文
kannushi　神主
Kannonji-shinden　観音寺新田
Kansei　寛政
Kantō　関東
karō　家老
Karuizawa　軽井沢
kashirabyakushō　頭百姓
Kashiwagi Koemon　柏木小右
　衛門

Kasuga　春日
Kasuga-shinden　春日新田
Katakura　片倉
Katsuyama　勝山
kawaramono　河原者
kawata　皮多，皮田
kawata tōryō　かわた棟梁
kawaya sōgashira　かわや惣頭
kegaretaru mono ni tsuki kome
　穢れたる物に付米
Keian　慶安
Ken　けん
kenchichō　検地帳
kengo　慶賀
Kengyō　検校
kenka ryōseibai　喧嘩両成敗
kerai　家来
kessho　闕所
Kichibei　吉兵衛
Kichijōji　吉祥寺
Kichisaburō　吉三郎
Kichitarō　吉太郎
Kii　紀伊
kimoiri　肝煎
Kinai　畿内
kinjū dōzen　禽獣同前(然)
Kinki　近畿
Kira　吉良
Kisaburō　喜三郎
Kita-Saku　北佐久
Kitasawa　北沢
kobyakushō　小百姓
Kodai　小田井
Kodaira　小平
kogashira　小頭
kōgi　公議
kōjō no oboe　口上の覚
kōjōsho　口上書
Kojūrō　小十郎
kokoro jidai　心次第
kokoro ni zen'aku no naki yue
　心ニ善悪ノ無ユヘ

koku　石
kokudaka　石高
kokugaku　国学
kokujin　国人
Komiyayama　小宮山
komononari　小物成
Komoro　小諸
Kōnoshita　神下
Koshigoe　腰越
Kōzuke　上野
kuchigaki　口書
kuchimai　口米
Kujikata osadamegaki　公事方御
　定書
kujiyado　公事宿
Kumamoto　熊本
kumanogoōhōin　熊野牛王宝印
Kumazawa Banzan　熊沢蕃山
kumi　組
kumigashira　組頭
kuniyaku　国役
Kurashiki　倉敷
Kurome　黒目
Kurume　久留米
kusaba　草場
kyōdōtai　共同体
kyokuji　曲事
Kyōto　京都
Kyūjirō　久次郎
kyūmai　給米
kyūri　久離，旧離
Kyūshū　九州
Kyūzaemon　久左衛門

Maebashi　前橋
Magoichi　孫市
Magoroku　孫六
Makibuse　牧布施
Maruko　丸子
matagi　狩獵
Matsudaira　松平
Matsumiya Kanzan　松宮観山

Matsumoto 松本
Matsumoto Hidemochi 松本秀持
Matsuo 松尾
Matsushiro 松城
mawaki まわき
meikun 名君
men 免
menwarichō 免わり帳，免割帳
meyasu 目安
mibun 身分
midomo 身共
Mikage-shinden 御影新田
Mimasaka 美作
Mimayose 御馬寄
Minamoto 源
Ming 明
Mino 美濃，御野
Miura Kaneyuki 三浦周行
Miya みや
miyaza 宮坐
mizunomibyakushō 水飲百姓
Mochizuki 望月
mōjin 盲人
momiko 籾子
Mon もん
monnami hitomasu 門並壱舛
Monoimi no ki 物忌の記
mōshioyobazu 不及申
Motoori Norinaga 本居宣長
mudaka 無高
mura 村
murahachibu 村八部
Murakami 村上
murakata 村方
murakata sanyaku 村方三役
murauke 村請
Mure 牟礼
Muromachi 室町
Musashi 武蔵
Musashino 武蔵野
Mushiage 虫明

mushuku 無宿
Musu むす
muyashiki 無屋敷
muza to むざと

Nagano 長野
Naganuma 長沼
Nagaoka 長岡
Nagase 長瀬
nagatazune 永尋
Nagatoro 長土呂
nagaya 長屋
Nagayoshi 長吉
nago 名子
naibun nite 内分ニて
naisai 内済
naisaku 内作
naisho ni 内所に
Nakae Tōju 中江藤樹
Nakano 中野
Nakanojō 中之條
Nakasendō 中仙道
nayosechō 名寄帳
nenbutsu 念仏
nengu 年貢
nengumenjō 年貢免状
nenguwaritsukejō 年貢割付状
nenkihōkōnin 年季奉公人
Niboku 二睦
Nichiren 日蓮
nigirimeshi 握飯
Niigata 新潟
Nikkō 日光
ninsoku 人足
Niremata 楡俣
Nishi Honganji 西本願寺
nobori 幟
Noto 能登

Ōashi 大足
Oda Nobunaga 小田信長
Odawara 小田原

Ōgaki　大垣
Ogoseimaichi　越生今市
Ogyū Sorai　荻生徂徠
Ōita　大分
Oiwake　追分
Ōjin　応神
ōjōya　大庄屋
Okayama　岡山
Oku　邑久
Okudono　奥殿
okurijō　送状
Okutama　奥多摩
Ōmi　近江
Ōmori Hisazaemon　大森久左
　衛門
Ōmotokyō　大本教
onbyakushō tsukamatsuri makari
　ari　御百姓仕り罷在
onnagata　女形
ore　をれ
osabyakushō　長百姓
Osaka　大坂
osamekatawaritsuke　納方割付
oshikome　押込
Ōshio Heihachirō　大塩平八郎
osorenagara　乍恐
Ōsumi　大住
ōtakamochi　大高持ち
otonabyakushō　長百姓
otsudo　越度
Otsukoto　乙事
Owari　尾張
oya　親
oyabun　親分
Ōzawa　大沢

rakushogishō　落書起請
ri　里
Rihei　理兵衛
Rinsai　臨済
Risaemon　利左衛門
Ritsuryō　律令

Rokuemon　六右衛門
rōnin　浪人
ryō　両
ryōmin　良民
ryōmyō　両苗

sabetsu　差別
Sadaemon　貞衛門
Sagami　相模
Saitama　埼玉
Sajihei　佐次兵衛
Sakai　酒井
sankinkōtai　参勤交代
Sanuki　讃岐
Sasaemon　佐左衛門
Sassa Narimasa　佐々成政
Sayama　佐山
Seijirō　清次郎
seishi o koto ni su　姓氏ヲ異
　ニス
sen　銭
Sen　せん
sendara　旃陀羅
Sengoku　仙石
senmin　賎民
seppuku　切腹
setta　雪駄，席駄
Settsu　摂津
shaku　尺
Shiga　志賀
Shige'emon　茂右衛門
Shigeshichi　茂七
shih　士
shihi　死皮
shijin　死人
shikitari yaburi　仕来破
Shikoku　四国
Shimabara　島原
Shimoda　下田
Shimogata　下県
Shimo-Ifuku　下伊福
Shimo-Kaize　下海瀬

Shimo-Kawarabayashi　下瓦林
Shimo-Okamoto　下岡本
Shimōsa　下総
Shimo-Sakurai　下桜井
Shimo-Wana　下和名
Shinano　信濃
shindenmura　新田村
Shin'emon　新右衛門
Shingaku　心学
Shingon　真言
shinheimin　新平民
shinkoku no fūzoku zehi nashi　神国ノ風俗是非ナシ
Shinran　親鸞
shinshimin　新市民
shinshō　身上
shinson　神孫
Shinzō　新蔵
Shionada　塩名田
Shiosawa-shinden　塩沢新田
Shirōemon　四郎右衛門
shishimai　獅子舞
shizai　死罪
shō　升
shōen　荘園
shōshin　商心
shōya　庄屋
shozokudanteki kyōgyōtai　小族団的協業体
shujen　庶民
shūmon aratamechō　宗門改帳
sō　惣
sōbyakushō　惣百姓
sōbyakushō nokorazu　惣百姓不残
sōbyakushōdai　惣百姓代
sōdanfuda　相談札
sōinaku　無相違
sojō　訴状
Sominshōrai　蘇民将来
sonae　備
Sōtarō　総太郎

Sōtō　曹洞
sōuke　惣請
Sugaura　菅裏
Sugito　杉戸
sukego　助郷
sumaki　簀巻
Sunpu　駿府
Suruga　駿河
Suwa　諏訪
Suzaku　朱雀

tabi　足袋
tafu　大夫
Tahee　太兵衛
taka　高
Takada　高田
Takai　高井
Takasaki　高崎
takawari　高割
Takayama　高山
Takeda Shingen　武田信玄
Takejirō　竹二郎
Tamada Naganori　玉田永教
tameshimono　試物
tan　反
Tanba　丹波
Tani Shinzan　谷秦山
Tanoguchi　田野口
tanomoshikō　頼母子講
Tanuma Okitsugu　田沼意次
tanwari　反割
Tarōshichi　太郎七
tatari　たたり（祟り）
Tateishi　立石
tatemae　立て前
Tatsugorō　辰五郎
taue　田植
Tayasu Munetake　田安宗武
tedai　手代
tega　手下
Tendai　天台
Tenjinbayashi　天神林

tenka dai ichi no gohatto 天下第一の御法度

Tenpo 天保

Terajima Ryōan 寺島良安

tetsuki 手付

to 斗

tobichi 飛び地

todai 斗代

Tōhoku 東北

tojime 戸締

Tōkai 東海

toko 屠沽

Tokubei 徳兵衛

tokubetsu 特別

Tokugawa Ieyasu 徳川家康

Tokugawa jikki 徳川実紀

Tokugawa seiken hyakkajō 徳川成憲百箇条

Tokugawa Yoshimune 徳川吉宗

Tokuzaemon 徳左衛門

Tomikura 富蔵

Tosa 土佐

toshiyori としより，年寄

Tosho 図書

toto とゝ

totō 徒党

Toyota 豊田

Toyotomi Hideyoshi 豊臣秀吉

tsubo 坪

Tsuchiya Chūemon 土屋忠右衛門

tsuguru naki 告無

tsuihō 追放

Tsunazawa 綱沢

tsurawari 面割

Tsuyama 津山

uchi 内

Uchitsuneishi 内常石

uchizuke 内付

Ueda 上田

Uesugi 上杉

ujigami 氏神

ukeru 請ける

Umaji 馬路

Umanosuke 右馬之介

Utsunomiya 宇都宮

Wada 和田

wagamama 我侭

Wakasa 若狭

wakibyakushō 脇百姓

wariban 割番

warichi 割地

Watanabe buraku 渡辺部落

Yaehara-shinden 八重原新田

Yaemon 弥右衛門

Yahei 弥兵衛

yaku 役

yakuya 役屋

yamabushi 山伏

Yamagata Shūnan 山県周南

Yamashiro 山城

Yamazaki Ansai 山崎闇斎

Yanagisawa 柳沢

yashiki 屋敷

yashikibiki 屋敷引

Yata 弥太

Yawata 八幡

Yayoi 弥生

yogore daiku よごれ大工

Yohachi 与八

Yōjirō 要治郎

Yokomi 横見

Yomase 夜間瀬

Yoshino 吉野

Yūan 元

zatō 座頭

zatō nakama 座頭仲間

Zenzaemon 善左衛門

zōhyō 雑兵

Glossary

bakufu, shogunate

bu, one fourth of a *ryō*

bunke, branch house in a lineage; a more neutral term than *kakae*, which explicitly expresses dependency

buraku, "hamlet"; refers to an outcaste (*kawata*) community, usually attached to a regular peasant village, *mura*

burakumin, modern term for descendants of outcastes, *kawata*

busen, cash payment in lieu of corvée

buyaku, corvée

chigyō, fief entrusted to landed retainers

chōgai, "off the [population] register"; officially removed from the community

chōnai, "on the [population] register"; under someone else as his dependent or co-resident

daikan, intendant

dannaba, territory encompassing a number of peasant villages where *kawata* operated; also called *kusaba*

deiri-suji, adversarial procedure privately initiated

dogō, rural magnate

domen, equalization. See also *jinarashi*

eta, "plentiful pollution"; outcaste, derogatory name for *kawata*

fudai, lifelong servant

genin, bond servant

gō, medieval district

goningumi, five-household group

goningumichō zensho, village laws drawn up by overlords

hatamoto, bannerman; shogunal fief-holding vassal

hinin, "nonhuman"; registered beggar

honbyakushō, titled peasant

honke, main family; patron of *bunke*, *kakae*

honne, real intention. Cf. *tatemae*

hyakushōdai, peasant representative

hyō, bale; 2.5 *hyō* = 1 *koku*

Hyōjōsho, Tribunal; highest bakufu court

ie, household

iekazuchō, household register

iewari, intravillage computation of corvée, fees, and so on, per household. Cf. *takawari*

irefuda, voting by ballot

jigeuke, "subcontracting" local communities, especially corporate villages in the sixteenth century, for delivering tribute to overlords; similar to the Tokugawa *murauke*

jinarashi, intravillage adjustment of tribute among households in times of partial crop failures to meet the set village quota; same as *domen*

jizamurai, landed samurai

kabu, a share in common intravillage rights of various kinds

kado(ya), dependent, usually living in separate quarters, ranking between *fudai* and *kakae*

kakae(ya), branch house in a lineage, usually not of a titled peasant

kakaeoya, main house; same as *honke*; often a lineage head and titled peasant

kakochō, temple list of memorial days of deceased parishioners

kandō, disinheritance; very similar to *kyūri*

kan(me), copper currency equal to 1,000 *mon*

kanmon. See *kanme*

kashirabyakushō. See *honbyakushō*

kawaramono, "riverbed people"; low-status persons, including *kawata* and often identified with them

kawata, "leather-/hide-plenty," "leather-/hide-paddy field"; leather worker, nonderogatory term for *eta,* outcaste

kenchichō, land cadaster

kimoiri, village headman

kobyakushō, small landholder

kogashira, official in outcaste *kawata* hamlet

kōgi, "public authority"; dignified and legitimizing reference to shogun and daimyo

koku, 4.96 bushels

kokudaka, tribute base of village or domain expressed in the equivalent of the putative yield in *koku* of rice

komononari, miscellaneous tribute other than rice

kuchimai, supplementary tribute to the basic rice tribute

kumi. See *goningumi*

kumigashira, kumi head, head of *goningumi*

kuniyaku, national corvée levied by overlords for shogunal projects

kusaba. See *dannaba*

kyōdōtai, community

kyūri, disinheritance, very similar to *kandō*

menwarichō, tribute list

mibun, status

miyaza, corporate shrine association

mizunomibyakushō, "water-drinking peasant"; landless or nearly landless peasant, tenant

mudaka, landless peasant, tenant

mura, village

murahachibu, ostracism

murauke, overlords' subcontracting of the village as a tribute unit

mushuku, "homeless"; nonregistered person, vagrant

muyashiki, "without a homestead"; refers to a nontitled peasant

nago, dependent, similar to *genin* and *fudai*

naisai, conciliation

nayosechō, name register

nengu, yearly rice tribute

nengumenjō, overlords' letter stating the yearly tribute rate

nenguwaritsukejo. See *nengumenjō*

nenkihōkōnin, indentured servant

ninsoku, porter

nyūsatsu. See *irefuda*

ōjōya, village group headman, overseer of several villages

osabyakushō, titled peasant

otonabyakushō, titled peasant

ri, 3.93 km.

ryō, gold coin (equal to 4 *bu*)

ryōmin, "good people"; a legal status in the Nara period

sankinkōtai, alternate attendance

senmin, "despicable people"; originally a legal status in the Nara period

shaku, 30 cm.

shinden mura, newly developed village

shōen, medieval estate

shōya, village headman

sō, corporate village

sōbyakushō, "all the peasants"; meaning all titled peasants

sōbyakushōdai, "all-peasant representative"; comparable to *hyaku-shōdai*

sojō, legal suit

sonae, army unit

sukego, portage corvée between way stations

taka, assessed value of land productivity

takawari, computation of corvée, fees, and so on, per holding size

tanwari. See *takawari*

tatemae, professed principle, "face," opposite of *honne*

tedai, assistant to intendant

toshiyori, elders

wakibyakushō. See *kakae*

wariban. See *ōjōya*
yaku, corvée and other burdens
yakuya, "corvée house"; titled peasant
yashiki, homestead, compound
zatō, registered blind person with a profession

Bibliography

Note: *Unless otherwise noted, the place of publication is Tokyo.*

JAPANESE-LANGUAGE WORKS

Primary Sources and Reference Works

Aoki Kōji 青木虹二. *Hennen hyakushō ikki shiryō shūsei* 編年百姓一揆史料集成. 17 vols. San'ichi shobō, 1979–93.

Burakushi yōgo jiten 部落史用語辞典. Edited by Kobayashi Shigeru 小林茂 et al. Kashiwa shobō, 1985.

Hozumi Nobushige 穂積陳重, comp. *Goningumi hōkishū* 五人組法規集. Yūhikaku, 1921.

Hozumi Shigetō 穂積重遠, comp. *Goningumi hōkishū zokuhen* 五人組法規集続編. 2 vols. Yūhikaku, 1944.

Ishii Ryōsuke 石井良助, ed. *Kinsei hōseishiryō sōsho* 近世法制史料叢書. 3 vols. Sōbunsha, 1959.

Kamo Mabuchi 賀茂真淵. *Kokuikō* 国意考. In *Kinsei Shintōron; zenki Kokugaku* 近世神道論; 前期国学, 374–93. Nihon shisō taikei 日本思想大系, 39. Iwanami shoten, 1972.

Kobayashi Shigeru 小林茂, ed. *Kinsei hisabetsu buraku kankei hōreishū: Tenryō o chūshin to shite* 近世被差別部落関係法令集: 天領を中心として. Akashi shoten, 1981.

Kodama Kōta 児玉幸多 and Ōishi Shinzaburō 大石慎三郎, eds. *Kinsei nōsei shiryōshū* 近世農制史料集. Vol. 1. *Edo bakufu hōreishū* 江戸幕府法令集. Yoshikawa kōbunkan, 1966.

Kokushi daijiten 国史大辞典. Edited by Kokushi daijiten henshū iinkai 国史大辞典編集委員会. 15 vols. Yoshikawa kōbunkan, 1979–94.

Komachi Yūhachi 小町雄八. *Jishūhen* 自修篇. In *Nihon keizai sōsho* 日本経済叢書, edited by Takimoto Seiichi 瀧本誠一, 19:427–500. Nihon keizai sōsho kankōkai, 1915.

Maeda Masaharu 前田正治. *Nihon kinsei sonpō no kenkyū* 日本近世村法の研究. Yūhikaku, 1952.

Motoori Norinaga 本居宣長. *Hihon tamakushige* 秘本玉くしげ. In *Motoori Norinaga zenshū* 本居宣長全集, vol. 8. Chikuma shobō, 1972.

Nagano-ken 長野県, ed. *Nagano-kenshi: Kinsei shiryō-hen, Vol. 2, Tōshin chi-hō* 長野県史: 近世史料偏, 2 : 東信地方. Pts. 1 and 2. Nagano-shi: Nagano-kenshi kankōkai, 1978–79.

Nihon nōsho zenshū 日本農書全集. 35 vols. Nōsangyoson bunka kyokai, 1977–81.

Nihon rekishi taikei 日本歴史大系, 3. *Kinsei* 近世. Edited by Kodama Kōta 児玉幸多, Nagahara Keiji 長原慶二, et al. Yamakawa shuppan, 1988.

Nihon shomin seikatsu shiryō shūsei 日本庶民生活史料集成, 14. *Buraku* 部落. Edited by Harada Tomohiko 原田伴彦 et al. San'ichi shobō, 1971.

Nihonshi jiten (kaitei zōho) 日本史辞典 (改訂増補). Edited by Kyoto Daigaku bungakubu kokushi kenkyūshitsu 京都大学文学部国史研究室. Sōgensha, 1960.

Nishinomiya-shi shi 西宮市史. Vols. 4 and 5. *Shiryò-hen* 史料偏, pts. 1 and 2. Nishinomiya: Nishinomiya shiyakusho, 1962–63.

Nomura Kentarō 野村健太郎. *Goningumichō no kenkyū* 五人組帳の研究. Yūhikaku, 1944.

Ogyū Sorai 荻生徂徠. *Seidan* 政談. In *Ogyū Sorai* 荻生徂徠. Nihon shisō taikei 日本思想大系, 36. Iwanami shoten, 1973.

―――. *Sorai sensei tōmonsho* 徂徠先生答問書. In *Ogyū Sorai*, edited by Bitō Masahide 尾藤正英. Nihon no meicho 日本の名著, 16. Chūōkōronsha, 1983.

Ōishi Hisataka 大石久敬. *Jikata hanreiroku* 地方凡例録. Edited by Ōishi Shin-zaburō 大石慎三郎. 2 vols. Kondō shuppansha, 1969.

Ono Takeo 小野武雄. *Edo bukka jiten* 江戸物価事典. Edo fūzoku zushi 江戸風俗図誌, 6. Tenbōsha, 1989.

Saitama-ken 埼玉県, ed. *Saitama-ken shi: Shiryō-hen* 埼玉県史: 資料編. 26 vols. Saitama-ken, 1979–91.

Satō Naokata 佐藤直方. "Satō Naokata sensei setsuwa kikigaki: 5-hen unzōroku, maki 2" 佐藤直方先生説話聞き書き: 五偏饂蔵録 · 巻2. Mukyūkai 無窮会, Tokyo.

Senshū Fujiatsu 千秋藤篤. *Eta o osamuru gi* 治穢多議. In *Buraku* 部落, edited by Harada Tomohiko 原田伴彦 et al. Nihon shomin seikatsu shiryō shūsei 日本庶民生活史料集成, 14. San'ichi shobō, 1971.

Tanaka Kyūgū 田中丘隅. *Minkan seiyō* 民間省要. In *Nihon keizai sōsho* 日本経済叢書, edited by Takimoto Sei'ichi 滝本誠一, 1:229–740. Nihon keizai sōsho kankōkai, 1914.

Tokugawa kinreikō kōshū 徳川禁令考後集. Edited by Ishii Ryōsuke 石井良助. 4 vols. Sōbunsha, 1959–61.

Tokugawa kinreikō zenshū 徳川禁令考前集. Edited by Ishii Ryōsuke 石井良助. 6 vols. Sōbunsha, 1959–61.

Secondary Sources

Akutsu Muneji 阿久津宗二. "Mura gitei ni tsuite no ichi kōsatsu: toku ni seisai sadame no shojirei" 村議定についての一考察: 特に制裁定めの諸事例. *Gunma-kenshi kenkyū* 25 (1986): 94–116.

Amino Yoshihiko 網野善彦. *Nihon no rekishi o yominaosu* 日本の歴史をよみなおす. Chikuma shobō, 1991.

Aoki Takahisa 青木孝寿. "Niboku iriaiken jiken to hanketsu no igi" 二睦入会権事件と判決の意義. *Buraku mondai kenkyū* 40 (1973): 34–70.

Aono Shunsui 青野春水. *Nihon kinsei warichiseishi no kenkyū* 日本近世割地制史の研究. Yūzankaku, 1982.

Arai Eiji 荒居英次. "Nengu waritsukejō no seiritsu" 年貢割付状の成立. In *Kinsei no jikata-machikata monjo* 近世の地方・町方文書, edited by Nihon komonjo gakkai 日本古文書学会, 228–55. Nihon komonjogaku ronshū 日本古文書学論集, 12 (Kinsei 近世 2). Yoshikawa kōbunkan, 1987.

Araki Moriaki 安良城盛昭. *Bakuhan taisei shakai no seiritsu to kōzō* 幕藩体制社会の成立と構造. Ochanomizu shobō, 1959.

Asao Naohiro 朝尾直弘. *Kinsei hōken shakai no kiso kōzō* 近世封建社会の基礎構造. Ochanomizu shobō, 1967.

———. "Kinsei no mibun to sono henyō" 近世の身分とその変容. In *Mibun to kakushiki* 身分と格式, edited by Asao Naohiro 朝尾直弘, 7–40. Nihon no kinsei 日本の近世, 7. Chūōkōronsha, 1992.

———. 朝尾直弘, ed. *Mibun to kakushiki* 身分と格式. Nihon no kinsei 日本の近世, 7. Chūōkōronsha, 1992.

Banba Masatomo 万羽正朋. See also Tsukada Masatomo 塚田正朋.

———. "'Buraku' no keisei ni kansuru kōsatsu: Shinshū ni okeru burakushi sobyō (1)" 「部落」の形成に関する考察: 信州における部落史素描 (一). *Shinano* 12, no. 5 (1960): 1–24. Reprinted in Tsukada Masatomo 塚田正朋, *Kinsei burakushi no kenkyū: Shinshū no gutaizō* 近世部落史の研究: 信州の具体像. Kyoto: Buraku mondai kenkyūjo, 1986.

———. "'Buraku' no seiritsu ni tsuite: Shinshū ni okeru burakushi sobyō (2)" 「部落」の成立について: 信州における部落史素描 (二). *Shinano* 12, no. 9 (1960): 45–62. Reprinted in Tsukada Masatomo 塚田正朋, *Kinsei burakushi no kenkyū: Shinshū no gutaizō* 近世部落史の研究: 信州の具体像. Kyoto: Buraku mondai kenkyūjo, 1986.

———. "'Buraku' no sui-i to mibun kisei no kyōka: Shinshū ni okeru burakushi sobyō (3)" 「部落」の推移と身分規制の強化: 信州における部落史素描 (三). *Shinano* 13, no. 8 (1961): 27–38 and 16, no. 9 (1964): 16–34. Reprinted in Tsukada Masatomo 塚田正朋, *Kinsei burakushi no kenkyū: Shinshū no gutaizō* 近世部落史の研究: 信州の具体像. Kyoto: Buraku mondai kenkyūjo, 1986.

———. "Mibunsei no teppai e: Shinshū ni okeru burakushi sobyō (4)" 身分制の撤廃へ: 信州における部落史素描 (四). *Shinano* 16, no. 12 (1964): 32–48. Reprinted in Tsukada Masatomo 塚田正朋, *Kinsei burakushi no kenkyū: Shinshū no gutaizō* 近世部落史の研究: 信州の具体像. Kyoto: Buraku mondai kenkyūjo, 1986.

———. *Nihon jukyōron* 日本儒教論. Mikasa shobō, 1939.

———. "Ueda-ryō nai ni okeru 'eta' soshō jiken" 上田領内における「えた」訴訟事件. *Shinano* 17, no. 11 (1965): 1–12 and 18, no. 3 (1966): 30–48. Reprinted in Tsukada Masatomo 塚田正朋, *Kinsei burakushi no kenkyū: Shinshū no gutaizō* 近世部落史の研究: 信州の具体像. Kyoto: Buraku mondai kenkyūjo, 1986.

Chihōshi kenkyū kyōgikai 地方史研究協議会, ed. *"Kaihatsu" to chiiki minshū: sono rekishizō o motomete* '開発' と地域民衆: その歴史像をもとめて. Yūzankaku, 1991.

Fujiki Hisashi 藤木久志. "Ikōki sonrakuron" 移行期村落論. In *Nihon chūseishi kenkyū no kiseki* 日本中世史研究の軌跡, edited by Nagahara Keiji 長原慶二 et al., 197–215. Tōkyō Daigaku shuppankai, 1988.

———. *Toyotomi heiwarei to sengoku shakai* 豊臣平和令と戦国社会. Tokyo Daigaku shuppan, 1985.

Fukaya Katsumi 深谷克巳. "Bakuhansei shihai to mura yakuninsō no kokugaku juyō" 幕藩制支配と村役人層の国学受容. *Shikan* 91 (1975): 13–23.

———. "Keian ofuregaki no kōsei to ronri" 慶安御触書の構成と論理. In *(Ronshū) Chū-kinsei no shiryō to hōhō* (論集) 中・近世の史料と方法, edited by Takizawa Takeo 滝沢武雄, 345–72. Tōkyōdō shuppan, 1991.

Furushima Toshio 古島敏雄. *Nihon hōken nōgyōshi* 日本封建農業史. Shikai shobō, 1941.

Fuse Yaheiji 布施弥平治. "Shiryō: Murahachibu no soshō" 資料: 村八部の訴訟. *Nihon hōgaku* 23, no. 3 (1957): 96–109.

Harada Seiji 原田誠司. "Kinsei zenki sonraku no shoruikei: Fukuyama hanryō o chūshin ni shite" 近世前期村落の諸類型: 福山藩領を中心にして. *Shigaku kenkyū*, no. 193 (1991): 1–28.

Harada Tomohiko 原田伴彦. *Buraku sabetsushi kenkyū* 部落差別史研究. Kyoto: Shibunkaku, 1985.

Hatanaka Toshiyuki 畑中敏之. "'Kawata' mibun to wa nani ka" 「かわた」身分とはなにか. In *Mibun to kakushiki* 身分と格式, edited by Asao Naohiro 朝尾直弘, 307–44. Nihon no kinsei 日本の近世, 7. Chūōkōronsha, 1992.

Hayashi Motoi 林基. *Kyōhō to Kansei* 亨保と寛政. Kokumin no rekishi 国民の歴史, 16. Bun'eidō, 1971.

Hiramatsu Yoshirō 平松義郎. *Edo no tsumi to batsu* 江戸の罪と罰. Heibonsha, 1988.

———. *Kinsei keiji soshōhō no kenkyū* 近世刑事訴訟法の研究. Sōbunsha, 1960.

Hirayama Kōzō 平山行三. *Kishū-han nōsonpō no kenkyū* 紀州藩農村法の研究. Yoshikawa kōbunkan, 1972.

Hozumi Nobushige 穂積陳重. *Goningumi seido* 五人組制度. Yūhikaku, 1902.

———. *Goningumi seidoron* 五人組制度論. Yūhikaku, 1921.

Ichikawa Takeji 市川武治. "Saku chihō ni okeru reizoku nōmin 'kakaebyakushō' no jittai" 佐久地方における隷属農民「抱え百姓」の実体. *Nagano*, no. 128 (1986): 5–14.

Ichikawa Yūichirō 市川雄一郎. *Saku chihō Edo jidai no nōmin seikatsu* 佐久地方江戸時代の農民生活. Nagano-ken, Minami Saku-gun Nozawa-machi: Saku Insatsujo, 1955.

Igeta Ryōji 井ケ田良治. "Hōkenteki sonraku kyōdōtai to mura okite: Tanba-kuni Hozu-mura gomyō shūdan no sonraku shihai" 封建的村落共同体と村掟: 丹波国保津村五菌集団の村落支配. *Dōshisha hōgaku* 同志社法学, nos. 58 (1960): 52–78; 61 (1960): 80–109; 62 (1960): 27–56; 65 (1961): 23–45; 70 (1962): 66–98; 75 (1962): 87–108.

———. *Hō o miru Kureo no me: rekishi to gendai* 法を見るクレオの目: 歴史と現代. Kyoto: Hōritsu bunkasha, 1987.

———. "Iriai sabetsu to buraku mondai" 入会差別と部落問題. In *Kindai Kyōto no burakushi* 近代京都の部落史, edited by Buraku mondai kenkyūjo 部落問題研究所, 168–98. Kyoto no buraku mondai 京都の部落問題, 2. Kyoto: Buraku mondai kenkyūjo, 1986.

———. "Kinsei kōki no buraku sabetsu seisaku" 近世後期の部落差別政策. *Dōshisha hōgaku* 同志社法学, nos. 110 (1969): 28–49 and 111 (1969): 53–84.

———. *Kinsei sonraku no mibun kōzō* 近世村落の身分構造. Kokusho kankō-kai, 1984.

———. "Kon'in sabetsu no rekishiteki shosō: Edo bakufu no hanketsu o tsū-jite" 婚姻差別の歴史的諸相: 江戸幕府の判決をつうじて. In *Kindai tennōsei kokka no shakai tōgō* 近代天皇制国家の社会統合, edited by Mahara Tetsuo 馬原鉄男 and Kakeya Saihei 掛谷宰平, 3–20. Kyoto: Bunrikaku, 1991.

———. "Kuchi-Tanba chihō no hisabetsu shūraku" 口丹波地方の被差別集落. In *Zenkindai Kyōto no burakushi* 前近代京都の部落史, edited by Buraku mondai kenkyūjo 部落問題研究所, 92–129. Kyoto no buraku mondai 京都の部落問題, 1. Kyoto: Buraku mondai kenkyūjo, 1987.

———. "Meiji kōki no kenri tōsō no ichi jirei: Mikaihō burakumin no byōdō iriai yōkyū" 明治後期の権利闘争の一事例: 未開放部落民の平等入会要求. In *Nihon kindai kokka no hō kōzō* 日本近代国家の法構造, edited by Nihon kindai hōseishi kenkyūkai 日本近代法制史研究会, 482–514. Bokutakusha, 1983.

———. "Mikaihō burakumin no iriaiken" 未解放部落民の入会権. *Minshōhō zasshi* 78, suppl. no. 1 (1979): 201–16.

———. "Mikaihō buraku to iriaiken: Kyōto-fu Kameoka-shi Hozu-mura no baai" 未解放部落と入会権: 京都府亀丘市保津村の場合. *Dōshisha hōgaku*, no. 136 (1975): 101–44.

Inoue Kiyoshi 井上清. *(Kaihan) Buraku mondai no kenkyū: Sono rekishi to kaihō riron* (改版) 部落問題の研究: その歴史と解放理論. Kyoto: Buraku mondai kenkyūjo, 1959.

Ishii Ryōsuke 石井良助. *Inban no rekishi* 印判の歴史. Akashi shoten, 1991.

Ishio Yoshihisa 石尾芳久. *Nihon kinseihō no kenkyū* 日本近世法の研究. Boku-takusha, 1975.

Kadomae Hiroyuki 門前博之. "Kinsei no mura to kinseishi kenkyū" 近世の村と近世史研究. *Rekishi kōron*, no. 95 (1983): 94–101.

Kanzaki Akitoshi 神崎影利. "Muranyūyōchō ni tsuite" 村入用帳について. In *Kinsei no jikata-machikata monjo* 近世の地方・町方文書, edited by Nihon komonjo gakkai 日本古文書学会, 414–21. Nihon komonjogaku ronshū 日本古文書学論集, 12 (Kinsei 近世 2). Yoshikawa kōbunkan, 1987.

Kanzaki Naomi 神崎直美. "Kōzuke-kuni no sonpō" 上野国の村法. *Gunma bunka*, no. 225 (1991): 39–55.

———. "Musashi-kuni no sonpō" 武蔵国の村法. *Tama no ayumi*, no. 65 (1991).

Katada Seiji 堅田精司. "Kinsei sonpō no henshitsu ni tsuite: Yamashiro-kuni Atago-gun Ichijōji-mura no baai" 近世村法の変質について: 山城国愛宕郡一乗寺村の場合. *Chihōshi kenkyū*, no. 34 (1958): 30–34.

Katsurajima Nobuhiro 桂島宣弘. "Hirata Kokugaku to gōnōsō" 平田国学と豪農層. In *Shūkan Asahi hyakka Nihon no rekishi* 週刊朝日百科日本の歴史, no. 91 (1988): 9/74.

Kobayashi Daiji 小林大二. *Sabetsu kaimyō no rekishi* 差別戒名の歴史. Yūzankaku, 1987.

Kobayashi Kei'ichirō 小林計一郎. "Shomin no myōji wa itsu goro kara tsukerareta ka" 庶民の苗字はいつ頃から付けられたか. *Nagano*, no. 99 (1981): 1–30.

Kobayashi Shigeru 小林茂. "Kinsei ni okeru buraku kaihō tōsō" 近世における部落開放闘争. *Rekishi kōron* 3, no. 6 (1977): 89–95.

Kobayashi Shigeru 小林茂, et al. "Zadankai: Kinsei hisabetsu buraku ni kansuru hōrei o megutte" 座談会: 近世被差別部落に関する法令をめぐって. In *Kinsei hisabetsu buraku kankei hōreishū: Tenryō o chūshin to shite* 近世被差別部落関係法令集: 天領を中心として, edited by Kobayashi Shigeru 小林茂. Akashi shoten, 1981.

Kodama Kōta 児玉幸多. "Kinsei ni okeru mura no zaisei" 近世における村の財政. In *Kinsei no jikata-machikata monjo* 近世の地方・町方文書, edited by Nihon komonjo gakkai 日本古文書学会, 344–82. Nihon komonjogaku ronshū 日本古文書学論集, 12 (Kinsei 近世 2). Yoshikawa kōbunkan, 1987.

———. "Hihyō to shōkai: Maeda Masaharu, *Nihon kinsei sonpō no kenkyū; furoku sonpōshū*" 批評と紹介: 前田正治「日本近世村法の研究, 付録村法集」. *Shigaku zasshi* 60, no. 9 (1951): 66–70.

Komonjo kenkyūkai dai ni han 古文書研究会第二班. "Genroku-ki no shūmon aratamechō o miru" 元禄期の宗門改帳をみる. *Mochizuki no chōmin no rekishi*, no. 12 (1988): 57–80.

Kuroda Toshio 黒田俊雄. *Nihon chūsei no kokka to shūkyō* 日本中世の国家と宗教. Iwanami shoten, 1975.

Kurozumi Makoto 黒住真. "Tokugawa zenki jukyō no seikaku" 徳川前期儒教の性格. *Shisō*, no. 792 (1990): 102–31. Translated, with an introduction by Herman Ooms, as "The Nature of Early Tokugawa Confucianism," *Journal of Japanese Studies* 20, no. 2 (1994): 331–75.

Kurushima Hiroshi 久留島浩. "Kinsei gun'yaku to hyakushō" 近世軍役と百姓. In *Futan to zōyo* 負担と贈与, 273–317. Nihon no shakaishi 日本の社会史, 4. Iwanami shoten, 1986.

Mae Kei'ichi 前圭一. "Kinsei chū-kōki ni okeru 'kawata' no keizai seikatsu" 近世中後期における「かわた」の経済生活. In *Burakushi no kenkyū: Zen kindai-hen* 部落史の研究: 前近代篇, edited by Buraku mondai kenkyūjo 部落問題研究所, 243–74. Kyoto: Buraku mondai kenkyūjo, 1984.

Maeda Masaharu 前田正治. "Hō to sonraku kyōdōtai: Edo jidai ni okeru sonpō o chūshin ni" 治と村落共同体: 江戸時代における村法を中心に. In *Hōken shakai to kyōdōtai* 封建社会と共同体, edited by Shimizu Morimitsu 清水盛光 and Aida Yūji 会田雄次, 169–214. Sōbunsha 創文社, 1959.

Maruyama Yasunari 丸山雍成. "'Keian ofuregaki' ron no sui-i to sono sonpi o megutte"「慶安御触書」論の推移とその存否をめぐって. In *Kinsei-kindaishi ronshū* 近世近代史論集, edited by Kyūshū Daigaku kokushigaku kenkyū-shitsu 九州大学国史学研究室. Yoshikawa kōbunkan, 1990.

Mase Kumiko 間瀬久美子. "Ishiki no naka no mibunsei" 意識のなかの身分制. In *Mibun to kakushiki* 身分と格式, edited by Asao Naohiro 朝尾直弘, 269–306. Nihon no kinsei 日本の近世, 7. Chūōkōronsha, 1992.

Minegishi Kentarō 峯岸賢太郎. *Kinsei mibunron* 近世身分論. Azekura shobō, 1989.

———. "Kinsei no hisabetsumin no tōsō" 近世の被差別民の闘争. In *Ikki no kōzō* 一揆の構造, edited by Aoki Michio 青木美智男 et al., 287–316. Ikki 一揆, 5. Tokyo Daigaku shuppankai, 1981.

Miyagawa Mitsuru 宮川満. *Taikō kenchiron* 太閤検地論. 3 vols. Ochanomizu shobō, 1959–63.

Miyajima Keiichi 宮島敬一. "Kinsei nōmin shihai no seiritsu ni tsuite: 1. Chūsei zaichihō no 'hitei' to 'naizai'" 近世農民支配の成立について: 1. 中世在地法の「否定」と「内済」. *Chihōshi kenkyū*, no. 171 (1981): 1–11.

Mizubayashi Takeshi 水林彪. "Bakuhan taisei ni okeru kōgi to chōtei" 幕藩体制における公義と朝廷. In *Ken'i to shihai* 権威と支配, 120–58. Nihon no shakaishi 日本の社会史, 3. Iwanami shoten, 1987.

———. *Hōkensei no saihen to Nihonteki shakai no kakuritsu* 封建制の再編と日本的社会の確立. Nihon tsūshi 日本通史, 2 (Kinsei 近世). Yamakawa shuppansha, 1987.

———. "Kinsei no hō to kokusei kenkyū josetsu" 近世の法と国制研究序説. *Kokka gakkai zasshi* 国家学会雑誌 90, nos. 1–2 (1977): 1–61 and 5–6 (1977): 1–63; 91, nos. 5–6 (1978): 73–110; 92, nos. 11–12 (1979): 52–122; 94, nos. 9–10 (1981): 57–105; 95, nos. 1–2 (1982): 59–92.

———. "Kinsei no hō to saiban" 近世の法と裁判. In *Chūsei no hō to kenryoku* 中世の法と権力, 144–71 Chūseishi kōza 中世史講座, 4. Gakuseisha, 1985.

———. "Kinseiteki chitsujo to kihan ishiki" 近世的秩序の規範意識. In *Chitsujo* 秩序, 109–55. Kōza Nihon shisō 講座日本思想, 3. Tokyo Daigaku shuppan, 1983.

———. "Kinsei tennōsei kenkyū ni tsuite no ichi kōsatsu: kinsei tennōsei no sonzai hitsuzensei ni tsuite no shogakusetsu no hihanteki kentō" 近世天王制研究についての一考察: 近世天王制の存在必然性 についての 諸学説の批判的検討. *Rekishigaku kenkyū*, nos. 596 (1989): 18–27, 597 (1989): 19–33, and 598 (1989): 57.

———. "Ritsuryō tennōsei ni tsuite no ichi kōsatsu (1)" 律令天王制についての一考察. *Tokyo-toritsu Daigaku hō gakkai zasshi* 30, no. 1 (1989).

Mizumoto Kunihiko 水本邦彦. "Bakuhansei kōzōron kenkyū no saikentō—Asao, Sasaki-shi no shigoto o sozai ni" 幕藩制構造論研究の再検討: 朝尾 ·

佐々木氏の仕事を素材に. *Atarashii rekishigaku no tame ni* (Minka Kyoto shibu rekishibukai kikanshi) 131 (1973): 13–23.

———. "Bakuhanseika no nōmin keizai" 幕藩制下の農民経済. In *Nihon keizaishi o manabu: 2. Kinsei* 日本経済史を学ぶ: 2 近世, 55–84. Yūhikaku, 1982.

———. *Kinsei no mura shakai to kokka* 近世の村社会と国家. Tōkyō Daigaku shuppankai, 1987.

———. "Kōgi no saiban to shūdan no okite" 公義の裁判と集団の掟. In *Saiban to kihan* 裁判と規範, 283–316. Nihon no shakaishi 日本の社会史, 5. Iwanami shoten, 1987.

———. "Murakata sōdō 村方騒動." In *Chūsei no minshū undō* 中世の民衆運動, 289–307. Chūseishi kōza 中世史講座, 7. Gakuseisha, 1985.

Mochizuki-machi kyōiku iinkai 望月町教育委員会. *Mochizuki no burakushi*, nos. 1–5 (1976–79).

———. *Mochizuki no chōmin no rekishi*, nos. 6–15 (1980–91).

Morita Yoshinori 盛田嘉徳. "Edo-ki ni okeru buraku e no shiteki kanshin" 江戸期における部落への史的関心. In *Kinsei buraku no shiteki kenkyū (1)* 近世部落の史的研究(1), edited by Buraku kaihō kenkyūjo 部落解放研究所, 303–34. Osaka: Kaihō shuppansha, 1979.

Nagano-ken 長野県, ed. *Nagano-kenshi: Tsūshi 4 (Kinsei 1)* 長野県史, 通史 4 (近世1). Nagano-shi: Nagano-kenshi kankōkai, 1987.

———. *Nagano-kenshi: Tsūshi 5 (Kinsei 2)* 長野県史, 通史 5 (近世2). Nagano-shi: Nagano-kenshi kankōkai, 1988.

———. *Nagano-kenshi: Tsūshi 6 (Kinsei 3)* 長野県史, 通史 6 (近世3). Nagano-shi: Nagano-kenshi kankōkai, 1989.

Naitō Jirō 内藤二郎. *Honbyakushō taisei no kenkyū* 本百姓体制の研究. Ochanomizu shobō, 1968.

Nakada Kaoru 中田薫. "Tokugawa jidai ni okeru mura no jinkaku" 徳川時代における村の人格. *Kokka gakkai zasshi* 34, no. 8 (1920). Reprinted in *Hōseishi ronshū* 法制史論集 2: 963–90. Iwanami shoten, 1938.

Nanba Nobuo 難波信雄. "Hyakushō ikki no hōishiki" 百姓一揆の法意識. In *Seikatsu, bunka, shisō* 生活, 文化, 思想, edited by Aoki Michio 青木美智男 et al., 43–88. Ikki 一揆, 4. Tokyo Daigaku, 1981.

Narusawa Eijū 成沢栄寿. "Rekishiteki ni mita mikaihō buraku no kaimyō" 歴史的にみた未解放部落の戒名. In *Shūkyō to buraku mondai* 宗教と部落問題, edited by Buraku mondai kenkyūjo 部落問題研究所, 158–87. Kyoto: Buraku mondai kenkyūjo, 1982.

Nishiwaki Yasushi 西脇康, "Kinsei zenki Mino Wajū chiiki no 'konō' to sonraku: Bakuryō Anbachi-gun Niremata-mura ni okeru kisoteki bunseki" 近世前期美濃輪中地域の「小農」と村落: 幕領安八郡楡俣村における基礎的分析. *Gifu shigaku*, no. 76 (1982): 41–82.

———. "Kinsei zenki no nengu sanyō to 'mura' chitsujo: 'Narashi' sanyō o meguru murakata sōdō no bunseki o tōshite" 近世前期の年貢算用と「村」秩序:「ならし」算用をめぐる村方騒動の分析を通して. *Shikan*, no. 106 (1982): 19–39.

Ochiai Nobutaka 落合延孝. "Kinsei sonraku ni okeru kaji, nusumi no kendanken to shinpan no kinō" 近世村落における火事・盗みの検断権と神判の機能. *Rekishi hyōron*, no. 442 (1987): 63–84.

Ōide Yukiko 大出由紀子. "Kinsei sonpō to ryōshuken" 近世村法と領主権. *(Nagoya Daigaku) Hōsei ronshū*, nos. 18 (1961): 1–31 and 19 (1962): 73–128.

Ōishi Shinzaburō 大石慎三郎. *Hōkenteki tochi shoyū no kaitai katei: 1. Kinsei jinushiteki tochi shoyū no keisei katei* 封建的土地所有の解体課程: 1. 近世地主的土地所有の形成課程. Ochanomizu shobō, 1958.

———. *Kinsei sonraku no kōzō to ie seido* 近世村落の構造と家制度. Ochanomizu shobō, 1968.

———. *Kyōhō kaikaku no keizai seisaku: Dai ichibu, Kyōhō kaikaku no nōson seisaku* 享保改革の経済政策: 第一部, 享保改革の農村政策. Zōhoban 増補版. Ochanomizu shobō, 1978.

Ooms Herman オームス, ヘルマン. *Sosensūhai no shimborizumu* 祖先崇拝のシンボリズム. Kōbundō, 1987.

———. "Yamazaki Ansai no 'Kamiyo o maki' ni okeru kaishakugaku—tenkeiteki ideorogii-keitai to shite" 山崎闇斎の'神代巻'における解釈学 – 典型的イデオロギ – 形態として. *Shisō*, no. 766 (1988): 7–18.

Ōtsuka Eiji 大塚英二. "Nenguwaritsuke to mura nyūyō no kōkai ni tsuite" 年貢割付とむら入用の公開について. *Shinano* 43, no. 9 (1991): 1–24.

Ozaki Yukiya 尾崎行也. "Chikuma-gun bakufuryō ni okeru goningumichō to goningumi no jittai: Chikuma-gun Ōashi-mura no baai" 筑摩郡幕府領における五人組帳と五人組の実体: 筑摩郡大足村の場合い. *Shinano* 16, no. 2 (1964): 45–60.

———. "Kenjo oboegaki: Kinsei nōson joseishi e no kokoromi" けん女覚書: 近世農村女性史への試み. *Mochizuki no chōmin no rekishi*, no. 8 (1983): 61–100.

———. "Kinsei sonraku naibu no mibun kaisō ni tsuite: Shinano-kuni Saku-gun Kodaira-mura kakaebyakushō mondai o chūshin ni" 近世村落内部の身分階層について: 信濃国佐久郡小平村抱百姓問題を中心に. *Nagano* 29, nos. 8 (1977): 752–68 and 9 (1977): 815–30.

———. "Mochizuki-machi no buraku no rekishi (1)" 望月町の部落の歴史 (一). *Mochizuki no burakushi*, no. 1 (1975): 31–67.

———. "Shinano-kuni Saku-gun ni okeru buraku no shiteki kōsatsu" 信濃国佐久郡における部落の史的考察. *Buraku mondai kenkyū* 18 (1964): 88–102.

———. *Shinshū hisabetsu buraku no shiteki kenkyū* 信州被差別部落の史的研究. Kashiwa shobō, 1982.

———. "Shinshū no nōmin to buraku" 信州の農民と部落. *Mochizuki no burakushi*, no. 4 (1978): 34–74.

———. "Shinshū Saku-gun Makibuse-mura Kenjo ikken—Kinsei nōson joseishi shikiron to shite" 信州佐久郡牧布施村けん女一件: 近世農村女性史式論として. *Rekishi hyōron*, no. 419 (1985): 45–66.

Saitō Yōichi 斎藤洋一. *Gorobe-shinden to hisabetsu buraku* 五郎兵衛新田と被差別部落. San'ichi shobō, 1987.

Saitō Yoshiyuki 斎藤善之. "Kinsei shoki no nōmin tōsō to muraukesei: nengukanjō sōdō o sozai to shite" 近世初期の農民闘争と村請け制: 年貢勘定騒動を素材として. *Rekishi hyōron*, no. 475 (1989): 42–60.

Sakai Uji 酒井右二. "'Sōbyakushōdai' kara 'hyakushōdai' e: zenki hyakushōdai no seiritsu o megutte" 「惣百姓代」から「百姓代」へ: 前期百姓代の成立をめ

ぐつて. In *Ronshū chū-kinsei no shiryō to hōhō* 論集中・近世の史料と方法, edited by Takizawa Takeo 滝沢武雄, 373–406. Tōkyōdō shuppan, 1991.

Sasaki Junnosuke 佐々木潤之助. "Kinsei nōson no seiritsu" 近世農村の成立. In *Iwanami kōza Nihon rekishi: Kinsei (2)* 岩波講座日本歴史: 近世 (二), 165–221. Iwanami shoten, 1963.

Sekigawa Chiyomaru 関川千代丸. "Shomin no myōji ni tsuite" 庶民の苗字につい て. *Nagano*, no. 3 (1965): 13–24.

Seta Katsuya 瀬田勝哉. "Shinpan to kendan" 神判と検断. In *Saiban to kihan* 裁判 と規範, 58–86. Nihon no shakaishi 日本の社会史, 5. Iwanami shoten, 1987.

Shibata Michiko 柴田道子. *Hisabetsu buraku no denshō to seikatsu* 被差別部落 の伝承と生活. San'ichi shobō, 1972.

Shimadani Yuriko 嶋谷ゆり子. "Kinsei 'honbyakushō' saikōsatsu no kokoro- mi" 近世「本百姓」再考察の試み. *Jinmin no rekishigaku*, no. 86 (1985): 13– 24.

Shirakawabe Tatsuo 白川部達夫. "Kinsei shichichi ukemodoshi kankō to hya- kushō takashoji" 近世質地請け戻し慣行と百姓高所持. *Rekishigaku kenkyū*, no. 552 (1986): 17–32.

Sugawara Kenji 菅原憲二. "Muranyūyōchō no seiritsu: Kinsei muranyūyō no kenkyū josetsu" 村入用帳の成立: 近世村入用の研究序説. In *Kinsei no jikata- machikata monjo* 近世の地方・町方文書, edited by Nihon komonjo gakkai 日本古文書学会, 383–413. Nihon komonjogaku ronshū 日本古文書学論集, 12 (Kinsei 近世 2). Yoshikawa kōbunkan, 1987.

Tahara Tsuguo 田原嗣郎. *Akō shijūrokushi-ron: Bakuhansei no seishin kōzō* 赤穂四十六士論: 幕藩制の精神構造. Yoshikawa kōbunkan, 1978.

Takagi Shōsaku 高木昭作. "Bakuhan taisei to yaku" 幕藩体制と役." In *Ken'i to shihai* 権威と支配, 309–41. Nihon no shakaishi 日本の社会史, 3. Iwanami shoten, 1987.

———. "'Hideyoshi no heiwa' to bushi no henshitsu: chūseiteki jiritsusei no kaitai katei" 「秀吉の平和」と武士の変質: 中世的自立性の解体過程. *Shisō*, no. 721 (1984): 1–19. Translated as "'Hideyoshi's Peace' and the Trans- formation of the *Bushi* class: The Dissolution of the Autonomy of the Medieval *Bushi*." *Acta Asiatica*, no. 49 (1985): 46–77.

———. "Kinsei Nihon ni okeru mibun to yaku: Minegishi Kentarō-shi no hihan ni kotaeru" 近世日本における身分と役: 峯岸賢太郎氏の批判に答える. *Rekishi hyōron*, no. 446 (1987): 90–108.

———. "'Kōgi' kenryoku no kakuritsu" 「公儀」権力の確立. In *Bakuhansei kokka no seiritsu* 幕藩制国家の成立, edited by Fukaya Katsumi 深谷克巳 and Katō Eiichi 加藤栄一, 151–210. Kōza Nihon kinseishi 講座日本近世史, 1. Yūhikaku, 1981.

Taoka Kōitsu 田岡香逸. "Murahachibu to tsuihō ni tsuite" 村八部と追放につ いて. *Chihōshi kenkyū* 12 (1954): 1–8.

Teraki Nobuaki 寺木伸明. *Kinsei buraku no seiritsu to tenkai* 近世部落の成立と 展開. Osaka: Kaihō shuppansha, 1986.

Tsuji Zennosuke 辻善之助. *Tanuma jidai* 田沼時代. Iwanami shoten, 1980.

Tsukada Masatomo 塚田正朋 [Banba Masatomo 万司正朋]. *Kinsei burakushi no kenkyū: Shinshū no gutaizō* 近世部落史の研究: 信州の具体像. Kyoto: Buraku mondai kenkyūjo, 1986.

Tsukada Takashi 塚田孝. "Kasōmin no sekai: 'Mibunteki shūen' no shiten kara" 下層民の世界 - 「身分的周縁」の視点から. In *Mibun to kakushiki* 身分と格式, edited by Asao Naohiro 朝尾直弘, 225–68. Nihon no kinsei 日本の近世, 7. Chūōkōronsha, 1992.

———. *Kinsei Nihon mibunsei no kenkyū* 近世日本身分制の研究. Kōbe: Hyōgo buraku mondai kenkyūjo, 1987.

———. "Kinsei no keibatsu" 近世の刑罰. In *Saiban to kihan* 裁判と規範, 88–131. Nihon no shakaishi 日本の社会史, 5. Iwanami shoten, 1987.

Uesugi Mitsuhiko 上杉允彦. "Kinsei sonpō no seikaku ni tsuite" 近世村法の性格について. *Minshūshi kenkyū*, no. 7 (1969): 80–106.

———. "Kinsei sonrakuron: kinsei sonraku to 'jichi'" 近世村落論: 近世村落と「自治」. In *Nihonshi kenkyū no shinshiten* 日本史研究の新視点, edited by Nihon rekishi gakkai 日本歴史学会, 175–93. Yoshikawa kōbunkan, 1986.

Wakamiya Yoshinobu 若宮啓文. "Hisabetsu buraku ni totte no kami to hotoke: Komoro-shi Arabori de no minzoku chōsa o chūshin ni" 被差別部落にとっての神と仏: 小諸市荒掘での民俗調査を中心に. *Nihon shūkyō to buraku sabetsu* 日本宗教と部落差別, special issue of *Dentō to gendai*, no. 73 (1981): 79–112.

Wakita Osamu 脇田修. *Kawaramakimono no sekai* 河原巻物の世界. Tōkyō Daigaku shuppankai, 1991.

Watanabe Hiroshi 渡辺浩. "'Goikō' to shōchō: Tokugawa seiji taisei no ichisokumen" 「御威光」と象徴: 徳川政治体制の一側面. *Shisō*, no. 740 (1986): 132–54.

Watanabe Hiroshi 渡辺広. *Mikaihō buraku no keisei to tenkai* 未開放部落の形成と展開. Yoshikawa kōbunkan, 1977.

Yamamoto Yukitoshi 山本幸俊. "Kinsei shoki no ronsho to saikyo: Aizu-han o chūshin ni" 近世初期の論所と裁許: 会津藩を中心に. In *Kinsei no shihai taisei to shakai kōzō* 近世の支配体制と社会構造, edited by Kitajima Masamoto 北島正元, 79–127. Yoshikawa kōbunkan, 1983.

Yokota Fuyuhiko 横田冬彦. "Kinsei sonaku ni okeru hō to okite" 近世村落における法と掟. *(Kōbe daigaku daigakuin bunkagaku kenkyūka) Bunkagaku nenpō* 5 (1986): 141–97.

———. "Kinseiteki mibun seido no seiritsu" 近世的身分制度の成立. In *Mibun to kakushiki* 身分と格式, edited by Asao Naohiro 朝尾直弘, 41–78. Nihon no kinsei 日本の近世, 7. Chūōkōronsha, 1992.

WESTERN-LANGUAGE WORKS

Works on Japan and China

Berry, Mary Elizabeth. *Hideyoshi*. Cambridge: Harvard University Press, 1982.

———. "Public Peace and Private Attachment: The Goals and Conduct of Power in Early Modern Japan." *Journal of Japanese Studies* 12, no. 2 (1986): 237–71.

Bix, Herbert. "Miura Meisuke, or Peasant Rebellion under the Banner of 'Distress.'" *Bulletin of Concerned Asian Scholars* 10, no. 2 (1978): 18–28.

———. *Peasant Protest in Japan, 1590–1884.* New Haven: Yale University Press, 1986.

Brown Philip C. *Central Authority and Local Autonomy in the Formation of Early Modern Japan: The Case of Kaga Domain.* Stanford: Stanford University Press, 1993.

———. "The Mismeasure of Land: Land Surveying in the Tokugawa Period." *Monumenta Nipponica* 42, no. 2 (1987): 115–55.

Bryant, Taimie. "For the Sake of the Country, for the Sake of the Family: The Oppressive Impact of Family Registration on Women and Minorities in Japan." *UCLA Law Review* 39 (1991): 109–68.

Burton, Donald. "Peasant Struggle in Japan, 1590–1760." *Journal of Peasant History* 5, no. 2 (1978): 135–71.

Chambliss, William. *Chiaraijima Village Land Tenure, Taxation, and Local Trade, 1818–1884.* AAS Monograph, 19. Tucson: University of Arizona Press, 1965.

Cornell, John B. "From Caste Patron to Entrepreneur and Political Ideologue: Transformation in Nineteenth and Twentieth Century Outcaste Leadership Elites." In *Modern Japanese Leadership: Transition and Change,* edited by Bernard Silberman and Harry Harootunian, 51–81. Tucson: University of Arizona Press, 1966.

Cornell, L. L., and Akira Hayami. "The *shūmon aratame chō*: Japan's Population Registers." *Journal of Family History* 11, no. 4 (1986): 311–28.

De Vos, George, and Hiroshi Wagatsuma. *Japan's Invisible Race: Caste in Culture and Personality.* Berkeley: University of California Press, 1966.

Fukuda Tokuzō. *Die gesellschaftliche und wirtschaftliche Entwickelung in Japan.* Munchener volkswirtschaftliche Studien. Stuttgart: J. G. Cotta, 1900.

Gay, Suzanne. "The Kawashima: Warrior-Peasants of Medieval Japan." *Harvard Journal of Asiatic Studies* 46, no. 1 (1986): 81–119.

Gluck, Carol. *Japan's Modern Myths: Ideology in the Late Meiji Period.* Princeton: Princeton University Press, 1985.

Haley, John O. *Authority without Power: Law and the Japanese Paradox.* New York: Oxford University Press, 1991.

Hall, John C. "Japanese Feudal Laws III: Tokugawa Legislation, Part IV, The Edict in 100 Sections." *Transactions of the Asiatic Society of Japan* 41, pt. 5 (1913): 683–804.

Hall, John Whitney. *Government and Local Power in Japan, 500 to 1700: A Study Based on Bizen Province.* Princeton: Princeton University Press, 1966.

———. *Tanuma Okitsugu, 1719–1788: Forerunner of Modern Japan.* Cambridge: Harvard University Press, 1955.

———. "Terms and Concepts in Japanese Medieval History: An Inquiry into the Problems of Translation." *Journal of Japanese Studies* 9, no. 1 (1983): 1–32.

Hane Mikiso. *Peasants, Rebels, and Outcastes: The Underside of Modern Japan.* New York: Pantheon Books, 1982.

Harafuji Hiroshi. "*Han* Laws in the Edo Period with Particular Emphasis on Those of Kanazawa *Han.*" *Acta Asiatica* 35 (1978): 46–71.

Harootunian, Harry. *Things Seen and Unseen: Discourse and Ideology in Tokugawa Nativism*. Chicago: University of Chicago Press, 1988.

Hayami Akira. "The Myth of Primogeniture and Impartible Inheritance in Tokugawa Japan." *Journal of Family History* 8, no. 1 (1983): 3–29.

Hayami Akira and Nobuko Uchida. "Size of Household in a Japanese County throughout the Tokugawa Era." In *Household and Family in Past Time*, edited by Peter Laslett, 474–513. Cambridge: Cambridge University Press, 1972.

Helm, Leslie. "A Long Haul for Japan's Plaintiffs." *Los Angeles Times*, January 14, 1991, A1 ff.

Henderson, Dan Fenno. *Conciliation and Japanese Law, Tokugawa and Modern*. 2 vols. Seattle: University of Washington Press, 1965.

———. "The Evolution of Tokugawa Law." In *Studies in the Institutional History of Early Modern Japan*, edited by John Whitney Hall and Marius Jansen, 203–29. Princeton: Princeton University Press, 1968.

———. "Introduction to the Kujikata Osadamegaki (1742)." In *Hō to keibatsu no rekishiteki kōsatsu* 法と刑罰の歴史的考察, edited by Hiramatsu Yoshirō hakushi tsuitō ronbunshū henshū iinkai 平松義郎博士追悼論文集委員會, 489–544. Nagoya: Nagoya Daigaku shuppankai, 1987.

———. *Village "Contracts" in Tokugawa Japan*. Seattle: University of Washington Press, 1975.

Hiramatsu Yoshirō. "History of Penal Institutions: Japan." *Law in Japan* 6 (1973): 1–48.

———. "Tokugawa Law." Translated by Dan Fenno Henderson. *Law in Japan* 14 (1981): 1–41. Originally published as "Kinseihō" 近世法. *Kinsei* 近世 3:332–78. Iwanami kōza Nihon rekishi 岩波講座日本歴史, 11. Iwanami, 1976.

Ikegami Eiko. "Disciplining the Japanese: The Reconstruction of Social Control in Tokugawa Japan." Ph.D. diss., Harvard University, 1989.

Irokawa Daiichi. "The Survival Struggle of the Japanese Community." In *Authority and the Individual in Japan: Citizen Protest in Historical Perspective*, edited by Victor Koschmann, 250–82. N.p.: University of Tokyo Press, 1978.

Ishii Ryōsuke. Review of *Conciliation and Japanese Law, Tokugawa and Modern*, by Dan Fenno Henderson. *Law in Japan* 2 (1968): 198–224.

Jameson, Sam. "Japan's 'Untouchables' Suffer Invisible Stain." *Los Angeles Times*, January 2, 1993, A24–A25.

Joly, Jacques. "L'Idée de shizen chez Andō Shōeki." Dissertation. Université de Paris VII, Unité Asie Orientale, 1991.

———. "Spontanéité et nature: Le cas d'Andō Shōeki. Comparatisme et récupération." *Revue Philosophique de Louvain*, vol. 92, no. 4 (1994): 546–69.

Joüon des Longrais, F. *L'Est et l'Ouest: Institutions du Japon et de l'Occident comparées (six études de sociologie juridique)*. Tokyo: Maison Franco-japonaise, 1958.

Keene, Donald. *The Japanese Discovery of Europe, 1720–1830*. Stanford: Stanford University Press, 1952.

Kelley, William. *Deference and Defiance in Nineteenth-Century Japan*. Princeton: Princeton University Press, 1985.

Kurozumi Makoto. "The Nature of Early Tokugawa Confucianism." *Journal of Japanese Studies* 20, no. 2 (1994): 331–75. Translated with a foreword by Herman Ooms. Originally published as "Tokugawa zenki jukyō no seikaku" 徳川前期儒教の性格. *Shisō*, no. 792 (1990): 102–31.

Lu, David John. *Sources of Japanese History*. 2 vols. New York: McGraw-Hill, 1974.

Macauley, Melissa. "Civil and Uncivil Disputes in Southeast Coastal China, 1723–1820." in *Civil Law in Ch'ing and Republican China*, edited by Kathryn Bernhardt and Philip C. C. Huang, 85–121. Stanford: Stanford University Press, 1994.

Maruyama Masao. *Studies in the Intellectual History of Tokugawa Japan*. Princeton: Princeton University Press, 1974.

McCallum, Donald F. *Zenkōji and its Icon: A Study in Medieval Japanese Religious Art*. Princeton: Princeton University Press, 1994.

McEwan, J. R. *The Political Writings of Ogyū Sorai*. Cambridge: Cambridge University Press, 1969.

McMullin, Neil. *Buddhism and the State in Sixteenth Century Japan*. Princeton: Princeton University Press, 1984.

Nakai, Kate Wildman. *Shogunal Politics: Arai Hakuseki and the Premises of Tokugawa Rule*. Cambridge: Harvard University Press, 1988.

Nakane Chie. *Kinship and Economic Organization in Rural Japan*. London School of Economics Monographs on Social Anthropology, 32. London: Athlone Press, 1967.

Neary, Ian. *Political Protest and Social Control in Prewar Japan: The Origins of Buraku Liberation*. Manchester: Manchester University Press, 1989.

Ninomiya Shigeaki. "An Inquiry concerning the Origin, Development, and Present Situation of the *Eta* in Relation to the History of Social Classes in Japan." *Transactions of the Asiatic Society of Japan*, 2d ser., 10 (1933): 47–154.

Ohnuki-Tierney, Emiko. *The Monkey as Mirror: Symbolic Transformations in Japanese History and Ritual*. Princeton: Princeton University Press, 1987.

Ooms, Emily Groszos. *Women and Millenarian Protest in Meiji Japan: Deguchi Nao and Ōmotokyō*. Cornell East Asia Series. Ithaca, N.Y.: Cornell University, East Asia Program, 1993.

Ooms, Herman. "Neo-Confucianism and the Formation of Early Tokugawa Ideology: Contours of a Problem." In *Confucianism and Tokugawa Culture*, edited by Peter Nosco, 27–61. Princeton: Princeton University Press, 1984.

———. *Tokugawa Ideology: Early Constructs, 1570–1680*. Princeton: Princeton University Press, 1985.

Prasad, Sajja A. *The Patriotism Thesis and Argument in Tokugawa Japan*. 3 vols. Samudraiah Prakashan, 1975–84.

Robertson, Jennifer. *Native and Newcomer: Making and Remaking a Japanese City*. Berkeley: University of California Press, 1991.

Rudorff, Otto. "Tokugawa-Gesetz-Sammlung." *Mittheilungen der Deutschen Gesellschaft für Natur- und Völkerkunde Ostasiens in Tokio.* Suppl. to vol. 5 (April 1889).

Scheiner, Irwin. "Benevolent Lords and Honorable Peasants: Rebellion and Peasant Consciousness in Tokugawa Japan." In *Japanese Thought in the Tokugawa Period, 1600–1868,* edited by Tetsuo Najita and Irwin Scheiner, 39–62. Chicago: University of Chicago Press, 1978.

Shively, Donald H. "*Bakufu* versus *Kabuki.*" In *Studies in the Institutional History of Early Modern Japan,* edited by John Whitney Hall and Marius Jansen, 231–61. Princeton: Princeton University Press, 1968.

Smith, Thomas C. *The Agrarian Origins of Modern Japan.* Stanford: Stanford University Press, 1959.

———. "The Japanese Village of the Seventeenth Century." In *Studies in the Institutional History of Early Modern Japan,* edited by John Whitney Hall and Marius Jansen, 263–82. Princeton: Princeton University Press, 1968. Reprinted from *Journal of Economic History* 12, no. 1 (1952).

———. "The Land Tax in the Tokugawa Period." In *Studies in the Institutional History of Early Modern Japan,* edited by John Whitney Hall and Marius Jansen, 283–99. Princeton: Princeton University Press, 1968. Reprinted from *Journal of Asian Studies* 18, no. 1 (1958).

———. *Nakahara: Family Farming and Population in a Japanese Village, 1717–1830.* Stanford: Stanford University Press, 1977.

Steenstrup, Carl. *A History of Law in Japan until 1868.* Leiden: E. J. Brill, 1991.

Takagi Shōsaku. " 'Hideyoshi's Peace' and the Transformation of the *Bushi* Class: The Dissolution of the Autonomy of the Medieval *Bushi.*" *Acta Asiatica,* no. 49 (1985): 46–77. Originally published as " 'Hideyoshi no heiwa' to bushi no henshitsu: chūseiteki jiritsusei no kaitai katei" 「秀吉の平和」と武士の変質: 中世的自立性の解体過程. *Shisō,* no. 721 (1984): 1–19.

Tanigawa Akio. "Excavating Edo's Cemeteries: Graves as Indicators of Status and Class." *Japanese Journal of Religious Studies* 19, nos. 2–3 (1992): 271–97.

Tonomura Hitomi. *Community and Commerce in Late Medieval Japan: The Corporate Villages of Tokuchin-ho.* Stanford: Stanford University Press, 1992.

Totman, Conrad. *Politics in the Tokugawa Bakufu, 1600–1843.* Cambridge: Harvard University Press, 1967.

Tsunoda Ryusaku, Theodore William de Bary and Donald Keene, comps. *Sources of Japanese Tradition.* 2 vols. New York: Columbia University Press, 1964.

Uchiyama Junzō. "San'ei-chō and Meat-eating in Buddhist Edo." *Japanese Journal of Religious Studies* 19, nos. 2–3 (1992): 299–303.

Upham, Frank K. *Law and Social Change in Postwar Japan.* Cambridge: Harvard University Press, 1987.

Vlastos, Stephen. *Peasant Protests and Uprisings in Tokugawa Japan.* Berkeley: University of California Press, 1986.

Walthall, Anne. "Edo Riots." Paper read at the Southern California Japan Seminar, UCLA, December 8, 1989.

———. "The Life Cycle of Farm Women in Tokugawa Japan." In *Recreating Japanese Women, 1600–1945*, edited by Gail Lee Bernstein, 42–70. Berkeley: University of California Press, 1991.

———. "Representations of Women in the History of Japanese Peasant Uprisings." Paper read at the Western Conference of the Association of Asian Studies, Long Beach, Calif., October 1989.

———. *Social Protest and Popular Culture in Eighteenth-Century Japan*. Tucson: University of Arizona Press, 1986.

———. "Village Networks: Sōdai and the Sale of Edo Nightsoil." *Monumenta Nipponica* 43, no. 3 (1988): 279–303.

Watanabe, Teresa. "Japan Casts Envious Look at U.S. Crisis Management." *Los Angeles Times*, May 7, 1995, A1 ff.

White, James. "Economic Development and Sociopolitical Unrest in Nineteenth-Century Japan." *Economic Development and Cultural Change* 37 (1989): 231–59.

———. "Rational Rioters: Leaders, Followers, and Popular Protest in Early Modern Japan." *Politics and Society* 16, no. 1 (1988): 35–70.

———. "State Growth and Popular Protest." *Journal of Japanese Studies* 14, no. 1 (1988): 1–26.

Yamamura Kozo. "Returns on Unification: Economic Growth in Japan, 1550–1650." In *Japan before Tokugawa: Political Consolidation and Economic Growth, 1500 to 1650*, edited by John Whitney Hall et al., 327–72. Princeton: Princeton University Press, 1981.

General Works

Andreski, Stanislav. *Military Organization and Society*. Berkeley: University of California Press, 1971.

Balibar, Etienne. "Paradoxes of Universality." In *Anatomy of Racism*, edited by David Theo Goldberg, 283–94. Minneapolis: University of Minnesota Press, 1990.

Beik, William. *Absolutism and Society in Seventeenth-Century France: State Power and Provincial Aristocracy in Languedoc*. Cambridge: Cambridge University Press, 1985.

Berreman, Gerald. *Caste and Other Inequities: Essays on Inequality*. Meerut, India: Folklore Institute, 1979.

———. "Social Inequality: A Cross-Cultural Analysis." In *Social Inequality: Comparative and Developmental Approaches*, edited by Gerald Berreman, 3–40. New York: Academic Press, 1981.

Bourdieu, Pierre. "Célibat et condition paysanne." *Études rurales*, nos. 5–6 (1962): 32–135.

———. *Ce que parler veut dire: L'économie des échanges linguistiques*. Paris: Fayard, 1982.

———. "The Force of Law: Toward a Sociology of the Juridical Field." *Hastings Law Journal* 38 (1987): 805–53.

———. *In Other Words: Essays towards a Reflexive Sociology.* Stanford: Stanford University Press, 1990.

———. *The Logic of Practice.* Stanford: Stanford University Press, 1991.

———. *Outline of a Theory of Practice.* Cambridge: Cambridge University Press, 1977.

Cannadine, David. "Cutting Classes." *New York Review of Books*, December 17, 1992, 52–57.

Castoriadis, Cornelius. *The Imaginary Institution of Society.* Cambridge: MIT Press, 1987.

Delacampagne, Christian. "Racism and the West: From Praxis to Logos." In *Anatomy of Racism*, edited by David Theo Goldberg, 83–89. Minneapolis: University of Minnesota Press, 1990.

Derrida, Jacques. "Force of Law: The 'Mystical Foundation of Authority.'" In *Deconstruction and the Possibility of Justice*, edited by David Gray Carlson, Drucilla Cornell, and Michael Rosenfeld, 1–67. New York: Routledge, Chapman and Hall, 1992.

Devyver, André. *Le sang épuré: Les préjugés de race chez les gentilshommes français de l'Ancien Régime (1560–1720).* Brussels: Éditions de l'Université de Bruxelles, 1973.

Foucault, Michel. *Discipline and Punish: The Birth of the Prison.* New York: Vintage Books, 1979.

———. "Nietzsche, Genealogy, History." In Michel Foucault, *Language, Counter-Memory, Practice: Selected Interviews and Essays*, edited and translated by Donald F. Bouchard, 139–64. Ithaca, N.Y.: Cornell University Press, 1977.

Kempton, Murray. "A New Colonialism." *New York Review of Books* 30, no. 19 (1992): 39.

Koziol, Geoffrey. *Begging Pardon and Favor: Ritual and Political Order in Early Medieval France.* Ithaca, N.Y.: Cornell University Press, 1992.

Laclau, Ernesto, and Chantal Mouffe. *Hegemony and Socialist Strategy.* London: Verso Press, 1985.

Levinas, Emmanuel. *The Levinas Reader.* Edited by Séan Hand. Oxford: Basil Blackwell, 1989.

Lévi-Strauss, Claude. *The Savage Mind.* Chicago: University of Chicago Press, 1966.

Lynch, John. *The Spanish American Revolutions, 1808–1826.* New York: W. W. Norton, 1973.

Lyotard, Jean-François. *Just Gaming.* Minneapolis: University of Minnesota Press, 1985.

Marx, Karl. *Grundrisse.* New York: Vintage Books, 1973.

Marx, Karl, and Frederick Engels. *The German Ideology.* New York: International Publishers, 1970.

Popkin, Samuel. *The Rational Peasant.* Berkeley: University of California Press, 1979.

Rout, Leslie B., Jr. *The African Experience in Spanish America: 1502 to the Present Day.* Cambridge: Cambridge University Press, 1976.

Scott, James. *The Moral Economy of the Peasant.* New Haven: Yale University Press, 1976.

Weber, Max. *Economy and Society.* Edited by Roth, Guenter and Wittich Claus. 2 vols. Berkeley: University of California Press, 1978.

Index

Designer:	Barbara Jellow
Compositor:	Asco Trade Typesetting Ltd.
Text:	10/13 Sabon
Display:	Sabon
Printer:	Maple-Vail Book Mfg. Group
Binder:	Maple-Vail Book Mfg. Group